ANCIENT MESOPOTAMIA

ANCIENT

Portrait of a Dead Civilization

MESOPOTAMIA

y A. Leo Oppenheim

Revised Edition
Completed by Erica Reiner

THE UNIVERSITY OF CHICAGO PRESS

Chicago & London

A. Leo Oppenheim, one of the most distinguished Assyriologists of our time, was editor in charge of the Assyrian Dictionary of the Oriental Institute and John A. Wilson Professor of Oriental Studies at the University of Chicago.

Erica Reiner is editor in charge of the Assyrian Dictionary of the Oriental Institute and John A. Wilson Professor at the University of Chicago. She teaches in the Department of Near Eastern Languages and Civilization and in the Department of Linguistics.

The University of Chicago Press, Chicago 60637
The University of Chicago Press, Ltd., London

Library of Congress Cataloging in Publication Data

Oppenheim, A   Leo, 1904–1974.
Ancient Mesopotamia: portrait of a dead civilization.

Includes bibliographical references and index.
1. Civilization, Assyro-Babylonian.   2.   Iraq—
Civilization—To 634.   I.   Reiner, Erica, 1926–
II.   Title.

DS69.5.06   1976   935   76-28340
ISBN 0-226-63186-9

Contents

Illustrations

Acknowledgments

This book could hardly have been written anywhere but in the stimulating atmosphere of the Assyrian Dictionary Project of the Oriental Institute of the University of Chicago. In that constant give and take of ideas and information, in that sustained drive for the understanding of the entire gamut of the Mesopotamian text material which determines our work, I have formed my views—preferences and idiosyncrasies alike. To the scholars, old and young, past and present, who have honored me by working with me on that project, I owe a deeply felt debt of gratitude.

I acknowledge with thanks the permission granted me by *Current Anthropology* to reprint in the chapter "Assyriology—Why and How," the original version of the article which appeared in Vol. 1, Nos. 5–6 (September–November 1960).

I would like to thank my colleague, Erica Reiner, for her careful reading of the manuscript of this book. The appendix, entitled "Mesopotamian Chronology of the Historical Period," was written by Dr. J. A. Brinkman, who also was kind enough to read the proofs of the book.

I am grateful to the Division of the Humanities of the University of Chicago for its contribution for secretarial expenses.

I wish to thank Paul Hamlyn, Ltd., for permission to include a number of plates from R. D. Barnett's *Assyrian Palace Reliefs*. The British Museum Photographic Service has given me permission to include plates from *Assyrian Sculptures in the British*

Museum (1914), by E. A. Wallis Budge; *Assyrian Sculptures in the British Museum* (1938), by Sidney Smith; and *The Sculptures of Assur-Nasir-Apli II, Tiglat-Pileser III, Esarhaddon* ... (1962), by R. D. Barnett and M. Falkner.

A. Leo Oppenheim

Preface to the Revised Edition

Since its first publication in 1964, *Ancient Mesopotamia* has remained the most distinguished presentation of the civilization of Babylonia and Assyria. The uniqueness and personal quality of the point of view presented in this cultural history have been amply emphasized in the reviews, and the book's impact can be measured by the literature stimulated by its first appearance. It is addressed to the educated layman, but it is also an indispensable tool for intellectuals and scholars interested in ancient civilizations. It is a textbook used in colleges and universities in the field of ancient history, and it is also a constant companion of the professional Assyriologist, who turns to it again and again to consider its insights and to find references in the extensive notes and bibliography. This latter function seemed so essential to the author that he had been keeping the critical apparatus current. When asked to prepare a revised edition, he welcomed the opportunity to bring the book up to date with material he had collected for ten years, and to revise some of the statements he had made.

It was characteristic of Leo Oppenheim constantly to reshape his view of Mesopotamian civilization; every new bit of information helped modify his perception of the essence of this civilization. He insisted that his subject was a "dead" civilization because, as R. M. Adams suggests, "for him, the death of his subject matter was somehow a precondition for its productive study, which then had to involve its painstaking, conscious recreation as a formed thing of the mind." All of Oppenheim's work was determined by his quest for what "makes" Mesopotamian civilization, the total understanding of which, he said, would always elude him, an observer from another civilization.

He pursued this elusive understanding through extracting all possible information from the ancient texts and organizing it into entries for the *Assyrian Dictionary*, a dictionary conceived by a previous generation of scholars as a thesaurus and which became under Leo Oppenheim an encyclopedia of Mesopotamian culture. Oppenheim also believed it his duty to attempt new formulations of his overall view of Mesopotamia. *Ancient Mesopotamia* is one such formulation, a picture intensely and intentionally personal, which is why, in the subtitle, he called the book a portrait. This being just one possible portrait, a few years later he sketched another, "The Measure of Mesopotamia," which appeared as the Introduction to his *Letters from Mesopotamia*.

Both these presentations show Oppenheim's preoccupation with and emphasis on what he called "central concerns." Though famous as a philologist—one of the foremost Assyriologists and the editor of the *Chicago Assyrian Dictionary*—Oppenheim preferred to call himself a cultural anthropologist who happens to work with a civilization whose records are in a dead language and a strange script, full of difficulties which too often claim the scholar's total attention. His aim was to make Mesopotamian records as commonly understood as classical ones, which when quoted can stay in the original Latin or Greek. For Oppenheim, texts were only a means to understand cultural history, and he thus greatly helped to establish Assyriology as a discipline of the cultural sciences. Contemporary approaches to the classical world influenced his thinking in many other ways too, as did the contributions of anthropologists from Lovejoy and Boas to Claude Lévi-Strauss.

Oppenheim was concerned with social and economic history from the time of his dissertation, on legal texts concerning rental agreements, to his last project, on the money economy of the temple in the Neo-Babylonian period. He often drew wide implications about bureaucratic or fiscal practices from a single term or an isolated document, yet he warned against simplification in polemical articles, whether directed at the economic theories of Karl Polányi, with whom Oppenheim collaborated for many years, or at the historical materialism of Soviet scholars.

Oppenheim also had a long-standing commitment to science and technology; he studied the material culture of the Neo-Babylonian period and published the monograph *On Beer and Brewing Techniques*. He then became increasingly fascinated with the aspirations and achievements of Mesopotamian technology and the Western and Eastern influences that shaped it, as is evidenced in his book *Glass and Glassmaking in Ancient Mesopotamia* (1970) and in his essay for the *Dictionary of Scientific Biography*, "Man and Nature."

Those who have been offended by the subtitle in Chapter IV of *Ancient Mesopotamia*, "Why a 'Mesopotamian Religion' Should Not Be Written," would do well to consult Oppenheim's articles on "Mesopotamian Mythology" or on the numinous and the terms used to express it, and to follow the model of his "Analysis of an Assyrian Ritual" (1966) which illustrates the approach to Mesopotamian religion that Oppenheim regarded as more fruitful than lists of gods or festivals.

Social and economic history, religion, and technology, however, are but aspects of the cultural history that was Oppenheim's prime interest. The exponents and transmitters of this culture were the Mesopotamian scholars and scientists. Understanding their status in society and their intellectual approach to their discipline promised to lead to the understanding of this dead civilization. Chapters V and VI of this book show Oppenheim's emphasis of this topic; his preoccupation in his last years with the "astrologers" at the royal court in Assyria is reflected in an essay printed posthumously in *Daedalus* (spring 1975) and in the numerous additions which Oppenheim made to these chapters.

Ancient Mesopotamia grew out of these shifting and recurring interests and methodological concerns. The book is not and was never meant to be a textbook that provides all the answers. It was meant to be a book that raises questions that will take many decades to answer. Therefore the revised edition is geared to supplying all the new material that can aid in the study of the subject, not to changing the book's basic outlook. In Oppenheim's words, the book was not meant to be "a synthesis, since such syntheses are misleading and necessarily personal, but rather a presentation which takes fully into account the breadth of variations and the phenomenological range either at one or more characteristic synchronic levels or in individual diachronic elaborations in order to show the essential internal developments. However, the amplitude does require a system of coordinates, in other words, the establishment of central concerns."

At the time of his death in July 1974, Leo Oppenheim had incorporated about half the material that he intended to include in the revision. The remaining material was sorted and marked for insertion at the proper places. My task was thus limited to inserting these additions and checking the references; only occasionally did I have to update the references or make a decision about material not definitively marked for integration.

Oppenheim did very little rewriting of the main text. The scholarly controversy aroused by the book only strengthened his belief that none of his provocative statements should be toned down in a new edition: the book was meant to make people think and argue. The results of his shifts of emphasis since *Ancient Mesopotamia* was first published are incorporated in the Notes to this revised edition. The scope of these notes reflects the concerns of Oppenheim's last decade, and their extent is a measure of the complexities he encountered.

This revised edition, then, while condensing in the Notes the new information we possess on Mesopotamian civilization, is a compendium both of the author's insights and of the vast amount of material that has become available since the first edition. In this way *Ancient Mesopotamia* can continue to serve as an up-to-date research tool for students and scholars alike.

It was Oppenheim's desire that John A. Brinkman revise his Appendix on Mesopotamian Chronology in the light of the latest historical evidence, and that John Sanders draw new maps. The contributions of both men are gratefully acknowledged.

ERICA REINER

Prefatory Note

The word "portrait" in the subtitle "Portrait of a Dead Civilization" is meant to convey, as reliably as can be expected of a programmatic statement, the kind of presentation of a civilization which I intend to give.

During the nearly twenty years in which this book has been in the making, a period of continuous rethinking and rewriting, the conviction grew in me that new ways had to be found to present Mesopotamian civilization. It became obvious to me that no amount of painstaking atomizing, no endless inventories under the pretense of objectivity, and no application of any of the accepted, over-all patterns were capable of presenting the data in a way that would convey the whole as well as its integral constituents. This could be done only by comprehending, reducing, and rendering in a more or less readable manner a characteristic selection of the staggering mass of diversified and very often unrelated facts which philologists and archeologists alike have extracted from the tablets and the sherds, the ruins and the images of Mesopotamia and have labeled and arranged in innumerable ways.

Portraiture, a selective approach, seems to offer such a way of presentation. A portrait aims at presenting an individual, not completely but in his uniqueness, and not only at a fleeting moment of time but also at that juncture where past experience encounters future expectation. Yet, to achieve such a portrait of a multifaceted civilization would require a degree of intimate and comprehensive knowledge we hardly possess of any ancient and alien civilization. In spite of this formidable obstacle, the technique of portraiture has been adopted as an incentive rather than as an end in itself. This allows us to present certain dominant characteristics and attitudes in Mesopotamian civilization as illustrations of its uniqueness as well as to delineate the fateful lines of strain and fatigue that constantly endangered its cohesion.

Any Assyriologist who has read through as many cuneiform texts as I have in pursuit of general understanding rather than on a quest for, let us say, linguistic features, will and must come to form a concept of Mesopotamian civilization differing in major as well as minor points from that which I offer here. After all, a portrait to be worth anything must contain as much of the portraitist as of his subject. Moreover, I must warn the reader that nearly every sentence in this book glosses over some essential and ultimately insoluble problem, and that what may seem complicated is still but an unavoidable simplification. I know quite well that my attitudes will be criticized as pessimistic, or nihilistic, or too bold, or simply foolhardy, and so on, but, correct as such judgments may be with regard to specific points, they will not deter me from the course I aim to steer between the Scylla of an easy and ready optimism and the Charybdis of the pessimism that accepts difficulties as an excuse for abandoning the quest for understanding. In other words, neither the easy joys of specialization nor the equally hedonistic escape into penetration centered on restricted data must hinder the advance toward an over-all synthesis of the field. Whenever possible, I have made clear what we know and what we have surmised from the few facts available. I have refrained from assuming unilinear developments that lead elegantly through the empty spaces of prehistory and converge on the few facts at hand. Such presentations make easy reading but do not contribute much; synthesis should be the goal only where we have to deal with a complexity and superabundance of individual data, as in well-documented historical periods.

The organization of this book is intended to correspond to a certain degree to its purpose as suggested by the subtitle. The first chapter provides the background for the "portrait," the second applies broad washes of color to achieve aerial perspective, and the third can be said to fix the linear perspective. The last three chapters give texture, depth, and highlights, if one may continue without overtaxing the metaphor.

To counteract the inherent and inevitable subjectivity of such a treatment, each chapter is provided with a more or less extensive bibliographic footnote. Its primary purpose is to offer the general reader references to books and articles that deal with the topics discussed, giving preference to opinions that differ from my own. It contains for the Assyriologist, moreover, references to cuneiform passages to substantiate specific statements.

Only sparing use has been made throughout this book of the practice of quoting translated cuneiform texts either in support of statements or in order to "let the texts speak for themselves." To take up the second point first, translated texts tend to speak more of the translator than of their original message. It is not too difficult to render texts written in a dead language as literally as possible and to suggest to the outsider, through the use of quaint and stilted locutions, the alleged awkwardness and archaism of a remote period. Those who know the original language retranslate anyhow—consciously or unconsciously—in order to understand it. It is nearly impossible to render any but the simplest Akkadian text in a modern language with a satisfactory approximation to the original in content, style, or connotation. A step nearer to the realization of the legitimate desire to make the texts "speak for themselves" would bring us, perhaps, an anthology of Akkadian texts, with a critical discussion of the literary, stylistic, and emotional setting of each translated piece.

To quote supporting textual evidence in translation only—to return to the first point mentioned above—would make the book much too long; such a procedure would necessitate lengthy philological commentary. It would also detract from one of the purposes of this book, namely to communicate with non-Assyriologists.

In a book of comparable outlook and scope dealing with European culture and its history, such terms as Rinascimento, scholastics, or the Wars of the Roses, such geographical names as Cluny, Oxford, Avignon, or Vienna, and reference to such personages as Luther, St. Augustine, Napoleon, or King Alfred the Great would be fully understandable to the reader. And he would also be expected to place such names immediately in a rather complex frame of reference. When, however, the reader of this book comes across such terms as Third Dynasty of Ur, Sargonids, and Chaldean kings, finds such place names as Larsa, Ugarit, and Kaniš, and the personal names Hattušili, Merodach-Baladan, and Idrimi, he will necessarily be at a loss. Since it would greatly hamper the manner of presentation to offer explanations at each instance, and since a systematic survey of periods, places, and personages would make hard reading, a glossary of names and terms appears at the end of the book (see p. 398ff.). The reader is also referred to the Appendix on Mesopotamian Chronology and to a map of the entire region.

This brings me to my final point. The immense problem of the extent, the validity, and the effect of the Sumerian legacy on Mesopotamian civilization cannot and will not be dealt with here. The Sumerians left their imprint in varying degrees on all things Mesopotamian. Their traces are palpable; they range from the most obvious, such as the preservation of Sumerian texts in certain cultic practices and the use of Sumerian as the vehicle of specialized literary expression, to the mass of individual Sumerian loan words in Akkadian texts, words that refer to all levels of literature, to all aspects of Mesopotamian civilization. There is Sumerian influence, real or seemingly real, in the social sphere, as in the concept of kingship and in the phenomenon of urbanization, and in the arts, in the motif repertory of the mythology and in monumental architecture and in the use of glyptic. To what degree of transformation and adaptation the religious life and its articulation in Akkadian Mesopotamia is ultimately indebted to Sumerian (or earlier) forms, we shall probably never know. Hence it would appear that a presentation of Mesopotamian civilization should include a presentation of its Sumerian background. Though this might be an ideal solution, a comparison with similar studies of medieval and modern Europe will show the reader that it is feasible only on just that level of vague generality and facile simplification which I am attempting to avoid. Everyone knows of the classical and the Old Testament fountainhead of Western civilization. Should a "portrait of European civilization" study both? Should it—and this is certainly defensible—separate Greek and Roman contributions, and in the Old Testament, the general Near Eastern and the genuinely Palestinian, and should one not go further and trace for Greece the ultimate Asiatic Ionian, the Dorian and Minoan sources, and, for Rome, the contributions of the Etruscans as against those of the Oscans, Sabines, and others? To embark on such a course of research would lead any scholar to inevitable standstill—although the mentioned peoples, their languages, and so on, are much better known than the Sumerians.

For exactly this consideration, I have turned my back on Sumer and moved into the more than two millennia of Akkadian evidence.

Introduction: Assyriology—
Why and How?

Sapere aude

It is now well over a hundred years since western European scholars succeeded in discovering the key to the writings that two long-vanished Near Eastern civilizations had left behind. These are the hieroglyphic inscriptions to be found on Egyptian buildings and objects, and the writings, in cuneiform script, on clay tablets and on stone objects found in and around today's Iraq.

Ancient Egypt always has been a strange and curious country, exciting much interest in the minds of its neighbors. For nearly two millennia after its disappearance, the inscribed walls of the impressive and unique ruins of the Nile Valley were successful in keeping alive some memory of Egyptian civilization. Everyone was familiar with the dramatic and memorable events concerning Egypt related in the Old Testament and the colorful and intriguing tales of Egypt recorded by Greek writers. There were, as well, the fairy tales the Arabs spun around the pyramids, buried treasures, and vengeful ghosts. When the fantastic Egyptian adventure of Napoleon and the quick and startling decipherment of the Rosetta Stone by Champollion threw open the buried civilization of Egypt and its ancient sites to the inquisitive eyes of European scholarship, a new world of undreamt-of complexity and appeal emerged, and the historic vista of man and his adventures was enlarged by many centuries beyond the point reached by the Old Testament and classical sources.

Mesopotamia, the land between two rivers, the Euphrates and the Tigris, was not nearly as fortunate as Egypt. There were no walls inscribed with mysterious and beautifully executed signs, hardly any precious objects to be collected as curiosities, only a few high, isolated, and dilapidated brick towers to which clung the name and the fame of the biblical Tower of Babel. The extensive ruins of the once famous cities of Babylon and Nineveh could not much impress the traveler. Their crumbling outlines had been buried for millennia under sand, mud, and huge layers of debris; the once fertile countryside had reverted to deserts and swamps, dotted with mounds—*tells*—to which, curiously enough, the Bedouins still referred with names that echoed the ancient designations of the cities whose sites they marked. Only by the towering stone columns of Persepolis, in the highlands of southern Iran, could the attention of the few European travelers be attracted when they visited the far-flung lands of the decaying Ottoman Empire. There, in Persepolis, they found impressive structures and statuary and—above all—inscriptions in an unknown writing that excited their curiosity.

It so happened that both events—the rediscovery of the world of ancient Egypt and the appearance of intriguing Mesopotamian wedge-writing on bricks, clay cylinders, stone slabs, and inaccessible mountain rocks—occurred at a propitious time. It happened at the moment when Western man was eager to step out of that magic circle, the field of energy that protects, preserves, and confines every civilization. At the end of the eighteenth century, Europe, the last of the great civilizations of a span of more than five millennia, had reached a convenient plateau before the upswing of technological, economic, and political developments produced the changes that have altered the course of human history. In that precarious interlude of collection and relaxation, Western man could suddenly perceive himself, his own civilization, and the civilizations around him. In fact, Western man became then and there, and for the first time, willing and able to appreciate and to evaluate with objectivity his own civilization, to correlate other civilizations, and to strive for an understanding of some over-all design and plan. In whatever romantic form that novel experience was cast, it must be taken as representing a new departure for inquiring mankind.

European scholarship extended to embrace not only alien and exotic civilizations but, with equal inquisitiveness and eagerness, turned to the civilizations of the past, and not only to its own past. Ruins and undeciphered writings suddenly changed from objects deserving only a passing interest to the rank of messages from vanished civilizations. They became a challenge to the ingenuity of the amateur, a worthy object of study for the scholar. They were considered as belonging to a field of intellectual endeavor in which the nations of Europe, in dignity, could compete for prestige—and for loot for their growing museums.

The ruins and writings of Mesopotamia began soon to speak volubly of the civilization that had created them more than four millennia earlier. The decipherers called the language "Assyrian." After a time it became evident that there was an Assyrian and a Babylonian dialect—we now refer to both as Akkadian—but the name Assyriology was retained for the field of study that deals with the language and its numerous dialects, all written with cuneiform signs on clay, stone, or metal.

In the heroic period of the new science of Assyriology, which lasted until the last quarter of the nineteenth century, various systems of writing using cuneiform signs had been deciphered, the main content of the royal inscriptions had been established, and the spades of the busily competing excavators had attacked many of the principal sites, which yielded objects of silver, gold, and copper and impressive statues and reliefs as well as the remnants of grandiose architecture. Above all, an abundant and steady stream of documents inscribed on clay came to light everywhere, from the Persian Gulf to Asia Minor, and even as far off as Cyprus and Egypt.

We cannot be concerned here with tracing the history of the

decipherment, that exciting battle in which the acumen of many scholars was pitted against the unheard-of complexities of several alien systems of writing and hitherto unknown languages, nor the rather sordid maneuvers of rival agents of European governments to obtain sites and objects, although this happens to be customarily presented and accepted as a major part of the history of archeology. What can and should be done here is to present Assyriology in its aims and its achievements.

The record of achievement is impressive indeed. The decipherment of the writings led to the development of a series of new disciplines concerned with the study of the civilizations that either had made use of one or more of the several systems of writing or had become known through them. Sumerology, Hittitology, and Elamitology are concerned with civilizations which used the writing systems, the study of the Hurrian and the Urartian languages as well as that of the remnants of the languages of early Asia Minor deals with languages and civilizations known indirectly through these writings. Essential contributions were made by all these disciplines toward the understanding of the background and the surrounding world of Mycenean, Palestinian, and Egyptian civilizations. Finally, new vistas were opened up by archeological study of the ancient Near and Middle East, which owes much of its success to the stimulus of decipherment of textual materials.

In Assyriology proper, to return to the focus of this presentation, the texts on clay tablets are far more valuable, far more relevant, than the monuments that have been discovered, although the latter, especially the famous reliefs on the walls of Assyrian palaces and the countless products of glyptic art, offer welcome illustration to the wealth of factual information contained on clay tablets, stelae, and votive offerings. The archeologist's contribution toward the elucidation of the Mesopotamian past bears primarily on that crucial millennium or more which preceded the earliest written documentation (i.e., before 2800 B.C.), and which only field and comparative archeologists are able to scan and to articulate through their intricate network of horizons and stratified levels. (In exceptional instances, however, and in small sites, the interplay of the archeologist and the epigrapher in Mesopotamia can yield important results.)

The cuneiform texts have given us a strangely distorted picture of more than two thousand years of Mesopotamian civilization. This picture is composed of abundant but very spotty detailed information and of rough and incomplete outlines of major political and cultural developments. All this theoretical framework, moreover, is torn to shreds again and again by immense gaps in time and space. It requires much patient work on the part of the philologist to hold these shreds together by a crisscrossing web of connections based on the slimmest textual evidence. He has to link minutiae to minutiae, analyze and correlate highly recalcitrant material, in order to gauge developments and to trace these trends through the ever-recurring blackouts of information.

Thus, we have come to know the names of hundreds of kings and important personalities, from the third-millennium rulers of Lagaš to the kings and scholars of the Seleucid period; we are able to follow the fate of dynasties and the personal fortunes of certain rulers, observe the rise and decay of cities, and discern, at times, the geopolitical situation within a chronological framework that—even for the early periods—is becoming more and more reliable. We now have at hand a number of codified laws, from the Sumerian to the Neo-Babylonian period, that can be related to a staggering number of private and public legal documents and illustrated by an equally extensive body of letters and administrative texts. This, in turn, has enabled the Assyriologist to realize period and local differences in legal practices and to observe changing social and political contexts; and it has provided him with new and unexpected opportunities for research. No other early civilization offers material on its economic history with such abundance and over such a long period of time. There has been preserved, as well, a considerable body of texts that are customarily labeled literary. We have one full-length Creation epic and a bevy of shorter ones, the rightly famous Epic of Gilgamesh in a late and very sophisticated version together with a number of earlier fragments and several tales about gods and heroes of divine extraction, their exploits, triumphs, and sufferings, often but not always harking back to earlier, Sumerian, prototypes. Their alluring contents and the obvious relationship of these stories to the thematic inventory and even to specific incidents of myths known from neighboring civilizations have given special importance to these texts in the eyes of Assyriologists and those scholars concerned with these civilizations, for the texts have evoked far more interest than have texts clearly religious in content, the numerous prayers, conjurations, and lamentations which have been collected. Still farther in the background of the attention of Assyriologists remains the immense bulk of the learned literature in cuneiform, consisting primarily of the writings of several types of diviners and of handbooks of Mesopotamian scholars, ranging from Sumero-Akkadian dictionaries to learned commentaries and theological speculation. Only a handful of Assyriologists has ventured into these realms, dry, monotonous, and difficult of access as they are.

Assyriology is definitely an arcane discipline. Behind a façade of painfully inadequate popularizations written for the interested but innocent layman, a small group of workers labors in an ever-enlarging field of research. Either in self-imposed concentration on a specific segment or a single approach, or compelled into such restrictions by the sheer bulk of the available data, these scholars have been at work now for nearly a century. Under such circumstances, one may well ask where we stand today in the process of interpreting, correlating, and digesting textual evidence, archeological findings, and monuments. Can we determine in some way whether the work that has been going on for such a long time in the universities of Europe, America, and Asia has made adequate use of that unforgettable intellectual experience offered Western scholarship by these inscriptions?

To answer this, I would like to establish what these tablets meant to those who wrote them. I do not want to assign them importance, meaning, and literary qualities derived, consciously or not, from our own culture-conditioned preferences. And there is another problem: What can these tablets possibly mean to us, of a late and alien civilization, to whom they were not meant to speak?

For the purpose of understanding what these tablets meant to those who wrote them, it is essential to realize that all written documents that come from Mesopotamian soil—and all those that are waiting to be dug up—reflect two distinct backgrounds. They must be carefully differentiated and each investigated in its own context if a relevant answer is to be given the question that has just been asked.

First, there is the large number of tablets that belong to what I will call the stream of the tradition—that is, what can loosely be termed the corpus of literary texts maintained, controlled, and carefully kept alive by a tradition served by successive generations of learned and well-trained scribes. Second, there is the mass of texts of all descriptions, united by the fact that they were used to record the day-to-day activities of the Babylonians and Assyrians. Both streams, of course, run side by side; each has only limited contact with the other. Still, one has to realize that the texts of the second level could never have been written without that cultural continuum maintained so effectively by the scribal tradition.

Parenthetically, it should be noted that the dichotomy which is offered here, primarily for the purpose of emphasizing a characteristic feature, is disturbed by texts which represent—as will be shown below, p. 22—the living literary creativeness of Mesopotamia. Such texts are fed to a considerable extent by the stream of tradition. They were not meant to be read but were communicated orally, and they were couched—even though they were on a different level of style—in the language of the day and the place.

In the tablets of the literary tradition we have a considerable body of texts which a class of scribes, organized in some loose way in local schools or families, considered a duty to copy carefully in order to keep the chain unbroken. And in this they succeeded for nearly two millennia. The desire to maintain a written tradition represents in itself an important culture trait of Mesopotamian civilization. One would expect the driving impulse for such an attitude to be the intention of preserving a body of religious writings or the wish to sustain one tradition against or in competition with rival traditions. But in Mesopotamia this continuity of tradition was achieved by a purely operational though highly effective circumstance rather than by ideological pressures: it was considered an essential part of the training of each scribe to copy faithfully the texts that made up the stream of tradition. The longer and more elaborate the training of a scribe—and long and elaborate training was quite natural in the larger cities, where more scribes were needed and more disciples available—the more extensive became his copying work. This led eventually to the accumulation of a large number of private collections, each containing larger or smaller sections of the text material that made up the stream of tradition. Personal preference, or the requirements of the training, naturally created an interest in assembling private libraries. There even seems to have existed a tendency among the various agglomerations of scribes, whether these were groups attached to or supported in some way by temples or palaces, to obtain missing texts from outside collections in order to replenish the body of material available to a school. In this way a number of scribes, widely scattered throughout Babylonia and Assyria, became owners of literary texts that they had copied themselves during their apprenticeship or out of personal interest. Consequently, copies of the same texts were kept in many different localities. This distribution, combined with the fact that the writing was on extremely durable clay tablets, maintained the major bulk of the texts as a literary corpus in actual use from the second half of the second millennium B.C. up to the periods of the Seleucid and even the Arsacid rulers of Mesopotamia, and subsequently kept them safe for us in the rubble of destroyed cities for another two millennia.

It seems likely that it will forever be a moot question to what extent this corpus of texts remained unaffected by changes during such an extended period of continuous transmission. Have certain texts been discarded, have others succumbed to the ravages of time and men? We know that all major and minor Mesopotamian cities were repeatedly destroyed by enemy action, and we know that the water table has been rising in lower Mesopotamia. Furthermore, a sizable number of the old cities of Mesopotamia are still inhabited today and therefore inaccessible to the spade of the archeologist. These potential and actual losses are counteracted to a certain extent by lucky accidents: clay tablets were sometimes used as fill, and entire archives have thus been preserved. Certain sites have remained undisturbed since victor and vanquished allowed the ruins to be forgotten and covered by dust and vegetation. Although we realize that we are to a large extent at the mercy of chance, we still have a duty to recognize the possibility that certain selective manipulations may have interfered with the handing down of traditional texts, or that new material may have been incorporated in the texts we have. This problem is extremely difficult, and no clear-cut solution should be expected. There exists, however, the definite possibility of approaching it in a rather promising way.

It so happens that the last great Assyrian king, Assurbanipal (668–627 B.C.), succeeded in assembling in Nineveh what has every right to be called the first systematically collected library in the ancient Near East. Nearly all the tablets that made up his collection are now in the British Museum. Many of them are published or reasonably well catalogued. Because the library was not that of an individual scribe or even a school or family, but, rather, was brought together upon a royal fiat from all over Mesopotamia, we are entitled to assume that the topical range of Assurbanipal's collection is representative of the main body, if not the entire content, of the scribal tradition. This assumption is borne out by a small but sufficient number of private tablet collections that come from such widely scattered cities as Assur and Harran in the north and Babylon, Nippur, Ur, and Borsippa in the south—collections that are distributed through time adequately enough to furnish essential controls. Further corroboration is offered by finds originating in scribal schools outside Mesopotamia proper, in which Akkadian and Sumerian were taught to foreign scribes in the course of their training.

With the exception of the late and highly technical astronomical texts from Babylonia proper, the contents of all these collections demonstrate that the picture offered by the library of Assurbanipal in Nineveh is basically representative. There exist, of course, inevitable discrepancies and gaps. The laws of probability militate against the preservation of small text groups and work havoc even with larger ones. In spite of the fact that less than one-fourth of the body of traditional texts has been preserved, and only too often in rather poor condition, and in spite of the selection that is produced by the accidents of survival, of discovery, and—not to be underestimated—the accidents of publication, the unified picture that results from the observation of these well-distributed collections entitles us to speak of the literary tablets of Mesopotamia as belonging to a coherent and continuous stream. When Assyriologists will be able to follow the fate of individual text groups through the history of their tradition, they will obtain more insight into the workings of this stream and, conceivably, light will be shed some day on ideological preferences and other attitudes that neither the content nor the wording of these texts is likely to reflect directly.

One more point bearing on the stream of tradition is to be discussed: What is the size of this body of texts?

The salient characteristic of all the ancient collections is the predominance of scholarly over literary texts, and, within the scholarly texts, the predominance of texts which Assyriologists call "omen texts." Such omen collections consist of endless, systematically arranged, one-line entries, each describing a specific act, a well-defined event, the behavior or feature of an animal, a specific part of its body, or that of a plant or of a human being, or the movements of the stars, the moon and the sun, atmospheric events, and other observable details, of unbelievable variety. Each case is provided with a prediction that refers to the welfare of the country or to that of the individual with respect to whom—such is the basic assumption—the event happened, if it was not purposefully provoked to obtain information about the future. The library of Assurbanipal contained more than three hundred tablets, each holding eighty to two hundred entries of the nature just described.

Next in size seems to have been a group of about two hundred tablets of a quite different nature. These contain lists of cuneiform signs and sign combinations with added readings as well as lists of Sumerian words with their Akkadian translations, organized according to various principles of arrangement and representing what may be termed a dictionary. They further include lists explaining rare and foreign expressions in Akkadian. In short, this group of tablets embraces in an encyclopedic form everything required for teaching scribes the native (Akkadian) and the traditional (Sumerian) languages. The bilingualism of the scribes is reflected in a large number of Sumerian incantations and prayers that are provided with interlinear Akkadian translations. The latter form a group that seems to have amounted to more than one hundred tablets.

About the same number of tablets contain cycles of conjurations for cathartic and apotropaic purposes as well as what is customarily called the "epic literature," fables, proverbs, and sundry small collections of varia and trivia that somehow have found their way into the body of "canonical" texts. One should stress that the epic literature (such as the Creation story, the Epic of Gilgamesh, of Irra, the stories of Etana, Anzu, and so on) amounts to only thirty-five to forty of the seven hundred tablets so far enumerated.

The existence of another two hundred or more tablets can be inferred with varying degrees of certainty from isolated fragments and such other indications as catalogues of tablets. As a safety margin dictated by general pessimism rather than by rational considerations, one may add one-third again to these nine hundred tablets in order to achieve something like an informed guess at the total number of tablets that were kept in Assurbanipal's palace at Nineveh. One may perhaps—but not necessarily—assume that a further projection beyond this estimate should be hazarded, so that fifteen hundred would represent, at a maximum, the entire corpus of cuneiform literature that embodied, at any time or place, what we call the stream of tradition.

To venture further guesses, such as to the number of lines which these tablets may have contained, is sheer folly, but there is little doubt in my mind that the sum total would leave the Rigveda (about the size of the Iliad) and the Homeric epics, as

well as the Old and New Testaments (which surpass the epics
only slightly as to the number of verses), far behind, and would
probably reach, if not exceed in bulk, even the size of the
Mahabharata with its 190,000 verses.

It should be added that these figures refer to individual texts
and not to the number of copies of these texts. In the royal
library at Nineveh there were as many as six exemplars for a
single text, which is a great help in filling in lacunae and in
reconstructing compositions. Since it was an essential part of the
training of the apprentice scribes to copy certain tablets, those
works that make up the primary curriculum are preserved
in many more copies than those that are part of the higher
levels of training, which only a small number of students
attained.

It now behooves us to outline what should be considered the
characteristic features of this corpus of texts, surveying it
without the professionally myopic outlook of the Assyriologist.

First, one has to point out that nearly all of these tablets were
at some early point in their history frozen into a specific wording
and an established arrangement of content. This process of
standardization began early (third quarter of the second
millennium B.C.) for certain key text groups—especially those of
the encyclopedic genre. It continued, successively affecting
other groups, until the scribes of Assurbanipal assembled and
copied individual tablets or small groups that had been in
restricted circulation, and combined them into topical arrangements, giving them definite titles and indicating their sequence
by numbers.

Standardization effectively maintained the original contents
against the pressures of changing concepts and attitudes, preserving obsolete text material that otherwise certainly would
have disappeared. For the Assyriologist this standardization is
the greatest boon. Normally, all he has to work with are
shattered fragments of tablets that come from several excavations and accidental finds, fragments which more often than not
contain lines that break off in the middle of the text or which
contain only beginnings and ends of lines. But due to the fact
that in the body of literary material nearly all identifiable

fragments, wherever they come from, go back to one standard-ized version, the Assyriologist is often able to reconstruct an entire text out of small fragments.

The contents of these tablets clearly indicate that the cunei-form literature which the Mesopotamians themselves considered essential and worthy of being handed down, concerned, directly or indirectly, the activities of the diviners and of the priests specializing in exorcistic techniques. Only a very small section contains what we, immersed in the Western tradition, like to call products of literary creativeness. One may, in fact, reasonably estimate that there are, at most, fifty or sixty tablets that contain what we are wont to call epic texts (the thirty-five to forty tablets already mentioned) plus rather platitudinous concoc-tions of practical "wisdom" as well as some prayer tablets whose diction and imagery seem to us to be distinguished by a certain tang of genuineness, though it is open to doubt whether this quality was instrumental in their inclusion in the stream of tradition.

The epic texts make a strong appeal to the esthetic tastes and ideological preferences of Western cultures, steeped as we are in literary and religious traditions that originated in Greece and in the land of the Bible, only to be transposed into a new key in medieval Europe. This has induced us, consciously or not, to make two obvious mistakes: We have been exaggerating the importance of such texts, although they are few and far between in Mesopotamian literature, and thus we judge the bulk of the tradition for its lack of the texts we are conditioned to appreciate.

In the fragments preserved, there is a noticeable absence of historical literature; that is, texts are lacking that would attest to the awareness of the scribes of the existence of a historical continuum in the Mesopotamian civilization of which they themselves and their tradition were only a part. To be sure, there are preserved a few late chronicles, lists of kings, a number of copies of very old royal inscriptions, a small group of texts that contain legends of early kings, and theological interpreta-tions of sundry historical events of the pre-standardization period. Nothing, however, was considered worthy of recording that would relate the literary and intellectual traditions in and for which these scribes lived with any co-ordinates of time, space, and socioeconomic realities.

The same detachment expresses itself in the complete absence of any polemic in this type of literature. All statements appear without relation to any background of ideological, religious, or even political stress or tension. This is not for lack of opportunity, because the ritual complaints in the prayers written or adapted for royal use, or the predictions in the innumerable omen passages, could easily reflect discontent or social criticism. These tensions are very much in evidence in Greek texts, where they are further accentuated by the didactic style of scholarly presentation. There was apparently no rivalry between schools, no clash between the Mesopotamian scribe's cultural outlook and that of those who lived around him, either in his own country or elsewhere. It is especially the latter contrast in both the Old and the New Testament that imparts a specific mood and intensity not only to pragmatic utterances but even to descriptive passages. The person of the scribe, his beliefs and ambitions, are conspicuously absent in cuneiform literature; no cognizance is taken of religious or philosophical insights; no constructive political thoughts are revealed and no awareness of man's role and claims in this world.

The explanation for all this is quite simple. What we have at hand in these twelve hundred or more tablets is but a reference library geared to the needs of the diviners and those specialized practitioners of magic who were responsible for the spiritual security of kings and other important persons. To this were added several sets of handbooks for educational and research purposes, meant to maintain the scholarly standards and the technical proficiency of these essential professions. By accident, and hardly for what we would call their merits, literary texts were carried along in the stream of tradition as part and parcel of the education of the scribes simply because the copying of such texts belonged to the traditional curriculum. The corpus has to be understood, appreciated, and utilized solely in terms of what it was meant to represent for those who created, maintained, and used it. And the literary texts have to be considered primarily from the point of view of their own position of importance within the stream of the tradition.

Assyriologists, however, always did, and still do, approach these texts from a quite different angle. They look for deeply meaningful cosmologies, for primeval wisdom, for the pomp of mythological exploits, the charm or crudeness of early social and economic patterns that supposedly reflect the growth of ideas beyond the ken of history, for legends and *historiae* and titillatingly different mores—in short, for what Western scholars in the "study of man" ever since Herodotus have expected to discover at the periphery of their own, and of course normative, world. And expectations of that sort are apparently fulfilled, to judge from the books concerned with Mesopotamian civilization produced by popularizers. Such an attitude affects Assyriological research work to varying degrees. There are scholars who are inextricably entangled in attempts to relate Assyriological data to the Old Testament in some acceptable way, and others who find in haphazardly collected instances, torn out of their ideological and stylistic context, convincing proof for whatever the fashion of the day is propounding in anthropology, the history of religions, or the field of economics. Even linguistically, the cuneiform texts have not been subjected to candid and unbiased investigation. Having been, quite early and correctly, tagged as a Semitic language, Akkadian was, and still is, mercilessly put on the procrustean bed of one or another Semitic language that is whimsically considered normative. Often this is done not out of methodological considerations or because of the range of the scholar's interest, but for reasons which seem rather to originate in a quest for a *raison d'être* for the entire field of Assyriology, not only in the eyes of other disciplines but also in the eyes of the scholars themselves. This psychological situation has yielded, and continues to yield, a number of biased articles and books. The same situation influences the research range of Assyriologists in a more subtle way. It exerts considerable influence—normally, at a sub-conscious level—on the selection of topics to be investigated. Thus are created or fostered preferences for the study of certain literary patterns, mythological motifs, or social and economic contexts that in some way either correspond to, or are strikingly different from, those to which our composite Western background has conditioned these scholars.

Let us return to the literary texts. Any evaluation with respect to topic inventory and style types should take into consideration the fact that there exists meager, but unquestionable, evidence of a rich and productive oral literary tradition in Mesopotamia. It seems to have flourished not only before the period in which the standardization, or "canonization," of the written tradition became effective, but also parallel and subsequent to it. We know, for instance, of the existence of cycles of songs, mainly love songs, that were cast, in the fashion of the ancient Near East, in intense and quasi-religious phraseology, but also of songs sung in battle and in praise of the king. We know of courtly tales and legends spun around kings both loved and feared, of popular stories with sometimes jocular and pungent undertones. Also in circulation were dire prophecies and political diatribes in poetic form as well as riddles and animal tales. Of all this we are informed mainly by isolated tablets containing texts that do not belong to the stream of tradition and were copied only by chance and survive in single copies. Nevertheless, that these have survived entitles us to assume the existence of several literary genres that belonged to a tradition different in content and probably also in purpose from the written tradition we propose to discuss. It is too simple to call that other tradition "oral," because the possibility has to be considered that a divergence between the written and the oral tradition was the consequence of either linguistic conditions or the emergence of a different writing material.

Let us first raise the question as to the social context of this other type of literature, its carriers and its public. As a habitat outside the stratum in which the stream of the written tradition was in evidence, one could reasonably suggest the courts of the kings of Babylon. The reason why we know next to nothing of this important and natural center of political, economic, and social life is simple: no literary text of importance came to light during the excavations of Babylon, due to the rise of the water table in that region, and no archeologist has ever happened to find the ruins of a Babylonian palace. We do know, however, that, in the second millennium, the courts of the kings of Ur, Isin, Larsa, and Babylon harbored both scholars and poets, and there is no reason to suppose that it was any different in the first, although there is hardly any indication available of this role of the royal courts of Babylon. There are several possible reasons for this scarcity of documentation: the lack of finds from Babylon, the use of perishable, wax-covered tablets that may go back further in history than we are now assuming, and the possibility that the Aramaic language became, in Babylonia, at an earlier stage than generally supposed, the vehicle for a literary tradition different from that written in Akkadian and on clay tablets.

Such suggestions are offered here solely to illustrate the essential fact that the traditional cuneiform which we have been discussing should not be considered the main or the sole product of the creative effort of Mesopotamian civilization. For its correct evaluation and an appreciation of its achievements and its importance, one has to realize its limitations in purpose, style, and content. One has to concede the existence of other types of literature in this civilization, genres that are of still undefined range, status, and import, even though the evidence is slim and often circumstantial.

By no means do the traditional texts offer the most important documentary material for the work of the Assyriologist. There exists—and very often deservedly in the front ranks of interest—an impressive bulk of cuneiform tablets that contain the records of the day-to-day activities of the inhabitants of Mesopotamia, from kings down to shepherds. In time span and geographical distribution, in bulk and in topical variety, they quite often surpass the traditional texts. These tablets fall into two sharply differing categories: records and letters. The great majority of the records deal with administrative transactions of all sorts. They originated in the realm of an elaborate bureaucracy that handled with technical skill and methodical consistency the affairs of the temple administrations of southern Babylonia (from Ur to Sippar, and from the end of the third millennium to the last third of the first millennium B.C.). Such records come to us also from the royal palaces all over the ancient Near East, wherever the Akkadian language and the cuneiform system of writing was in use, that is, from Susa, north of the Persian Gulf, to Ugarit and Alalakh, near the Mediterranean coast. To a much lesser extent, clay tablets record private legal transactions, such as sales, rentals, and loans as well as marriage contracts, adoptions, wills, and so on. There exist, also, a number of international agreements scattered through a period of one millenium. The letters likewise fall into two groups, those dealing with administrative and political matters and those concerned with private and personal affairs. The latter are far less numerous and are restricted to specific periods and contexts.

We again feel obliged to venture a reasonable guess as to the number of these records and letters. It can be said that the material already published, together with that known to be in the possession of several of the larger museums, amounts to about 40,000 to 50,000 tablets. This estimate refers to tablets written in, or predominantly in, Akkadian. Sumerian administrative and legal documents may run easily to more than three times that number.

What information do these texts contain? How and to what degree can this information be utilized for the understanding of Mesopotamian life and customs? Is this the raw material the historians of law and of economic institutions dream of? Are these the texts that will clearly reveal what those who wrote them, and those for whom they were written, thought about themselves, their world, their gods?

Unfortunately, clear and easy answers to these questions cannot be expected. The potential usefulness of this source of information is severely curtailed by a number of factors. These texts cover a wide area geographically and a very long period of time, so that their large number is sharply reduced when one's research focuses upon a point in time and space and upon a specific problem. Again, the coverage of these texts is very irregular. Large areas and periods are blacked out for a variety of reasons, and only rarely is it possible to obtain insight into developments on a larger scale in time or into regional differences on a synchronic level. The picture that any investigation based on such material can obtain consists of a number of spots of light. It is as if a narrowly confined beam of light haphazardly illuminated this or that city between the Persian Gulf and the Mediterranean Sea at infrequent and irregular intervals during two millennia, leaving everything else in darkness. It is true that, within the beam, complex institutions and political situations appear as the background against which we may observe history in the making—administrators at work collecting and appropriating taxes and services, merchants engaged in far-flung commercial activities, and farmers and bankers arguing endlessly about debts. Personalities appear, and the rise and fall of families can be observed, but, in most instances, for only two or three generations before darkness sets in again. Very rarely, where excavations have been persistent and fruitful or our luck has willed it, we have a continuous series of spotlights illuminating the history of a city, such as in Nippur and Assur, in Ur, and, to a certain extent, in Sippar.

An equally important obstacle to the utilization of this rich body of material is of a philological nature. This holds true, though for different reasons, for both the records and the letters. Administrative documents were written solely for internal use; their diction is terse, abbreviated, and full of mysterious technical terms. It is a delicate and difficult task to establish the meanings of terms that, in the course of time, often underwent subtle changes and to reconstruct their institutional and economic background. Yet only by doing so can one hope to infuse some life into the strictly formalistic style of ledgers, lists, and receipts. Without a carefully established frame of reference, without our knowing who delivered and who received, and under what title and claim goods and services were allocated, administrative texts yield only a meager harvest of personal names, a technical vocabulary elaborately describing staples and raw materials, and an opaque residue of unintelligible words from the bureaucratic language of the period.

Quite different but equally forbidding are the philological difficulties that hamper the study of the letters. Most of them are written by, to, or for officials, including the king. Their topics are reports, requests, and executive orders in administrative and legal matters; their diction ranges from voluble protests and insincere excuses to cutting remarks and invective. In the private letters—and there alone in cuneiform texts—we often come in contact with the spoken language instead of the formalized phraseology of religious texts, the technical jargon of scholarly literature, and the careful archaizing and stylized verbiage of historical texts. In quick-shifting, emotion-charged, pregnant sentences, topics are introduced and abruptly dropped, and allusions are made to situations known only to the correspondents. Emphasis, irony, rhetorical questions, veiled threats, unfinished sentences, and imprecations run the gamut of syntactical finesse to mold the diction of these letters to such expressiveness that it remains beyond the ken of the philologist accustomed to the inane formalism of conventional literary texts.

This characterization of the material available in cuneiform sources applies to all but one rather substantial group, the historical texts. This term is commonly applied to the royal inscriptions, on which most of what we know of Mesopotamian history is based. They represent an important and valuable source material, it is true, but when one searches for information other than names of kings and places, for more insight than can be offered by repetitious descriptions of victories and the pompous phraseology of triumph, these inscriptions are disappointing. The reason lies in two important stylistic features, often overlooked. First, only a small fraction of these documents was written for the purpose of recording and conveying information to be read; on the contrary, they were buried carefully in the foundations of temples and palaces or engraved in other inaccessible places. Second, generally they are couched as communications from the king to his deity, reporting on warlike deeds and building activities. This is especially true for the later group of Assyrian and Babylonian royal inscriptions which represents an ingenious adaptation of an earlier prototype that, fundamentally, had the form of a votive inscription. As votive inscriptions, these historical texts are extremely interesting, but the information they yield is of little import. In combination with king lists and treaties, they serve to outline roughly the course of historic events, but they cannot bring us very near to an understanding of Mesopotamian history. From what social, economic, or other situations sprang the aggressive *élan* of Assyria, the tenacity and the staying power of Babylonia? What pressures guided the continuous struggle of both civilizations in their search for a livable and workable form in which their political and spiritual preferences could materialize with that stability which was to them an eternal dream and which eluded both of them time and again?

Documentary evidence of the type here described can be handled in two ways: either through a process of sustained synthesis on a specific and restricted level that singles out certain data and analyzes and interprets them in detail, or through an over-all synthesis that aims at the creation and constant re-creation of a picture that is to embrace the entire civilization, either diachronically or synchronically. The latter kind of synthesis should give direction and impetus to further research by pointing out the frontiers of knowledge and should convey, ultimately, an image of the field and of work done, in progress, or to be desired to both the Assyriologist and all scholars who care to know about Assyriology.

In both these kinds of syntheses, we have made little effort and had less success. With regard to the first kind, one has to remember that the Assyriologist has at his disposal but a small section of material. Any new excavation and any other find can endanger and perhaps overthrow the conclusions he has reached. This can place a severe strain on the creative activity and the scholarly *élan* of those who do not find it easy to discard carefully worked out conclusions. Of course, the classical scholar may also have to face new and surprising data, but only exceptionally can such data be compared in scope and relevance to what the Assyriologist has every right to expect. Another hazard, touched on above, concerns the difficulty of synthesizing data coming from an alien civilization, a civilization that is reflected solely in the dull and distorting mirror of documents written in a language long dead. It is necessary, but extremely difficult, to free oneself from one's own ingrained concepts in attempting to organize data pertaining to another civilization.

But in what other way can a Western scholar evaluate the tenor, mood, and sincerity of a polytheistic religion or comprehend the delicate complexities in the workings of alien institutions that only inadvertently shed light on the numerous questions he has to ask? And if the wrong questions are posed, the answers obtained surely will be wrong or at least misleading.

With regard to an over-all synthesis that purports to embrace the entire field, the following procedure usually has been applied. All extant data that can be easily and, for the most part, uncritically collected are projected, in complete disregard for chronological, regional, and contextual differences, upon one level in time and one dimension in space within a framework that reflects nothing but the cultural background of the scholar at work. When one thus "synchronizes" and "consolidates" an array of data, one can achieve rather easily what the undemanding reader and the layman would term reasonable coverage. When all data are summarily pigeonholed into the conventional framework of such headings as "king," "temple," "religious life," "mythology," "magic," "family," and so on, the goal of the presentation is believed to have been reached. It is, of course, easy to shrug one's shoulders over such glib popularizations and leave them to marginal scholars and certain loquacious archeologists, but one has to confess that this attitude on the part of an Assyriologist would border on cowardice. The battle for synthesis is the battle he is to fight, and this battle should be considered his *raison d'être*, even though it is a battle that can know no victorious outcome. The battle as such must be the task of the Assyriologist.

Typically, however, we tend to escape into peripheral skirmishes. The field of Assyriology has grown so wide and so complex that not more than a handful of scholars can claim to be at home in its manifold domains. Most Assyriologists restrict their interest to apparently well-documented subdivisions and often select, in premature specialization, a specific area as their field of research. Such work is more likely to yield a feeling of satisfaction, achievement, and security than the continuous endeavor to keep abreast of the incessant changes created by the afflux of new texts, new interpretations, and new meanings.

Consequently, the scholarly journals in the field of Assyriology are devoted to learned editions of individual texts, if not fragments of text, and of small groups of documents, and technical discussions of a selection of small-scale problems that happen to be the fashion of the day. Even important additions to our text material are rarely presented in systematic correlation to an over-all frame of reference.

If what has been said sounds like a long-winded preamble intended to offer the Assyriologist a panacea and a new way, let the reader be assured that I do not believe that the diagnosis of our malaise allows for simple medication.

There are, none the less, indications of the direction in which one must look to remedy the situation here outlined. Spectacular successes in the interpretation of cuneiform texts dealing with mathematics and astronomy are quite obviously the result of close co-operation between the Assyriologist and the mathematician and astronomer interested in the history of his discipline. And it is no accident that in both these instances the initiative came from outside the field of Assyriology. Similar, if not so spectacular, successes have been experienced in the study of legal documents from Mesopotamia; here again, stimulus came from the historian of law.

This may be, at last, the solution of many problems that beset Assyriology. Perhaps the descriptive linguist will help us throw off the fetters that are hampering our progress in the understanding of both the Sumerian and the Akkadian languages; the historian of medicine may well contribute essentially toward the understanding of numerous medical texts in cuneiform that so far have not received adequate treatment; and the historian of technology will show us the way in which we should investigate, for example, the tablets describing the manufacture of colored glass and help us to understand the elaborate technical terminology referring to the science of metallurgy. But in this respect one must not stop at the physical sciences. Assyriologists need the understanding and sustained co-operation of interested scholars in economics, the social sciences, and, above all, in cultural anthropology, in order to achieve a better understanding of the institutional structure of Mesopotamia and especially of the religion, or better, the religions, of the entire region that have been handed down to us in countless documents.

And the Assyriologist need not be afraid that his discipline will enjoy only an ancillary role in such collaborations—quite the opposite will be the case. No history of science and technology that claims scholarly status can be written when its author has to rely on inadequate translations of cuneiform texts pertaining to his subject. The Assyriologist should become aware that he holds the keys to a potential wealth of information covering more than two millennia of one of the first great civilizations. If he is in need of a *raison d'être*, here it is.

All this is not meant to be a "programme," but neither should it be simply called wishful thinking—it is a way, well worth considering, out of the stagnation from which we suffer, a stagnation of which the most salient symptoms are the shrinkage of topics selected for research, the "flight into specialization," and the scarcity of students who once used to stray from theology into the perhaps greener pastures of a new and venturesome discipline.

If the new directions here surveyed mean that Assyriology will eventually move away from the humanities and nearer to cultural anthropology, I shall shed no tear. The humanities have never been successful in treating alien civilizations with that tender care and deep respect that such an undertaking demands. Their conceptual tools are geared to integration on their own terms and to assimilation along Western standards.*

* For a critical review of the attitude expressed in this section ("Assyriology—Why and How"), the reader is referred to D. J. Wiseman, "The Expansion of Assyrian Studies: An Inaugural Lecture" (School of Oriental and African Studies, University of London, 1962).

I The Making
of Mesopotamia

THE BACKGROUND

THE SETTING

THE ACTORS

THE WORLD AROUND

Early in the fourth millennium B.C. there occurred in southwest
Asia a phenomenon of lasting importance for the history of
man: the appearance in quick succession of a group of culture
foci. Among them were those which were eventually to give
rise to the self-contained and characteristic civilizations which
we may identify by the names of the river valleys that harbored
them: the civilizations of the Indus Valley, Euphrates Valley,
and Nile Valley. Apart from these, a number of smaller foci
came into evidence at that time, or somewhat later, in the same
region. Equally endowed with characteristic features and unique
formulations, they seem to have been either hampered and
stunted or delayed in their internal evolution by factors of
geopolitical or accidental nature. Elam, South Arabia, and Syria
offer examples, though others may still be buried under the

countless *tells* of the entire region. One essential feature of the phenomenon seems to have been the accretion of satellite civilizations in locations peripheral to the river valley civilizations. Typically, they originated through contact between the principal or nuclear civilization and new ethnic groups with their own cultural traditions. Here, the much later Hittite and Urartian formulations offer obvious examples, and we may well expect more such instances to become known or to be recognized.

The Background

The unique concentration of culture foci extending from the upland tributaries of the Indus to the first cataract of the Nile seems to have blossomed forth from a far more extensive welter of anonymous, incipient, and locally restricted small centers. In these man had achieved, in the preceding millennia, a fusion of his demands and expectations with the ecological and technological realities of the setting, which he translated into that specific way of life we term rather inadequately village culture.[1] From such villages, diversified as they must have been in that wide arc of land, the river valley civilizations are separated by a gap which we are as yet unable to bridge with theories or narrow with new information.

With their persistent dynamism and their innate directional pressure, the great civilizations represent a new departure. Both timing and location suggest strongly the existence of some internal relationship which presents an important challenge to our inquisitiveness.

Southwest Asia as such does not form a natural unit. It includes a wide variety of geographical and ecological conditions, such as alluvial river valleys, highlands and swamps, grazing land on flanks of hills, piedmont regions and fertile mountain valleys, as well as arid stretches, even extensive deserts of stone and sand. It is only partially isolated from surrounding territories. Offshore islands along the seas lessen the terror of the endless horizon, and the mountain chains, though sometimes formidable, are interrupted by passes that prevent complete isolation. There are only a few natural and effective boundary lines, such as the backbone of the mountains sweeping westward from the Pamirs, the Caucasus Mountains, and the expanse of the Indian Ocean, although the much less impenetrable bodies of water, the Black, Aegean, and Mediterranean seas provide a rather effective insulation toward the north and the west. How then were the regions in which these several civilizations came into being linked together?

Quite possibly, accident and the spade of a lucky archeologist will offer us, one day, if not the solution, such novel material as will direct our research into a rewarding channel. For the time being, however, we must look in another direction. It seems that the domestication of a number of plants and animals, as a stage in the history of man in southwest Asia, had achieved its main and most important results in the millennium or more preceding the period we are interested in. These plants and animals, as well as the entire inventory of techniques necessary to utilize them effectively, were distributed variously over the entire range of land we are discussing and constituted a unifying bond which should be made the object of intensive investigation.[2] Botanists and zoölogists will have to combine efforts to locate the centers of domestication, to trace the lines of diffusion, and to study the transitions that led, for example, to the cultivation of domestic grasses, the keeping of herds as a way of accumulating wealth, and the raising of fruit trees, such as the date palm. The climatologists will establish and date earlier climatic changes that will allow us insight into the lines of communication open or closed at specific periods between these several culture foci. The work of these scholars will be furthered—and, of course, complicated—by the fact that Mesopotamian records mentioning these plants and animals, as well as tools, will actually elucidate the period in which writing was as yet unknown, particularly since a considerable section of the Sumerian vocabulary bearing on the material culture of Mesopotamia contains terms and designations that do not seem to be Sumerian and do not belong to any early Semitic (proto-Akkadian) language. These words may conceivably echo one or more much older language substrata and thus relate to the previous carriers of what we propose to term Euphrates Valley civilization. Moreover, there is ample evidence in the geographical names along the two rivers and in many names of the deities customarily associated with the Sumerian pantheon that they may belong to that same older language or to several of them. Definite possibilities are thus offered to reach beyond the Sumerian of the earliest texts for evidence bearing on the relations that link Mesopotamia to the east, the north, and the west. All this is, admittedly, extremely difficult and may not bring satisfactory results, especially as what remains of the Indus Valley civilization is not likely to yield evidence of a linguistic nature. Yet, one might venture along this line of approach by utilizing as a source of information pre-Sumerian terms (see p. 49) dealing with the social and economic spheres of life and other terms referring to stones, plants, and animals. The main purpose in discussing this avenue of research is to draw the reader's attention to the fact that the civilization that arose in Mesopotamia was not an isolated phenomenon and that it cannot be separated from the world into which it grew.

Another observation which bears on the prehistory of this civilization is suggested by the fact that it was of a composite nature. In this respect, linguistic discoveries to date do not adequately reflect the complexities of the background. As we have seen, the Sumerian language extends our horizon beyond the Akkadian, which takes us barely beyond the last centuries of the third millennium; both yield evidence of borrowed words that reflect one or more preceding culture levels. In addition to these, the commingling of words of obvious Semitic origin indicates the presence of speakers of more than one early Semitic language either along or near the course of the Euphrates. Akkadian itself, as the first recorded Semitic language, offers a meager and restricted picture in its earliest material (known as Old Akkadian), due in part to the nature of its subject matter and its style. This linguistic homogeneity does not attest, necessarily, to a similar ethnic background. The Akkadian language, as we know from its history through nearly two millennia, had a remarkable ability to resist foreign influences, even those we know to have been strong and pervasive. Thus it cannot be ruled out that the Semitic component of Mesopotamian civilization was as complex and diversified in that very early period as it was, for example, in the middle of the second and of the first millennia, when Semites who did not speak Akkadian ("Western Semites" and "Arameans") exercised considerable political and cultural influence but left hardly any trace in the Akkadian texts of these periods.

In repeated fusions Mesopotamian civilization was, then, built up in several layers. In each of these layers novel situations, borrowed concepts, and essential reinterpretations of tradition-bound expressions were cast into familiar molds and adjusted to fit the range of expression considered adequate for the specific subject matter, be it in the realm of economics, social and political life, theology, or *belles lettres*. And exactly as any phase or attitude of Mesopotamian civilization at a given moment in history represents an amalgam of diverse strains, so should every facet of its earliest expressions—whether objects, buildings, or words—be regarded *a priori* as the complex finial in which converge several lines of development rather than representative of early and "primitive" attempts toward formulation. However far we go back in time, we must not assume that we have reached a cultural stage in Mesopotamia that one would be justified in characterizing as "primitive."

The Setting

Babylonia and Assyria lay within that stretch of more or less fertile soil which, peripheral to the huge arid subcontinent of Arabia, sweeps northwest from the marshes and the shores of the Persian Gulf along the rivers and the ranges of the Zagros to fuse into the plateaus and hills that pile up toward the Taurus and the Lebanon and lead to the Mediterranean Sea and, southward, to Egypt. The Euphrates, especially in the last third of its course, sharply marks off the fertile land from the arid territory extending beyond its western bank, but the Tigris hardly forms a boundary. This situation, of course, had its political consequences. The frontiers between Mesopotamia and the mountain regions that accompany the Tigris to the northeast and the upper Euphrates to the north never became stabilized. In fact, they constituted the line of contact between Mesopotamia and those regions that proved more or less effective links with the flatlands of inner Asia. Through the passes of these mountains came such essential materials as metals (especially tin), precious stones, aromatic matter, and timber, all in great demand in the lowlands, where increasing prosperity based on agriculture made its inhabitants feel the lack of such materials. Only rarely were these contacts peaceful. The mountain tribes exerted a continuous pressure against the inhabitants of the plains, whose resistance depended on their momentary political and economic situation. At times, the mountaineers entered the plains as workmen or mercenaries, at others they infiltrated as bandits or descended *en masse* to conquer cities and kingdoms and to rule over them. This menace evoked different reactions in Babylonia and in Assyria. The Babylonians, probably in continuation of the Sumerian attitude as illustrated by the setting of the Enmerkar story (see Glossary), seem to have exercised a civilizing influence which stimulated the growth of hybrid buffer states in the zones of contact or assimilated existing civilizations there. Elam, with its capital Susa, in the plains, and Lullubu, in a mountain valley of strategic importance, exemplify the results of this Babylonian policy. Assyria, however, in order to obtain security from invasions, attempted consciously and consistently to colonize and eventually to subjugate the regions which harbored these menacing tribes. The constant fighting of the Assyrian kings on this "mountain front" will occupy us later.

Toward the southeast, the Persian Gulf with its littoral and islands formed a frontier of Babylonia that functioned as barrier as well as an avenue of communication in the course of Mesopotamian history. The shipping lanes of the gulf for a time formed a tenuous but rather effective link with the east—whether this was Oman, or Magan and Meluhha, still further out—through which came new plants and animals as well as timber and precious stones. For some undetermined reason these links failed to function for about a millennium, from the Hammurapi period to the downfall of Assyria.[3]

The Euphrates, with vast reaches of desert lands on its western bank, formed the south and southwest border. Due to ecological conditions, contacts occurred sporadically in the south (perhaps along the littoral) and, more regularly and effectively, along the middle course of the river. Through certain corridors of approach, repeated invasions and a continuous process of infiltration brought smaller and larger Semitic-speaking tribes into the region between the rivers and even across the Tigris. Sheep and donkey nomads, they either settled in some kind of semipermanent camp or moved with their animals between summer and winter pastures.[4] Their cultural contribution to Mesopotamian civilization—apart from the language which an early group brought along—remains still to be determined but should not be underestimated. The nomadic element as such—whatever specialized and specific way of life this term may cover at any given time—provided an extremely important factor, the influence of which made itself felt in many aspects of Meso-potamian civilization. Certain phases in the political and social history of the region, certain attitudes toward war and overland trade and, above all, to urbanism can be explained only as an expression of nomadic outlook.

The last frontier to be enumerated here is that toward the west. As yet, its importance in the development and possibly also in the origins of Mesopotamian civilization cannot be gauged. Neither is it possible as yet to trace the several com-ponents of the complex of influences to which Asia Minor, the Mediterranean coast, and even the islands beyond the coast are bound to have contributed through the Syrian intermediary. Several well-traveled roads supported a process of continuous give and take, intensified at times by conquest and political incorporation, a contact that was maintained even in times of war and turmoil through essential trade routes between the bend of the Euphrates and the cities of the littoral of the Mediterranean Sea.

It is customary to designate the two principal local formula-tions through which Mesopotamian civilization speaks to us by the political terms Babylonia and Assyria. This north–south dichotomy is to be found in all the evidence available for our investigation, either overtly or hidden under a consciously applied Babylonization in Assyria. The Babylonian formulation of Mesopotamian civilization is a little older than the Assyrian and shows more obviously the influence of its Sumerian component, while the Assyrian, which developed under quite different political, social, and ethnic pressures, remained throughout its entire history receptive toward the sister civilization to the south. This receptive attitude in Assyria was subject to an ever-deepening and embittering ambivalence which pervaded the political, religious, and intellectual life of Assyria. The relationship to Babylonia provided Assyria with a fateful challenge which affected the very core of its existence. We shall repeatedly have occasion to point out in detail what this complicated relationship meant to Assyria as a state, as a community in search of self-expression, and as a bearer of the common Mesopotamian civilization.

The heartland of Babylonia was downstream from present-day Baghdad or, better, from the point where the two rivers, the Euphrates and the Tigris, approach each other so closely as to leave a stretch of only about twenty miles between them. It was not situated in the alluvial plain between the two rivers, but rather on the banks along several courses of the Euphrates that fanned out in a number of channels during the known history of the region. At times, Babylonia reached beyond the Tigris, into the flatlands and the foothills of the Zagros range, generally along the eastern tributaries of the Tigris. Its political and cultural influence extended upstream along both rivers, on the Euphrates as far as Mari and beyond, on the Tigris as far as Assur. Only when seen from the west, from the shores of the Mediterranean, does "Mesopotamia" mean a land between two rivers.[5]

The heartland of Assyria is less well defined. Without natural frontiers, Assyria was engaged in a constant process of expansion and retraction, expanding from a region along the middle course of the Tigris further east toward the piedmont, into the fertile valleys upstream and downstream along the Tigris, and to the southwest, across Upper Mesopotamia, as far as the large bend of the Euphrates, the gateway to the riches and the marvels of the west. As quickly as Assyria was able, at times, to expand in

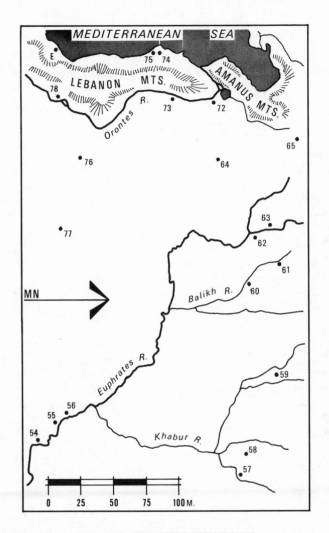

SYRIA AND THE UPPER EUPHRATES

E Tripoli
54 Mari (Tell Hariri)
55 Dura-Europos (Salihiyah)
56 Terqa (Tell Ashāra)
57 Tell Brak
58 Tell Chagar Bazar
59 Guzana (Tell Halaf)
60 Harran (Sultantepe)
61 Urfa (Edessa)
62 Til Barsip (Tell Ahmar)
63 Carchemish
64 Aleppo (Haleb)
65 Sam'al (Zenjirli)
72 Alalakh (Tell 'Atshānah)
73 Qarqar
74 Ugarit (Ras Shamra)
75 Latakia
76 Qatna (Mishrifah)
77 Tadmur (Palmyra)
78 Kadesh

these three directions, as suddenly could it retract to its heartland. In systole and diastole, the Assyrian hub kept the entire
Near East in a state of unrest for about a millennium. Where
the sources of this dynamism were located, we cannot tell.

The two rivers represent the most salient topographical
feature of Mesopotamia and furnish us, moreover, in addition
to that of Egypt, with another agricultural civilization in the
ancient Near East dependent upon irrigation, thus offering the
opportunity for revealing comparisons.[6] The Tigris and Euphrates both descend from the Armenian mountains, fed by a
number of mountain streams. The courses of some of these
tributaries are, at one place, only fifteen miles apart, making it
thus practically impossible to reach Mesopotamia without
crossing either the Tigris or the Euphrates. After breaking
through the last hills, the courses differ widely in direction and
character. The Tigris flows swiftly east and then southeast
parallel to the Zagros ranges, passing near Nineveh, Calah,
and Assur—all three capitals of successive Assyrian empires. It
enters the plain upstream from Samarra and touches Opis and
Seleucia, the last capital of Babylonia. Downstream, its course
underwent many changes in the historic period, which pre-
vented the growth of permanent settlements on its banks. It
once emptied directly into the Persian Gulf, but it now joins the
Euphrates to form the Shatt-al-ᶜArab. All its tributaries rise in
the eastern mountains: the Khoser that flows past Nineveh, the
Upper or Greater Zab that joins the Tigris near Calah, the
Lower or Lesser Zab, the Adhem and two other tributaries that
flowed at times through densely populated regions—the
Diyala [Akk. *Mê-Turna(t)*, *Turna(t)*] and the Duweirig [Akk.
Tupliaš]. Quite different is the course of the Euphrates. When
it leaves the mountains it runs southwest and reaches a point
where only ninety miles separate it from the Mediterranean
Sea. Then it turns south in a wide bend and, beyond Carchemish,
eventually southeast, receiving only two tributaries, the Balikh
and the Khabur on the left bank. It reaches the alluvial plain
below Hit, near the Tigris. The wide loop formed by the two
rivers makes Upper Mesopotamia an island, and indeed it is
today called Gezirah by the Arabs. From Hit, the river runs a

course which, although it changed from time to time, is studded
with old cities as far as the marshy regions of the southeast,
where the river empties into the Persian Gulf.[7] The Euphrates
carries less water than the Tigris; its current is much slower and
permits navigation much further upstream. Annual flooding is
characteristic of both rivers and deeply influenced all life in
Babylonia proper, where alone it was of vital importance. The
two rivers follow a similar pattern: autumn rains in the uplands
cause a general swelling of the water through winter and spring
till the melting snow in the Armenian mountains makes the
crest of the flood reach the plains in April and May, the Euphrates cresting later than the Tigris. The water subsides in
June, and the level sinks to its lowest in September and October.
Thus, the timing of the inundation in Mesopotamia is not nearly
as favorable for cereal agriculture as is the case in Egypt, where
the flood occurs at such a time that the fields can be planted
after the water has receded and its fertilizing mud has been
deposited. Since the flood stage is reached so late in the season in
Mesopotamia, it was essential to prepare dikes and levees to
protect the green fields from the water. It required special
earthworks to store the water and to distribute it where and
when it was needed. Equally important, the late flooding
increased the tendency of the soil toward salinization due to
rapid evaporation in the increasing heat.[8] This progressive
salinization of irrigated soil cuts down its yield and after periods
that may vary in length, necessitates the relocation of agricultural territories. Changes of that nature, of course, deeply affect
the prosperity of a settlement or an entire region. They eventually cause disturbing shifts in the density of the population.
There is still another detrimental feature caused by the lateness
and the swiftness of the annual flooding of the Euphrates. The
mud suspended in the swollen river was far less fertile than that
carried by the Nile, and, since it could not be immediately
deposited on the fields in any quantity, it clogged the canals
that carried the water inland. This silting diminished the
capacity of the watercourses. The canals had to be re-dredged or
replaced by new ones. For these reasons, the digging of new
canals and the resettlement of the population on new soil

formed an essential part of the economic and political program of a responsible sovereign, rivaling in importance the maintenance of the dikes.

Two ecologic conditions can be discerned in Mesopotamia: first, the landscape of the alluvial plains piled up by the two rivers which push their accumulation of silt into the Persian Gulf. The continuous rise of the ground is counteracted by a tectonic sinking movement which, together with other circumstances, causes a rise in the water table.[9] This rise not only robs archeologists of much of the lower strata (especially early Old Babylonian), now impossible to excavate, but also increases the speed of salinization of the topsoil wherever it is irrigated. The higher land of this type is suitable for pasture (especially in spring) and, when irrigated, for cereal agriculture, gardening, and, in the south, for the growing of date palms, which have a high tolerance to brackish water. In low-lying regions, cane grows in the numerous swamps. The so-called Marsh Arabs use cane with great ingenuity, by itself and in combination with clay, for house and boat-building, thus maintaining a semi-aquatic way of life along the rivers and on man-made earth platforms in and around swamps.[10] The other landscape is that of the fertile valleys in the hills and along the tributaries of the Tigris where sufficient rainfall permits the growing of a good crop of barley and where even today the yield equals, if not surpasses, that of the irrigated fields in the plain. There is sufficient pasture to raise sheep and goats for additional food and income, and there is stone for building purposes, and, at one time at least, there was timber. The region around the sources of the Khabur River, a tributary of the Euphrates in central Upper Mesopotamia, was especially fertile because of its volcanic soil.

As in all the countries from the Pamirs to the Nile, the domesticated grasses formed the mainstay of sedentary life, from the earliest village level to the metropolis of the latest period of the ancient Near East. These were barley, emmer-wheat, wheat, and millet. Of these, millet was of the least importance (in contradistinction to India and Africa), and barley was utilized much more than wheat. In fact, one can easily

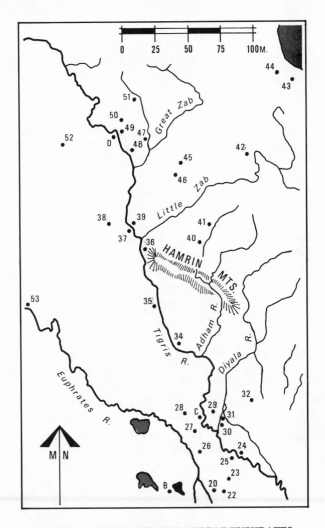

THE UPPER TIGRIS AND THE MIDDLE EUPHRATES

B	Karbalā'	30	Ishchali	43	Hasanlu
C	Baghdad	31	Khafājah	44	Kelishin
D	Mosul	32	Eshnunna (Tell Asmar)	45	Arbela (Erbil)
20	Babylon	34	Samarra	46	Kalzu (Qasr Shamamok)
22	Kish (Tell Akhimer)	35	Tikrit	47	Balawat (Imgur-Bēl)
23	Cutha (Tell Ibrahim)	36	Ekallātu	48	Calah (Nimrud)
24	Ctesiphon	37	Assur (Qal'at Sherqāṭ)	49	Nineveh (Kuyunjik)
25	Seleucia	38	Hatra (Al-Hadhar)	50	Dur-Šarrukin (Khorsabad)
26	Sippar (Abu Habba)	39	Kar-Tukulti-Ninurta	51	Bavian
27	Tell ed-Dēr	40	Nuzi (Yorghan Tepe)	52	Nemed-Ištar (Tell Afar)
28	Dur-Kurigalzu ('Aqarquf)	41	Arrapha (Kirkuk)	53	Anat (Ana)
29	Tell Harmal	42	Tell Shemshāra		

observe a connection between the preferred grasses and other domesticated plants: Mesopotamia proper is the land of barley, beer, and sesame oil, while toward the west one reaches the "Kulturkreis" of wheat, wine, and olive oil—all clearly in evidence in texts from Assyria, and even more frequently mentioned in those from Alalakh and Ugarit, and in the Old Testament. With barley goes unleavened bread and other dishes prepared from this versatile grain, while wheat is used in leavened bread and various sweetmeats. The ground seeds of the sesame[10a]—also known in the Indus Valley civilization— yield a rather pungent oil which together with fats of animal origin (tallows and some kind of butter preparation) provided the principal source of energy. Leguminous plants do not seem to have been of great dietary importance in Mesopotamia; in fact, they appear only rarely in first-millennium texts as against those of the Ur III period. The most frequently mentioned vegetables are various kinds of onions, garlic, and leeks; turnips are rare. Equally essential seem to have been aromatic and spicy seeds, such as watercress, mustard, cumin, and coriander; they were used together with salt to enliven the dull and monotonous fare of soupy cereal dishes. Flax was grown for its fiber rather than for the oily seeds that were used as medicine. As for fruit trees, the date palm was of primary economic importance and yielded the most popular supply of sweet food. Honey was rare and apparently collected mainly from wild bees. The date palm as one of the earliest domesticated plants of southern Baby- lonia—no wild-growing species has been discovered—requires the services of the horticulturist in pollination if a substantial crop of dates is to be harvested. Its fruit can be easily preserved and represents an essential source of the calories needed in the diet of a working population. In the first millennium an alcoholic beverage was prepared from dates, replacing the barley malt beer of the periods up to the middle of the second millennium. Vineyards were cultivated as a rule only in Upper Mesopotamia, though there is some evidence of the use of dried grapes and wine in the south during the very early and very late periods. Other fruit trees were rarely grown; apples, figs, pears, pome- granates, and some kind of plum are mentioned, but their cultivation seems to have had no economic importance. It has to be borne in mind that our texts deal nearly exclusively with essential staples produced for temple and palace, or on large estates in private or feudal tenure. There must have been a number of domesticated plants raised in small fields and gardens which supplied additional food to certain strata of the population. It should be noted, furthermore, that the inventory of domesticated plants remained stable throughout three millennia, although the Persians are said to have introduced rice into Babylonian agriculture.

Turning now to domestic animals, it is clear that their selection was dictated by a desire for a ready supply of fresh meat. Goats, sheep, pigs, and other animals, such as stags and antelopes, are mentioned early. Goats, sheep, and pigs were easily domesticated, yielding not only their meat but also—an unplanned but highly important result—their wool (sheep) and hair (goats); but stags and antelopes proved a failure. Such experiments in domestication, which are also attested in the Old Kingdom of Egypt, ceased in Mesopotamia with the Ur III and the early Old Babylonian periods.[11] Goats and sheep were kept in large flocks under the supervision of shepherds, who were either in charge of herds belonging to temple or palace or took care of the animals for the owners, who received a fixed share of the proceeds. The latter practice appears mainly in the first millennium B.C.

Several breeds of Bovidae are represented by early Mesopotamian artists, though not differentiated in economic documents. Their relation to eastern breeds as well as to those apparently native to western regions is still a moot question. They were used primarily as animals of traction for plowing, rarely for pulling wagons, and also before the threshing sledge. In herds they seem to have been kept only by palace or temple, due, no doubt, to the necessity of moving herds to winter pastures. Milk, made into various kinds of cheese, and butter prepared for storage (ghee) are well attested.

Among the Equidae, the donkey was always the beast of burden and rarely used for riding.[12] As the last of the Equidae which came into Mesopotamia, the horse is mentioned from at least the Ur III period onward. Its main use was to draw war chariots which, in the course of the second millennium, evolved into a very efficient weapon. The horse acquired added military importance when the Assyrians introduced cavalry into their army after the ninth century B.C. Mules of various crossbreeds were known and appreciated.

As for domesticated fowls, we meet a different problem; from the Sumerian period to the Persian, geese and ducks are frequently mentioned and likewise a type of partridge (perhaps the francolin), a bird called *kurkû*, and others, yet it cannot be established how far one can speak in these instances of true domestication.[13] But the fowler or bird keeper is mentioned frequently in texts, and we know of the practice of fattening the birds with dough.[13a]

Mention should also be made of the dog, which seems to have been kept as pet and as the helpmate of the shepherd; the use of hounds is also attested.

Kings kept lions in cages or pits from the Ur III period on, but only Assyrian rulers mention that they hunted them, and they liked to be represented in this dangerous exploit. Nimrod, "the mighty hunter," was an Assyrian king.[13b] Elephants (along the middle Euphrates and the Khabur), wild bulls, and ostriches were likewise pursued by these royal hunters, who at times kept wild animals in parks and reported with pride on their charges.[14] Apart from this Assyrian royal custom—to be exact, apart from royal and ritual hunting—the chase to obtain animals for food or to diminish the number of predators on the flocks was not practiced in Mesopotamia.

The fish in rivers, swamps, lakes, and the sea were used on a large scale as food dried or preserved in salt only up to the middle of the second millennium B.C., and that with markedly decreasing frequency. The economic texts up to the early Old Babylonian period enumerate large quantities of a variety of fish in contexts that indicate the importance of the fishing industry for the community. The lexical texts corroborate the popularity of fish with their endless lists of fish names. Later and Assyrian texts, however, rarely speak of fish and fishing. The word fisherman even came to denote, in Neo-Babylonian Uruk, a lawless person.[15]

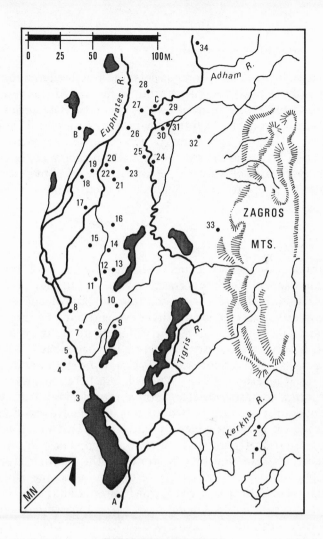

BABYLONIA AND ELAM

A Basra
B Karbalā'
C Baghdad
1 Choga-Zanbil
2 Susa (Shush)
3 Kisiga (Tell Lahm)
4 Eridu (Abu Shahrain)
5 Ur (Mugaiyar)
6 Kutalla (Tell Sifir)
7 Larsa (Senkereh)
8 Uruk (Warka)
9 Lagaš-Girsu (Telloh)
10 Umma (Djokha)

11 Šuruppak (Fara)
12 Kisurra (Abu Hatab)
13 Adab (Tell Bismaya)
14 Drehem (Puzriš-Dagan)
15 Isin (Bahriyat)
16 Nippur (Tell Niffer)
17 Marad (Wannah-was-sadum)
18 Dilbat (Dulaim)
19 Borsippa (Birs Nimrud)
20 Babylon
21 Hursagkalama
22 Kish (Tell Akhimer)
23 Cutha (Tell Ibrahim)

24 Ctesiphon
25 Seleucia
26 Sippar (Abu Habba)
27 Tell ed-Dēr
28 Dur-Kurigalzu ('Aqarquf)
29 Tell Harmal
30 Ishchali
31 Khafājah
32 Eshnunna (Tell Asmar)
33 Der (Badrah)
34 Samarra

Bactrian camels and dromedaries came in as foreign animals,[15a] normally as booty; monkeys from India and Africa were also known; and in the Amarna letters we find a Babylonian king requesting from the Egyptian pharaoh (Amenophis IV) lifelike (possibly stuffed) specimens of Egyptian "animals that live either on land or in the river"—probably meaning the crocodile or hippopotamus.[16] Clearly, the king had heard of these strange animals and wanted to see and exhibit them in his palace.

The Actors

Before speaking of the "actors" that are known to have appeared on the stage on which was enacted what we call Mesopotamian civilization, it should be stressed that our knowledge is based almost exclusively on documentary evidence and that the groups we are able to single out and to differentiate are characterized as such only by their use of a specific language that happens to have been preserved in writing. We cannot define and describe the racial or ethnic groups. The relation between these three categories, linguistic, racial and ethnic, is exceedingly complex in Mesopotamia and still far from being sufficiently investigated. Although it is rather generally understood that racial, ethnic, and linguistic categories only rarely correspond in such complex civilizations, attention may be drawn to the fact that even the written texts offer no reliable testimony as to the language actually used by the society which produced them. This is especially true for Mesopotamia, where, more often than we like to assume, an extreme and consistent traditionalism separated the language written by the scribe from that spoken by him and by others around him in daily life.

Many peoples passed through Mesopotamia, and quite a number left documents in writing. From the time when the linguistic affinities of the inhabitants of Mesopotamia become clear until the end of their political independence, the most important settled inhabitants in the south are known as Sumerians, Babylonians, and Chaldeans, and in the north and west as Assyrians, Hurrians, and Arameans. Of the invaders who succeeded at times in establishing themselves in parts of Mesopotamia, we have written evidence that ranges from word lists, isolated words, and lists of personal names to an impressive and diversified corpus of literature. Here can be enumerated the Quti, the western Semites (Amorites), the Kassites, the Elamites, and the Hittites. The Elamites and Hittites came into Mesopotamia only for short raiding expeditions; there must have been others who have left their traces in that considerable number of early (up to the end of the second millennium) personal names that cannot be assigned to any known language, i.e., neither to the Sumerian nor to any Semitic dialect. More traces of such groups appear in sections of the Sumerian and Akkadian vocabulary that do not seem to have belonged originally to either of these languages. When the conquest of Nineveh by the Medes (612 B.C.) and that of Babylon by the Persians (539 B.C.) brought the political independence of Mesopotamia to an end, the subsequent history of the region still followed the same pattern. Alexander the Great conquered Babylonia, which was at that time a satrapy of the Persian Empire under the Achaemenids; the Parthians, coming down from the Iranian plateau, put an end to the rule of the successors of Alexander—the Seleucid kings, who had made Seleucia on the Tigris the capital of the realm. The Parthians in turn fell—after half a millennium—to the Persians, at that time under a Sassanian dynasty.

The first intelligibly written documents from Mesopotamia (from Uruk, Ur, and Djemdet-Nasr) are in Sumerian.[17] It is quite likely that the Sumerians had adapted for their own use an already existing system and technique of writing. This seems to have been the creation of a lost and earlier, either native or alien, civilization, which may or may not have had some relation to the foreign elements in the Sumerian vocabulary, the topographical names of the region, and, possibly, the names of the gods worshiped there. The Sumerians were only one of several ethnic groups to which a proto-Akkadian group speaking some early Semitic dialect also belonged. Out of these elements grew by coalescence and accretion a Mesopotamian civilization. It seems to have arisen within an astonishingly short period, and persisted in various minor and major transformations for more than three millennia, having an important effect on surrounding civilizations and stimulating others into specific reactions. The linguistic affiliation of Sumerian is still completely obscure. It represents possibly only one of several languages spoken by groups which must have moved from the mountain regions through lower Mesopotamia in the formative centuries of the protohistorical period. In Uruk, in southern Mesopotamia, Sumerian civilization seems to have reached its creative peak. This is pointed out repeatedly in the references to this city in religious and, especially, in literary texts, including those of mythological content; the historical tradition as preserved in the Sumerian king-list confirms it. From Uruk the center of political gravity seems to have moved to Ur. Then began the continuous process of upstream advance that may have started in Eridu and reached out eventually as far as Assur on the Tigris and Mari on the Euphrates. Political aspiration and economic potential pushed forward in that direction, incorporating new cities and regions which became politically predominant, while the older areas retracted, congealed, and even fossilized. Thus the political centers were on the move from Ur to Kish, to Akkad, to Babylon, and eventually to Assur. In Assyria a parallel dislocation made itself felt; the capital shifted from Assur to Calah and then to Nineveh. The movement in the south exhibited another strange feature: it allowed at times a power vacuum to appear, a period of reversal to become noticeable. The city of Nippur lay in such a vacuum for a time, as did the city of Sippar, further to the north. Eventually the entire south lapsed into stagnation, abandoning the political initiative to the rulers of the northern cities. The succession of events shows recurrent irregularities which indicate the repeated efforts of the south (Ur III and Larsa) to seize political and cultural leadership again, and illustrate the intensity of the underlying struggle. The growing preference given to the use of the Akkadian language instead of the Sumerian reflects only inadequately the scope of the conflict, which was neither racial nor political but rather one between two social and spiritual ways of life. These tensions are related to certain essential changes in the structure of Mesopotamian civilization, such as the rise of royal power and the concomitant decline of the temple's position, the shift from the city-state concept and the pertinent interurban relations to that of a policy of supremacy on a geopolitical horizon, and changes in the family structure, the full scope of which is still unknown. Neither language affiliations nor political aims separated the changing attitudes through which the Sumerian formulation of Mesopotamian civilization disappeared in an internal breakup. The rich literature of that period could well furnish us with some information if one could rid oneself of the preconception that everything written in Sumerian necessarily reflects "Sumerian" as against "Semitic" civilization.

The subject matter of Sumerian texts ranges widely, from administrative documents (Uruk, Ur, Fara, and the immense bulk of the Ur III texts from Ur, Nippur, Telloh, Drehem, and Djokha), royal inscriptions (predominantly from the rulers of Lagaš), and literary works, such as hymns, lamentations, conjurations, and prayers, to law codes, legal decisions, proverbs, and myths, coming to a large extent from Nippur. The transfer to Akkadian occurred in stages; certain text groups, for example those originating from the palace (the codes and royal inscriptions), appear first in the new medium, others disappear altogether (the legal decisions, the royal hymns, with only a few exceptions) or are provided with interlinear Akkadian translations (conjurations and so forth), others reappear, transposed into a new key (mythological and epic texts) in Akkadian. The entire transference from Sumerian into Akkadian was, needless to stress, far more complex and interconnected a process than the preceding statement can suggest. It also had a far-reaching influence on the subsequent history of Mesopotamian civilization.

Most important in this respect is the fact that the transfer was incomplete. During the last third of the Old Babylonian period the translation of Sumerian texts stopped and such texts as remained extant in Sumerian were retained within the literary tradition in their original language, while new texts added to the literature were in Akkadian. The transfer was, so to speak, frozen in the act. This state expressed itself in the carefully maintained bilinguality of the scribes who could produce royal inscriptions in the Ur III style until the time of Assurbanipal, when political considerations required it, who for more than fifteen hundred years learned endless lists of Sumero-Akkadian word equations and grammatical forms, who provided Sumerian texts with explanatory and pronunciation glosses, and apparently did not shy away from occasionally manufacturing a Sumerian text. The successful effort of the Mesopotamian literary tradition to keep alive the language of Sumer as a scholarly and, in certain respects, as a sacred language—after it had disappeared as a living language in the first third of the second millennium—endowed Mesopotamian literary tradition with a remarkable resilience.[17a] For some time, it could even withstand the consequences of the replacement of Akkadian by another Semitic language, the Aramaic, and permitted the successful transplantation of the entire tradition into the centers of learning of Assyria, even into those outside the capitals.

With the appearance of cuneiform texts written in Old Akkadian, the dialect of the early Semites, who seem by that time to have settled in—or penetrated into—the region upstream from the Sumerian centers, the first bids for over-all political power in Mesopotamia were made. First a ruler of Umma (Lugal-zagesi), then one of the still unidentified city of Akkad (Sargon of Akkad), further north, embarked upon a policy of expansion and conquest. We will never know what specific economic, social, or ideological changes caused this shift in political outlook. The successes of these kings henceforth had a dominant influence on the political concepts and claims of Mesopotamian rulers. Not only did the Sumerian dynasty of Ur (called Ur III) follow Sargon's example, but the Assyrian kings of the next millennium or more took him as their prototype and the image on which to model their political aspirations. The Ur dynasty itself succeeded in creating a realm carefully and systematically articulated as to the distribution of authority and political responsibility, with governors in outlying provinces such as Elam, Mari, and far-off Assyria.[18] Though apparently more solid in structure than the suddenly expanding and unstable dominion of Sargon and

Naram-Sin, the splendor of Ur proved equally short-lived. The Akkadian language continued to replace or, at least, compete with Sumerian, or to restrict its application to certain realms of life such as administration, specific types of literature, and so on. With the rise of the dynasties of Isin, Larsa, and, eventually, Babylon, political power moved again toward the north. Moreover, a linguistic shift becomes evident at this period, the first half of the second millennium B.C. On one hand, we can observe the inroads the Akkadian (now the Old Babylonian dialect) made in the centuries between the beginning of the dynasty of Larsa (2025 B.C.) and the end of the dynasty of Babylon (1595 B.C.) into the scribal tradition; on the other, we encounter an increasing number of Semitic, but not Akkadian, personal names in historical, legal, and administrative documents. The importance of this period for the history of Mesopotamian civilization can hardly be overestimated. The kings have their inscriptions written in Akkadian as well as Sumerian, and their scribes begin to realize the artistic possibilities of the Old Babylonian dialect in literary composition. On closer scrutiny, we are able to differentiate within this dialect subdialects and distinctive literary levels. The Old Babylonian which appears now is a new dialect in the sense that, linguistically, it is markedly different from Old Akkadian, which was spoken and written up to the collapse of the dynasty of Ur III. The difference between Old Babylonian and Old Akkadian extends, however, beyond linguistic features and embraces the paleography, the system of writing (e.g., the selection of signs), and the physical aspects of the texts (such as form and size of the tablets). All these changes bespeak an essential change in the schooling of the scribes and the tradition of their craft.

We may thus distinguish at this formative stage of the Akkadian Mesopotamian tradition three levels of linguistic differentiation—Old Akkadian, Old Babylonian, and an intrusive West Semitic dialect, with whatever this differentiation may imply. The oldest level is that of Old Akkadian, attested in Mesopotamia proper, in the regions east of the Tigris from Susa to Gasur (Nuzi), and on the middle Euphrates (Mari), as far as our present knowledge goes. Since a number of linguistic features and scribal practices link the Old Assyrian spoken in Assur, on the Tigris, with Old Akkadian, one may well suggest that we consider these two dialects as belonging to a branch of the Akkadian which I propose to call—mainly for want of a better descriptive term—the Tigridian branch. It seems to have been spoken along that river from whence its speakers penetrated into Babylonia proper, held at that time (the last third of the third millennium B.C.) by the Sumerians. In its northern and somewhat later (Old Assyrian) form, this branch of the Akkadian spread into the mountain ranges of the Zagros and even into Anatolia. We contrast Old Akkadian, Old Assyrian, and whatever kindred dialects may turn up one day, with the *sit venia verbo* Euphratian branch whose speakers moved downstream along the Euphrates into Babylonia and spoke what we call Old Babylonian. This distribution in space and time assumes that the speakers of the earlier dialect, the Tigridian, moved—as all later Semites did—from northern Arabia across the middle course of the Euphrates and eastward across the Tigris into the region between that river and the mountain ranges. The subsequent—Euphratian—infiltration remained along the river which we have proposed to use as a kenning for this wave of immigrants.

In Mesopotamia proper, Old Akkadian was thus replaced by Old Babylonian, which represents the second and most important of the above-mentioned levels. Its importance is primarily due to the fact that it eventually became the literary language of the Mesopotamian tradition, which spread far beyond the limits reached by Old Akkadian. Nearly contemporary with the rise of the second ("Euphratian") level appears evidence that a sizable and politically dominant section of the population of Mesopotamia seems to have used a new and different Semitic language, usually called Amorite, the third level. The pertinent evidence consists almost exclusively of personal names of a new type. Needless to say, we must not assume that personal names represent the extent of the "Amorite" contribution to Mesopotamian civilization. We can only state that, for some reason, they alone are reflected directly in written documents. One of the peripheral dialects related to Old Akkadian, as has just been suggested, was spoken in and around Assur; it succeeded in maintaining itself and in growing for more than a millennium in several stages of internal development against the constant pressure of the language of the Mesopotamian literary tradition. Assyriologists are wont to set this dialect apart from the Babylonian of the south, as Assyrian. They insist, furthermore, on treating both dialects, the Babylonian and the Assyrian, as being of equal status and applying to them the same tripartite division, differentiating Old, Middle, and Neo-Assyrian and Old, Middle, and Neo-Babylonian. But such a symmetrical arrangement distorts the actual situation.

It would be better to assume a primary and a secondary contrast. The primary contrast is that between the literary dialect, to wit, Old Babylonian, and the several dialects in which are recorded the transactions of the administration, the correspondence of private persons and officials, and the proceedings in court from the Old Babylonian period onward, in Assyria as well as in Babylonia, until the disappearance of the cuneiform system of writing. During the entire period, the Old Babylonian dialect remained (with minor changes) in Babylonia—and also in Assyria, after its acceptance there—the sole vehicle of literary creativeness.

The secondary contrast manifests itself only within the non-literary texts. They fall into geographically distinct groups. These groups show, quite by accident, a distribution in time which favors the traditional division into three stages. Thus, we call simply Old Assyrian the texts coming nearly exclusively from Anatolia (Kultepe), which forms, in fact, the northern branch of what we have just dubbed Tigrido-Akkadian, and we call Middle Babylonian the administrative texts and letters written in the middle of the second millennium in the south, in Nippur, Ur, and Dur-Kurigalzu. The texts of similar nature coming from the Assur of roughly the same period and later are termed Middle Assyrian although a wider gap separates them from the Old Assyrian than intervenes between Old and Middle Babylonian. The large body of administrative letters, texts, and legal documents that come from Uruk, Nippur, and from Sippar, and, to a smaller extent, from Babylon, Borsippa, and Ur, are referred to as Neo-Babylonian. This last represents a dialect used in Babylonia proper from the seventh century on, with its earliest evidence coming, strangely enough, from the royal archives in Nineveh in Assyria.[19] Other texts in the same archives comprise most of the material we call Neo-Assyrian, although Calah and other sites contribute texts in this dialect.[20]

Each of the text groups mentioned has a special setting, a characteristic content, style, and scribal practice, and cannot be characterized solely by linguistic features. Each deserves a special investigation that keeps such differentiations carefully in mind. Only rarely are the listed dialects used as vehicles for literary purposes. Occasionally, a writer attempts a consciously new creation which does not fit into the framework of the traditional corpus of literary texts, or he uses the dialect for political purposes. Inevitable, of course, are the traces of the influence which these dialects exerted here and there on the spelling, grammar, and the lexicon of the traditional texts. We intend to show what the style and the content requirements of the royal inscriptions owe in one way or another to the living tradition of the special setting of each of the dialects. Much work is still to be done in analyzing adequately the individual groups of texts that dot the history of the Akkadian language. In the long run, this may prove more fruitful than the practice of disposing of such problems by assuming unilinear developments and scholastic schemes.

It is hoped that the preceding digression has contributed toward an understanding of the crucial half millennium in Babylonia between the earliest texts in Akkadian and the end of the Hammurapi dynasty. The entire political and intellectual history of the region was under the influence of what happened during that period.

The rise and establishment of a literary tradition in a dialect different from the one apparently used by the group in political power was to repeat itself twice again under better known circumstances, several hundred years later. In both instances, languages new and alien to the region failed nearly completely to leave traces. The incoming groups that spoke one or more West Semitic dialects, in the first half of the second millennium, and those who spoke one or more Aramaic dialects, less than a millennium later, all bowed to the language of the country they had invaded or where they held political power. This is also true of the Kassites in the middle of the second millennium. In the case of the Kassites and Arameans, we know that the gap between the culture of the invaders and that of the settled and more highly developed peoples upon whom they descended was quite substantial, so it is not surprising that the invaders, even though they wielded the political power, should abandon their own language and adopt that of the culturally more advanced people whom they controlled. The situation in the earlier instance is not so clear. We know very little of the West Semitic, "Amorite," invaders, neither their military strength, their relative cultural standing, nor the specific social situations in which they brought their weight to bear.[21]

From the earliest period, with wandering groups descending from the plateaus and deserts, to the final Arabic invasion which created that *tabula rasa* on which a new way of life was to be outlined in Mesopotamia, Semites have constituted the overwhelming majority of the population. As tribal groups in search of new pastures, as bands of warriors attracted by the lure of the rich "Gardariki" ("city land" as the Nordic warriors called Russia), they moved in a steady stream, mainly from Upper Syria through what seems to have been specific corridors leading either to the south or across the Tigris to the east. Apart from their linguistic differences, the several groups of invading Semites can also be characterized according to their attitude toward urbanization, the crucial social and political feature of Mesopotamia. Some of them were evidently ready to move into existing urban settlements and might even have contributed at times toward the phenomenon of urbanization itself; others preferred to drift through the open country and to settle in small and ephemeral encampments, a practice which continued from the earliest to the most recent period in Mesopotamian history. The latter groups always remained reluctant to pay with either taxes or *corvée* labor and military service for the security granted by a more or less effective central authority. They constituted an element that continually fomented unrest and resistance. We do not know how the settlement of the first groups of Semites in the protohistorical period came about. Wherever documents speak to us, we find these groups well installed quite early in cities from Assur to the north of Nippur; they do not seem to have participated in the settling of the "deep south." The next invaders—speaking Old Babylonian—seem to have exercised their influence in a smaller and a more coherent territory, although this is to be taken as hardly more than an impression. Their relation to the third wave—that group which shows its presence solely by its novel personal names—remains quite unknown. The aforementioned Amorites might well represent a more warlike society, which we know exercised influence over vast stretches of land, practically from the Mediterranean to the Persian Gulf, most likely through a ruling warrior class. The Amorites seem to have been of a different social structure from the earlier groups of Semites that reached Mesopotamia. Such a group—as we know them from parallels in history—can hardly be expected to have exercised any influence on the language of the conquered people and would be ready to respect any culture level that they considered superior to their own. Still, there is the possibility that these ruling Amorite warrior families are worthy of closer attention than is given them by modern Assyriologists, interested only in their language as attested in their personal names. Since so little is known of them, one might suspect, *a priori*, that much, if not most, of the essential changes to be observed in Mesopotamian political concepts after the spectacular collapse of the empire of Ur may be ascribed to their influence. These changes include the shift from a city-state concept (including dominion over other cities and leagues of cities) to the concept of a territorial state, the growth of long-distance trade relations through private initiative, wider horizon in international politics, and the manipulation of political situations in swiftly shifting allegiances. Here, one can feel at work the directness of personal decisions unhampered by the cumbersome way in which tradition-bound city rulers, accustomed to quarrel only over arable ground or pastures, must have been moving. Such organizers as Hammurapi of Babylon, who, with novel ideas, decidedly changed the social structure of the country to support his army, and such an empire-builder as Šamši-Adad I, who fought desperately and in vain to fuse far-flung stretches of Upper Mesopotamia into a territorial state, are the new types of political ruler on the Mesopotamian scene. One might speculate as to the extent that a "nomadic" background fostered the development of such concepts and whether the tenacity of tribal family-relations helped support and maintain an international network of contacts between the rulers. The very fact that as late as King Ammiṣa-duqa, the penultimate ruler of the Old Babylonian dynasty, a differentiation is evident, in an official edict (see below, p. 222), between "Akkadians" and "Amorites," proves that, socially and economically, a serious contrast must have been in evidence in Mesopotamia throughout the entire rule of the dynasty.

A new and far more intensive wave of Semitic tribes made itself felt throughout the ancient Near East nearly half a millennium later. Beginning with the twelfth century B.C., we meet these Aramaic-speaking tribes from the Euphrates to the coastal regions of the Mediterranean Sea; they penetrated along the Euphrates, downstream, into Babylonia proper, even moving—as their predecessors had done—across the river into the regions along and beyond the Tigris. Their behavior followed a somewhat different pattern.[22] In the northwest they did not accept Mesopotamian civilization, neither its language nor its characteristic system of writing; in the southeast, however, they seem to have come under Babylonian influence, as a rule accepting Akkadian personal names, and, initially at least, also Akkadian writing and language. But eventually their language and technique of writing won out.

In the course of their acculturation in and around Syria, they retained their own language, using an alphabetic script of Western extraction—first attested in Ugarit—on stone, leather, and sherds. It remains far from clear to what degree the cultural traditions of the states along the seaboard and the "East Luwian" principalities in northern Syria became related to those of the Aramaic intruders. Mesopotamia, especially Babylonia, must have lost the capacity to bring about the acculturation of such migrants outside the zones of immediate contact. The adjacent civilizations began writing monumental inscriptions and administrative documents in their own language and script, and clay as a writing material disappeared outside of Mesopotamia but for Elam and, for a short period, Urartu. The Akkadian language and writing were, at this time, clearly on the downgrade from their ecumenical importance during the Amarna period.

Assyria, being the most dangerous enemy of the Arameans, could hardly be expected to influence them. Much of the Aramaic migration was drawn into the power vacuum in upper Syria and along the Euphrates, where the city-states and smaller kingdoms, always threatened by Assyrian aggression, became an easy prey for the newcomers. There the inevitable acculturation took place in rather diversified patterns. Although the Assyrian kings, after centuries of bloody fighting, again succeeded in forcing their way to the Mediterranean through the Aramaic bloc, the ascendancy of the Aramaic language, which began shortly after their coming to Mesopotamia, remained unchallenged in the ancient Near East. Supported by the alphabetic system of writing with ink on parchment, leather, and some kind of papyrus-like writing material, Aramaic gradually spread downstream into the heartland of Mesopotamia, slowly but inevitably sapping the strength of the old (cuneiform) scribal tradition of that region. The role of the Arameans in Mesopotamia proper is difficult to evaluate. On one hand, they brought about an ever-increasing de-urbanization in the peripheral regions, outside the old and larger cities, which led to the rise of a corona of minor tribal states at the very gates of such cities as Babylon, Uruk, Nippur, Ur, and Borsippa; on the other hand, the Arameans assumed the role of champions of the Babylonian cause against Assyrian domination and eventually led, quite successfully, the liberation movement that culminated in the rise of the Chaldean dynasty under Nabopolassar and his son Nebuchadnezzar II, achieving for Babylonia its final but short triumph—rule over the entire ancient Near East.

Lastly, one should mention in this enumeration of Semites in Mesopotamia that contact with the Arabs of the desert, prior to their irruption into Mesopotamia and the adjacent regions in the seventh century A.D., was, in the main, only slight and incidental to the continuous expansion of the Neo-Assyrian Empire. It is quite likely, although it cannot be documented, that the Arabs, beside the Nabateans, participated during the last centuries of the first millennium B.C. and some time thereafter in that network of overland trade relations which eventually stretched from Medina, Petra via Tadmur (Palmyra), and Damascus to Vologesia in southern Babylonia, following in the main the old trade route that linked the Mediterranean to the Persian Gulf.

Among the foreign peoples passing through or penetrating as conquerors into Mesopotamia, the Hurrian-speaking groups are by far the most important because their own tradition was persistent enough to resist the influence of the Akkadian language and, to an undetermined yet considerable extent, that of Mesopotamian civilization. They are in evidence all over Mesopotamia—as is indicated by their characteristic personal names—at least as early as the end of the third millennium. For unknown reasons they rose to political and cultural importance in the eastern section of Mesopotamia in a development of which the main and crucial phase is hidden by the lack of documentation available for the period we refer to as the "Dark Age." But the vestiges of Hurrian political power, Hurrian institutions, and their language and art, dating from before and—largely— after the gap, are in evidence everywhere, from Mari, the valleys of the Zagros and Armenia across Assyria, into Anatolia and to the littoral of the Mediterranean. Hurrian influence on the specific Assyrian formulation of Mesopotamian civilization appears to have been especially important. It is particularly difficult to gauge this and other, non-Hurrian, influences on Assyria as it emerged from the Dark Age because certain Assyrian circles strove to emulate Babylonian standards in the realm of religious practice, in institutional behavior, and even in language.

Quite different was the relationship that developed between the Kassites, a mountain people, and the Babylonians. Kassite rulers sat on the Babylonian throne for about half a millennium, though they kept their native names only from ca. 1700 B.C. to 1230 B.C. We are somewhat at a loss to evaluate the range and depth of their influence on Mesopotamian civilization as a continuum, mainly for lack of documentation. The Kassites accepted rather consistently the existing forms of expression and the admitted pattern of private, official, and religious behavior and even went beyond that—as zealous neophytes do, or outsiders, who take up a superior civilization—by favoring an extremely conservative attitude, at least in palace circles. An excellent gauge of these aspirations are the royal inscriptions of the Kassite period, which return, with their pointed terseness, to the traditional pre-Hammurapi dynasty pattern. The slightly dramatic and effusive style of the inscriptions of the First Babylonian Dynasty was discarded, as was much, if not all, of the social reorganization effectuated in that period, and—last but not least—its political aspirations. At the same time, far more care was bestowed on the continuation of the scribal tradition and, above all, on the preservation of the existing corpus of literary and scholarly texts. Kassite personal names, the names of some of their gods, a vocabulary fragment, and a number of technical terms represent all that remain of the Kassite language.

The Elamites, who exercised considerable political influence in southern Mesopotamia in periods of crises or lack of governmental control, failed to influence Mesopotamia to any appreciable degree. Theirs was a civilization that grew up from native roots but was fatefully overshadowed by Mesopotamia. We shall discuss this relationship in the next section of this chapter, as well as that of the Hittite civilization to the Mesopotamian. The Hittites themselves are known to have made only one invasion into Mesopotamia, a short razzia that reached Babylon about 1600 B.C.

Eventually one should mention the Quti people, whose invasion and short rule in southern Mesopotamia are reported by Sumerian sources. This, by the way, is the only incident in cuneiform texts which describes with outspoken hatred a triumph over the invader; it is comparable only with the hatred of the Egyptians for the Hyksos. A short series of royal names in the language of the Quti and a word here and there in a lexical text are all that remain of their language.

For the sake of completeness rather than for their significance, we must point out the few Greek transliterations of Akkadian and Sumerian words and phrases that have been found on clay tablets in scratched-in Greek letters.[23] Possibly Greek interest in cuneiform texts and the fading civilization of Mesopotamia found expression in Greek writings at the Seleucid court. Yet, if this were the case, it must have been much less extensive both in scope and size, compared with what we know the interest in Egyptian civilization to have been at the court of the Ptolemies. Not much interest in Mesopotamia is in evidence in the extant Greek sources. But we must recall that the soil of lower Mesopotamia destroyed all parchments and papyri, so our lack of Seleucid evidence may be due to this factor.

The World Around

During the nearly three millennia of its documented history, Mesopotamia was in continuous contact with adjacent civilizations and, at times, even with distant civilizations. The region with which Mesopotamia was in contact either directly or through known intermediaries stretches from the Indus Valley across and, at times, even beyond Iran, Armenia, and Anatolia to the Mediterranean coast and into Egypt, with the immense coastline of the Arabian peninsula and whatever civilization it may have harbored as the Great Unknown. The drift and intensity of these contacts varied, of course, and the reasons for these variations cannot always be ascertained. Generally speaking, one may state that in this region some kind of osmotic pressure from east to west was effective from the earliest periods. It is well known that domesticated plants and animals and related technological practices moved through Mesopotamia from some far off center of Eurasian diffusion, possibly around the Gulf of Bengal. There are, in the historical period, unmistakable indications of trade contacts via shipping lanes between southern Mesopotamia (mainly Ur) and those regions to the east to which the Sumerian and early Akkadian inscriptions refer as Magan and Meluhha. Through such intermediate stations as the island of Bahrain (Sum. and Akk. *Telmun*) in the Persian Gulf, important raw materials, copper ore, ivory, and precious stones came by boat from coastlands that cannot be identified but which may have been near or beyond Oman. At any rate, the contacts were well established, and we know of an official interpreter of the Meluhhan language living in the period of the empire of Akkad.[24] When unknown events interrupted this link to the east, the terms Magan and Meluhha assumed a mytho-geographic connotation and referred (from the second half of the second millennium on) to southernmost ends of the ecumene, to the Egypt ruled at that time by an Ethiopian dynasty; Meluhha came to be known as the homeland of people of dark complexion. The contacts seem to have been effective in the earlier periods (up to the end of the third millennium); only much later, in the Persian and Seleucid periods, did they reach a comparable intensity. The interruption of the gulf trade may have been caused by changes of a political nature that affected either the intermediary or the eastern country that furnished the goods for the trade to Ur. And very probably the Mesopotamian attitude toward foreign contacts had undergone a change. With the increasing unrest and wars that ushered in the downfall of the Hammurapi dynasty and the narrowing of the political outlook, a progressive rigidity in Mesopotamian civilization seems to have created a resistance to foreign influences. Contacts with the outside world in the realm of trade were restricted to the royal level. The trade carried on by private initiative (even though at times with the support of temple and palace), as attested earlier in Ur (across the Persian Gulf) and Assur (to and within Anatolia), was replaced after the middle of the second millennium by the exchange of gifts between kings conveyed by royal emissaries. This created a rather effective control on imports, whether raw materials, goods, or ideas. It was a time of technological stagnation. In Babylonia, it was not relieved by the influx of craftsmen and artists as prisoners of war, as was increasingly the case in Assyria. The equilibrium that was evident in the Kassite period, after the experiments of Hammurapi had either run their course or been discarded, created a social texture characterized by a lack of inner dynamics. The static attitude inherent in a non-revealed religion and the steadily diminishing economic influence of the large sanctuaries contributed toward this paralysis. This state of affairs is, to a certain degree, illustrated by the extant works of Mesopotamian, especially Babylonian, art, which furnish a sensitive indicator in spite of their innate traditionalism. The break in this stagnation seems to have come in Babylonia through a shift in the geopolitical situation: Babylonia, liberated from Assyrian dominion with the help of Aramean tribesmen, was able to conquer the Assyrian Empire. This victory coincided with the increasing pressure exercised by the Iranian peoples on Mesopotamia, a development that was in some way connected with the disappearance of whatever obstacles had stood in the way of contacts between India and the Levant. Even before Cyrus occupied Babylon in 539 B.C., the economic texts from the great sanctuaries in Sippar, Babylon, and Uruk offer evidence of trade relations that reached to the Mediterranean (Cilician iron) and even as far as Greece. Persian domination ushered in the first period in the ancient Near East in which the geographic horizon extended beyond the limits of the past.

Assyria, until its dramatic collapse and heroic end, had an entirely different connection with the world that surrounded it. The Hurrian experience had been of decisive consequence for Assyrian development. It is unlikely that we shall ever be able to gauge adequately the extent and depth of foreign influence on Assyria. The motif inventory of Assyrian art does not necessarily represent an adequate indicator; the palpable Hurrian influence on the Assyrian cult may well have been restricted to specific religious and social aspects, but Hurrian—and other non-Mesopotamian—influences were not as far-reaching and as conflict-provoking as that exerted by Babylonia. The serious emotional conflict in Assyrian civilization in relation to Babylonia deeply influenced the internal and foreign policies of both countries. In Assyria, moreover, this conflict had consequences of an existential nature. There were circles in Assyria which looked toward Babylonia for an example and for the formation of a self-image. The most famous deities of the Babylonian pantheon became part of the Assyrian pantheon, and Babylonian scribal tradition was accepted, cultivated with professional care, and maintained with astonishing success. Various forms of political associations with Babylonia had been experimented with for more than half a millennium in order to create either an alliance, a joint dominion, a protectorate, or even to make a subjugated province out of the homeland of a civilization which was, to many of the Assyrian kings, the paragon of cultural achievement. Two causes contributed to deprive these Assyrian aspirations of any lasting success. In Assyria proper, the pro-Babylonian attitude was restricted to certain circles at court, although it must be admitted that these circles were influential and powerful, affecting not only ideological but also economic, or, more exactly, commercial interests. Evidence of the opposing anti-Babylonian forces, though certainly they were tenacious, is more difficult to find in the records, but it is clear that they were effective enough to counterbalance the forces favoring Babylon. A priori, one could assume that there was a "nationalistic" tendency in the official hierarchy of the army, and possibly also in the administration of the realm; the role of the sanctuaries is impossible to establish, because the main body of our information comes from the thoroughly "Babylonized" Assur, while a presumably native-oriented Assyrian sanctuary like the temple of the Ištar in Arbela has not yet been touched, buried as it is under the modern town. In Assyria there was a strong sense of participating in a common and native way of life which repeatedly proved persistent enough to survive military defeats and foreign domination. Who the carriers were who kept the political and cultural tradition and the Assyrian language alive through the eclipses of political power is extremely difficult to say. The right answer would reveal to us the very fountain-head of Assyrian strength and staying power. At any rate, these forces were often effective, able to remove pro-Babylonian kings, revise drastically the foreign policy toward Babylonia, and keep alive and foster the fateful ambivalence in the Assyrian attitude toward Babylonia until the end of the empire.

In non-political respects, Assyria was open to foreign ideas and stimuli. This is evident in its technology, as well as in the iconography of its monuments and other artistic products. Assyrian texts openly admit the importation of superior foreign techniques (e.g., in metallurgy, in architecture, in the use of glazes). They mention with pride that singers and musicians were among the prisoners taken in the west, and among the craftsmen brought back from Egypt appear bakers, brewers, shipwrights and cartwrights, even veterinarians and dream interpreters. Non-Babylonian influences with which Assyria came into direct contact are difficult to analyze. Several, and probably quite distinct, cultural elements are in evidence; we lump them conveniently together as Hurrian. There might well have been genuine acculturation in certain instances and the acceptance of specific culture traits in other instances. The complexity is reflected in the Hurrian loan words to be found in Assyrian dialects, covering a wide variety of topics from the names of dishes and pieces of apparel to those of officials and institutions. These foreign elements were incorporated apparently without conflict into the Assyrian way of life in spite of the strategic situation which made Assyria the eternal enemy of all those mountain peoples among whom Hurrian civilization was either preserved or to whom it became adapted.

The most appreciative acceptance of Mesopotamian civilization in the world that surrounded it expressed itself in the growth and flowering of a group of satellite civilizations. These appeared in peripheral locations and were hybrid in nature, with Mesopotamian elements in clear dominance and native traits often difficult to detect and to isolate for special study. They are, from east to west, the Elamite civilization, with its capital Susa; the Urartian, in the region of Lake Van; and the Hittite, with its Anatolian capital, Hattuša. The first had the longest duration; it lasted nearly as long as Mesopotamian civilization itself; the second is attested for only about two centuries, and the last, the Hittite, for seven hundred years or more. No systematic investigation dealing with the problem of the general structure of these hybrid formations has yet been made. The subject is fraught with complications, since the evidence is both linguistic and archeological, and the non-Mesopotamian constituent of the hybrid civilization is often composed of elements not clearly identifiable. Although they differ in essential respects, a number of attitudes are common to all these civilizations: they accepted the Mesopotamian system of writing (cuneiform signs on clay), and, to varying degrees, Mesopotamian language and literary tradition. With this went a transfer of a sizable amount of religious, cultural, and social terminology which, in time, entailed to some extent a transfer or an adaptation of concepts foreign to these civilizations. This also holds true of literary patterns, style requirements, and esthetic standards, which often were accepted or adapted by the native literature as far as it was written. Another common feature is the onesidedness of the relationship—Mesopotamia is always giving; not even in its relation to Elam, with which intimate and direct political contacts existed for a long time, can we discern any appreciable influence of Elam on Babylonia. Elam certainly, and Urartu most probably, had systems of writing that were native to their respective regions and were discarded in favor of the Mesopotamian system. With respect to the Hittite civilization, the situation is somewhat more complicated; there the native (hieroglyphic) system persisted and even survived the alien (cuneiform), whose preservation was apparently linked to a specific political and ethnic constellation with the collapse of which it disappeared, while the native system maintained itself into the seventh century B.C. Under the stimulus of an imported literary tradition, a native literature could grow up in any of these civilizations, but only in the Hittite did it reach an impressive degree of complexity and diversity; it even led to the creation of novel literary genres. In Urartu and in Elam, the native texts paralleled their Akkadian prototypes quite slavishly—at least according to the evidence we have. Such lack of originality, nevertheless, facilitates to a considerable extent our study of these native languages. Only with regard to the Hittite has scholarship been able to achieve to a degree that penetration and understanding that sheds light on native concepts in the religious and political spheres and thus enables us to gauge influence and resistance, the growth of pseudomorphic adaptations, and the creation of new concepts. For the Elamite the situation is complicated by linguistic difficulties—as against the Hittite which, as an Indo-European language, is relatively easy of access—and by the scarcity of texts for the crucial periods. Even the Akkadian texts coming from Susa are of little help because they are all rather specialized, as if the use of Babylonian had been admitted only for specific purposes. They leave large and essential sections of the native social, economic, and intellectual life untouched. Linguistic difficulties recur in Urartu, and, moreover, the documentation in both the Urartian and the Akkadian (Assyrian) language is meager as to content and extent. In all three civilizations, however, the archeological evidence shows few traces of foreign influence. Only in the realm of writing (technique and subject matter) was Mesopotamian influence irresistible. Incidentally, since Egyptian writing undoubtedly got its start under the stimulus of the Mesopotamian, the persuasive influence of the latter was in evidence even in early days.

The time element with regard to these three civilizations—Elamite, Hittite, and Urartian—is both important and revealing. Elam is definitely in a class by itself, as a result of its propinquity to Babylonia.[25] Its "Mesopotamization" dates at least to the Akkad period, and contacts were rarely interrupted, down to the time the Achaemenid kings found it appropriate to display trilingual inscriptions, in Persian, Elamite, and Babylonian. The situation in Urartu is quite different because this country belonged to those incipient hybrid civilizations which arose for a short flowering in the early first millennium B.C. under Assyrian influence in the mountain regions from Asia Minor to the Caspian Sea. While most—including those of the Manneans and the Medes—left us but scanty archeological evidence, the Urartians alone seem to have produced inscriptions (first in Assyrian and later in their native language) and an impressive number of buildings, sculpture, and *objets d'art*.

The Hittite acceptance of certain aspects of Mesopotamian civilization must be considered as representing only one local development—the best attested in many respects—of a phase of expansion through which this civilization passed in the first half of the second millennium. In the preceding centuries Akkadian inscriptions appeared on rocks in the mountain valley of the Lullubu in the Zagros, on statues in early Mari on the Euphrates, and, later on, were carried by the traders of Assur on clay tablets to Anatolia (Kaniš). During the Old Babylonian period,

Akkadian was written on clay in Mari and in certain mountain valleys, in Chagar Bazar on the trade route through Upper Mesopotamia, in Alalakh, and probably in other localities throughout this region, which served as intermediate centers of redistribution for the spread of this novel technique of communication. Whether or to what extent the Hurrians were instrumental in this process cannot yet be established, but their role might well have been crucial in this respect. So far, many of these places have escaped the spade of the archeologist and the far more effective searchings of native diggers for gold, statues, the fertilizing soil from ruins, and easily salable tablets. From such a center the Hittites must have received their cuneiform system of writing, which differs sharply in certain features from the one used only a short time before by the Assyrian traders in that region and from the one used by the scribes of contemporary Babylonia. Later on, the collapse of political power in Babylon, the disappearance of Mari, and the eclipse of Assur did not prevent the Akkadian and the cuneiform system of writing from spreading even further and becoming the internationally accepted diplomatic language of the West, from Hattuša, the capital of the Hittite Empire, across Syria and Palestine, including Cyprus, to the Egyptian capital in Amarna, nearly two hundred miles up the Nile. Akkadian was taught everywhere in a characteristic way, entailing the study of Sumerian to a certain extent and specific writing habits and even literary forms, each essential to the correct training of a Mesopotamian scribe. This, in varying degrees of thoroughness, we know to have been the case in the Hittite capital, in Alalakh, and also in Ugarit; it may well have been practiced in other cities which we have not discovered as yet. The scribes in all these capitals were well able to write letters for their masters to allies and overlords, to their dependencies, and to their governors either in the native language of their correspondents or in the Akkadian of the period, which was understood everywhere. They also established a bureaucratic organization to keep the accounts of the master's treasury and to record legal transactions patterned, however irregularly, on Babylonian prototypes. These legal documents deal with international agreements and with royal transactions and those between private persons of a certain class. We have such texts from Alalakh, Ugarit, and Nuzi, offering unbelievably rich source material. Only rarely and never successfully—according to Mesopotamian standards—did these scribes tackle what we call royal inscriptions; few literary texts are in evidence, although we have some from Amarna, Qatna, Hazor, and Nuzi. Even a site as near to the center of diffusion as Mari gives us only a few royal inscriptions whose contents exceed the minimal traditional formulation, and next to nothing in the way of literary texts.

It may well be assumed that more sites of this period will be discovered and that they will yield more texts and complicate an already complex issue. I do not foresee the unearthing of other satellite civilizations but rather the discovery of several smaller centers comparable to Nuzi or Alalakh, centers from which Hurrian rulers administered their realms, at times stretching from the piedmont of the Zagros (Nuzi) to the approaches of the Mediterranean coast. Among them might be one or even more that may turn out to be a capital of a Hurrian or Mitanni kingdom, a find which would fill a gap in our picture. The Hurrians accepted the Akkadian system of writing in a way that urges us to presume the existence of a center of learning of essential importance. What Hurrian texts we have today from Boghazkeui, Amarna, Mari, and other places, the number of Hurrian technical terms from Nippur and Ugarit over a period of nearly a millennium, not to speak of the widespread dissemination of Hurrian personal names, constitutes an impressive corpus of evidence. In addition to this, we have rich archeological material and an iconographic inventory of startling proportions. Proper evaluation of all this material is essential to bridge the gap between Mesopotamia and the civilizations to the north, northwest, and the west. This evaluation would be greatly facilitated if we could unearth the center of Hurrian culture.[25a]

A civilization of the magnitude and duration of the Mesopotamian cannot but exercise a radiation pressure which only formidable geographical barriers are able to screen off. We must therefore assume a halo-like peripheral zone about the satellite civilizations, a zone into which a number of Mesopotamian objects, ideas, and practices slowly infiltrated or were brought as spoils by booty-laden mountaineers returning from razzias into Mesopotamian territory, carried by traders, or remained after the short-lived attempts of Babylonia and Assyria to create buffer states by colonizing the unruly tribesmen. Mesopotamian influence, in varying degrees of intensity, must have spread and been diffused along routes much further into and beyond the Iranian plateau, Afghanistan, and the littoral of the Caspian Sea and that of the Aegean than we have any well-documented reason to believe.[26]

The coexistence of civilizations of a status equal to that of Mesopotamia was quite rare, but Ugarit seems to have been such a case. There, the technology of the Mesopotamian system of writing (cuneiform signs on clay) was applied to a system that represents a revolutionary advance: an alphabetic script the sequence of whose letters is already much the same as that of our alphabet.[27] This script was used to record a native literature, to administer a complex bureaucracy, and to write down legal transactions, but at the same time there were scribes well-trained in the Mesopotamian way of writing in Akkadian; in addition, Hurrian was written in Ugarit in both the Ugaritic alphabet and the Mesopotamian cuneiform system. In Ugarit, we also encounter Hittite documents in cuneiform as well as art objects bearing dedications in Egyptian hieroglyphs. It must have been a truly international center, a clearing house of ideas and merchandise. Whatever the native and alien components of this civilization on the shore of the Mediterranean may have been, they exercised considerable influence toward the south, in Palestine, a region that was apparently only slightly touched by the radiations of Mesopotamian civilization.

We happen to know more of Palestine than of any other sections of the ancient Near East—the best documented civilizations, Mesopotamia, Asia Minor, and Egypt, excepted. One can well say that the Old Testament reports with unrivaled excellence and thoroughness on the period following the eighth century B.C. and throws light in various degrees of reliability on certain events of the preceding three or four centuries. Even so, the crucial period during which one could have observed the effect of Mesopotamian influence (middle of the second millennium) is not covered by any primary evidence in the Old Testament. Later on, when the political influence of the growing Assyrian empire makes itself felt, when Assyrian kings and, later, Nebuchadnezzar II came as conquerors, the same body of texts provides us with a small but important number of references to Mesopotamia proper. Due to the culture differential between the two civilizations, and no less due to the polemic attitude of the Bible, the Old Testament gives us a unique opportunity to observe Mesopotamia from the outside. In this respect, the Bible contains remarks that are far more revealing and exact than, for example, the travelogue of Herodotus on Babylonia. While Mesopotamian influence on the Old Testament is either secondary (via Ugarit or other, still unknown, intermediaries) or accidental, the Old Testament itself served as a vehicle for the transmission to the West of a number of literary concepts and culture traits of Mesopotamian extraction.

Finally, one has to draw attention to the not yet sufficiently appreciated role of Hellenistic Egypt as a point of diffusion for Mesopotamian ideas: Babylonian astrology as well as astronomy moved from Egypt to the West; this parallels the spread of Assyrian art—in itself at that stage a highly syncretistic phenomenon—via Asia Minor to Greece, and that of Assyrian court ceremonial via Persian and Sassanian practices into Byzantium and eventually to Europe. Still unexplored are the contacts between Hellenistic Babylonia and India—and even the Far East.

All told, very few and then mainly secondary cultural achievements of Mesopotamian civilization were preserved and incorporated in the general trend of development that ran westward. This is also true of Egypt, the other representative of the great and primary civilizations of the ancient Near East. It places in proper relief the miraculous intensity and strength of that light that originated in the backland hills along the easternmost shores of the Mediterranean.

CHAPTER **II** *Go to, let us build us a city and a tower!* (GENESIS)

THE SOCIAL TEXTURE

ECONOMIC FACTS

"THE GREAT ORGANIZATIONS"

THE CITY

URBANISM

A primary characteristic of Mesopotamian societal structure appears to have been the absence of any non-economic status stratification, if one disregards the unique status of the king and excludes the slave population that was at all times rather small and in private hands. This statement will doubtless have to be qualified somewhat for specific regions and periods where alien influences are in evidence. The absence of a warrior class, which often arises as a result of foreign conquests, is especially noteworthy. Whatever articulations reminiscent of "feudalism" occur in the Babylonia of the outgoing second millennium B.C.

have royal officials as carriers. Moreover, no special status—except possibly that incidental to being connected with a sanctuary—set apart priests or scholars, nor were there any tensions between them and the laity. (We shall discuss somewhat later the position of the king, distinguishing Babylonian from Assyrian practices.)

The Social Texture

One has to differentiate between slaves who belonged to private persons and serfs who were owned by the "great organizations," the palace and the temple. Slaves in private possession were either born in the house, acquired by purchase, or—rarely—as shares of booty taken in war and distributed among the soldiers; or they were recruited from among debtors and their wives and children. Foreign slaves, mainly slave girls, were imported for their skills and other qualities. Slaves born in the house seem to have enjoyed a special status, at least in the Old Babylonian period, as did native-born slaves. There are no laws known to protect slaves against maltreatment by their masters, nor are such cases ever mentioned. Runaway slaves, however, were rather rare.[1] The custom of adopting slaves who were to be manumitted at the death of their elderly adoptive parents after they had taken care of them in their old age and buried them properly, suggests that the relationship between master and slave was one of trust with mutual obligations. This is clearly borne out by the use of the master-slave terminology in the religious literature to express exactly these aspects of the god-man relationship. The marking of slaves was rare in earlier periods—with the exception of slaves who were habitual runaways—but they seem to have had a characteristic hairdo. In certain regions, moreover, slaves outside their master's home had to wear fetters as a sign of bondage. The provenience of the slave (native or foreign-born) affected his legal status in various ways, as we know from Old Babylonian (Codex Hammurapi) and Middle Assyrian texts.[2] In the Neo-Babylonian period, slaves with the name of their owner branded on the backs of their hands are frequently mentioned, and adoptions have become extremely rare. This, together with the following development, point out a certain change in the master-slave relationship. From texts of the Neo-Babylonian period we learn that slaves were often allowed to work for their own living under the obligation of making monthly payments in silver (*mandattu*) to their masters. The masters often articled slaves to learn profitable crafts in order to increase their worth and, consequently, their masters' wealth.[2a]

That slaves were held only in small numbers in private households seems to be partly due to the specific nature of their relationship to their masters and partly to the absence of any interest in industrial production on the home level, a characteristic of the Greek city-dwellers. Such production was restricted in the ancient Near East to the great organizations, that is, ultimately to the manor-level, the house of the ruler or the god. The Mesopotamian city-dweller neither possessed nor desired to create a market for goods or objects that slaves could produce within his home, such as garments, baskets, and pottery. The ultimate reason or reasons for this attitude are difficult to ascertain (see below, p. 129). (Persons described as slaves of the king or the palace seem to have had an entirely different position. They will be discussed later in connection with other persons of restricted liberty who appear in similar social contexts.)

The position of the free citizen in Mesopotamia is well known with respect to his immediate family but rather hazy with regard to any other social unit. Through innumerable legal documents from the Sumerian to the Seleucid period we know the individual as father and son (adopted or natural), as brother (as set forth in legacies), and as husband (as mentioned in marriage and divorce texts). From these documents we can glean information as to local peculiarities, historical changes, and the adaptations of legal practices to specific social relations. Although most of the legal aspects of these relationships have repeatedly been studied, many problems still beset our understanding of the Mesopotamian family. The Akkadian kinship terminology is not revealing. In Sumerian the terminology seems to indicate a slightly greater complexity, but not enough is known to permit revealing comparisons or the investigation of substratum influences in this respect. Generally speaking, it can be stated that the family unit in Akkadian Mesopotamia was rather small and restricted, although it is evident that in the earliest period, as well as in certain marginal regions in southern Babylonia in the middle of the first millennium, clanlike or even tribal organizations of some sort existed. In Neo-Babylonian times, a measure of family consciousness is shown by the use of ancestral family names for identification purposes.[3] This coincides not accidentally with an increased emphasis on gentility, already in evidence somewhat earlier for certain professions.

The head of the family had one wife; only in the Old Babylonian period do we hear of a second wife, of lesser rank.[3a] We obtain most of our information from texts of the Old Babylonian period and especially from Neo-Assyrian documents and royal inscriptions. Emphasis was placed on the virginity of the bride solely in the Neo-Babylonian period, as far as we can gather from the few extant marriage documents. Such indications suggest a change in the relationship between the sexes from the Old to Neo-Babylonian period, in harmony with the observation that women had a higher social position in the early period, when they could act as witnesses and be scribes. In the south, the first-born son received a preferred share in the paternal estate, and in the Old Babylonian period, provisions were made to insure the daughters' dowries and the younger brothers' marriage expenses. Normally, brothers held in common the inherited fields and gardens to prevent their division into small lots. In the early period they often lived with their families in their father's house. Foreign influence on this simple family structure can readily be observed in peripheral regions, such as in Nuzi and in Susa, just as certain vestiges of even earlier customs, such as the position of the mother's brother, maintained themselves in the early Babylonian tradition. While the Mesopotamian family could be enlarged only by adoption, the peripheral texts, from Susa to Ugarit, speak of incorporating outsiders as "brothers" (adoptio in fratrem) into a family structure that apparently had different social and economic dimensions.[4]

Unattached individuals belonged in this social setup typically in the categories of refugees—displaced and runaway persons—for whom we have in Akkadian a number of terms and who evidently were able in some way to maintain themselves in the cities, as the rather frequent use of the personal name *Munnabtu*, "refugee," shows.[4a] As a rule, however, such persons did not seek refuge among the natives of a city but attached themselves to the great organizations, if their personal skill was in demand, or joined that part of the population that lived outside the urban settlements. The importance and role of the rural settlements and their relation to the city people will be discussed presently.

It remains uncertain to what extent foreigners—non-citizens or non-natives—were admitted into the city.[4b] Typically, their status must have been diplomatic, that is, dependent on their relation to the palace. Foreign emissaries, traders, political refugees, and others were able to move in and out under royal protection or could even be incorporated into the royal household. It is probable that, to some extent, non-citizens were allowed to settle in the *kāru*, the harbor of the city, a section outside of the town proper. They enjoyed a special administrative, political, and social status. The institution of "sojourners," or resident aliens, allowed to live within the city, which is known to us from the Old Testament, appears in Mesopotamia only in the west where a text from Ugarit speaks of "the citizens of the city of Carchemish together with the people (allowed to live) within their gates."[5] At those periods of Mesopotamian economic history when much of the overland trade was in private or semiprivate hands (see p. 90), a special section (*bīt ub(a)ri*) within the city wall seems to have been set aside for foreign visitors or merchants, e.g., the "Street-of-the-People-from-Eshnunna" in Sippar. Evidence from the Nippur of the Persian period might indicate the practice of having foreigners, and certain social classes (also craftsmen), live in separate quarters or streets, since they are all said to be under the supervision of special officials (see p. 81). An observation on the relation to foreigners may be in order in this context: the concept of, and terminology relating to, hospitality are conspicuously absent in Mesopotamia. This contrasts with the Old

Testament, where the nomadic background can be readily adduced as explanation, but presents an instructive similarity to Greece—not the Greece of Homer and its reflection in literature, but that of the *polis*, with its aversion to the non-citizen and all its discrimination, economic as well as social, against the alien.

Since family ties were generally ineffective in Mesopotamia and clan-relationships not in evidence in cities, other forms of association assumed their function in providing status and protection for the individual. Such associations could be professional, religious, or political. The last was doubtless the most important in Mesopotamia, insofar as one can term a political association the group of citizens who live together in a city and form a unit. This type of association will be dealt with, at length, in the fourth section ("The City") of this chapter.

Of religious associations in Mesopotamia we know very little. The concerns which normally give rise to associations of this kind, namely the care for the souls of the dead by means of funerary offerings and rituals, and also the maintenance of specific cults in conflict with generally accepted forms of worship, are absent in Mesopotamian cities. This does not exclude the possibility that some sort of relationship existed, at one time or another, between those persons who called themselves, on their own seals, servant or handmaiden of a certain deity. If there were such relationships, they were neither formalized nor, to our present knowledge, of much social or economic importance.[5a]

Professional associations were both numerous and important. Specialized crafts can evolve a tradition within families or clans as well as within the staff of a sanctuary, according to the demands made on them in specific economic and social situations. Within the symbiosis that came into existence during the urbanization of southern Mesopotamia (see p. 113), groups of craftsmen of divergent social backgrounds must also have come to some sort of consolidation for the usual economic reasons. We have to differentiate between guildlike associations of craftsmen and merchants, and professional groups consisting of certain highly trained experts in exorcism and divination techniques. The evidence for the former is complex, and one has to be very careful not to apply terms and patterns of Western origin in dealing with them. In the Old Babylonian period, "guilds" of brewers, smiths, and other trades were organized under a palace overseer, designated by a Semitic term in Sumerian, u g u l a, Akk. (w)aklu; it seems, however, that such associations were part of the palace or temple organization rather than organized to function independently—or, at least, were incorporated into these organizations. Independence—in the sense of the independence of the medieval guild—is unlikely for economic reasons, such as the difficulties of procurement of raw materials and the absence of a market economy, to mention only the most important problems. One might derive some enlightenment in this respect from the fact that the Old Babylonian merchants (tamkāru)—that is, overland traders—were likewise organized under an aklu.[6] From what we know of these merchants, they represent a typical example of the kind of administrative unit that is bound to develop in a societal structure such as the Mesopotamian. Between the opposing modes of integration characterized, on one hand, by an organization that was tight-knit and bureaucratic (the palace or the temple) and, on the other, by an association of individuals of more or less equal status who acted corporately as well as individually (the city), an intermediate zone was bound to develop that, as if by a law of nature, was attracted to the centers of power and assumed various forms of peripheral coexistence.

In whatever direction such a development took place in Mesopotamian cities, important crafts—those of the smith, the carpenter, the brewer—seem to have achieved some kind of independence within and among the organizations. They served the community with their products and their skills to a degree that must have depended largely on the internal political equilibrium with the temple and palace. Thus the overseers of the "guilds" achieved social status and a large measure of power, a position by which they could not fail to realize—quite legitimately—personal enrichment. We know this is true, for instance, of the merchants of Old Babylonian Larsa, who, of course, represent only an extreme case. The much poorer overseer of the musicians, who had but little of value to sell or hire, represents the opposite end of the scale. It is quite possible that the number of persons who appear in Old Babylonian legal texts as "overseer" of this or that craft had little to do with the work going on but rather were persons of status, deriving income or influence from their function as officials. From the early Neo-Babylonian period onward, we find frequent use of the names of professions as ancestral names ("family names"), a valuable indication that a wide variety of craftsmen had enjoyed a certain status in the preceding period. Again, one has to stress that special situations must have developed with respect to each and every one of these crafts. A case in point is offered by references in late Neo-Babylonian texts to the "city" of the tanners and the "city" of the metalworkers, referring to the special quarters to which certain crafts were either restricted or in which they were concentrated for mutual convenience. We know, moreover, that in Nippur of the Persian period special officials were in charge of such professions as those of the butchers, merchants, joiners, boatmen, and weavers; but it is important to note that officials having the same title in Nippur were also responsible for foreigners (Cimmerians, Urartians, natives of Tyre and Malatya) and of other social groupings. However, this may have been due to the special position of Nippur or an administrative regulation imposed by a conqueror (the Persians) on a quite different traditional organization.

The only genuinely independent associations in Mesopotamia seem to have been those of certain learned professions such as the *mašmāšu*, the expert in exorcism and related apotropaic rituals, of whom we are best informed, and similar arrangements may well have existed for the divination experts (*bārû*), and perhaps for the physicians and the scribes. Again, one has to caution against the transfer of findings and conclusions from one context to another, however related or parallel they may appear to us. The *mašmāšu* and the *bārû* had to fulfil certain requirements to enter the profession and the association; these requirements refer to descent, physical perfection, and to an appropriate and extensive training. There might even have been examinations (*maša'altu*), quite possibly competitive (*tašninti ummâni*). Little in this respect is known of the other learned professions, except for the scribes (see n. 17, chap. vi).

Since we shall treat the city at length in a later section of the present chapter, we may turn now to the relationship between that section of the total population which lived in cities of all sizes and that which either occupied more or less permanent agglomerations of huts and encampments outside the cities or drifted with their herds or were for other reasons steadily on the move between one city and another. This contrast between city-dwellers and those in the open country cuts across the fabric of Mesopotamian society and represents an eternal source of conflict. As such it was of fateful influence on the political development in Mesopotamia. The tension, city against surrounding country, affected the history of the region but should not be regarded as a typically Mesopotamian phenomenon, since the entire ancient Near East had to face this problem in varying intensity and in several periods, and had constantly to strive for any solution, however unstable, that could be found.

It can hardly be said that the two "strata" were at any time isolated; they maintained a constant interchange of persons, goods, and ideas in spite of their spatial separation. The palace, of course, the temple, and the hard core of city-dwellers in the large and old cities had only occasional contacts with the people in the open country, who subsisted on the yield of this environment and were not to be forced into sedentary conditions. Between these two groups there were important fluctuations comprising smaller or larger segments of the population of the cities as well as of the open country. Difficult economic and political situations were liable to crowd out of the cities such persons as delinquent debtors, power groups defeated in intracity striving, defectors from the great organizations, and others. In the open country, they joined the inhabitants of abandoned villages and settlements who had been driven into a seminomadic way of life by the deterioration of the soil, the breakdown of facilities for irrigation, or because they had rebelled against taxes and rents. The number of these was increased by infiltrating groups from the mountains and the deserts around Mesopotamia. Thus the ranks of this fluctuating element of the population could swell at times of crisis to a dangerous degree, even engulfing the cities, and—if led by an energetic and efficient political or military leader—it could transfer the rule over the city, and even that over the entire country, into the hands of outsiders or newcomers. Whenever linguistic differences appear between the city and such power groups in the rebellious hinterlands, or more exactly, between the dialect used to write official documents in the city and that actually spoken by the group in command, we have the impression of sudden foreign invasions, bringing kings bearing foreign names to the throne. Such dramatic changes need not have been the result, necessarily, of foreign invasion but could have been brought about by a rather slow economic and political process of increasing social unrest which would not be reflected in extant documents. The most effective remedy against these potentially dangerous elements were projects of internal and frontier colonization which only a powerful king could set afoot. The inscriptions of such kings speak triumphantly of the ingathering (*puḫḫuru*) of the scattered, the resettling (*šūšubu*) of the shiftless on new land, where the king forced them to dig or re-dig canals, build or resettle cities, and till the soil, pay taxes, do *corvée* work to maintain the irrigation system, and—last but not least—perform military service. We shall see how the situation just outlined, characterized by the tension between city and open country, contributed to the curious lack of political stability in Mesopotamia. This is especially true in Assyria, where cities were always few and far between and where the power of the central authority depended, to a large extent, upon its ability to overcome the innate resistance of a large section of the population toward integration into a territorial state with a strong central administration.

Economic Facts

The economic basis of Mesopotamian society throughout its entire development was primarily agricultural. Supplementary income was derived from trade in wool, hair, and leather. What can be termed industrial production in the ancient Near East up to the Muslim Middle Ages is concerned exclusively with the weaving of textiles and related activities. In Mesopotamia weaving on such a scale was done only in the workshops of the great organizations, private households producing hardly enough for their own use.

The cultivation of most cereals and large-scale planting of date palms was done on several levels: on extensive temple and palace land either directly (i.e., managed and staffed by the organization) or farmed out; on private land, the extent of which we cannot gauge readily, and in small plots where the city poor, nomads, and shepherds succeeded in raising crops. The proportionate amount of land held by each of these types of producers is impossible to establish and undoubtedly varied greatly according to the period, the region, and the condition of the soil. The variations in the pattern of distribution must needs have had far-reaching effects on the economy of the country. Knowledge concerning the proportionate distribution would bring to an end the perennial discussion as to whether *Staatskapitalismus* or other form of social organization for managing large holdings of real estate, or some form of private enterprise, was predominant.[7] Since all pertinent information is based on the meager written evidence and supplemented by inference, the nature of the text material is bound to influence our judgment. Bureaucracies necessarily leave more written evidence than family or clan organizations and private persons, so that the picture we obtain can hardly ever be trusted to correspond to facts. Moreover, all evidence adduced and interpreted cannot but be vitiated, consciously or not, by the emotionalism inherent in the political and intellectual tensions of today, with which the entire problem is fraught.

The progressive salinization of the intensively irrigated soil in Babylonia, the silting-up of the canals (carriers and distributors alike), and the weakening of the dikes necessitated constant surveillance. The temple and the palace, which were able to afford the capital investment needed to carry on this work, increased in size and importance. The steady decline of the influence of the temple from the middle of the second millennium, and the corresponding increase of land holdings in some kind of feudal tenure under royal charter, must likewise have brought about essential economic dislocations, just as did the increased role of capital in the last half of the first millennium in hands that seem to have been "private" within the customary limits of that term in the ancient Near East. Here the "banking house" of Murašû may furnish a case for such capital assuming the responsibilities held in the course of Mesopotamian history successively by village communities, the temples, and the palace, by investing in new land.[8]

A valuable source of information concerning the ownership of land in Mesopotamia, as well as the utilization of the labor force, comes from the numerous texts that record the renting of farmland, from the early Old Babylonian period until the late Persian. No systematic study of these documents is available, but one fact is obvious: the size of fields rented out—as a rule by city dwellers—to private individuals or partnerships increases continuously in the course of time until it reaches its maximum in the Neo-Babylonian and later texts. A corresponding development reveals evidence of a decline in use of slaves, serfs, and other menials to work the land under overseers responsible to a central organization to which the personnel belongs. Of course, such a statement has to be qualified as to period and region. Royal domains are very spottily attested. The most extensive evidence, coming from Kassite Nippur, has not been fully published as yet.[9] Since corresponding material from the preceding (Fara) and following periods is either not available in sufficient number, or not adequately studied, we remain in the dark as to the extent of royal holdings. Old Akkadian texts suggest that royal property was then managed as bureaucratically as is suggested by the Kassite evidence. A decided change in this respect is indicated by a small group of Neo-Babylonian documents pertaining to the lease of extensive farmlands to private persons by the king himself and his family (the Babylonian king Nabonidus and his son Belshazzar), which is quite unique in Mesopotamia. The development here suggested seems to have been fostered to an unknown degree by the practice of the royal administration of using the services of "capitalists" to finance income due from fields and gardens as taxes, a practice that can be observed in the large cities (Nippur and Uruk) beginning with the Persian period.

There is another point to be made with regard to the cultivation of cereals and sesame in Mesopotamia, one that relates to the difference between southern Babylonia and northern Assyria. Land seems to have been held in the south either by the great organizations or by private absentee owners living in the cities who usually rented it out to poor tenant farmers. Farmers who lived on their own fields are the exception. The necessity for the reclamation of land in order to create new sources of supply can hardly have given rise to lasting communities of farmers. On the new land, colonists worked under duress for the king or any other absentee owner or manager. In the north, however, in Assyria, in the Zagros valleys, on the plateaus, and up into Syria, farmers seem to have lived mainly in some sort of village community which was held either in feudal tenure or in private possession by a lord of the manor—the king, his high officials, or members of his family. These owners formed the thin layer of a ruling class, of "feudal" lords—either native or foreign—that could be replaced by newcomers without affecting the economic structure of the country. City-dwellers, concerned with tilling the soil around their city and acting as overland traders or capitalistic entrepreneurs, were concentrated in the very few cities of the region, where they were protected by special royal privileges. We shall have more to say of this characteristic arrangement in Assyria and Upper Mesopotamia.

As important as the problem of the ownership of land for the characterization of Mesopotamian economics is that of the use of silver as a means of exchange and payment, and as a standard. Again, over-all studies based on textual evidence are conspicuously lacking. Throughout the entire known history of Mesopotamia, silver was used as a standard, except for two interesting and nearly contemporaneous but short-lived intermezzi, the Middle Babylonian period, when gold and silver were valued equally, and the Middle Assyrian period, when tin, at least in Assur, became the medium of exchange.

As a means of payment, silver was used in ingots and un-specified forms that required weighing at each transfer. Not until the Seleucid conquerors were coins used—Greek coins which, characteristically enough, were again weighed rather than counted, though value was placed on their quality and on the ruler under which they were struck.[10] From the inscriptions of Sennacherib (704–681 B.C.), we learn through a casually used simile of the casting of small copper coins; but we know nothing of their use from legal and administrative texts of the period.[11] This may represent, however, another instance of western (here Lydian) influence on Assyria. During the Old Babylonian period, payments for real estate, slaves, goods, and services seem to have been only rarely made in silver, although prices as a rule are quoted according to that standard. Specific allusions in texts support this assumption, and since no concern at all is expressed in Old Babylonian legal documents as to the quality and fineness of the silver used in payment, the silver probably did not change hands. In contrast, in the Neo-Babylonian period, the legal texts make careful use of a complex terminology for the purpose of establishing precisely the quality of the silver given or expected. Since silver had to be imported and certain taxes (ever since the Ur III period) were paid in that precious metal, one realizes that in the Old Babylonian period the palace controlled the circulation of silver effectively as long as private overland trade did not upset the silver balance. Accumulations of silver as treasure seem then to have been restricted to palace and temple, from which the metal might have reached other strata of the population. Still, the dowry lists and precious objects mentioned in the wills of that time bespeak clearly the rarity of silver and gold.

On the subject of individual wealth, one may draw attention to a source of information on Old Babylonian Mesopotamia that has not yet been investigated thoroughly. These are the omen texts that reveal within their gamut of expectations and apprehensions (as reflected in the prognoses) a remarkable degree of economic mobility: poor people expect to become rich; the rich are afraid of becoming poor; both dread interference from the palace administration. It is difficult to ascertain how far and in what specific contexts the impression of economic mobility which these texts convey corresponds to reality.

Another problem important for an appreciation of Mesopotamian economics has to be taken up now. This was the practice of making capital—staples or silver—a commodity for the use of which interest was charged. This practice constitutes a trait peculiar to Mesopotamia, a characteristic feature that is rejected in regions west of Mesopotamia just as much as, e.g., the practice of drinking beer instead of wine, of using sesame instead of olive oil.

In a letter from Ugarit we read in the awkward Akkadian characteristic of these texts one of those revealing sentences that shed more light on the economic life of the time than hundreds of monotonous and lengthy tablets: "Give [in the meantime] the 140 shekels which are still outstanding from your own money but do not charge interest between us—we are both gentlemen!"[12] This curious and unique reference to a status situation mentioned for the purpose of influencing an economic relationship acquires meaning and significance when one connects it with a passage in Deuteronomy, 23:20 (and in Leviticus, 25:36–37), "Unto a stranger thou mayest lend upon usury; but unto thy brother thou shalt not lend upon usury." We see that both the Ugarit letter and the passage from the Old Testament exhibit the same disinclination to use capital as a commodity. Among the Old Assyrian traders, however, the taking of interest and of compound interest is completely acceptable. Of course, they prefer to pay interest at the rate "one brother charges the other."

It is well known that the biblical attitude toward what we translate as "usury" has had a far-reaching and fateful impact upon the economic history of the West. The prohibition of usury was taken over by the early Church and maintained in force with remarkable inflexibility through the entire medieval period in the face of all the pressure generated by slowly but profoundly changing economic conditions. Only the dislocation of the ideological background of the medieval civilization in Europe—the Reformation—was able to break the stranglehold of the traditional attitude of the Church upon the economic life of Europe. Throughout the long theological discussions in scholastic as well as in popular literature (up to the seventeenth century), "capitalistic" concepts of money were often linked with the name of Babylon, a name representing a city rich and materialistic, an eminently efficient social and economic organization. The importance of our passage from Ugarit lies in the fact that it compels us to reconsider our evaluation of the contrast: biblical versus Babylonian ethics, in terms of economic rather than moral considerations. The references in Western texts, i.e., those from Syria and Palestine, indicate that there the economic situation was diametrically opposed to that of Babylonia. What caused the difference?

Here is one possible explanation. Economic integration was effectuated in Babylonia (i.e., southern Mesopotamia as against Assyria and the West) to a large extent in terms of a storage economy so constituted as to be self-supporting, with a center in either the palace or the temple. I would like to stress that this does not—and probably never did—represent the only existing means of economic integration in that region. In fact, a symbiosis seems to have evolved between the storage centers and a layer of the population engaged in independent economic activity either as individuals or as a group of persons of equal status. The coexistence of divergent systems of integration, storage versus private economy, seems to have created or favored the use of money, that is, surplus staples. Money, or its equivalent in goods, is used under such circumstances as a tool and as a means of exercising economic pressure by making it a commodity to be rented and paid for. For reasons which we cannot explain, the storage economy originally lacked the means of contacting the world around it for those raw materials which fate had denied to the locale, such as stone, metal, and timber. Due to background or predilections, the groups outside the magic circle of the storage system were sufficiently mobile and commercially minded to serve the center as such means of contact and to be paid for their services. Thus a symbiotic arrangement could well have supplied the needs of both parties and created an economic climate which, among other consequences, favored the urbanization that occurred so early and efficiently in this region. In the northwest, in Assyria and Syria, the homeland of the village communities, capital circulated only among the elite of the population, a group of equal status, whether it was ethnically identical with the villagers or represented a layer of conquerors. There, money could not be used to exercise economic pressure (between private initiative and storage center inertia), and the taking of interest was socially, and therefore morally, unacceptable. This, by the way, holds true also for Greece and even for Rome, and demonstrates again the uniqueness of Mesopotamia in a world that evolved quite different forms of economic integration on which were based different moral codes of behavior.

The Old Testament speaks often and with hatred and contempt of Babylon's and Nineveh's merchants, which again points out—as unerringly as only bitter hate can do—an important feature of the economic life in Babylonia that was rejected in the West. We know very little of how trade was enacted within a Mesopotamian city. Of course, real estate (houses, fields, and gardens) were bought and sold, and there was income from temple offices (prebends) or shares thereof, and from slaves and even children, quite rarely animals (bovines and donkeys) and a very small number of mobilia. But staple transactions are not recorded as sales, and foodstuffs are never mentioned in any context that would suggest a form of trade. For the problem of the market, reference should be made here to the discussion on page 129.

What the Bible refers to as alien and objectionable is overland trade, for which Mesopotamia was apparently famed.[13] The same aversion against this type of trade is expressed in Vergil's *omnis feret omnia tellus* (Ecl. IV 39) which sees in autarchy an ideal economic situation. Evidence for this kind of trade, with its important political connotations, comes from nearly every period and region that has given us documentary evidence in cuneiform.

On principle, two types of foreign trade, as well as intercity trade, have to be distinguished. First is the export of industrial goods, which in Mesopotamia means, as we have seen, textiles produced by serfs in the self-contained organizations of temple or palace to create the means of exchange needed for importing metal, stone, lumber, spices, and perfumes. The second is a carrying trade between foreign cities, trading outposts, and barbarian tribes who lacked the prestige, the political power, and the initiative necessary to engage in trade relations on the basis of treaties. Both types of trade are attested around the Persian Gulf and in Asia Minor before the Dark Age as well as along the Euphrates route into the Mediterranean littoral before and after that period. There were certainly other regions in which this and similar types of trade were carried on, but we lack documentary evidence. In both instances, trade contributed directly or indirectly toward the raising of the living standard in Mesopotamia and—above all—helped to increase the spreading influence of Mesopotamian civilization.

The inventories of the traders (*tamkāru*) of the period before the Dark Age speak often of the importation of a large variety of luxury goods and essential raw materials, apparently for the court of the king and the temple of the god, but there is never a direct mention of export activities. Trade seems to have been conducted on a purely administrative level, and private initiative or gain was not openly admitted. In the Old Babylonian period that followed, the role of the *tamkāru* became clearly more complex in the south, the range of his activities increased, and there is reason to believe that the traders in royal service (especially those of Larsa) were allowed to grow rich. The degree of the trader's freedom of disposition and individual financial responsibility and initiative can not yet be established with any clarity. Only from the Ur of the early Old Babylonian period have we evidence that the importers of copper from beyond the Persian Gulf transacted their business by pooling their funds and by sharing the risks, the responsibility, and the profits. These texts repeatedly mention the *kāru*, a merchant organization with a seat and a legal status of its own, outside the city proper.

We are best informed, for a short period before the Dark Age, about the Old Assyrian merchants who settled in Kaniš in Anatolia. Merchants are known to have had settlements in other localities of that region and along the communication lines to Assur, although no textual evidence has been found there.

Their numerous letters, accounts, and legal documents (amounting now to more than 16,000 texts, all but 2,000 unpublished) have been found in Kaniš, in Boghazkeui, and, in very small numbers, outside of Anatolia.[14] No text of that kind has yet been discovered in Assur proper, the very center of the trade organization. All the texts show the merchants in at least two roles: handling the export of textiles manufactured in or traded through the town of Assur, and acting as intermediaries between mining and smelting centers and distributors in the copper and iron trade within Asia Minor. Their reports on their dealings with native rulers, and on their business activities with other merchants and with natives, give us most of our information about Asia Minor at the beginning of the second millennium. One cannot fail to notice the freedom of movement of these traders, the security of communication without reference to any military protection, the large returns in silver and gold which their activities yielded, and, above all, the pride of the merchants in their social status, and in their high ethical standards. The picture given by the tablets unearthed at Kaniš is one which is rare in the economic history of the ancient Near East and finds its analogy only in the Phoenician cities of the Iron Age and in the Nabatean caravan trade of the first centuries of our era. We still do not know what historic circumstances fostered this short-lived flowering in Kaniš; it lasted little more than three generations. It may well have been the self-interest of the native kinglets and their needs rather than a political power that protected these traders.

Additional international trade relations are reported in Mari texts; they link the Persian Gulf, with its island emporium Telmun, via the Euphrates, Aleppo, and the Orontes valley, to the Mediterranean. Mari seems, furthermore, to have been a station on the tin trade route (between inner Asia and the Mediterranean) which somewhat earlier was in the hands of Assyrian merchants. Tin was, of course, essential for the manufacture of bronze, and it could be had in quantity only from sources outside Mesopotamia, reaching there through the hands of many intermediaries. Mari trade was apparently operated on a different level from that of Ur and Kaniš; caravans enjoyed royal protection and brought foreign merchants from court to court, granting them something similar to diplomatic status.

After the Dark Age had passed, a situation similar to that attested in Mari is encountered all over the ancient Near East. Merchants of the type found in Kaniš, Assur, and probably also in Ur have disappeared. The traders have become royal emissaries carrying precious gifts from one ruler to the other and are sometimes called *ša mandatti*, a designation which seems to refer to the source of their capital.[14a] There exist treaties to guarantee their protection and to limit their activities, which apparently could be combined with private initiative. The risks seem to have become considerable; we begin to read in the correspondence from Amarna and the documents from Ugarit and Boghazkeui about attacks on caravans and the murder of merchants. Trade relations between the Hittite capital Hattuša in Anatolia, Ugarit, Alalakh, and Mesopotamia proper seem to have been surprisingly intense in view of the instability of the political situation and the dangers of overland communication.[15] Strangely enough, cuneiform texts, soon after the Amarna period, are silent with respect to trade and traders, and this silence extends, for all practical purposes, to the very end of the Babylonian empire.[15a] Still, one cannot assume that trade relations ceased through that millennium, especially since they are known to have flourished greatly in the subsequent period when Arameans and Arab tribes handled the extensive caravan traffic in the triangle between the Mediterranean, the Red Sea, and the Persian Gulf, not to speak of the routes leading deep into central Asia. There are a sufficient number of allusions scattered through the texts of the entire millennium to make this absence of any direct references to trade still more conspicuous.

The following is additional evidence that bespeaks the continuous existence, if not the steady growth, of foreign trade in, through, and around Mesopotamia. From a recently discovered inscription, we learn that Sargon II (721–705 B.C.) was the first Assyrian ruler who succeeded in forcing Egypt to open trade relations with his country and that he considered the fact so important as to mention it in an inscription.[16] Egypt had to abandon its traditional isolation—its "sealed-off frontiers," as

Sargon puts it tellingly—after a successful Assyrian campaign that took place on Egypt's Palestinian border.[16a] Here we have another indication that Assyria was interested, i.e., participated, in international trade relations. Later, according to a well-known inscription of Sargon's grandson, Esarhaddon (680–669 B.C.), the inhabitants of the city of Babylon, rebuilt by Esarhaddon after his father, Sennacherib, had destroyed it, are again granted the privilege of unrestricted trade with the entire world.[17] This passage shows that the Babylonians had lived and probably thrived into the reign of Sennacherib, i.e., during a period of political impotence, on overland trade. One receives the impression that both Babylonian and Assyrian trade had changed at the beginning of the first millennium from the old export-import to the more profitable carrying trade. It thus could well have linked the East, the countries accessible via the Persian Gulf and those whose goods came across the Iranian plateau, to the Mediterranean Sea. It is no coincidence that at this time the long-interrupted contact with the East was taken up again; the island emporium of Telmun reappears, after nearly a millennium of eclipse, in cuneiform sources; and Sennacherib plants Indian cotton in his royal garden. At the western end of the trade route were the cities of the Phoenician coast, Sidon and Tyre, whose struggle against Assyria is often recorded in royal inscriptions. The Neo-Babylonian kings—Nebuchadnezzar II, Neriglissar, and Nabonidus—who continued the Assyrian imperial policy after the fall of Nineveh, fought in Cilicia, dealt with Phoenician cities, and traveled deep into Arabia in an unprecedented way. It is certainly no accident that the *rab tamkāri*, "chief trader," was a high official at the court of the Babylonian kings, an office which was held under Nebuchadnezzar II by a man called Hanūnu, i.e., Hanno, a typical Phoenician name.[18]

The lack of any written evidence for first-millennium trade is not easily explained. It may be suggested that the entire trade was in Aramaic hands and that these merchants used papyrus and leather as writing material. After all, only a very small fraction of the private legal acts was recorded in cuneiform on clay even during the Neo-Babylonian period when this technique continued to be used mainly by the temple administrations of Sippar, Ur, Babylon, and others. More difficult even than the problem of the traders is the question of the merchandise handled by them, and the geographical extent of trading. We do not have answers to these questions.

"The Great Organizations"

In every civilization the network of social interaction is articulated within established channels that are co-ordinated in a characteristic and unique manner. For Mesopotamia, one such pattern of integration found its most direct expression in the city. This pattern maintained its effectiveness through three millennia of history. In order to study and to analyze it adequately, its composite nature has to be recognized as an essential feature and the components have to be investigated, first separately and then in their relationship to one another. Let us distinguish two essential components: first, the community of persons of equal status bound together by a consciousness of belonging, realized by directing their communal affairs by means of an assembly, in which, under a presiding officer, some measure of consensus was reached as it was the case in the rich and quasi-independent old cities of Babylonia; second, an organization of persons entirely different in structure and temperament from the community just mentioned, whose center and raison d'être was either the temple or the palace, either the household of the deity or that of the king. Both were closed-circuit organizations in which goods and services were channeled into a circulation system and where the entire personnel was integrated in a hierarchic order. It seems advantageous to approach these two great organizations first for a discussion and an analysis and then to treat the city itself and its relationship to the temple and palace.

Before discussing the differences between palace and temple, certain common features should be pointed out. Each derived its income primarily from agricultural holdings, either directly or through payment of rent and taxes; secondarily, from what the workshops of the organization produced; and, lastly, from what was offered by the pious worshipers of the god and gifts prompted by the respect or fear shown by the king's allies and tributaries. A central administration received all income and disposed of it by redistributing what was not set aside for storage according to a pattern that was dictated for the palace by political considerations and, for the temple, by custom. Both administrations supported by means of food rations, oil, clothing allowances, and a number of other benefits the managerial personnel who directed, administered, and controlled the work, the deliveries, and the payments. The reason the systems differed only in certain specific instances was simply that both temple and palace remained households, the temple that of the deity, the palace that of the king. The deity is conceived as residing in his cella, to be fed, clothed, and cared for appropriately, just like the king on his dais. King and god alike were surrounded by a personnel which we call respectively courtiers and—quite inappropriately—priests, who called themselves slaves in relation to their master. The menial work was performed either by slaves or to a much larger extent by persons of restricted freedom (serfs) who were obliged to devote either all or a part of their time and work to the central authority.[18a] The number of these attendants, officials, serfs, and slaves varied greatly according to the importance and status of the "household" to which they belonged. Prisoners of war swelled their ranks, as did free citizens in times of famine who attached themselves or their children to such households. The splendor and luxury displayed in temple and palace demanded not only materials which had to be imported but attracted artists and craftsmen and others whose talents could serve them best in these cirumstances.

The provenience of such a large body of serfs—especially in the early (pre-Sargonic) temples as those of Lagaš—should give considerable concern to the social historian. To speak here of conquered and subjugated population strata offers a much too obvious answer, which moreover has no base in the known history of the region. It is thinkable that we might be faced here with a phenomenon which is more restricted locally than we are accustomed to assume and which might be the expression of a specific socio-ideological situation in which certain groups of the population expressed their relation to the deity in terms of menial service dedicated to the god's household. What legal or pious fiction or what economic or social pressure conditioned this attitude, we shall probably never know.

All these common features should not make us forget the far-reaching differences which separated the temple from the palace, and the wide range of variations that must have existed among the individual palaces and temples throughout the millennia of history over the extensive reaches of Mesopotamia proper (from Ur and even Eridu to Dur-Šarrukin) and the regions under Mesopotamian influence (from Susa to Alalakh). The specific requirements of cults in the sanctuaries, the size of their endowments, the rank of their deities, and their relationship to the king determined the style in which the temple functioned. Royal largess, rather than the returns of its agricultural investments and the pious generosity of its worshipers, often, and especially in the later periods, provided the means the temple could utilize for the purpose of displaying the wealth of the deity. The extent of the realm and the political and military effectiveness of the king bore directly on the size of the establishment. The desire of every powerful ruler to build a new palace made palace architecture at all times a revealing mirror of the creative aspirations of the period. Palace personnel reflected in number and quality the power of the ruler, and—if we knew more about it—would also offer us a good picture of the internal politics of his time. Still, it seems that personal talents and achievements permitted a higher degree of mobility for the individual within the necessarily hierarchic organization of the royal household than in that of the deity where status and concomitant wealth depended mainly on descent, although individual initiative could certainly successfully manipulate inherited and acquired wealth.

A discussion of the palace as a functioning socioeconomic institution must be introduced by clarifying the position and function of the Mesopotamian king. If properly documented, a study of Mesopotamian kingship would easily fill a book far longer than the present one, and even a prolonged discussion of this topic would keep us from achieving our goal, to present, if possible, all aspects of Mesopotamian civilization without undue stress on any one of them. But since kingship has been the topic of two recent studies (see bibliographical footnote), it can be dealt with here somewhat succinctly.

From the point of view of Mesopotamian civilization, there was only one institution in the modern sense of the word: kingship. As a main characteristic of civilized living, it was of divine origin. The divinity of kingship expresses itself differently in Babylonia and Assyria. In Babylonia, from the time of Sargon of Akkad until the Hammurapi period, the name of the king was often written with the determinative DINGIR ("god"), used normally for gods and objects intended for worship. We also know, from Ur III texts and, sporadically, from later documents, that statues of deceased kings received shares of the offerings in the temple.[19] The sanctity of the royal person is often, especially in Assyrian texts, said to be revealed by a supernatural and awe-inspiring radiance or aura which, according to the religious literature, is characteristic of deities and of all things divine. A number of terms refer to this phenomenon; among them the probably pre-Sumerian term *melammû*, something like "awe-inspiring luminosity," is most frequent,[20] while other terms stress the quality of *tremendum* inherent in this accepted phenomenon. The royal halo is also referred to in Middle Persian (Sassanian) texts as *xvarena*, in late classical as *aura*, and a corresponding nimbus is pictured about the living emperor as late as in early Christian representations. This *melammû* terrifies and overwhelms the enemies of the king but is said to be taken away from him if he loses divine support. The royal apparel underlines the divine aspect of kingship; the horned miter with which Naram-Sin is represented and the *kusītu* garments of the Neo-Assyrian kings are similar to those worn by images of the gods.[21]

The special relationship which—according to royal propaganda—existed between the king and his god was said to materialize in the successes of the ruler in war and in the prosperity of the country in peace. It was often couched, especially in the Sumerian period, in terms of family relationships. The scribes and artists of the courts loved to elaborate on this *topos* in their hectic and adulatory style in royal hymns (almost exclusively Sumerian) and panegyric passages in royal inscriptions. We do not intend to discuss in detail this type of literary reference to the king and his position but rather intend to dwell for a moment on the deep-seated differences between the Babylonian and Assyrian concept of kingship. Sumer must be omitted from this presentation, because the relationship evolving between the l u g a l ("king") and the e n ("high priest") is too complex and as yet too ill-defined to be mentioned but in passing.[22]

The essential fact concerning the Assyrian king is that he was the high priest of the god Aššur. As such, he performed sacrifices and was in a position to influence both temple and cult. The Babylonian king was admitted into the cella of Marduk but once a year, and then only after having put aside his royal insignia. The Assyrian king, as far as we know, was crowned anew each year, the ceremony accompanied by shouts of "Aššur is king!" The Assyrian kings only reluctantly, and apparently for reasons of prestige, assumed the designation *šarru*, "king," which is perhaps a foreign term in Akkadian, like *basileus* in Greek.[23]

It was an Assyrian custom to have the king act as eponym (*limmu*) on a par with the highest administrative officers of the realm. Years were not counted in Assyria as regnal years of the king as was the case in Babylonia, but differentiated by the name of a high official who acted as eponym. The king himself gave his name to the first year of his own reign and the officials of the realm, in a traditional sequence, to the subsequent years, after which the king could again be the eponym for one year. A possible explanation for this custom could be that the king was originally only the *primus inter pares* of an amphictyonic league of sheikhs, as we know the kings of Hana to have been, and possibly also those of Naʾiri. Assyrian tribal chieftains could well have lived around the sanctuary of the god Aššur and acted there, at an early period at least, as kings and priests, each for one year. As a matter of fact, it seems that in theory—and probably originally in practice—the eponym, or ruler of the year, was determined by lot.[24] Such a lot through which the eponym of the year 833 B.C. was chosen is preserved; it bears the following inscription: "O great lord, Aššur! O great lord, Adad! this is the lot of Jaḫali, the chief intendant of Shalmaneser, king of Assyria, [governor of] the city of Kipsuni, of the countries ..., the harbor director; make prosper the harvest of Assyria and let it be bountiful in the eponym [established] by his lot! May his lot come up!" We may assume that, originally, the official whose lot came up was considered chosen by the god to be his priest, or to perform some essential priestly function in connection with the new year. Later, the sequence of officials was determined by rank and tradition rather than by lot. In fact, the kings of the Neo-Assyrian period seem to have spurned this native practice and have not always and in the above-outlined sequence assumed the office of eponym.

As priest, the Assyrian king participated, actively or as object, in numerous and complex rituals which are described in great detail in certain texts. His person was carefully protected from disease and especially from the evil influence of magic because his well-being was considered essential for that of the country. For this reason, Assyrian kings, as we know from the letters in their archives, were surrounded by a host of diviners and physicians. All ominous signs were observed and interpreted with regard to their bearing on the royal person. Complex rituals existed to ward off evil signs, and at least one instance is known in Assyria where a fatal prediction was counteracted by the stratagem of making another person king (called šar pūḫi, "substitute king") for one hundred days and then killing and duly burying him so that the omen should be fulfilled but fate cheated and the true king kept alive.[25] Access to the king was carefully regulated, even for the heir apparent, to avoid untoward encounters, and in each Assyrian palace was a room, adjacent to the throne room, for ritual ablutions of the king.

The Assyrian coronation ritual prescribes that the court officials deposit their symbols of office in front of the new king and leave their place and join the suite of the king, thus indicating that they resign their positions, to be reappointed by the newly crowned king.[26]

The case is quite different in Babylonia. We happen to have a list of the entire personnel of the court of Nebuchadnezzar II. He was surrounded by the administrators of his palace and of his realm, by bureaucrats and vanquished kings who lived at his court, whereas the officials of the Assyrian king seem to have been primarily executors of his commands. After the Middle Babylonian period, the Babylonian and Assyrian kings often had viziers (the Akkadian term means "chief of the chancellery") whose names are given in the king lists; in Assyria, this happened only in the late period.[27] There the crown prince normally assumed the role of chief administrator of the realm, which was ruled from the "palace of the administration" (*bīt ridûti*).

The problem of succession was important in both countries. Babylonian historical sources mention only rarely that a usurpation actually took place; but many predictions contained in the omen collections show that the revolt of high officials and royal princes was not exceptional. The events after the death of Nebuchadnezzar II until the usurpation of the throne by Nabonidus illustrate such incidents, and there is a letter of Samsuiluna which indicates that he took over the throne before the death of his father Hammurapi, who was ill.[28] In Assyria, much stress is placed on the legitimacy of the ruler, and long genealogies often appear in the royal inscriptions, displaying the pride of the kings in their royal ancestors. In view of such exhibits, it is more than strange that some Assyrian kings pointedly avoid mentioning their fathers and ancestry, as if they were not of royal lineage, although we know from other sources that this was the case. This deviation leaves the impression that there existed in the Assyria of the end of the second and the beginning of the first millennium B.C. two ideal ruler types, one who derived authority from the divinely guarded lineage that extended deep into the past of Assyria, and the other who saw in the very success of becoming king the approval of the gods of Assyria, who had elevated him as the man chosen for this task. The more interesting ruler image is the latter, that of the "self-made man." The older Sargon, who rose from "an ark of bulrushes" to become the most famous ruler in Mesopotamian history, was given a purely mythological background whereas Idrimi, self-made king of Alalakh, and likewise

Ursa, self-made king of Urartu, represent themselves proudly as heroes.[29] Such coexisting ideals illustrate once again the complexity of the Assyrian background.

The position of the Mesopotamian king in war was that of leader of the army. Very few Assyrian kings entrusted an army to such a top military official as the *turtānu*, who by his rank commanded one half of the entire military might. Even the achievements of the *turtānu* were frequently reported by the king in the first-person singular. In peace, the king's responsibilities were predominantly social; in the historical period, only the Assyrian king had definite cultic obligations, as we know from a very diversified body of ritual texts that describe in detail the king's part in certain cultic acts, either recurrent in nature or provoked by circumstances. In the early titulary of the Babylonian kings, we find reflections of a much earlier stage, in which the king, as the representative of the community, seems to have been duty bound to participate in certain ritual activities.[30] (A probably late practice involving the Babylonian king at the festival of the New Year shows him in a rather peculiar role, discussed on p. 122.)

As for his social responsibilities, the Mesopotamian king had to guarantee legal protection for the underprivileged and was expected to discharge these duties by establishing and maintaining proper legal procedures and hearing appeals. Traditionally, he promulgated laws and price regulations to correct abuses and, above all, to change existing practices according to the needs of those adversely affected by them. In certain instances, the king devised new regulations for the protection of certain strata of the population or guided the judges in making decisions in cases involving a conflict of interests. The king as a lawgiver disappears, however, with the Old Babylonian period, and at the same time there is a cessation of royal attempts to promote the general welfare by the remission of certain debts and by regulating the rate of interest, the wages and fees for essential services, and the prices of staples.[31] Certain of these regulations, in this period, seem to have been still within the responsibilities of the temples; after the Dark Age, such regulations are rare.

Of course, contacts with foreign countries in times of peace were likewise a royal privilege. Diplomatic and trade relations were always managed by the king and the officials designated for that purpose.

As for the relationship between king and his subjects, one can say that obedience to the proper authorities was considered by the people of Mesopotamia as a main characteristic of civilized living on the same level as worship for the gods. In the descriptions of the strange ways of the unsedentary section of the population this attitude is mentioned together with certain eating habits and burial customs as culture traits which separate the civilized from the uncivilized.[32] The legal and practical implications of this relationship are difficult to delineate. The exemptions granted by the kings to certain officials, estates, and even cities give us some insight as to the burden that the royal service could impose on individuals and communities. There were not only direct taxes, the nature and extent of which are, unfortunately, quite unknown, but also obligations to perform all kinds of services for the palace and its officials, to keep up roads and canals, and to serve in the army, about which we also know next to nothing. All this must have varied greatly according to local conditions and the power of the authorities to enforce the execution of work and deliveries. The omen texts are again revealing in those predictions which refer to contacts between king and subject; they show a definitely dark picture, with the palace acting harshly and unjustly, with seizure and imprisonment.

Still, the Mesopotamian kings were anything but Oriental despots. The Assyrian kings—of whom we happen to know more than we do of their Babylonian counterparts—were always careful not to offend their high administrative officials, whose loyalty to the dynasty they at times had to secure by oaths and agreements to insure the succession of the crown prince, and who were quite ready to revolt against a king if they did not approve of his policies. Throughout the intrigues and machinations of the court, reported in the royal correspondence of the Sargonids, there is no mention of terrorism or of death sentences. Important segments of the population were protected by their status as citizens of the old, privileged cities against any encroachments by the king, and it can be assumed that similar arrangements existed between administrators and those governed all over the realm. There are no traces anywhere of any popular reaction against royal administration, as is discernible in the Old Testament both in fact and in political aspirations as they manifest themselves in messianic ideals.

As for the king and his family, one should note first that the term "queen" was only applied to goddesses and those women —in fact, only the queens of the Arabs—who served as rulers. The chief wife (called with deferential circumlocution "she-of-the-palace") and the royal concubines lived, at least at the Assyrian court, in a harem guarded by eunuchs. Their way of living was carefully regulated by royal edicts. We know from a number of letters written at the court in the last period of the Assyrian kingdom that the influence of the king's spouse and his mother was politically important at times.[33] All are over-shadowed, however, by the fame of Semiramis, the widow of Šamši-Adad V and probably a Babylónian princess, who seems to have ruled the country during the minority of their son, Adad-nirari III, and even later, when she continued to maintain her title as queen and had her name mentioned on monuments beside that of her son, the ruling king.[34] A number of stories about her by Greek authors are preserved.

The king's palace represented an organization of major economic importance within the Mesopotamian city. Into it poured the tribute of subjugated and even of distant peoples, the yield of royal estates, and the products of royal workshops. From its storehouses had to be fed and clad, according to their status, the members of the royal family, the administrative officials of country and palace, the personnel of the royal household, the standing army and a host of serfs, slaves, and others who depended on the palace for their living. As for its origin, it is difficult to determine whether the palace organization developed solely from manorial roots, whether it is to be considered, in certain respects, as an offshoot of the early Sumerian, if not pre-Sumerian, temple organization, or whether it is to be related to alien, non-Mesopotamian political concepts. We are rather poorly informed about the administration of the palace. A small number of Old Akkadian administrative documents, a body of material coming from Nippur of the Middle Babylonian period, and eventually the Neo-Assyrian texts coming from Calah and Nineveh—few in number—are all we have. To supplement these three main sources are isolated Old Babylonian documents and a large section of the material found at Chagar Bazar, Alalakh, Ugarit, and Nuzi, which remain to be investigated as to their bearing on the nature of the administration of a palace.

A redistribution system of the magnitude of the Mesopotamian palace organization almost certainly conflicted in some way with that of the temple organization in Babylonia, and yet nothing is known of any stress between them. Apparently the temple organization was on a steady decline after the Sumerian period, and the palace organization, grown rich and complex in a territorial state, overshadowed it increasingly as time progressed. The increase in documents coming from the temple administration of Neo-Babylonian Uruk and Sippar does not prove necessarily that these temple organizations were more than locally important. It is possible that the administrative acts of the realm were already at that time recorded with ink on parchment and are therefore lost to us.

From the point of view of architecture and ground plan, the Mesopotamian palace shows certain specific features: the throne room in which the king received ambassadors and other visitors, the large courtyard in front of it, and a spacious hall, perhaps used for official banquets, a purpose suggested by an Assyrian text which contains instructions for such a feast, to be attended by the king and his nobles. Living quarters for the king and his entourage, as well as storage rooms, were built around these principal areas. A comparative study of excavated palaces has not been made, although it would yield information about local differences and variations in design from one epoch to another. The building or rebuilding of a palace is often described in Assyrian records in considerable detail. It seems that every important city had a palace although quite often rather as the seat of the residing representative of the central administration than as the abode of the king, and that in certain capitals a number of them were built by successive rulers.

The history of the Mesopotamian temple as an institution is very much in the dark, although there is no scarcity of text material, especially for the Sumerian (primarily from Telloh) and the Neo-Babylonian (from Uruk and Sippar) periods.[34a] Unfortunately, these documents are concerned exclusively with the lower personnel of the sanctuaries, the workers and craftsmen who received wages and rations, and with the accounting for material for the manufacture of specific objects. The temple was organized as a typical redistribution system with its characteristic double aspect, incoming rents and gifts and outgoing rations and wages. Income was derived primarily from invested gifts, i.e., from land donated to the temple by kings, and only secondarily from occasional dedications of the spoils of war, precious objects, and, above all, prisoners of war.

Only from the Neo-Babylonian period have we evidence that the worshipers dropped small gifts of silver into boxes at the entrance of the sanctuary, a custom which is mentioned in the Bible.[35] We happen to have this information because the kings levied a tax on the income of the temple and even had an official in the sanctuary for the protection of their interests. For this time we have two large temple archives at our disposal—that of the Šamaš temple in Sippar and that of the Ištar sanctuary Eanna in Uruk. They reveal quite different aspects of the temple economy of the first half of the first millennium B.C.: while the Uruk texts throw much light on the management of the agricultural holdings of the temple, those from Sippar (still largely unpublished) show, interestingly enough, the impact of the rising money economy on the temple organization. Of the higher echelons of the temple administration we know very little. It seems that the *šangû*-priest (literally, perhaps, chief priest) headed the administrative side of the sanctuary's activities, while the *enu*-priest may have related the temple and its community to the deity in ways which differed from sanctuary to sanctuary. A priestly hierarchy in the customary sense of that term is nowhere attested, and we do not know whether heredity or qualification were decisive in appointments and what the procedure for such appointments was. Apart from the persons needed to run the temple's business, the scribes and overseers of all kinds, the cultic aspect required, as well as the chief priest and perhaps his assistants, only those exorcists and experts in divination who were essential for the proper functioning of both the temple and the palace. Larger sanctuaries probably had some division of labor for the rituals and processions required by their specific practices, which we must assume to have varied greatly according to the nature of the deity who was thought to live in the sanctuary. The scribes who served the temple administration kept up the tradition by teaching their craft in the time-honored way of having apprentices copy old texts. Thus the temples played a rather important role in keeping up the literary tradition, even though they had no libraries of their own.

The role of the temple in relation to the community, as far as it can be ascertained, was twofold; certain social responsibilities were assumed by the sanctuary, and certain cultic services were rendered to the community as a whole but hardly to the individual. The temple endeavored in various ways to correct the grievances of the economically underprivileged. This was done in the Old Babylonian period by establishing standards of weights and measures to prevent the victimizing of the poor and by standardizing the rate of interest, whose fluctuations had been constantly used in favor of the creditor. In general, the temple sought to set an example, to establish norms and just standards. Quite frequently in the Old Babylonian, and sometimes in later periods, we find the temple granting small loans without interest in cases of hardship.[36] From administrative documents coming from Neo-Babylonian Uruk, we learn about parents dedicating their children as oblates to the temple to save their lives during a famine, and there are indications that this also happened in earlier periods.[37] The temple used these oblates and their descendants by letting them follow their callings and receiving income from them, as was often done at that time with slaves.

What cultic services were rendered by the temple to the community which harbored it is not clear. The administration of oaths and perhaps ordeals should be mentioned first, because these practices are well attested, especially in the Old Babylonian period. It does not seem likely that the temple provided cultic assistance to private persons at any moment of their lives, from birth to burial. Diviners, exorcists, and other professional persons of the type we are wont to call priests may have had this function, but spiritual power was not invested in them through the temple with which they may or may not have had a connection or through their relationship with those who consulted them. Solely training and personal potential gave them status and authority. The basic function of the temple for the community seems to have been its mere existence in the sense that it linked the city to the deity by providing a permanent dwelling place. The house in which the god lived (see below, p. 186ff.) was maintained and provided for in due form in order to secure for the city the prosperity and happiness which the god's presence was taken to guarantee. Beyond that, the common man was given the opportunity to admire only from afar the glamor of the image displayed in the background of the sanctuary, which he himself was not permitted to enter, at least in Babylonia.[38] Or he was a spectator when the images were carried in processions which displayed the temple's wealth and pomp, and he participated in the collective joys of festivals of thanksgiving and in expressions of ceremonial mourning. The only person in the community who had the right to claim the cultic functions of the temple under specific circumstances was the king (see p. 102). A chasm similar to that between the temple and the individual worshiper separated the king from his loyal subjects.

The building and the constant maintenance of the sanctuaries was a royal prerogative and obligation. From victorious kings the temple expected a share in the booty, especially precious votive gifts to be exhibited to the deity in the cella and the dedication of prisoners of war to increase the labor force of the temple. Under the tutelage of the priests, from the Old Babylonian period onward, kings were made to see that the building of larger and more sumptuously decorated sanctuaries with higher temple towers was an essential part of their duty toward the god, an expression of thanks as well as a guarantee of future successes. The Assyrian kings performed their duties in this respect much more energetically than was the case in Babylonia. The basically different position of the king in Assyria expresses itself in the repeatedly attested influence he exercised on the cult, such as the creation of new images. Similar attempts of Nabonidus to introduce cult changes in Babylonia—whether involving a tiara for the sun god or something as important as preference for the cult of Sin in Harran—led to violent reactions to such innovations.[39] Open conflict of this kind is extremely rare, but one should not assume that the development which finds royal commissaries on the administrative boards of the most famous temples in the Neo-Babylonian period came about apparently without clashes of interest. On the same boards—though evidently only when they acted in judicial functions—appears also the assembly of the citizens of the town that harbored the sanctuary. In short, the relationship between temple, king, and city was extremely complex during the millennia of our documentation, although, more often than not, it fails to throw light on this essential aspect of Mesopotamian civilization. The relationship must clearly have been enacted on several distinct levels, those of power politics and economics and of cult being only the most obvious ones. While the temple strove for economic independence secured by agricultural holdings and sufficient manpower, the king also had to maintain and increase the fiscal base of support of the palace, i.e., of the state. The role of the city itself, that is, of the assembly of free citizens, is far less clear; the assembly might well have been instrumental in keeping the clashing interests in line. Eventually, of course, it profited from the existing tensions.

The City

The complex of social institutions that grew out of the phenomenon of urbanization has attracted more and more attention in the last decades. Obviously, a civilization like the Mesopotamian, whose records go further back than those of any other, should be the perfect area of research for a pertinent investigation. In fact, a large number of cuneiform texts bearing directly or indirectly on this topic is invitingly at hand. The information this material contains, if properly interpreted, could be supplemented by what the Old Testament and Greek sources yield, in particular on the topic of incipient urbanization. Although the Bible and Greek sources are much later in terms of absolute chronology, they are, strange as it may seem, older than even the earliest Sumerian documents bearing on the city, that is, in terms of the relative chronology of the phenomenon "urbanization."

An important and as yet not fully recognized fact concerning the problem of urbanization has to be pointed out before we can embark upon a more detailed study of this topic. Urbanization is not the only social pattern which can articulate the political and social structure of a civilization, and lead to the development of large-scale political bodies and eventually to what we term political history. As important as the growth and the consequences of urbanization are, the undeniable trend against urbanization has to be credited with an important share in the development of the historical events in this part of Asia. The anti-urban tendencies in and, for the most part, around Mesopotamia have to be recognized as social and political facts, exactly as does the trend toward living in cities, if one is to achieve a genuine understanding of the history of the time between the first emerging city-states and the conquest of Mesopotamia by the Arabs.[40] In a perennial battle characterized by sudden reverses and a persistent instability of political power, the pattern of the events in this region was shaped by pro- and anti-urbanization tendencies. Urbanization created and tenaciously maintained cities which evolved into centers of political gravity but which evoked in turn anticentralization reactions in certain strata of the population. These strata, because of tradition or previous experience, show definite and often effective resistance not only against living in settlements of greater complexity than the village but also against the power—be it political, military, or fiscal—that an urban center was bound to exercise over them.

The urbanization process as such in Mesopotamia is totally beyond our reach. The cities appear quite early with toponyms that belong to one or the other of the several languages spoken there before the emergence of either the Sumerians or the Akkadians. For unknown reasons, the center of urbanization lay in southern Mesopotamia. It may even be said—and probably must be said although no conventional proof can support it—that there alone within the entire ancient Near

East spontaneous urbanization took place. It is true that cities rose here and there around royal residences, trading settlements (ports of trade), wells, and certain sanctuaries, but nowhere do we find such an agglomeration of urban settlements as in southern Babylonia—and so early in history at that. In this dark and remote period originated the basic attitude of Mesopotamian civilization toward the city as a social phenomenon. This attitude is one of unconditional acceptance of the city as the one and only communal organization. There is nothing here of that resentment against the city which in certain passages of the Old Testament still echoes the nomadic past with nostalgia and which goes hand in hand with the rejection of that type of storage agriculture that forms the basis of a redistribution system.[41] Neither are there in these cities any vestiges or even memories of a tribal organization such as have left their unmistakable imprint on Muslim cities. What is more, even that antagonism between city-dwellers and those who live in the open countryside, which is characteristic of many urban civilizations, cannot be found in the cuneiform sources. Only nomadic invaders and the uncouth inhabitants of the Zagros mountains are sometimes despised as being devoid of the essential qualities of civilized people with regard to personal behavior, the care for the dead, and willingness to submit to organized government.

Such enemies of the Assyrians as dwelt in cities and were ruled by kings were considered equal and are never referred to as barbarians, "Asiatics," or the like. The detailed and interested descriptions of foreign countries and their particular achievements which appear in certain Neo-Assyrian royal inscriptions (concerning Urartu and Egypt) give evidence for this attitude.[42]

A passage in a Sumerian poetic text written in praise of Ur asserts that even a native of Marhaši—a mountain region of Elam—becomes civilized when living in Ur, so proudly certain were its inhabitants of achieving the acculturation of any *paganus*.[43]

On the social level, the solidarity of a Mesopotamian city is reflected in the absence of any status or ethnic or tribal articulation. Constituted as an assembly, the community of citizens, though as a rule only of the old, rich, and privileged cities, administrated the city under a presiding official.[44] Although no direct indications are available, one may well assume that, at least originally, the assembly included every householder, with the eldermen playing an important role. Quite rarely do we find (e.g., in an Old Babylonian text) that only its most important persons (*qaqqadāt āli*) act in a special capacity for the city, or that, in an unusually serious matter, the important persons of Assur address a letter to the king together with its lesser citizens.[45] Some kind of oligarchic tendencies cannot have failed to appear in an assembly of this type, which was not "democratic" in the Western sense of this much abused term, but functioned rather like a tribal gathering, reaching agreement by consensus under the guidance of the more influential, richer, and older members. These assemblies—here we have to telescope a complex and lengthy development—write letters to kings and receive missives from them; they fight for their exemptions and privileges and have them confirmed by the king. They also make legal decisions, sell real estate within the city that has no private owner, and assume corporate responsibility in cases of murder or robbery committed even outside the city, within a specified distance. We know about the last point from instructions (found in Nuzi) given to the mayor of a city, from the Hittite laws, and from Deuteronomy 21:1ff. The region outside the city wall and probably also outside the suburbs was denoted by various terms (*pan ṣēri, erṣetu, limītu, talbītu, pāṭu*) and seems to have included farms and manors belonging to the inhabitants of the city (see p. 129).

To repeat, the city harbored within its walls not only the community of citizens but the temple and the palace. An answer as to how two such discrepant socioeconomic patterns (city *v.* temple-palace) could develop in the same ecological context and yet establish a symbiosis which proved extremely successful and long lasting, would bring us much nearer to the primary forces which influenced the rise and the development toward urbanization.

A number of suggestions offer themselves only too easily and should be mentioned here—mainly *sed ne taceatur*. The natural

tensions between villages of settled fishermen and hoe-agricul-
turists with bovines for traction, a few donkeys, sheep and pigs,
and seminomads who moved up and down along the rivers
with large herds and also raised cereals on occasion, could
have provided a stimulus. One can also think of sacred localities
that served as central meeting places for a region inhabited
by seminomadic groups; there was one such in the Sippar
of the early Old Babylonian period or, much more uncertain,
in the earliest Nippur in mid-Babylonia. Interacting developments, such as increased agricultural production through
systematic engineering, the growth of fortified power centers,
together with the increasing contacts among settlements and
tribal areas, to mention only a few of the possible contributing
factors, encouraged the growth of cities. What is perhaps most
significant in this flowering is that it was not one city which
evolved or several centers distant from each other, but an
agglomeration of cities. Such important towns as Eridu, Ur,
Larsa, and Uruk were actually in sight of each other, and that
without natural boundaries separating them.

In view of the composite character of the Mesopotamian city,
the nature and character of the community itself and the
peculiar relationship between intracity and intercity economic
integrations, I venture to offer another hypothesis: The community of citizens was originally made up of owners of landed
property, fields, gardens, and manorial estates situated along
natural canals and depressions, that could be easily improved
by simple irrigation methods and on which a labor force of
family members, serfs, and slaves produced food and the few
essential goods necessary to supply the lord of the manor,
whose status may have been that of a conqueror, his family,
and retainers. With growing prosperity, and also for prestige
purposes, the landed owners began to maintain "town houses"
at nearby sanctuaries and eventually moved their main residence into the agglomeration of dwellings that grew up around
the temple complex. This rather natural development may or
may not have been accelerated by pressures generated by an
enemy or by the deterioration of the soil. It resulted in the
emergence of a community of persons of equal status living in

symbiosis with a cultic center and later also with a center of political power of increasing influence, the palace of the king. The new city-dwellers went on relying primarily on their out-of-town farms for food and supplies, so that the market place as a means of economic integration was very slow to gain what little importance it eventually assumed in Mesopotamia. Since each household produced its own needs (in its manor), it was profitless to engage in home manufacture of goods for sale to other households, for which reason the number of slaves was kept low. Being of the same status—differing only in individual wealth—the city people rather easily achieved a *modus vivendi* in dealing with affairs that affected them as a community. Their commercial activities centered in the management of their rural holdings and, if capital was at their disposal—either accumulated through partnership or borrowed from the temples—they concerned themselves with intercity trade, managed, curiously enough, from a special locality, the harbor, outside the city proper. It is as if the intracity and the intercity economies had to be kept apart either for status reasons or in order to maintain the specific economic and social climate of the community. The latter is especially worthy of note when one contrasts it with the deeply agonistic mood of the Greek city where an ever-enlarging arsenal of complex and elaborate practices was needed to keep the city government functioning in the face of the ambition of certain individuals, who wished to assume control and to exercise power over their fellow citizens. The very presence of the great organizations in the Mesopotamian city seems to have created an equilibrium of forces and an over-all harmony that endowed the city with the longevity which the Greek *polis* could not achieve.

It should be clear by now that the hypothesis I have proposed relies heavily on parallels offered by the known history of the Greek cities of the fifth and fourth centuries B.C. and on certain aspects in the development of the Italian cities of the early Renaissance. Such a parallel development, however, is possible and even suggested—so it seems to me—by the evidence outlined above.

Amid the many problems and questions which probably will

never find an answer, one certainty stands out: exactly as one has to recognize the Greek *polis* as an unique type within the range of city types created by the process of urbanization, so the Mesopotamian u r u fully deserves to be treated as *sui generis* by the historian of civilization.

In the terminology of Sumerian and Akkadian no distinction is made in respect to the size of the settlement; village and city are both called u r u in Sumerian and *ālu* in Akkadian, indeed this term applies to every permanent settlement consisting of houses made of sun-dried mud bricks and sometimes even to agglomerations of huts and other forms of shelter constituting an administrative unit. Only manors (é, uru . še = *kapru*)[45a] and certain ill-defined rural settlements (é . duru$_5$, *ḫaṣāru*, etc.) were differentiated from these "cities." An enclosing wall seems to have been the rule but was not a prerequisite. In this the u r u was like the *polis*, which was not necessarily walled. We shall have to explain what these defensive ramparts imply (see p. 127). A situation on a water course was indispensable for the existence of the settlement, and any change in the course of the river had fateful consequences for the city if the citizens did not undertake to redig the river bed. Outside the walls of some cities, but belonging to it, was often situated, for unknown reasons, a sanctuary of a special type, called the New Year's Chapel (*bīt akītu*). Once a year, the image of the principal deity of the settlement was carried in a procession to the sanctuary, accompanied by throngs of worshipers. In certain instances, a sacred road through a special gate linked the outlying sanctuary to the temple. Doubtless we would obtain an important insight into the prehistory of the u r u city concept if we could understand why this chapel was placed outside the city walls.

The typical Sumerian city, and probably most of the later cities, consisted of three parts. First, the city proper, often called in Akkadian *libbi āli* or *qabalti āli*, terms which in some cases refer only to the oldest section of the city. This is the walled area which contains the temple or temples, the palace with the residences of the royal officials, and the houses of the citizens. The city was administered from the "gate," or "gates" in larger settlements, where the assembly of citizens or of the pertinent city quarter (called *babtu*, d a g . g i₄ . a) convened and the mayor exercised his office. To each gate was assigned a precinct within the city. Next came the "suburb," in Sumerian the "outer city," (u r u . b a r . r a) in which we find agglomerations of houses, farms, cattle folds, fields, and gardens, all of which provided the city with food and raw materials. We do not know how far these outskirts extended or whether they were protected in any way by secondary walls or only by the fortified outposts (*kidānu*) that are mentioned in the Neo-Babylonian period. When the Old Testament speaks of the three days it took to cross the city of Nineveh (Jonah 3:3), the reference may be to the green reaches of the outer city. Third, there was the harbor section, the k a r in Sumerian, *kāru* in Akkadian, which functioned, beyond its actual use as a harbor, as the center of commercial activity, particularly that concerned with overland trade. It thus corresponded in function as well as in name to the *portus* of the early Middle Ages. The *kāru* had administrative independence and also a separate legal status important for the citizens transacting business there. In the *kāru* lived the foreign traders; there they had their stores and were provided for by the tavernkeeper of the *kāru*. This shows again a difference between the u r u city concept and that of, e.g., Syria and Palestine where, in Damascus and Samaria, the foreign merchants had their "factories" within the town (but see below). We know of the activities of the *kāru* from tablets found in Ur and from the *kāru* of the town Kaniš and a number of other towns in Anatolia. The tablets from Ur show the *kāru* of a Mesopotamian city, those from Anatolia speak of Assyrian merchants in foreign cities.

Of course, this threefold articulation is not in evidence in every city, and we must keep in mind individual differences caused by special circumstances and the accidents of history. Especially noteworthy is the city of Sippar, on the periphery of the urbanized region, famed as the oldest of the Babylonian cities and probably a port of trade between the sheep nomads of the desert and the inhabitants of the urbanized stretches along the Euphrates. It seems that the most important nomadic tribes had permanent encampments at Sippar, if indeed the city did not originally consist of a cluster of just such encampments (called Sippar-Jaḫruru, Sippar-Amnānûm, Sippar-Arūru, Sippar-ṣēri). Sippar possibly followed a more Western type of urban agglomeration, as indicated by the fact that the "factory" of the traders of Isin existed within the city.[46] Atypical was Nippur, in the center of Babylonia, which, like Sippar, never was the seat of a dynasty, let alone of an important king. Both cities seem to have figured in trade relations, Sippar in the Old Babylonian and Nippur in the Late Babylonian period; both are very old, but Nippur, especially in early times, was considered a sacred city.

While the typical city enjoyed a modicum of prosperity slightly above the subsistence level, real prosperity came to a Mesopotamian city only when it had in its midst the palace of a victorious king. Then the spoils of war, the tribute of subjected cities, and the gifts of intimidated neighbors were added to the stores of the ruler and distributed among the hierarchy of the army and the bureaucracy, thus raising the standard of living of the entire community. The sanctuaries then grew rich, were sumptuously decorated, and received grants in land and workers. The desire to decorate palace and temple attracted traders, who brought into the economy of the capital not only typical imports (metals, timber, precious stones) but also luxury items (certain spices, perfumes, wines, finery, rare animals).

Only a few of the Babylonian cities had more than one or two short periods—and many none at all—of such intense flowering. From this affluence they relapsed into a drab and wretched existence, the people living among ruins, the sanctuaries dilapidated, and the city walls crumbling. Debt-ridden, in the hands of rapacious administrators, the inhabitants were an easy prey for invading enemies and the raids of those who lived in the open country. The texts excavated in Ur tellingly illustrate a progressive deterioration from the wealth of the period of the kingdom of Ur III to the provincial poverty of the Middle and the Late Babylonian period. Still, even after a destruction of a city or in the face of complete desolation, the remainder of the inhabitants tended to cling to the ruins of their city and to preserve its name across the millennia to the present day, as is the case of Nippur (Niffer). The metropolis of Babylon was not abandoned completely for a full millennium after its last destruction. Other capitals—Ur, Larsa, and Assur—disappeared. Akkad rose to an early and short-lived prominence as the capital of the first Mesopotamian empire but soon lost its importance. That it was lying in ruins in the Neo-Babylonian period we know from the remark of a scribe interested in archeology who copied an inscription he found on a brick among the ruins of Akkad. The site of Akkad has not been found to this day.

Within the life span of Mesopotamian civilization, new cities founded by royal volition and for political or military purposes appear in Assyria or where Assyrian kings extended their rule. In Babylonia proper, we encounter only small fortresses established by kings against possible invasions or fortified seats of government (Harmal). This country had to wait until the downfall of its national sovereignty before it saw new cities, such as Seleucia and Vologesia, rise. It had always been the policy of Babylonian as well as Assyrian kings to organize into settlements those elements of the population who lived outside the cities. Complete urbanization of the realm was one of the chief aims of royal policy throughout the Near East until the Roman period. This policy hastened the general trend from the city state to the territorial state and favored the ascent of the capital at the expense of the other cities of the realm. Forced urbanization of outlying sections resulted in a pacification of the country and allowed the safe passage of caravans engaged in overland trade and served to freeze nomadic or unsettled populations into a controllable way of life in order to protect already urbanized regions against invasion or infiltration. Furthermore, such endeavors, which we would term projects of internal and frontier colonization, increased agricultural production and provided the administration with tax income, corvée workers, and soldiers. Hellenistic and, later, Roman cities along the trade routes from Arabia to the Caspian Sea and eastward to the Punjab, illustrate the scope and the results of such a policy of planned urbanization.

In Babylonia, the redigging of old and silted-up canals and the building of new ones had to precede any attempt to turn or to return certain elements of the population to a sedentary agricultural life in once-abandoned settlements or in new fortified places. In Assyria, the kings often created cities on virgin soil as new capitals (Kar-Tukulti-Ninurta, Kar-Šulmanašaridu, Dur-Šarrukin), to be populated by retainers, members of their administration, and craftsmen captured in wars, but they also claimed conquered cities, renaming and repopulating them with prisoners of war or deported peoples in order to secure Assyria's hold on new territory.

A thin network of routes stretched through the open country from trading center to trading center. It was considered a tell-tale sign of economic collapse when grass grew on the route, a *topos* which recurs in the Book of Judges 5:6. The building of roads for purely military purposes, such as the pacification of rebellious regions, was practiced only by Neo-Assyrian kings. The upkeep of roads was considered a royal responsibility and *corvée* labor from adjacent villages was required to care for them. A Sumerian royal hymn speaks of stations erected along such roads as do Neo-Assyrian itineraries (*mardītu*).[48]

Different terms for several types of smaller settlements were used in different periods and regions, and manors and tribal agglomerations, especially in the Old-Babylonian period, are recognizable by their characteristic names, of the type *Bīt-PN*, "house [i.e., estate or manor] of *PN*." The countryside was strewn with the abandoned sites of cities, *tells* (mounds), which date from the earliest periods onward. They bespeak invasions, economic changes, and the neglect of an irrigation system or its natural end, caused mainly by salinization of the soil and the silting of watercourses. Fortresses established in outlying or unruly areas often have names of the type *Dūr-RN* or *Kār-RN*, i.e., "fortress of [King] *RN*" or "wall of *RN*." Occasionally we find an extensive wall construction meant to seal off a dangerous frontier, such as Šu-Sin, the Sumerian king of 'Ur III, built against the invading Amorite tribes, and, much later, the Median wall across the gap between the Tigris and Euphrates which served a similar purpose. Apart from the coming and going of army contingents, of caravans with donkeys carrying loads from city to city, of foreign envoys traveling under military protection, and of royal messengers, there was little other traffic on these routes. Traveling was made dangerous by marauding deserters, groups of migrants, runaway slaves, and wild animals, and there seem to have been very few periods in the history of the region when private letters could be sent from city to city (as in the Old Babylonian period) or a private person could move around freely.

In these Mesopotamian cities there grew a concept of citizenship which was either the result or the driving force of the urbanization process itself. The institutionalization of this way of living in cities of this kind has every right to claim our attention as a specific expression of Mesopotamian civilization. The cuneiform documents of the end of the second millennium and the first half of the first millennium B.C. contain a number of isolated indications which, taken together, reveal that a small number of old and important cities enjoyed certain privileges and exemptions with respect to the king and his power. They apparently had a legal status which differed in essential points from that of any other community. In Babylonia, these cities were Nippur, Babylon, and Sippar; in Assyria, the old capital Assur and, later, Harran in Upper Mesopotamia. In principle, the inhabitants of these "free cities" claimed with more or less success, depending on the political situation, freedom from *corvée* work, freedom from military service (or perhaps from certain types of military service, see below), as well as a tax exemption which we are not able to define in specific terms. These privileges were neither new nor exceptional. Even certain persons with restricted liberty,[48a] mentioned in the administrative texts of the Sumerian empire of Ur III, were said to be exempted from carrying earth, and the name of a year in the reign of king Išme-Dagan of Isin records as a special achievement that the inhabitants of Nippur were exempted from military service and the paying of tribute (gú) in silver and gold.[49] This shows that the resistance against the claims of a central authority for services of its subjects is characteristic not only of a non-urbanized group (cf. the warnings of Samuel in I Samuel 8:11ff.), but also one of the aspirations of city-dwellers.[50] We shall return to the matter of fiscal exemptions.

The privileges of the inhabitants of these cities were under divine protection. Their legal status was referred to as the *kidinnūtu* ("status of being under the aegis of the *kidinnu*," probably some kind of standard), and the inhabitants themselves are called "people of the *kidinnu*." In both instances, the word *kidinnu*, a term with both religious and legal implications, denotes an object placed at the gateway of such a city as a symbol of divine approval and protection which safeguarded the status of the citizens.[51] Our information concerning this institution comes from a text known as the *Fürstenspiegel* (cf. pp. 123f.) and from references in Neo-Assyrian royal inscriptions which deal with the military and political situation in the conflict between Assyria and the nationalistic resistance in southern Babylonia. Although it is only fragmentary, we have the "Charter of Assur," the only one of its kind preserved, in which an Assyrian king, in this instance Sargon II, confirmed the privileges of the city after a period of civil war and rebellion. The *Fürstenspiegel* enumerates the privileges of the inhabitants of Nippur, Babylon, and Sippar in case of lawsuits. No fines or imprisonment can be imposed upon them by the king, nor can he dismiss their claims. They are protected, furthermore, against carrying the hod and doing *corvée* work when called up, even when all the country is summoned. Their plowing cattle must not be taken away by the king, nor can a tax be levied on their flocks; nor need they provide feed for the king's horses. Historical references often evoke the issue of the *kidinnu* status of Babylonian cities, an issue which was, from Sargon II to Assurbanipal, of primary importance for Assyria in its fight for the effective control of Babylonia.

Most of our information concerns the fiscal and personal privileges of the inhabitants of these cities but fails to show us the actual functioning of the institution, especially its historical development. We learn that only native-born citizens could claim the *kidinnūtu*. Yet there is a letter written by the inhabitants of Babylon to Assurbanipal in which it is asserted quite pointedly that even a dog is free when he enters the city of Babylon.[52] This argument seems to have been brought forth in the heat of discussion and should not be taken to mean that the air of the city makes those who breathe it free, as was said of the medieval European cities. Revealing of the status of these privileged city-dwellers is a passage in the ritual texts describing the ceremonies performed during the New Year's festival in Babylon. On that occasion, the king was permitted to enter the innermost sanctuary, but he could do this only after the high priest had taken from him all the insignia and *indumentaria* of kingship and humiliated him by slapping his face and pulling his ears. Then the king had to crouch down and, in a formal prayer, assure Bel, the god of the city, that he had not committed any sin during the year, that he had not been negligent toward the sacred city and its sanctuary, and, further, that he had not offended a person enjoying the status of *kidinnu* by slapping his face.[53] This startling statement, appearing in a royal confession of political capital sins, shows us the importance attributed to human dignity unusual in the ancient Near East and, for that matter, in other early civilizations in the west. The citizens of Babylon and other Mesopotamian cities appear thus to have become a class set apart from and above the rest of the population not for ethnical or economic reasons but solely because they were natives of certain cities.

Apart from privileges, there were also obligations. But of the latter we know only by chance. When Esarhaddon, king of Assyria, speaks of the events which led to his rise to kingship over Assyria, he complains that his rival brothers fought among each other for the throne and that they "even drew the sword within the city of Nineveh, which is a godless thing to do."[54] One has to take this phrase as indicating that the great cities of Mesopotamia knew what the European West called *Burgfriede*, i.e., the divinely protected prohibition of the use of weapons within the confines of the privileged settlement.

It is extremely difficult to answer the obvious question concerning the specific conditions and causes which generated and fostered the development of such a social situation. The essential features, namely, the fiscal and personal exemptions of the inhabitants of the Mesopotamian cities, are not unique. We have already mentioned some parallels from the Sumerian periods, and we have pointed out that the granting of tax exemptions and preferential treatment with regard to *corvée* work and military service to certain landed owners and tribal chieftains or to sanctuaries had become common practice for the Babylonian kings of the last half of the second millennium b.c. We know about this from a certain type of inscribed stone monument, called *kudurru,* "boundary stone," which lists privileges similar to those of the privileged cities granted by the king to temples and faithful servants, out of piety or out of political necessity. The stones are provided with reliefs representing sacred objects (see p. 197), thus placing the property on which they were erected—and its privileged status—under divine sanction and protection.

What the *kidinnu* erected at the city gate was for an entire city, the *kudurru* appears to have been to agricultural holdings. Both these technical terms are unknown up to and including the Hammurapi period and appear only after the Dark Age. The weakened central authority of the Middle Babylonian period was evidently ready to cede to persons of special status and to sanctuaries its right to collect taxes, to levy soldiers and workers, and to use the services of its subjects. When this happened, those who carried the burden only changed their master. But when cities were exempted, the citizens themselves profited. For this reason any connection between the *kudurru* status and the *kidinnu* status is only superficial. The special status of the cities mentioned must be connected with the very fountainhead from which urbanization originated but cannot be proved, for we lack written evidence. The problem can only be stated.

There were certainly fluctuations in the ability of the citizens to enforce their rights. Most of what we know about the *kidinnūtu* comes from a period in which the internal political situation was adverse to the king or in which the cities occupied a key position in an international conflict. The content of the *Fürstenspiegel* illustrates the former, the fight of Assyria against Babylonian nationalism the latter situation. The cities of Babylonia were ready to accept Assyrian political supremacy over the country; they could thus safeguard their widespread commercial activities and maintain their privileges as the price of their collaboration. The open country of Babylonia, populated mainly by Aramaic tribes of more warlike character, the Chaldeans (see p. 162), and the priesthood of the main sanctuaries were violently nationalistic and anti-Assyrian. Still, the proud self-reliance of the cities and their dignified display of confidence, as revealed in the correspondence of that period, cannot have been solely the product of a passing political situation. It must have had its roots deep in the consciousness of status shared by all inhabitants; we find the same attitude in Assur and even in Harran, both with a historical background quite different from that of Babylonian cities.

We have indications that the cities of the Phoenician coast achieved a type of internal social organization which in Greek political terminology would have been called an aristocracy. There, as well as in certain texts referring to the citizens of Assur, we come across a concept of a ruling town patriciate, a concept alien to the attitude generally accepted of placing the city under the authority of a king. We cannot attempt to establish in which relationship the *kidinnūtu* status of the Babylonian cities has to be placed to this "western" city concept. Nor can one say what was the attitude of the early fortified cities of the Nile delta, before the unification of Egypt, toward kingship, but we can point to a meaningful artifact of that period. A schist palette shows the king as the Horus bird destroying several fortified cities, reflecting the eternal conflict between the city and the king, a conflict which seems to have been as virulent around the Mediterranean as it was conspicuously absent in southern Mesopotamia. The Syrian foes of the rebuilding of Jerusalem characterized their opposition against cities with a well-turned phrase in Ezra 4:13 when they wrote to Artaxerxes, king of Persia, that a walled city "will not pay tribute, custom, or toll and in the end it will endamage the revenue of the kings."

To counteract the loss of revenue when cities were able to realize such exemptions, the Assyrian kings resorted to the building of new cities, either as capitals of the realm or in strategically important regions (see above, p. 118). Sargon of Akkad is said by the legend to have applied this policy more than a millennium earlier in Babylonia, when he built a new city, in fact, a "new Babylon," as his capital. The enraged god of the real Babylon, Marduk, thereupon put a horrible curse upon Sargon. Clearly the story is apocryphal, but its aim is to show that Sargon had intended and actually achieved as the first Mesopotamian king the fundamental policies that were to make Assyria great. He not only founded a new capital but created a large palace organization (amounting to 5,000 persons), had natives of his city rule his provinces, erected stelae in conquered regions, and, in short, set a pattern of royal behavior which was to be taken up later by the Middle Assyrian kings but was not acceptable at that time in Babylonia. It therefore may not be an accident that Sargon's name was adopted by more than one Assyrian king. Perhaps the situation that existed in Babylonia proper at the time of Sargon of Akkad was parallel to the one which developed later in Mesopotamia between Babylonia and Assyria, with the Sumerian-speaking agricultural south and its city states pitted against northern Babylonia (Kish, Akkad, and perhaps Sippar) held by the warlike immigrants from the deserts who spoke Old Akkadian.

Urbanism

Urbanization as a social phenomenon creates in every civilization in which it materializes a characteristic projection in the physical design of the typical urban settlement. The arrangement of the private and the public buildings of a city and that of the intracity arteries of communication and fortifications reflect the needs as well as the aspirations of the community as they find their realization within the existing frame of the ecological and the technological contingencies of period and region. Indeed, it would be a fascinating task to correlate the specific features common to the urban patterns of a given civilization with the important social, economic, and religious attitudes of its founders. We must except, however, established foreign city patterns which are at times imitated or maintained for extraneous reasons, such as the world-wide diffusion of the gridiron pattern.

Although this correlation probably can never be achieved, the existence of such relations should always be kept in mind.

From the beginning we are greatly hampered, in Mesopotamia, by the lack of written documents bearing on our topic; urbanism can be studied with satisfactory results only where archeological reports coincide with literary records and both are sufficiently diversified and elucidative with respect to the process of urbanization. In the known story of early mankind, these ideal conditions are best approximated in the history of the Greek city—to be more precise, the history of that unique phenomenon, the *polis*. Only there are we able to follow the urbanization process in its characteristic stages: from its inception—conceived as and typified as *synoikismos*—to its short-lived but splendid success, and on to its political failure and protracted fossilization, which was destined to preserve its seed for later civilizations. All these data survived only because the people who lived in these cities were alert and articulate enough to understand, describe, and interpret the process. And what is more, they succeeded in recognizing the problem which concerns us in this section: the relationship between the physical features of a city and the behavior and ideological patterns of its inhabitants. It was Aristotle (*Politics* IV, xi) who formulated with stunning conciseness: "A citadel is suitable for oligarchies and monarchies; a level plain suits the character of a democracy; neither suits an aristocracy, for which a number of different strongholds is preferable." Nowhere in the literary records from Mesopotamia will we find such insight and readiness to appraise one's own characteristic ways.

Apart from this shortcoming there is a lack of pertinent archeological evidence from Mesopotamia. Many ancient cities of these regions are still inhabited; for example, Aleppo-Haleb and Erbil. Even the ruins of abandoned cities—Babylon, Sippar, and Nippur—succeed by the sole fact of their extent and accumulation of debris in discouraging the explorations of even the best endowed expeditions. And archeologists prefer digging for monuments to spending time in following the endless walls of cities with their spades or disentangling the network of crooked streets in a residential section. Still, we are much better off in Mesopotamia than are the Egyptologists, with the exception of their one—clearly atypical—city, that of

Akhnaton, today's Amarna; all others have completely vanished.

There is one last but important cautionary remark to be made: in the ancient Near East we are confronted, as we have repeatedly seen, with a remarkable variety of civilizations, each of which created a distinctive assemblage of urban features. These assemblages were blurred, distorted, and reduced by repeated invasions and the more important though less tangible influence of internal social and economic changes and the effects of fashions and the preferences of kings, and this to a degree which is often impossible to gauge, rendering most conclusions hazardous.

In the following pages a number of specific features of the Mesopotamian city will be discussed and an attempt will be made to connect them with the ideological attitudes they may reflect. This approach allows full use of the extant evidence, in spite of limitations we have just pointed out.

From the third millennium B.C., the distinguishing mark of a city in the Near East—with the possible exception of Egypt—seems to have been the presence of a rampart. It was the duty of the king to keep the walls in good repair and—correspondingly—to tear down those of conquered cities. This raises the question whether the fortified city—as against a fortress erected for military reasons—represents an innate or an acquired feature in this region and civilization. Large-scale fortifications are by no means an essential characteristic of cities in general. The Greek *polis* was conspicuously slow in resorting to fortifications in spite of—or in opposition to—the impressive cyclopean walls and castles of Mycenean origin. The Minoan cities on Crete seem to have dispensed with walls and towers during the entire flowering of their civilization. There exists a definite aversion to fortified cities whenever a nonurbanized group conquers an urban civilization; thus we see the king pictured on Egyptian slate palettes as a bull or a falcon destroying the fortified cities of the Nile delta in the course of the unification of the country, and we have a parallel in the smashing of the cities of the Indus Valley by the Vedic Indians under their god Indra, to whom they gave the epithet *puramdara*, "fortress-destroyer," which corresponds to the Greek *poliorketes*. Since such attitudes are not evident in early Mesopotamian sources, and since the articulation of a Sumerian town into city, suburb, and outside harbor or port of trade reflects the existence of a definite borderline between the city and what was beyond, it seems reasonable that the circumvallation of the Sumerian city was typical. Still, there were atypical cities, such as Sippar, and others in the south— such as Lagaš—that represent accumulations or, better, clusters, of settlements, where an urban core seems to have "citified," and thus incorporated, the surrounding settlements. As for the role of fortifications in the complex development that led the settlements in the South toward urbanization, we are again completely in the dark.

The walls of the cities in the ancient Near East were, in fact, more than a demarcation line between the city and the open fields, more than a prepared line of defence. They were the dominant feature of urban architecture. Their size and arrangement proclaimed the importance and might of the city, their gateways displayed its wealth with a monumentality intended to impress the visitor and ward off the enemy. The carefully maintained walls were placed under the protection of deities and given long and propitious names.[55]

The elaborate gateways had yet another function as the town's "civic centers." Here, probably on a place (rebitu) next to the gate inside the city, the assembly met and made decisions and the mayor administered the town or, at least, that quarter to which the gate led. Here, the victorious conqueror used to erect his statue to remind everyone of the loyalty owed to him, and here he stationed his garrison. From the popular names of these gates, not their long-winded official designations, we learn about the city quarter to which they belonged. Examples are the "Gate of the Metalworkers" in Assur and the "Gate of Sheep and Goats" in Assur and in Jerusalem (Neh. 3:3), as well as the "Refuse Gate" and the "Spring Gate" in Jerusalem (Neh. 3:14). Attention should be drawn to the "Fish Gate" in Jerusalem, where the inhabitants of Tyre used to come to sell their fish and "all kind of wares" (Neh. 13:16). In only certain of these respects does the function of the open space at the gate correspond to the Greek *agora*.

The important problem of how the inhabitants of such cities

were supplied with food and consumer goods is difficult to solve. References to markets are rare and show a definite distribution in time and region that must not be disregarded. A market gate is mentioned in Kaniš and in one Old Babylonian letter at the beginning of the second millennium; much later, in Neo-Babylonian tablets, a "market gate" refers to a locality rather than to its function. Equally seldom does one come across a reference to a market like the one in an early inscription from Susa which indicates that a tariff of prices was exhibited there.[56] Specific information that buying and selling were done at the market gate comes only once and in a late inscription of Assurbanipal.[57] From Sippar of the Old Babylonian period we have a term (*bīt maḫīrim*) for what appears to be a small shop, possibly for luxury items.[58] From all that, one gains the impression that the institution of the market was at home outside of Mesopotamia, in Elam, and in Anatolia—the Hittite word for city, *ḫappira*, is etymologically connected with that for market. In Mesopotamia it seems to represent a late development, stimulated by the extraordinary size of the cities, which led to the creation of supply markets. Thus, the institution of markets, meant to link together those who live outside the city and the city-dwellers for the exchange of their products, be these food or goods, was in Mesopotamia clearly of limited and marginal importance. This is again one of the features of urban Mesopotamia which may have its roots in the genesis of the city itself. It confirms to a certain extent what has been suggested above (p. 112) concerning the relationship between the city-dwellers and the arable land around the city.

In certain periods and regions of Mesopotamia the palace of the king, the administrative center of the empire, and the temples form part of the circumvallation. We propose to treat this deviation as an essential variation of the urban pattern which may reveal underlying ideological attitudes and shed some light on the process of urbanization. In general it can be said that in Mesopotamia we do not encounter an accentuation of the center of the city. Whatever geometric shape is given to the ramparts, there is no urban center formed by palace, temple, or market place.

In the old cities of the alluvial plains—with the exception of the Babylon of the Chaldean kings—we observe a significant separation between the temple and the palace and the gate or gates. The main sanctuary, with its temple tower, courts, propylea and chapels, the granary and storehouses, and the living quarters of its personnel are encircled by a wall or an enclosure and separated from both the palace and the main wall. Temple and palace are surrounded by residential sections shot through with a maze of winding streets, as we can see in the Ur of the Old Babylonian period, the best example known. When one leaves the alluvial plain, proceeding upstream toward Upper Mesopotamia, Syria, Asia Minor, and Palestine, the separation between temple and palace disappears. They have moved together and now often form an urban unit either occupying a central position or becoming part of the circumvallation. Where temple and palace are close together, the single rampart that surrounds them and their several dependencies, the treasury, the barracks of the royal bodyguard, is a striking indication of their relationship to each other and to the outside world. The citizens settled outside the enclosure and were protected, as a rule, by a second line of walls. This urban pattern can be called the citadel city. It must be stressed that such a layout could also result from a specific development which must be recognized if the pattern is to be analyzed as an expression of definite ideological attitudes. A citadel city, for instance, could be simply the result of the growth of a small settlement. The inner city, with the palace and temple, once may have contained all the inhabitants as well, while the outer city was built when the pressure of the increasing population called for an enlargement of the city proper or an incorporation of its suburbs. Depending upon the terrain, the inner city became the upper city, the outer and newer city a lower city, as happened in Assur and Hattuša. The progressive accumulation of debris in the older section can create a mound for the inner city and leave the outer and later city on a lower level, as it had in Carchemish.

The situation is further complicated by the preference in certain regions for settling on hilltops even when level ground was available nearby. Such a preference is to be considered a culture trait and may or may not be connected with the requirements of the cult. These cities are sometimes the only type of urban settlements in a region; in other instances they appear in conjunction with cities on level ground, as is the case in Palestine, where the "cities that stood on hills" are mentioned beside the "cities of the plain" (Joshua 11:13). Zenjirli, a "new city" in northern Syria, was situated on level ground, its builders evidently having spurned adjacent sites on hills even though better suited for defense. In Mesopotamia, Assur, on a cliff overlooking the Tigris, represents the southernmost example of a city that probably grew from a nuclear hilltop sanctuary and its adjacent settlement. From Assur upstream, in the piedmont, in the hills of the Zagros, and to the northwest, cities seem to have had this position. This is borne out by the hieroglyphic Hittite pictogram for "city," which shows a steep hill.

A hill city can be enlarged by incorporating low-lying settlements without resulting in what we have dubbed a "citadel city"; nor must such a process be compared with the growth of Greek cities. The typical acropolis of a Greek city contains the oldest sanctuaries, which were later replaced in the lower city by new temples that came to surpass the first in cultic importance and splendor. The acropolis itself then lost its civic function and became merely a part, though an important part, of the city's fortification system. This was not possible in the ancient Near East where the numinous presence of the deity is so precisely located that the sanctuaries cling forever to the same spot. The essential difference between a hill city and a citadel city can be found in the wall which surrounds temple and palace and thus created a city within a city and shut out the settlements of the ordinary people. This inner or sacred city has been able to survive as a specific pattern of urbanism until today in Eurasia; we find it in the Kremlin of Moscow and the "Forbidden City" of Peking. The term *kirḫu*, which is used to refer to this feature of Mesopotamian urbanism, is neither Akkadian nor Semitic and thus clearly suggests that the citadel city represents an alien feature. It refers to a part of a city in texts from Mari, Chagar Bazar, and Nuzi; it is mentioned with respect to towns in Armenia and appears earlier on a victory stela erected by an unidentified Babylonian king. He records the conquest of Arrapha with the words, "I entered its *kirḫu* and kissed the feet of the god Adad. I reorganized the country." This shows that the *kirḫu* of Arrapha contained the temple and probably also the palace. The sacred nature of the inner city of Carchemish is illustrated by the report of a Hittite king concerning the siege and conquest of that city. He expressly states that he pillaged and destroyed the lower city but spared what he called in Hittite *šariẓẓiš kurtaš*, the "upper city," and there worshiped the gods.[59]

What is the meaning of the fusion of temple and palace into one unit in the citadel cities as against their separation in the cities of the alluvial plain? Can it be taken to express the role of the king as high priest in the cult of the nation's main deity? We find this fusion in all the capitals of Assyria, and the pertinent ritual texts show us convincingly the cultic importance of the king and high priest. The same situation occurs in Hattuša, whose citadel harbors both palace and temple and where the king as well as the queen were busily engaged in all sorts of ritual activities of a public nature.[60]

In Babylonia proper there are traces of a somewhat similar arrangement, but they are found only in the early Sumerian period, when the position of the ruler was conceived of as that of the vicar of the city's deity. With the secularization of royal function and power, the king's residence became separated from the temple complex. Still later, the king was allowed to enter the inner sanctuary only once a year, during the course of the New Year's festival (see above, p. 122).

When we investigate the position of the citadel within the circumvallation of these cities, we come upon a dichotomy: the older cities have the citadel in their center, but the new ones, especially those built by Assyrian kings as their new capitals (Calah, Nineveh, and Dur-Šarrukin [Khorsabad]), place the entire citadel complex in such a way that it straddles the circumvallation of the settlement. In this peripheral location, both palace and temple are often raised above the plain by means of a terrace the height of the city wall, which forms a rectangle around the city. Three characteristic traits of this novel urban arrangement can be singled out: first, the adoption of the citadel; second, its position on the wall; and third, the rectangularity of the ramparts. Each trait invites comment, as does their integration into a perfect whole, which offers us a very early instance of city planning, of creating a novel pattern in Mesopotamian urbanism. We have already discussed the citadel concept, but we must add that the Assyrian kings evidently considered the citadel as such a distinctive expression of their concept of kingship that they adopted it in every new city they built as residences for themselves. They separated palace and temple from their subjects not only by means of a wall surrounding the citadel but also by a difference in level. The citadel becomes an essential part of the wall it straddles. Strangely enough, the entrance to the citadel is always through the lower city; the king cannot leave the palace without passing through the city.

Before we attempt to explain this extraordinary arrangement in Assyrian cities, a word should be said concerning Babylon. In that city alone we find a royal palace as part of the fortification system, a deviation from the Babylonian pattern of city design. The explanation seems to be that Nebuchadnezzar II, who built this palace, intended to follow the Assyrian prototype. This fits quite well the general situation, which is characterized by the ascendancy of Babylonia over the ancient Near East as heir and successor of Assyria. In one essential point, however, Nebuchadnezzar II did not follow the Assyrian example: his palace has no physical connection with the temple. The sanctuary of Marduk was near the center of the city; only the king's palace was on the ramparts.

Normally, the wall of a Mesopotamian city is arranged in wide curves or in rectilinear, mostly quadrilateral, and often symmetrical designs. Ovaloid shapes occur in the southern cities of Ur and Uruk and in Arslan-Tash in northern Syria; Der shows a triangular outline; Babylon of the late period may have been diamond-shaped, but it is not fully excavated. There are the irregular rectangles of Guzana (Tell Halaf) and of Sippar, and the trapezoid of Nineveh. Of square cities in Mesopotamia we may also mention Dur-Šarrukin and Calah. The irregular outlines of Nippur are shown on the only extant map of a Mesopotamian city, preserved on a clay tablet.

Square, rectangular, and round cities are typically new foundations; these forms clearly represent abstractions, natural only in planned cities. We have only one example of a round city obviously planned that way. This is Zenjirli (Sham˒al) in northern Syria, dating from the end of the second millennium. The outer wall forms a nearly perfect circle, studded with exactly one hundred wall towers, and encloses an inner city, also circular, containing a palace, a temple, barracks, and so on. All this bears the imprint of overly ambitious urban planning, since no traces of habitation have been found in the confines of the outer city. Round cities were built frequently after the collapse of the Babylonian and Seleucid empires. There is the Hatra of the Parthians—the last refuge of the Assyrian gods—with a square inner city; Ctesiphon; and eventually, of course, the round city of the Khalif Manṣoor, Baghdad.[61] The latter shows the natural street arrangement of a round city—radial streets. More examples can be found in Iran, 'one of the last regions of the ancient Near East to be urbanized systematically. Apart from the mythical twelve-walled Ecbatana of Herodotus, we have the Sassanian capital of Firuzabad and such impressive sites as Darabjird (with radial streets), Herat, Isfahan, and others.

It has been repeatedly asserted that both rectangular and round city plans have as their prototype such military encampments as those represented on Assyrian reliefs. These stockades form either a circle or an oblong rectangle with rounded corners. In fact, symmetrical enclosures forming simple geometric figures are the customary way in which migrating tribes or armies arrange their camps. The encampment of the Twelve Tribes and the *campus* of the Roman army are the best known examples. Representations of Assyrian military camps, rectangular or round, show the royal tent, together with the sacred standards, consistently placed off center, in fact quite near to the stockade which surrounds the rows of tents. The location of the royal citadel, with its palace and temple, within a planned Assyrian town closely approximates this layout, differing solely by its incorporation in the wall and the raising of its level. Unlike the Roman camp, where the commander's tent occupies the very center, the arrangement in Assyria seems to correspond to that which was typical for the private house in Mesopotamia. In a quite characteristic spatial arrangement, the living quarters of the owner occupied the south side of the square yard, with storage rooms on adjacent sides of the square, the entrance to the street being placed as far as possible from the living quarters.

Mesopotamian temple architecture often shows aversion to any clear spatial separation of the sanctuary, the "house of the god," from the walls of the close, but also avoiding any central location. In the same way, the king assumed the most protected position within the encampment of his army. In the city, the stockade became turreted walls of brick, the royal tent and its portable shrine became palace and temple, and the houses of officials, craftsmen, and workers filled the square made by the walls of the new city.

There exists only one example of a new if small fortified city from as early as the Old Babylonian period: Tell Harmal (ancient *Šaduppum*) near Baghdad. The very fact that the city had only one gateway near which the main buildings seem to have clustered shows that it was little more than a fortified camp of a ruler, probably of a conqueror.[62]

In the new cities of Assyria, planned after the layout of a military camp, we have the first known instance of the influence which fortification techniques exercised everywhere on the development of new cities, erected as they were for military purposes. The influence of military installations on the planning of cities has remained a dominant factor in the development of urbanism in all those regions of the Western world which, at some time, were conquered or occupied by Roman armies. The layout of the Roman army camp determines the basic spatial organization of countless cities in western and southern Europe, as well as in the Near East and in North Africa. This influence was exercised either directly, whenever a city grew upon the original campsite, or indirectly, when planned cities were built by European kings in the medieval period. What is more, it can even be asserted that urbanistic thinking and planning were carried on in military terms even when applied to the chiliastic and utopian speculations and aspirations of Western man. Several parallel strands in the Western tradition come from that direction, from the camping arrangements around the Tabernacle of the Israelites in the wilderness and the glory of the heavenly Jerusalem; the ideal city of Plato; and the utopian urbanism of the last two or three centuries. The development was especially accentuated by the concept of the *ecclesia militans* which is ultimately responsible for Campanella's *Civitas solis*, Andreae's "Christianopolis," and their descendants.

Expansion through colonization has furnished the opportunities on internal and external frontiers for the materialization of ambitiously projected urban designs. One may refer to the Greek colonies of the fifth and fourth centuries B.C., the Roman colonies of the third century and later, the German colonies on the frontiers against the Slavs, the new cities, *bastides*, in France and England during the thirteenth century A.D., and the sudden, world-wide, expansion of Western colonization which founded, in the space of thirty years, Batavia (1652) in the far East Indies and Philadelphia (1682) in the New World in identical urban layouts.

We should proceed, after this excursus, to another, equally important and essential feature of a city, planned or not: the arteries of internal communication, to wit, the arrangement of the streets which linked the various centers to the gateways and provided access to the dwellings of the inhabitants. The Minoan cities of Crete and the cities created in the pattern of the Roman military camp offer two extreme instances of street arrangement. The layout of a Minoan city seems to be characterized, apart from the absence of a circumvallation, by a sprawling maze of houses nestling against each other and haphazardly meandering streets in ever-changing widths, all in the semblance of cellular growth and, at least to our eyes, without regard to basic function. The complex and labyrinthal palaces, though distinguished by a rectangular open space in front of them, seem not to be integrated with the communication arteries of the city. Quite different is the rigid symmetry of a city following the arrangement of a Roman camp, where the two main thoroughfares cross each other at right angles in the administrative center and where the main streets lead to the four gates in a coaxial arrangement, imposing their determined regularity upon the secondary streets of the city. The Greek cities turned to urban planning in repairing the ravages caused by war and in building new cities as colonies in the fourth century B.C. They thus had a unique opportunity to realize their urban aspirations. As a result they produced a curiously close-meshed and rigid grid of streets, an arrangement traditionally linked with the name of Hippodamos of Miletus in Asia Minor. This grid was laid out without directional accent and without the stress distribution which the natural flow of traffic seems to demand. The web thus created spreads somewhat aimlessly, with sovereign disregard for the lay of the land, through the city area, around which was flung an impressive but irregular line of stone ramparts which, exactly like their gateways, remained without relation to the layout of the streets.[62a]

As for the arrangement of the streets in Mesopotamian cities and their relation to the gateways, we have little archeological evidence on which to draw. A small section of Adab has been excavated but in an unreliable way. For investigation we have only a limited section of Ur containing residential quarters and their streets. The streets of Ur show a tendency toward standard-ized widths and approximately rectangular crossings. Here and there, some of the streets turn unpredictably, but these may have developed from lanes which once curved their way across unused land, ruined areas, or even fields and gardens. One has to remember that the large cities of the ancient Near East often contained such empty areas, due to fluctuations in the density of population and the dislocation of residential sections in the course of the many centuries of their life-span. An analogous tendency toward regularity in the network of streets is also evident in the large cities excavated in the Indus Valley, at Mohenjo-Daro and Harappa. These do show more differentia-tion in the widths of the thoroughfares. One can hardly fail to realize that the use of bricks created in Mesopotamia, as well as in the Indus Valley, a natural inclination toward rectangularity in building, whereas such building materials as mud or rubble had to be forced into a rectangular pattern.

But were the new cities of the Assyrian kings laid out in a regular rectangular pattern, a grid? Unfortunately, neither the private dwellings of Dur-Šarrukin nor those of Kar-Tukulti-Ninurta or Calah have been sufficiently uncovered so as to give us an answer to this question. There are a number of considerations which make it likely that the streets were arranged in a grid pattern. The desire of any military planner is to lodge soldiers or workers in regularly arranged barracks or lots, exemplified, for instance, by the workmen's quarters in Kahun (in the time of Sesostris III) and Amarna (in the time of Amenophis IV), in Egypt, and the workers' barracks in the citadel of Harappa. Such arrangements are natural in encampments where the camp discipline—an important phase of pre-urbanization social experience—requires the leader to allot campsites on an equitable basis but also according to rank and status. Military as well as court ceremonials emphasize such regularity for the battle array, for the train of royal attendants, and for the layout of the necropolis, as we know from Egypt where the tombs of the courtiers are set out in neat rows, placed rectangularly. The asymmetrical disposition of gateways in the circumvallation—e.g., in Dur-Šarrukin, where there are two gates on three sides of the square and one gate on the fourth, the citadel side—does not speak against a regular arrangement of streets, because as has been indicated, even the Greek cities of the Hippodamic grid do not link streets to gateways.

A valid argument for the existence of a grid comes from Urartu, in the region of Lake Van, where a planned town was discovered.[63] Although the town remained unfinished, it has a quadratic grid of streets measuring five meters in width, with the exception of one main street seven meters wide. The stone walls are too low to show traces of gateways. All houses were built at the same time and in uniform size, but the walls now stand only one course high and there are no potsherds to be found; the work was clearly abandoned at an early stage. This town, which seems to be somewhat older than Dur-Šarrukin, shows very convincingly how such cities were built in Mesopotamia, although it is by no means certain that the Urartian kings imitated Assyrian prototypes here. Whether the application of the grid system of streets, which originated in the Ionian cities of Asia Minor in the fourth century, was influenced by Urartu or its successors and imitators cannot be decided. Independent origin of such a grid system is quite possible, as the Italian *terramare* cities show.[64]

In connection with this discussion of the system of streets, we have to return for a moment to the sacred road (see above, p. 115) as far as it is in evidence within the city walls. The remains of such a processional road have been excavated in Babylon, Assur, and Hattuša, and we know from literary records that there was one in Uruk. In the Hittite capital, this road links the temple, the palace, and the out-of-town sanctuary, but in Mesopotamia proper its function was to lead the annual procession from the main sanctuary of the city to a special sanctuary outside the city on the occasion of the New Year's festival. The sacred road was well paved and, in Babylon, was provided with splendid decorations along its course as far as the famous Ištar Gate through which it passed. It should be noted that the entire setting of this *via sacra* shows a surprising lack of concern with perspective in spite of its manifest monumentality. In Babylon as well as in Hattuša, it makes a 90° turn, which should be contrasted with the boulevard character of the Egyptian sphinx-flanked avenues and with the straight sacred of Peking that leads from the Forbidden City to the Altar of Heaven. This avoidance of the vista as a feature of monumental architecture in Mesopotamia is also evident in the use of staggered door openings (placed *en chicane*) and the absence of any stress on coaxial arrangements on a non-utilitarian scale. It seems to represent an essential characteristic of the architecture of the period and region as against that of Egypt. The interest in the vista provided by long avenues with co-ordinated and symmetrically disposed buildings and spaces dominated the urbanism of Mesopotamia and the ancient Near East only when Greek, and especially Roman, principles of urban planning became an influence.

We should mention finally a passage from the inscriptions of the Assyrian king Sennacherib which attests to the interest of certain kings in the improvement of their cities. Sennacherib tells us with considerable pride of his having the streets of Nineveh straightened and the square next to the city gate widened. We even have two stelae from Nineveh which inform us that he had enlarged one of the narrow streets of the city to make it a royal road; that to encroach upon the new avenue when building new houses was to be punished with death by impalement; and that the inscribed stelae were erected expressly to mark the width of the new street, which is given as 62 cubits.[65] It may well be assumed that the new royal road led from the citadel to one of the city gates which, as the text indicates, had been remodeled, probably to co-ordinate road and gateway in width and direction. Through this *via triumphalis* the king intended to enter his palace when returning from annual (and always victorious) campaigns.

A few words should be said concerning the size and the appearance of these cities. With regard to their size it is advisable to present reliable measurements of the occupied area rather than to indulge in conjectures concerning the number of inhabitants. The largest city was undoubtedly Babylon in the Chaldean period; its area covered 2,500 acres. Then follows Nineveh, with 1,850 acres, while Uruk was somewhat smaller, with 1,110 acres. Other cities are much smaller: Hattuša, the Hittite capital, occupied 450 acres; Assur had only 150 acres. Among the royal cities, Dur-Šarrukin was 600 acres, Calah, 800 acres. Athens had 550 acres at the time of Themistocles; one has to keep in mind that it was unusually large and populous for a Greek city. Aristotle (*Politics*, III, iii) repeats a saying about the wondrous size of Babylon: ". . . at the time of the capture of Babylon, it was three days before a part of the city was aware of the fact." This reflects the same implied criticism of large cities that we encounter in the Book of Jonah (3:3): "Nineveh was an exceeding great city of three days' journey." Greek and Biblical aversion against very large cities had different roots: the Greek political thinkers realized, quite correctly, that their type of democratic rule could not work in cities over a certain well-defined size, and in the Old Testament there is everywhere a latent disapproval of city life, especially with respect to large agglomerations.

The extraordinary extent of the larger capitals, Babylon and Nineveh, could well have been a secondary development caused by a rare and atypical increase in the population of these cities. As such, it represents a special phase in the history of the Mesopotamian city, and one on which we have very little material.

Little can be said of the appearance, the "skyline," of the Mesopotamian city. Only isolated pictorial representations of individual and identifiable cities have come down to us; most of the representations of cities on Assyrian reliefs are hopelessly schematized and of little worth. Even they, however, show the difference between the walled city and the lower houses of the suburb; and they show the monumental gateways, the turreted and crenelated walls which often form a double rampart, the military use made of the lay of the land, of watercourses, and so on. Exceptionally, we find the features of a specific city reproduced with valuable details, such as the relief which shows Muṣaṣir, the conquered Urartian city, with its strange pillared temple and its multistoried buildings.[66] On a damaged slab we have the city of Babylon in an interesting perspective, which would be enlightening were the upper part not missing.[67]

Few of the cities of Mesopotamia were distinguished by specific topographical features, such as Assur on its cliff, approached by a monumental stairway (mušlālu), Borsippa, situated on both sides of a lake, and Babylon, made unique by its size, its bridge over the Euphrates, and the height of its famous tower.

The cities of the plain and the new cities, with flat-roofed, windowless, one- and two-story buildings, characteristic temple towers with blue glazed tops, and endless brick walls with crenelations and towers, were quite unlike the citadel cities of the piedmont and mountain regions, which were situated on hilltops and surrounded by complex circumvallations on substructures, with high towers.

Within the ramparts were a maze of streets, alleys, and dead-end streets, filled with the "busy hum of man," with street vendors but without beggars,[68] domestic animals could be encountered, cripples and prostitutes.[69] Indeed, the noise and bustle of a city day, the eternal coming and going, was effectively contrasted by the poets with the quiet nights when the city slept under the starry sky, behind locked gates.[70] Only the night watchmen made their rounds. But we do not know whether their song sounded through the empty streets, as it did in Jerusalem, where they answered the call of the sleepless: "Watchman, what of the night?" (Isaiah 21:11).

CHAPTER **III**

Regnum a gente in gentem transfertur

(JESUS SIRACH)

HISTORICAL SOURCES OR
LITERATURE?

AN ESSAY ON BABYLONIAN
HISTORY

AN ESSAY ON ASSYRIAN
HISTORY

Only few cuneiform texts expressly purport to write what, in the traditional Western sense, we would call "history." Many more refer to actual happenings for purposes other than that of merely recording these events. Our first task is to separate the former from the latter, the historiographic texts from the large corpus of documents which Assyriologists are wont to call "royal inscriptions." The historian studying Mesopotamia has to consider, in addition, an array of sundry literary compositions which offer for one reason or another what one might term historical information. In all instances, we have to keep foremost in our mind that even strictly historiographic documents are literary works and that they manipulate the evidence, consciously or not, for specific political and artistic purposes.[1] Even these few texts that are patently more reliable than others, whose aim is mainly literary, cater to preconceived ideological requirements. In short, nearly all these texts are as wilfully unconcerned with the "truth" as any other "historical text" of the ancient Near East.

Historical Sources or Literature?

Mesopotamian historiography—in the strictest sense—covers a stretch of only about half a millennium, that is, from the time of Tiglath-Pileser III (744–727 B.C.) in Assyria and Nabu-naṣir (747–734 B.C.) in Babylonia to the year 264 B.C., the thirty-eighth of the Seleucid Era (Antiochus I Soter). In annalistic form a number of chronicles present the events of many of these years, although often in a very fragmentary way. The data clearly exhibit the restrictions imposed by the nature of the text type; they are concerned with war and peace, and they record the death of kings and members of the royal family in factual and terse form. Needless to say, they are often of great importance to historians for the data they provide of Mesopotamian and at times of Old Testament and Greek history. Some of the chronicles display their literary ambition by offering a *historia mundi*. They record in accepted style a selection of events before the Dark Age and offer a series of striking episodes that were apparently considered "historical," in the sense in which Herodotus uses the term. From these chronicles can be gathered highly interesting episodes from the times of Sargon of Akkad to Ilušuma of Assyria and Sumuabum of Babylon, and from Irra-imitti of Isin to a very early Kassite king, Agum.

As a unique case of strictly contemporary recording of events, on a day-to-day basis and with a restricted local outlook, we may mention the astronomical diaries—unpublished still but for a few fragments—which record the death of important persons, plagues, fires, and other calamities occurring in Babylon as well as prices of commodities and the water levels of the

Euphrates—all as an appendix to observations of the movements of the planets.[2]

As a more relevant expression of the consciousness of history, the texts customarily called king lists present themselves. They begin with that mythical moment "when kingship descended from heaven" and give us in great number the names of kings and their capitals and the length of time they reigned. In a rather complete sequence, the entire known history of Babylonia and Assyria is reflected in several such lists of kings. They bridge the gaps of documentation with a string of names and reach beyond the period of the Diadochi to the beginning of the Arsacid domination, maintaining the traditional Sumerian formulations even to that late date.[3] Their typology is rather complex; variations appear in the arrangement of entries and summaries. Apart from indication of the length of reigns and division into dynasties, they contain remarks—at times cryptic—on outstanding events (especially for the oldest period) and also the names of certain high officials.[4] One text co-ordinates the reigns of the kings of Assyria and Babylonia; but what is preserved of it sheds light only on the last centuries of the co-existence of the two countries. On another level, the same awareness of a historical continuum speaks to us out of occasional references in royal inscriptions that indicate in more or less exact figures the number of years that had passed since a specific historical event. It is generally assumed that the scribes relied for information of this type on king lists and on two related text types of utilitarian purpose; the date lists of the Old Babylonian period (about one thousand different dates)[5] and the several types of eponym lists which cover with some interruptions much of Assyrian history.[6] In Babylonia, from the Akkad period until the Dark Age, every year derived its name from an event that had occurred in the preceding year, a system of dating that made it necessary to keep lists of such names in order to establish their correct sequence. To us, the usefulness of these year names is restricted to a certain extent by their rigid formalism, which admits mention only of victories and pious acts of the ruling king, such as dedications of sumptuous gifts to the sanctuaries, the inauguration of important priests and priestesses, and the rebuilding of temples. These formulas display more pious phraseology than factual precision and are more concerned with the description of precious objects than with recording specific events. Still, the skeleton of far more than half a millennium of history is preserved for us in such year names. The Assyrians, as well, drew up lists because they identified the years of the reign of a king by means of a continuous sequence of the names of high officials of the realm who served as eponym officials. Some of these lists contain short remarks in which references are made to campaigns or to calamities. The value of these eponym lists for the historian is inferior to that of the Old Babylonian date lists.

Although clearly written from a pro-Assyrian point of view, what seems to be the historical preamble of a treaty between Assyria and Babylonia provides us with an interesting survey of the political relations between these two countries as reflected in border regulations and dynastic marriages from the early fifteenth to the early eighth centuries. This report (dubbed "synchronistic history") bespeaks a serious interest in history dictated by political exigencies.

We turn now to documents of an entirely different nature, purpose, and origin. From such early kings as Mesannipadda of Ur to the Greek ruler Antiochus I Soter, we have objects which bear dedicatory inscriptions of the kings of Sumer, Babylonia, and Assyria.[7] These inscriptions range from a few signs on a clay cone to the many columns on the rock of Behistun. Bricks, prisms with hundreds of lines, stone slabs, beads and statues, gold and silver objects, reliefs, and many other carriers sing the praises of gods and kings, glorify their makers' deeds and achievements, and clamor to the gods for health, long life, fame, and booty.

Two types may be differentiated, inscriptions that are placed on the objects which the kings dedicated to the gods, and inscriptions on objects to be incorporated into temples or palaces that were thus dedicated. The latter do not bear dedicatory inscriptions on their surfaces as did Egyptian buildings but had the carrier of the message—a clay prism, a clay nail, a brick inscription—hidden under mortar or within the wall or beneath the foundations. The longest and most explicit Assyrian royal inscriptions discovered to date were imbedded in the substructure of a temple or a palace, safe from human eyes and only to be read by the deity to which they were addressed. Only a limited number of royal inscriptions on reliefs, stelae, or rocks were placed where—theoretically at least—they could be read.

At the outset of a complex and diversified stylistic development, the writing on such objects consisted of a short dedication addressed to a deity, identifying the donor, the object, and the occasion of the donation.[8] Soon, these dedications blossomed in unparalleled extravagance. Royal titles grew to include strings of honorific and semimythological verbiage incorporating epithets that strove to sum up the king's victories and achievements; the address to the deity was extended in hectic hymnic exaggeration—but the dedication of the object or building retained its key position in this flood of words. It cannot be our task here to dissect the development of this type of text, to trace the lines that lead from early Sumerian formulations to the numerous barrel-shaped cylinders of the Chaldean kings, or to analyze the complexities of the Assyrian evolution with its many innovations and elaborations—not to speak of the texts from peripheral regions that in many instances imitate Mesopotamian patterns with interesting variations. Such an investigation, all the same, would shed light on political concepts and their development, which are often reflected in the type of inscription preferred in a specific epoch. All that can be offered at this point are such observations as bear more or less directly on the main topic of this chapter: are these texts historiography or a special type of literary production?

The great majority of royal inscriptions were not written in order to convey information to the beholder. Even those stelae that proclaim the kings' victories to posterity could hardly reach the public. The following consideration should qualify and bear out this statement. Such texts as the inscription of Aššurnaṣirpal II describing in detail the banquet held upon his accession to the throne,[9] or that of Nabonidus offering an apologetic account of his rise to kingship,[10] are written on stone stelae which were meant to be set up in a locality accessible to everyone. Still, one cannot deduce from this practice that the inscriptions on such stelae were meant for dissemination. The cylinder of Nebuchadnezzar II, which adds to a conventional Neo-Babylonian royal inscription a systematic list of the official hierarchy at his court,[11] was buried, as such cylinders were, in a foundation box of the palace. Although it does contain information that has no immediate relation to the dedication of a building, this information was not intended for reading. Since the information on the supposedly openly displayed stelae of Aššurnasirpal II and of Nabonidus is of the same type as that on the buried cylinder of Nebuchadnezzar II, we must assume that the inscriptions were not there for the purpose of being read by the observer any more than those on the buried cylinder. What distinguishes the stelae from the cylinders, is that the stelae were to be displayed, while the cylinders were deposited within the building not only to dedicate it but also to convey information to a future king who intended to rebuild the temple, as these texts often expressly state. All cylinders, prisms, cones, and brick inscriptions were hidden in walls and foundation boxes. Formally, these texts as well as inscribed reliefs placed in dark corridors of royal palaces and rock inscriptions carefully carved in inaccessible spots, are addressed to the deity; they report the king's victories and his piety and demand blessings in return. For this very reason they are written in a highly stylized language, often poetic and exuberant; they mention only carefully selected happenings and use a restricted vocabulary. Both Assyrian and Neo-Babylonian inscriptions of that tenor must be taken to reflect literary patterns cultivated in their respective settings. The Assyrian royal inscriptions show several new departures in their development; thus one finds, beginning with Arik-den-ili (1319–1308 B.C.) and Shalmaneser I (1274–1245 B.C.) an annalistic arrangement; in Tiglath-Pileser I (1115–1077 B.C.) we have long-winded and solemn invocations as introductions, short and hectic paeans between the descriptions of individual campaigns, and a triumphal hymn at the end. After Adad-nirari II (911–891 B.C.), who introduces his annals with pompous self-praise in an overlong introduction, the style changes and the introits become formal and restrained.

Later, one can observe in the inscriptions of Sargon II (721–705 B.C.) a preference for extremely poetic and stilted parlance; in those of Assurbanipal (668–627 B.C.) the inclusion of episodic happenings; in Esarhaddon's (680–669 B.C.) and Sennacherib's (704–681 B.C.), other peculiarities. One thus gains the impression that these inscriptions were written for the king himself. The scribes and poets at court created for him his own image as hero and pious king; they show him in these texts as he wanted to see himself. In this respect, the royal inscriptions of the Hammurapi dynasty, of the Assyrian kings (from the end of the second millennium on), and of the Chaldean kings apparently assumed the function of the royal hymns that we have from the kings of Ur III and their early Babylonian emulators (from Ur-Nammu to Abi-ešuh).[11a] The preference of the poets and bards at court seems to have shifted from the production of hymns in praise of the king to the composing of royal inscriptions for exactly the same purpose. It is quite possible that hymns to the ruler continued to be composed, but they were not incorporated into the corpus of the literary tradition and, if preserved in fragments, are not sufficient in number to attract our attention. The relationship of the royal inscriptions to the literary production of a given period and place is for the same reason difficult to investigate. Nevertheless, the very inscriptions that offer us a chance to fill out the skeleton of historical facts contained in king lists, year names, and eponym lists provide us at the same time with important insights into the literary aspirations of the courts at which they were written.

Only when the royal inscriptions are linked with their literary background can their diversification and their continuous stylistic changes be explained. We see the kings of the Hammurapi dynasty enumerate the blessings they expect in return for their piety; the Chaldean kings—with the exception of Nabopolassar's reference to his victory over Assyria—avoid mentioning their adversaries and specific victories, unlike the early Babylonian and, above all, the Assyrian practice. Nabonidus, to give an example of a novel feature, enlivens inscriptions with dialogues in which gods, priests, dead kings, and workmen appear, and Samsuiluna offers a unique inscription in which the gods in heaven speak of him.[12] To turn back to Nabonidus, he quotes in scholarly fashion the texts of the documents his workmen had excavated from the ruins of temples he was in process of rebuilding. He even gives us on one such occasion the text of an inscription of a Kassite king that would otherwise have been lost.[13] His preference for mentioning and, at times, reporting his own dreams represents another novum. To terminate this random sampling of the style of the royal inscriptions, let me point out Assurbanipal's repeated descriptions of his training and his achievements as a scholar and a soldier which—one-and-a-half millennia later—include a *topos* from the Sumerian royal hymns. This illustrates the continuity and tenacity of a living literary tradition other than that literary tradition frozen and preserved in the royal library of Nineveh. Anyone who intends to write a history of Mesopotamian literature that is more than an inventory of extant fragments will have to consult these living, changing royal inscriptions.

Mesopotamian scribes were conscious of the importance of the inscriptions to be found on statues and votive objects, but for antiquarian and literary rather than for historical reasons. We have a number of copies (from the Middle Babylonian through the Neo-Babylonian period) of older inscriptions, often imitating their script. To this interest we owe much of what we know today of the Old Akkadian period and the rule of the kings of Ur III. The use of such historical material for purely ideological purposes appears early in the Old Babylonian period. Scribes began to collect the inscriptions (e.g., of the sanctuary of Tummal in Nippur)[14] to illustrate their belief that pious rulers received divine favors and those who did not respect the temple fell by divine interference—an important theme throughout the ancient Near East. They also recopied actual or invented letters of outstanding kings in extraordinary situations. The names as well as deeds, crimes, and victories of famous rulers seem to have been kept alive through some oral tradition that must have centered in sanctuaries rather than in palaces. The interest of the palace in tradition was by nature short-lived and geared to matters of immediate concern, but the scholars, administrators, and experts living in the temple were prone to keep stories alive that enhanced the importance of the sanctuary or record, in lamentations, its destruction. From such a body of written and unwritten stories must come all the proverbial sayings, the king lists and the chronicles and, above all, the references in the omen collections to the famous kings of old.[15] Among them is Ku-Baba, a female innkepeer who founded the third dynasty of Kish; Šulgi, the most powerful king of the third dynasty of Ur; and Irra-imitti, of the dynasty of Isin, who died a strange death—to mention only the best-known personages. On a different level of literary creativeness, these tales grew into legends that attached themselves to founders of dynasties or kings who fell from power in a spectacular way, such as Sargon of Akkad and Ibbi-Sin of Ur.[16] Sargon remained a semimythical king throughout much of the second millennium. The story of his birth and exposure, his rescue from a basket floating down the Euphrates, his rise to power, and, last but not least, his campaigns, adventures, victories, and reverses, and his conquest of the West was read in Amarna in Egypt, in Hattuša in Anatolia, and even translated into Hurrian and Hittite. The text of the epic šar tamḥarim deals with the gesta of Sargon; the exploits of his son Naram-Sin are retold in what was once called by Assyriologists the Cuthean legend. Here again, the topos of desperate situations which the king turns into victories is in evidence, and the warrior-king is shown as victorious in such far-off regions as Asia Minor and the island of Telmun. Copies come from the capital of the Hittites (in Akkadian) and some fragments, much later, from Nineveh and Sultantepe.[17]

Not only kings of the distant past but, under certain circumstances, also kings of the present and the still living past could appear in literary texts when extraordinary events characterized their rule. Such events seem to have been the military triumph of Tukulti-Ninurta I,[18] who was the first Assyrian king to conquer Babylon; the destruction of that famous city by the Elamites (under Šutruk-Nahhunte); and the spectacular successes of Nebuchadnezzar I, king of Babylon, against the Elamites. On the other hand, the Babylonian poets and scribes had a difficult task explaining the tragedy of Babylon abandoned by its god Marduk and conquered by enemies. Thus, the famous raid of the Hittite king Muršili gave rise to literary texts in which Marduk speaks, like a king in a royal inscription, of his westward journey[19]—as his image is carried off in that direction—and of his eventual return. A conquest of Babylon seems to have given stimulus to another poetic creation, known to us as the Epic of Irra. There, in contrived and inelegant diction, the catastrophe of Babylon is blamed on the fumblings of minor gods ruling the country—and of mankind—during the absence of Marduk on an essential errand. The poem is one of a group of creations in a similar vein bespeaking a resurgence of literary interest— in the critical half millennium from Nebuchadnezzar I (1124–1103 B.C.) to the famous king who assumed the same name (Nebuchadnezzar II, 604–562 B.C.)—in a Babylonia that once again began a slow rise to power and glory (see below, pp. 159 f.).

Much easier was the task of the Assyrian poets and courtly bards when they had to extol the victories of such a great king as Tukulti-Ninurta I over the Kassite rulers of Babylonia. This truly historical epic shows the same delight in descriptions of battle and carnage, the same vilification of the enemy and ecstasy of triumph that one often finds, somewhat tempered by repetition, in the royal inscriptions of contemporary and later Assyrian kings.

Another Babylonian ruler, whose strange behavior and dramatic downfall attracted attention outside Babylon, achieved such fame that he is still remembered. This was Nabonidus, the last king of Babylon. In part due to his conflict with the temple of Marduk, for he allegedly interfered in religious matters and preferred the god Sin and his temple in far-off Harran, in part due to his protracted and still mysterious absence in the oasis cities of Arabia and his curious and unkingly behavior in face of the impending attack of Cyrus, Nabonidus became in the eyes of his contemporaries the "mad" king of Babylon. We have a strange text written apparently at the end of the political independence of Babylonia which vilifies Nabonidus and praises Cyrus as the liberator of the oppressed sanctuaries. Here the king of the Persians is not considered a foreign invader but the savior who delivered Babylon. The form is poetic, arranged in strophes, and the text lists with venom the sins of

Nabonidus against the old temples and against the old capital in taking up residence in the Arab city of Tema. Nabonidus is accused of ignorance and blasphemy, and his most hated officials are mentioned by name. The same spirit of hatred speaks out of the text of a barrel-shaped clay cylinder which resembles a foundation deposit but certainly never served as such. The text describes, moreover, the triumphal entry of Cyrus into Babylon in near-messianic terms.[20] In no other document written in cuneiform do we come across such intensity of political antagonism, and one cannot but wonder what acts of Nabonidus brought about such a violent reaction. In the Old Testament—but not in the scrolls from the Dead Sea—the *topos* of the "mad king of Babylon" was transferred from Nabonidus to his much better known and more famous predecessor, Nebuchadnezzar II.[21]

In all these instances, references to literary *topoi*, historical facts, and historical situations are so densely interwoven that the historian is not only faced with philological difficulties but also with the far more complex problems of style and literary influence as they mold and distort the report for specific purposes. All this in no way precludes that at times a serious artistic interest expresses itself in the presentation of the realities ("mimesis") of a scene or a setting, of the acts of men and their reactions and emotions. Such passages are rare outside the story of the adventures of Idrimi, and the descriptions of peoples and places contained in certain Neo-Assyrian royal inscriptions. And even then the cuneiform texts fail by far to reach the degree of superb objectivity, the empathic understanding and sense for history which is displayed in the story of David as told in the books of Samuel.

An Essay on Babylonian History

During the nearly two millennia of recorded Babylonian history, the country experienced only two short-lived climaxes of political power. They occurred, perhaps not quite accidentally, at the outset and at the very end of that tremendous span of time. Two famous names characterize the two periods, that of

Sargon, king of Akkad (ca. 2310 B.C.), and that of Nebuchadnezzar II (604–562 B.C.).

The best documented periods, however, are not the ones of these Babylonian kings but the reigns of Hammurapi (1792–1750 B.C.) and his immediate predecessors and successors. Only for two centuries of this dynasty do we obtain some insight into the mechanics of government, the workings of the administration, and into certain essential aspects of the social and economic life. Observation of the law code of Hammurapi gives us a unique opportunity to study the gap between facts and aspirations. Sargon and Nebuchadnezzar II can be seen only through the distorting mirror of their own highly stylized self-presentations. What administrative documents of Sargon and legal texts written under Nebuchadnezzar II we possess, combined with what legends and chronicles tell us about these two kings, hardly allow us more than a glimpse of the underlying social, economic, and intellectual contexts.

When Uruk fell to Lugalzagesi, and when, a little later, his adversary, Sargon of Akkad, achieved for the first time a new type of unification of Mesopotamia, a fateful and decisive change occurred in the history of the entire region. Political power moved away from Uruk, the focus of classical Sumerian civilization, and from a new center a political structure began to evolve, different in kind from that customary among city-states. Sargon's claim to fame, in legends and tradition, is based on that achievement, although he may not have been the first to provide the impetus for this development. He became the exponent of imperial aspirations, of expansion beyond the natural spheres of influence in a world of city-states. He evolved —or allowed to grow—an extensive palace organization which seems to have gone beyond the limitations of a royal "household." The palace was supported by taxes, which were levied and collected by a centralized bureaucracy, and manned by a personnel of which military service was expected. In spite of the long reigns of both Sargon and his grandson Naram-Sin (93 years together), in spite of their famous victories and fabulous achievements, their dominion seems to have been denied inner stability and lasting consolidation. It was disrupted by invading Quti mountaineers, who were, in turn, defeated by a king of Uruk (Utuhegal). The Neo-Sumerian empire of Ur (conventionally termed Ur III) took over the heritage of Sargon in a distinctively different key. For one hundred years, the kings of Ur ruled Mesopotamia either directly or through provincial governors, who sat in Susa as well as in Mari and Assur and defended their realm against invaders from the mountains and the deserts.[22] Ur flourished, embellished with sumptuous temples and palaces, and trade routes led to it from across the mountains and from the sea, demonstrating both the prosperity and the security that in Mesopotamia is concomitant with effective royal power. Abundant documentation, still far from being exhausted as a source of information, illustrates the functioning of a complex hierarchy of officials, and a final flowering of Sumerian literature characterizes the period. The empire collapsed with long-remembered spectacularity, succumbing apparently to increasing internal stresses and the pressure of the nomads from the west, rather than to an invasion from Elam. Slowly but irresistibly, the center of political gravity moved upstream, through Isin and Larsa, to settle in a small town attested only sporadically before Ur III. It was called Babylon.[22a] The several stages of that move occurred in a period of great upheaval.[23] It was contemporaneous with the final acceleration of the shift from the Sumerian to the Akkadian language, with the influx of foreign elements on several distinct social levels, and with the progressive fragmentation of the country. It was accompanied, at the same time, by an enlargement of the political horizon, which now stretched effectively from Telmun and Susa to Anatolia and the littoral of the Mediterranean, thus provoking and favoring the exchange of goods and ideas throughout the entire Near East. In short, a highly interesting period which we are still not able to define with precision as to temper and to analyze adequately as to constituents. Since it is not the task of this section to recount the history of Mesopotamia, we may turn our attention to Babylon, to the Babylon of Hammurapi (1792–1750 B.C.).

Babylon, in the hundred years before Hammurapi, during which five kings of his family sat on the throne, had led an inconspicuous existence, conquering and losing this or that not-too-distant city (particularly Kish) and making rather ineffective campaigns along and beyond the Tigris. It is quite likely that Babylon had not always been independent of more important southern centers, Isin and Larsa. The rise to power began, apparently, with the father of Hammurapi, Sin-muballiṭ, the last of the rulers of that dynasty to have an Akkadian name. He directed his efforts toward the south (victory over Ur and Larsa, the conquests of Isin and Ešnunna), because to the north was Šamši-Adad I of Assyria, an important political and military power. With Hammurapi a change occurs in the names of the kings of this dynasty; they all assume foreign (i.e., Amorite) names as if to stress their non-Akkadian background. When Hammurapi became king, it is said that he "entered the house of his father." With the death of Šamši-Adad I of Assyria, Hammurapi seems to have grasped the opportunity to undertake a policy of military expansion. The names for the seventh to the eleventh years of his reign record the defeat of Uruk and of Isin, the destruction of Malgium, and an invasion into Emutbal across the Tigris. This burst of warlike activity was apparently followed by a period of peace, since the year names up to the twenty-ninth year of Hammurapi's reign do not refer to conquests but indicate an era of consolidation and organization. All this, of course, might be deceptive, because defeats and the progressive deterioration of a ruler's political power can hardly be expected to find expression in the names given the years. It is therefore not surprising to find Hammurapi, from his thirtieth year to the year of his death, engaged in nearly continuous warfare. His wars had clearly become defensive in nature; the very first of the last series of year names strikes what one may well call an ominous note: "Year in which the leader, the beloved of Marduk, organized [through] the power of the great gods [the empire of] Sumer and Akkad after having defeated the army which Elam—[coming] from the frontier of Marhaši, together with Subartu, Gutium, Eshnunna, and Malgi—had raised in masses." Similar coalitions are referred to in the year 32 (Eshnunna, Subartu, and Gutium) and the year 37 (Sutium, Turukku, Kakmu, and Subartu). Offensive wars led to the victory over his former ally,

Rim-Sin of Larsa (year 31), the leveling of the walls of Mari (year 35), and the defeat of Eshnunna (year 38), but one cannot fail to gain the impression that in these and in subsequent years the events reduced rather than maintained or extended the realm of Hammurapi, to which he now likes to refer with the old designation "Sumer and Akkad." The last two year names show him clearly on the defensive, and that rather near his capital; the year 42 is named after a wall built along the Tigris and Euphrates, and the next speaks of an earthen wall built to protect—as an emergency measure probably—the town of Sippar. Only one badly damaged letter throws some light on the end of Hammurapi.[24] In it his son Samsuiluna writes (TCL 17 76) to a high official with respect to the circumstances that accompanied his accession to the throne: "The king, my father, is s[ick] and I sat myself on the throne in order to [...] the country." Then, Samsuiluna announces his first royal act, the customary remission of debts to certain groups of the population, an act to which the Mesopotamian kings resorted periodically to remedy the constant economic maladjustment of their country. Whatever course history took in the ensuing one hundred and fifty years, during which five more kings of the same dynasty ruled in Babylon, the city itself remained the capital, while all former seats of power became provincial cities. This transfer of power was recognized everywhere but in the deep south, where inaccessible marshes and poor communications create a natural refuge for ethnic groups out of power and separatists. The south became a backwater, whatever ephemeral attempts were made to reclaim political power by the dynasty of the Sealand. A process of encystment took place that preserved much of its cultural heritage during the more than half a millennium before new and vigorous cities rose there again.

The years between the death of Hammurapi and the end of the dynasty saw the formation of the Old Babylonian literary tradition, the consolidation of the Sumerian legacy within that formulation of Akkadian Mesopotamian civilization which had evolved in Isin and Larsa. Couched in this formulation, the literary tradition was able to survive the cataclysms of the

Dark Age. It was carefully maintained by the conservativism of the Kassite period and transmitted to Neo-Babylonian and Neo-Assyrian scribes. The Assyrians were aware of their indebtedness to the Old Babylonian period, as we know from a letter addressed by a scribe to an Assyrian king (probably, Assurbanipal), in which he reports that he had brought from Babylon some tablets from the times of "Ammurapi, the king."[25]

One cannot possibly mention Hammurapi without referring to his code of laws,[25a] whose contents and social aims present a unique view of the Mesopotamia of that period. Still, one should bear in mind that this code—as well as other, earlier, Akkadian and Sumerian codifications—does not show any direct relationship to the legal practices of the time. Its contents are rather to be considered in many essential respects a traditional literary expression of the king's social responsibilities and of his awareness of the discrepancies between existing and desirable conditions. Ultimately, such codes represent an interesting formulation of social criticism and should not be taken as normative directions in the manner of post-biblical and Roman law.[26]

With the conquest of Babylon by the Hittite king Muršili (ca. 1600 B.C.) the Dark Age began, continuing through the reign of the nineteenth king (Burnaburiaš II, 1359–1333 B.C.) of the next dynasty, the Kassite, to rule in Babylonia. Again, we shall not dwell upon the numerous problems concerning the chronology of that period, nor shall we investigate the gradual emergence of a politically important Babylonia or the tensions that developed between this country and an increasingly expanding Assyria.

The following statement might serve to characterize the period: while the literary tradition and what pertained to it was evidently securely enough imbedded in the intellectual and spiritual continuity to survive the span of nearly a millennium, social and economic traditions underwent serious changes and readjustments which we are not always able to state in positive terms. Although the caprices of survival of adequate documentation place us in a difficult position to gauge the nature of such changes, a number of more or less sensitive indicators suggest their general trend. Such are the increased economic role of the palace organization, the decreasing influence of royal authority, the disappearance of private economic initiative and of all vestiges of social reforms—or experiments—that characterize the Hammurapi period. Even though the role of the palace may be emphasized because we have chanced upon a palace archive in Nippur, much smaller finds from Dur-Kurigalzu and from Ur do support the characterization just offered. Numerous land grants, styled and exhibited in a specific form, show by their very designation, *kudurru* (boundary marker), which has not been attested before, that they represent a novum.[27] They reveal an administrative articulation of the country that reminds us forcibly of feudalism. But this designation, in no way to be taken literally, is solely an inadequate and popular approximation, in the way the term democracy is usually applied. The exact nature of the administrative and social context of the time of the earlier and genuine *kudurrus* is still to be examined and presented. The scarcity of legal documents related to private commercial activities (such as the buying and selling of real estate) or the making of wills and marriage settlements, the absence of documents referring to the hiring of persons and services, and the making of loans—so plentiful in earlier times—emphasize the decline of private initiative and show through their deeply changed phraseology and vocabulary that we are dealing here with an economic world grown different.

The victory of Nebuchadnezzar I (1125–1104 B.C.) over the Elamites ushered in that half millennium through which Babylonia, first slowly and with many setbacks, then with ever-increasing momentum, rose again to power. This movement which continues with Nabu-naṣir (747–734 B.C.), whose role and impact is still beclouded by lack of evidence, culminated in Nabopolassar, the first king (625–605 B.C.) of a new dynasty which was to become for a short time heir to the Assyrian supremacy over a large section of the ancient Near East. Much of that span of time is as dark an age as the Dark Age itself. Our sole information comes from the short and stereotyped royal inscriptions, which echo those of the pre-Hammurapi period, from the king lists, from Assyrian royal inscriptions that speak of conflicts with Babylonia, and from kindred documents.

The crucial event of the period, the event that gave impetus to Babylonia's rise to power and influenced decisively the entire history of the region, is the appearance of the Chaldeans on the Babylonian scene.

In the ninth century B.C., we begin to hear of a country called Kaldu and of its inhabitants, the Chaldeans. They seem to have lived in a region of swamps, lakes, and canebrakes along the lower course of the two rivers between the shores of the Persian Gulf and the southernmost cities of Babylonia. This region, in which they relied on agriculture, mainly date growing, fishing, and some horse breeding for their livelihood, was divided into tribal areas called "houses." Each "house" (bītu) was under the leadership of a chieftain who, at times, called himself king. But the regions were ill-defined and the political strength of the chieftain depended primarily on his personal influence. The largest of these tribes was located south of Borsippa. Its name was Bit-Dakūri, and its neighbor further to the south was called Bit-Amukani. Along the Tigris, we have Bit-Yakin, large and important because of its proximity to Elam, whence came weapons and money, enabling the tribe to make difficulties for the government in Babylon. We know, furthermore, of smaller tribes, the Bit-Adini, somehow connected with the Bit-Dakuri, and the Bit-Šaʾalli and Bit-Šilani. Their geographical isolation and perhaps their social organization kept them away from the life as lived in the old cities. They seem to have either participated in or profited from the overland trade that had to move through the territories they held. The only indication that the Chaldeans spoke a language of their own is a small number of foreign names, probably in a dialect of Aramaic, the language which they probably used; most of the persons mentioned in historical texts and in letters have good Neo-Babylonian names. For reasons not yet clear, the Chaldeans are in the texts always differentiated from the Aramean tribes settled in the higher terrain upstream along the Euphrates and especially along the Tigris.

Certain characteristics of the Chaldean way of life become evident when one studies the conflicts between the Assyrian

Empire and Babylonia when the latter was at war with Assyria or ruled by an Assyrian king or his Babylonian puppet. Evidence for Babylonia's struggle for liberation from the Assyrian yoke comes mainly from Assyrian royal inscriptions, which one has to interpret carefully in order to see the Babylonians as a people fighting for independence, not as they are presented as incorrigible rebels and perfidious enemies. Especially revealing are those letters found in the royal archives at Nineveh which contain reports, complaints, and accusations sent by officials, soldiers, spies, and partisans engaged in the Assyrian fight for control of southern Babylonia. The following picture results from even a cursory study of the evidence: the Chaldean tribal groups, loosely connected with some prominent chieftain, shifted allegiance according to the distribution of military strength and fought to maintain their independence from each other and the Assyrians who tried desperately to police the area. In groups of ever-changing size, the Chaldean tribes refused to pay taxes or to render services to the government and if not bought off were ready to waylay caravans and to attack and plunder settlements and small cities. The Chaldeans must have come to some kind of agreement with Babylonian city-dwellers when the Assyrian kings attempted to control the region, probably by placing garrisons in key cities and by guarding their lines of communication.[28] This military situation made the Chaldeans, despite their anti-urban bias, of necessity the champions of the anti-Assyrian movement and the defenders of national independence in Babylonia, while it created within the cities a pro-Assyrian party, the party of those Babylonians who wanted peace and security for the sake of their fields and gardens, for their ships and caravans. For these reasons, the large cities, especially Nippur, remained to the very end faithful to Assyria.

The Chaldean kinglets were well prepared for the type of warfare required. Sudden attacks and flights, guerilla tactics and infiltrations, together with a complete disregard for sworn treaties with the enemy, made the task of the Assyrian army, moving among a population of doubtful loyalty, very difficult. Elam was always ready to grant refuge to defeated rebel leaders, to supply the tribes with weapons and even with troops whenever its own rather unstable internal situation allowed an effective and sustained anti-Assyrian policy. Nothing illustrates the situation better than the career of that indefatigable rebel king, Merodach-Baladan II. He appears first under Tiglath-Pileser III as king of the Sealand, claiming royal descent (from Eriba-Marduk of the early eighth century B.C.), and paying homage to the Assyrian king in the company of other Chaldean chieftains. With help from Elam, he made himself king of Babylon (721–710 B.C.) while Sargon II, who had just usurped the Assyrian throne, had to fight the Elamite army at Der, without, however, winning a victory. Merodach-Baladan conveniently came too late for the battle—exactly as did the Chaldean king Nabopolassar in 614, when the Medes took Assur by assault. The Assyrian setback allowed Merodach-Baladan to remain king of Babylon until Sargon II returned in 710 to make himself king of that city. Sargon was not strong enough to refuse recognition to Merodach-Baladan as king of Bit-Yakin. Next Merodach-Baladan reappeared under Sennacherib to oust a Babylonian king (703 B.C.). He sought—planning now in "global" terms—to ally himself with every potential enemy of Mesopotamia, and to incite to rebellion the Assyrian vassals in the far west. We know that he wrote letters to that effect which an embassy brought with a present to Hezekiah of Judah (Isaiah 39:1–8). Sennacherib reacted with all his energy and ruthless persistence; in three campaigns he took Babylon, forced Merodach-Baladan into exile in Elam, and in a seaborne invasion destroyed the cities along the Elamite coast, where Chaldean exiles used to organize rebellions in Babylonia. Merodach-Baladan disappeared, but his fight for Babylonian independence was taken up, three generations later, by another leader, Nabopolassar (625–605 B.C.), who succeeded where Merodach-Baladan had failed, for Assyrian power and military strength were rapidly collapsing.

What makes these Chaldean warrior-kings so fascinating to us is that they help us to understand how and under what circumstances kings with Amorite names had come to power at an earlier time, before the rise of the first dynasty of Babylon (see

above, p. 156). Although the parallel here suggested is as unsatisfactory as such parallels always are, the rise of the Chaldeans
to power, the effect of the personal dynamism of certain kings
among them, and the attempts of the central government to
combat the intruders all may be taken to correspond in some
way to the events that brought the Hammurapi dynasty to
power. Of course, it would be rash to liken Sin-muballiṭ to
Nabopolassar and Hammurapi to Nebuchadnezzar II, but one
can hardly close one's eyes to the similarities in events and
personalities.

Under Nabopolassar's son, Nebuchadnezzar II, Babylonia
invaded and took over the provinces of the Assyrian Empire
from the Mediterranean Sea to the Persian Gulf. Nebuchadnezzar was married to Amyitis, the daughter of the king of the
Medes, and thus Babylonia was protected by an alliance with
that kingdom. Quite in Assyrian style, the Babylonian king
began then to appear annually with his army to collect tribute
and to conquer and punish recalcitrant cities such as Jerusalem in
597 and 586 B.C. He repeatedly fought with the Egyptian army.

The last ruler of Babylonia, Nabonidus (555–539 B.C.), provided a somewhat queer "finis" to the independence of Babylonia (see above, p. 152). Cyrus moved into the capital without
encountering resistance and treated Nabonidus with his characteristic leniency toward defeated kings. This was the end of
Babylonian sovereignty, but that the spirit of the country was
not yet dead is brought home by the fact that two later pre-
tenders to the Babylonian throne took the magic name of
Nebuchadnezzar.[29]

An Essay on Assyrian History

A contrast dominates Assyrian history; the periods before and
after the Dark Age of Assyria, the eclipse under foreign domination, differ in essential respects. On the surface, these contrasts
are obvious: the early period lacks that spirit of military aggressiveness which is so characteristic of the later; in its place we
meet an efficiency in organizing overland trade relations and
internal commercial activities that is not conspicuous in the

documents of the period after the Dark Age. Moreover, a considerable body of alien influences can be found superimposed upon a native Assyrian tradition when the country emerges from the dark centuries. On the other side of the ledger is the preservation of the linguistic tradition, of specific social institutions such as the Assyrian concept of kingship and certain basic aspects of the religious life, e.g., the cult of Aššur, to mention only the obvious. By probing further one finds that but for some shreds of royal inscriptions and what little information we derive from the "Cappadocian" tablets on the economic role of the temple of the national god, we still know next to nothing of the civilization of the Assyria of the early kings. One also finds that the Assyrian formulation of the Mesopotamian civilization of the subsequent periods presents a multi-layered agglomeration of Hurrian and Babylonian influences interspersed with solid blocks of genuine Assyrian attitudes and concepts that had not died out. Not only is the structure of the civilization of Assyria far more complex than that of Babylonia, but it shows a different mood and direction altogether. Differences in habitat and in the nature and the intensity of alien influences alone cannot account for this divergence.

Assyrian history begins with a governor of the kings of the third dynasty of Ur residing in Assur. The most important royal personage of the Assyrian period before the Dark Age is Šamši-Adad I (ca. 1813–1781 B.C.), who was not of Assyrian extraction. The more than two hundred years before him are documented to a large extent by the three generations or more of Assyrian merchants attested as doing business in Anatolia (Kaniš, Boghazkeui, Alishar, and probably, but not directly attested, elsewhere in that region) and in the region of Kirkuk.[30] We are completely without information as to the developments and the circumstances which led to this commercial expansion; we know only that the conflicts resulting in the emergence of the Hittite kingdom, a novel political and military power in Anatolia, put an end to these activities either directly or by interrupting the freedom of communications that had maintained these traders for so long. The merchants' settlements quickly withered away. According to many indications, Šamši-Adad I was a foreign conqueror who seized Assur and attempted to create a territorial state in Upper Mesopotamia, which he seemed to have ruled from his palace in Šubat-Enlil.[31] He organized his realm as a conqueror who relies on his energetic followers to handle a population accustomed to a different way of life. He founded new settlements, brought in new agricultural methods, and attempted to raise the living standard of his subjects—but with his death, the empire quickly disintegrated. His son, Išme-Dagan, could hold on only to Assur, and soon that city too was lost and disappeared from the historical scene for many centuries. At that time Babylonian power was on the upswing under Hammurapi, and the entire region from the Persian Gulf to Ugarit was seething with political activity and criss-crossing tensions and relations. Although Assyria apparently disappeared under foreign domination, it is worthy of note that the official king list, which alone spans the gap in the historical tradition with its string of names, mentions six rulers who called themselves either Šamši-Adad (three kings) or Išme-Dagan (again three kings) during the four centuries that elapsed between the death of Šamši-Adad I and the accession of Aššur-uballiṭ, the first Assyrian ruler of stature. There exists no better indicator for the importance of a ruler and his political and military program than the choice of such names. It also indicates that the Assyrian political tradition was kept alive during this dark period, just as was the native dialect.

The victory of the Hittite king Šuppiluliuma (ca. 1380–1340 B.C.) sealed the doom of the Mitanni kingdom, of which Assyria seems to have been a vassal for a prolonged period. This victory brought Syria under Hittite influence and enabled Assyria to become independent and to fight for a place among the nations of the Amarna age and thereafter. The following centuries represent the formative period in which Assyria had to develop concepts of foreign policy for defensive as well as for offensive purposes.

As a result of the rising military might of successive Assyrian empires, these concepts determined, to a fateful extent, historical developments in the entire Near East. Assyrian foreign policy now had three fronts. The first was the perpetual line of conflict that separated Assyria from the mountain peoples. Attacks, extermination, or forcible resettling in new cities were combined with the building of strategic roads and fortresses, with varying success. At best, Assyria could obtain soldiers from the mountains and import horses needed for the cavalry that was becoming increasingly important militarily; but, for the most part, security from small-scale invasions was Assyria's typical gain on this front. Continuous contact in war and peace produced some sort of acculturation in the frontier zone which both facilitated colonization and created "nationalistic" satellite civilizations in the buffer region. The battle on that front was eventually lost when, after more than half a millennium, the Urartian buffer state which, on several previous occasions, had posed a dangerous threat to Assyrian holdings in Upper Syria collapsed. This event seems to have destroyed the restraints that held in check the Scythians, other people on the move, and invaders from the mountains.

It was equally difficult and eventually impossible for Assyria to keep the second front, that against Babylonia. The political situation that evolved between Assyria and Babylonia in the post-Amarna age, apparently gave a specially bitter turn to the relationship between the two states. It may have been, originally, Hittite intrigues that set Babylonia against Assyria, just as the Egyptians encouraged Assyria to exercise pressure against the Hittite kingdom, but this does not seem to explain in rational, i.e., political and economic, terms the aggressive attitude of Assyria toward her southern neighbor. At the first conquest of Babylon, the Assyrian king, Tukulti-Ninurta I (1243–1207 B.C.), carried off in triumph the statue of Marduk. This act may have begun the "Babylonization" of Assyria. We have already dealt with the ambivalent attitude of the Assyrians toward Babylonian civilization (see pp. 65 f.) and have pointed out (see p. 161) the gradual extension of Assyrian power down to the Persian Gulf, probably to establish a corridor between Elam and Babylonia. The eventual liberation of the entire region came about after the Medes destroyed the tottering Assyrian Empire.

On the third front, that against the west and toward the

Mediterranean Sea, the "Upper Sea" in Akkadian parlance, Assyria was relentlessly on the offensive. The drive toward the sea proceeded in several stages through a barrage of larger and smaller Aramaic principalities: Carchemish was reached by Adad-nirari I (1305–1274 B.C.) and again by his son Shalmaneser I (1273–1244 B.C.); Tiglath-Pileser I (1114–1076 B.C.) advanced as far as Palmyra (Tadmur); Shalmaneser III (858–824 B.C.) laid siege to Damascus, but only Tiglath-Pileser III (744–727 B.C.) was able to conquer it. This constant Assyrian advance posed an immediate threat to the small kingdoms of Judah and Israel so that all fluctuations in Assyrian military potential beginning with Tiglath-Pileser II (966–935) B.C., a contemporary of Solomon, are reflected in the political stability of Syria and Palestine and eventually in the content and mood of certain books of the Old Testament.[32]

By means of institutionalized annual campaigns, the Assyrian kings, beginning with Arik-den-ili, succeeded in building a series of more or less ephemeral empires. These often collapsed suddenly—usually at the death of the king—but were again and again reconquered, to be enlarged and more carefully organized. The ability to recuperate quickly and to gain added strength should be considered as characteristically Assyrian as the curious instability of the governmental structure. We have already suggested that the Assyrian Empire, when it functioned adequately, was based primarily on the integration of small administrative units, villages, manors, new cities settled with colonists, and garrisoned conquered cities. Military might was harshly used to maintain that income, consisting mainly of a steady supply of manpower, services, and staples, and to guard communications between these units and the administrative centers. Any weakening of these functions due to internal political stress (between, for example, the king and his high officials) endangered the lines of supply and interrupted the superimposed coherence. Eventually, the empire collapsed and fell into fragments governed by local interests. While this may explain the mechanics of the process, the perseverance of the Assyrian kings in reorganizing their hold over these units remains a problem. The few attempts made to offer explanations in terms of typical nineteenth-century concepts of economic and racial—and climatic—determinism are best passed over in silence. There seems to have existed within a small circle of Assyrians, particularly the natives of the town of Assur, the intense conviction that it was their duty to reimpose the lost coherence, to increase its effectiveness, and to enlarge its basis. This constant and hectic pressure for enlargement should not be considered the prime mover; it was often the consequence of the progressive exhaustion of the homeland and the old provinces. The need for expansion bespeaks solely the weakness of the system. The fact that the exhaustion of the country was constantly being remedied bespeaks ideological, i.e., religious roots, and we have to look for an institution that was able to survive all reverses. Such considerations lead us to the sanctuary of the god Aššur and to his king and priest and suggest rather strongly that originally, at least, the sanctuary had a claim to taxes and services on all groups that worshiped in the "Assyrian triangle." To collect what was due the sanctuary must have constituted an essential part of the duties of the priest—and king—a duty that gave economic stimulus and ideological impetus as well as religious sanction to his claims. This explanation, of course, rests solely on what little evidence is available and understandable (see pp. 99 f.). For the time being we assume that in that very complex and *sui generis* position of the sanctuary of Aššur and in the function of his priest lie the fountainhead of the purposeful and tenacious energy that kept Assyria alive and fighting to its very end.

It is not our task here to follow the ups and downs of Assyrian might. Suffice it to point out some of the culmination points and the changes that occurred in the course of its rise and fall. When Tukulti-Ninurta I reached out toward the Euphrates, the west, and toward the south, Babylon, the first high point was reached. The movements of Aramaic-speaking groups shattered the efforts of the Assyrian kings toward the organization of their realm. A short-lived resurgence was possible for Tiglath-Pileser (1114–1076 B.C.), and a new spirit of aggressiveness is evident in the inscriptions of Tukulti-Ninurta II (890–884 B.C.) and Aššurnaṣirpal II (883–859 B.C.). Aššurnaṣirpal II and his son Shalmaneser III pushed toward the Mediterranean coast in spite of the fierce resistance of the Aramaic states of the region (battle of Qarqar, 853 B.C.), receiving tribute from Israel and the Phoenician cities. Both kings battled the dangerous enemy to Assyrian ambitions which had arisen in the kingdom of Urartu; at the same time the Chaldean danger began to loom in southern Babylonia. Tiglath-Pileser III (744–727 B.C.) was another outstanding conqueror. He applied the age-old method of large-scale deportation of vanquished peoples and extended his influence even into Arabia; two queens of the Arabs sent tributes to him.[33] He carried the extension of Assyrian rule into Syria and Palestine, which aroused a new enemy of Assyria, Egypt. Sargon II spent nearly his entire reign reconquering the countries which Assyria had lost at the death of Tiglath-Pileser III, and his own death in the field again brought general defection and rebellion. Assyrian rule was far from being securely based; nearly every king had to fight the opposition of large sections of the ancient Near East. In fact, resistance against Assyria seems to have been growing steadily throughout the region. Sargon's son Sennacherib (704–681 B.C.) was murdered by his sons in an uprising, after a life spent in fighting enemies and rebels on all three fronts. Esarhaddon (680–669 B.C.), usurped the throne and had to pacify Assyria as well as to fight against new enemies from the mountains, the Scythians and Cimmerians. He was eventually compelled to attack and invade Egypt. At his death on the march to reconquer Egypt, the change of ruler occurred without trouble. Esarhaddon had attempted to solve the perennial "Babylonian problem" by making one son, Assurbanipal (668–627 B.C.), king of the realm and another son, Šamaš-šum-ukin, king of Babylon. After a respite of some sixteen years, during which Assurbanipal conducted only minor campaigns, Šamaš-šum-ukīn succeeded in forming a formidable alliance of all enemies of Assyrian rule from Elam to Israel. It took Assurbanipal four years of civil war to subdue the rebels and to destroy Babylon once again, only forty years after its systematic destruction by Sennacherib. Punitive campaigns followed against the Arabs and against Elam, ending with the sack of Susa. The sources for Assyrian history cease to speak to us for the last dozen years of Assurbanipal's rule. It seems that the empire had already begun to disintegrate during his lifetime, and it disappeared with appalling speed under the short-lived rule of his successor and son.[34] While Nabopolassar, representing a Babylonia turned aggressor, took Mesopotamia proper, the Medes under Cyaxares descended upon Assyria from the Iranian plateau, took Assur, the old capital, in 614 and eventually Nineveh (612 B.C.).

There remains a strange and heroic epilogue. Some segments of the Assyrian army held out for a time in Harran, waiting in vain for the help of Egypt. Egypt only now had begun to realize the danger of losing Assyria as an ally against Babylonians and Medes alike. There was even for a short time an Assyrian king in Harran, but the history of a mighty Assyria had run its course.

CHAPTER IV *Nah ist—und schwer zu fassen der Gott* (HÖLDERLIN)

WHY A "MESOPOTAMIAN RELIGION" SHOULD NOT BE WRITTEN

THE CARE AND FEEDING OF THE GODS

MESOPOTAMIAN "PSYCHOLOGY"

THE ARTS OF THE DIVINER

In lieu of a chapter on Mesopotamian religion, which the reader has every right to expect in a presentation of Mesopotamian civilization, I intend to deal here solely with three specific aspects that seem important and representative enough to be singled out for comment and for which suitable and sufficient documentary evidence is available. The reader should be forewarned that this section is predominantly negative in tone and outlook and be reminded that apparently well rounded and

171

pleasingly complete presentations of Mesopotamian religion in English, German, French, and Italian are by no means lacking—as a glance at the bibliographical footnote to this chapter will show.

Why a "Mesopotamian Religion" should not be written

As a general statement covering the underlying problem, let me present some of the reasons that have convinced me that a systematic presentation of Mesopotamian religion cannot and should not be written.

These reasons are of two orders—the nature of the available evidence, and the problem of comprehension across the barriers of conceptual conditioning.

Evidence for Mesopotamian religion—to use this complex term *grosso modo*—is archeological as well as textual. The archeological evidence consists of the remnants of buildings and structures that served cult purposes, such as shrines, temples, and temple towers, and of objects of worship, in the widest sense of this term, from images to charms.

The immense ruins of the temple towers of the large cities, especially of southern Mesopotamia, not only made Babylonia famous but, to a large extent, have helped to maintain the fame of its civilization. Yet even today—and this I offer as a warning—we do not know the purpose of these edifices. We have excavated these towers and studied their impressive construction from a technical point of view; we know their names and the Akkadian terms that refer to their parts; we know their histories—but we do not know what they were for. As for the temples, we are, of course, aware that the temple's cella harbored the image of the deity, that antecellas, propylea, courtyards, passageways, and major and minor gates were related in such a manner as to serve the personnel of the sanctuary and the worshipers that thronged into it periodically, and that they were built to display the power and wealth of the deity and to harbor and protect its staff and its treasures. The essential questions as to their meaning, questions that go beyond the description of what we see and beyond the—apparently—obvious functions of the several units that made up the sanctuary complex, cannot be answered. The monuments of a forgotten cult, of a cult we know only through a few written documents, can reveal, even if perfectly preserved, only a fraction, a dim reflection, of the cultic activities which they served. Their mechanics and functioning, and the meanings which motivated the enactments of the cult, remain removed from us as if pertaining to another dimension. A simple example will illustrate this point: if the monuments of Western Christianity were preserved for some distant and alien generation or a visitor from outer space, what could they possibly reveal of the essential tenets of that faith? The cathedrals, campaniles, the domes and baptisteries, towers, cloisters, and closes would remain mute; their iconography and carefully preserved skeletons—obvious objects of worship—would induce archeologists to propound fantastic theories to be harmonized with whatever conclusions they might draw from the general layout of the buildings, their structural and dimensional peculiarities, and their unbelievably complex and misleading display of decorations and statuary. It is legitimate, of course, to draw conclusions concerning the relationship between the deity and its worshipers and the deity and its characteristic abode when written sources, explicit about such problems, are available. But even then one cannot link in a convincing way the architectural forms or their functional uses to ideological situations and essential spiritual requirements, unless primary and derived forms are carefully separated distinguishing superstructures from basic and ideological concepts. Form, function, and creative elaboration, the three inevitable variables of each feature, have to be traced painstakingly in every instance. The most exacting examination of material remains of a civilization as dead and removed as that of Mesopotamia, with its written evidence so difficult of understanding, does not and cannot yield results that allow us better to understand the function and meaning of the buildings. And yet this effort is sometimes made, and a scholarly literature has evolved that derives conclusions from, for example, the emplacement of the image with regard to the axis of the cella and the doors, from the orientation of the sanctuary, and from other features of the buildings.[1]

Less obvious but by no means less misleading are conclusions based on a study of iconographic evidence. What can be conjectured from rare reliefs and from the few extant fragments of images and cheap replicas intended for private worship does not bring us much closer to the meaning of these images. These representations indicate that the Mesopotamians avoided non-anthropomorphic figures of the sort that are known from India and Egypt, but this is already evident from texts listing the gods and their epithets. Not even a perfectly preserved image could indicate to us what it meant for the priest and the pious, how it functioned as the center of the cult, what its *Sitz im Leben* was for the community. All that, however, we are able to obtain, to a limited degree, from written sources, as we intend to show in a later section of this chapter dealing with the images.

As to iconographic material—reliefs, seals, clay plaques— which is likely to shed light on Mesopotamian religion, one can think, *a priori*, of narrative representations meant to illustrate the story of a deity. Such representations do not seem to have had any important role in Mesopotamian religion. The world of the myth remains relegated to the level of literary creation throughout the entire known history of Mesopotamia. Only quite early and in marginal instances do representations seem to allude, secondarily, to written myths. The heroic or otherwise extraordinary achievements of the deity are not expressed as acts but rather are sublimated and symbolized. Non-narrative, non-objective formulations that bear in some way on the cult as enacted in the sanctuary are displayed in what we call heraldic symbols—often animal-shaped—which acquired sanctity through processes totally beyond our comprehension; furthermore, they may visualize—often in the form of weapons and other objects—formulaic statements concerning the deity and the world of man which are, today, out of our reach.

Before we turn to the documentary evidence bearing in general on the religious life of Mesopotamia, a material that in its riches seems to hold the promise of much information, let us raise a principal question; What conceivable light can a body of texts shed, synchronically, on the perplexing diversity of what we are wont to call "Mesopotamian religion," or, diachronically, on the entangled millennial history of this or that cult center or cult practice? To what extent and with what degree of reliability can written sources impart to us that accumulation of cult practices, of tradition-bound individual and group reactions to things considered sacred, to such existential facts as death, disease, and misfortune; in short, how truthfully do they reveal what is commonly meant by religion?

Three types of cuneiform texts (and some other text groups and passages) are important for an understanding of this and related problems. The three groups are prayers, mythological texts, and ritual texts. Let us now inquire into their usefulness for our purposes.

Prayers in Mesopotamian religious practice are always linked to concomitant rituals. These rituals are carefully described in a section at the end of the prayer which addresses either the praying person or the officiating priest—rather, "technician"—in order to regulate his movements and gestures as well as the nature of the sacrifice and the time and place it should be undertaken. Ritual activities and accompanying prayers are of like importance and constitute the religious act; to interpret the prayers without regard to the rituals in order to obtain insight into the religious concepts they may reflect distorts the testimony. Just as the acts and offerings of the prayer are fixed, with little variation and few departures from the small number of existing patterns, so the wording of the prayer exhibits a limited number of invocations, demands and complaints, and expressions of thanksgiving. Such material succeeds in conveying something of the mood and the emotional climate of Mesopotamian religion in spite of the repetitious diction of these prayers and their elaborate synonymy, but does not contain much information for our area of inquiry.

The prayers contain no indication of an emotion-charged preference for a specific central topic such as, for example, the individual in relation to spiritual or moral contexts of universal reach, the problem of death and survival, the problem of immediate contact with the divine, to mention here some *topoi* that might be expected to leave an imprint on the religious literature of a civilization as complex as the Mesopotamian.

One obtains the impression—confirmed by other indications—that the influence of religion on the individual, as well as on the community as a whole, was unimportant in Mesopotamia. No texts tell us that ritual requirements in any stringent way affected the individual's physiological appetites, his psychological preferences, or his attitude toward his possessions or his family. His body, his time, and his valuables were in no serious way affected by religious demands, and thus no conflict of loyalties arose to disturb or shake him. Death was accepted in a truly matter-of-fact way, and the participation of the individual in the cult of the city deity was restricted in the extreme; he was simply an onlooker in certain public ceremonies of rejoicing or communal mourning. He lived in a quite tepid religious climate within a framework of socio-economic rather than cultic co-ordinates. His expectations and apprehensions as well as his moral code revolved within the orbit of a small urban or rural society.

Two principal topics appear in the prayers, verbalizing the experience of the divine and expressing in a quasi-mythological way the self-experience of the worshiper. The latter is important and characteristic, and deserves further discussion (see pp. 198–206). The first is no less important, but it does not seem to represent an equally characteristic expression of Mesopotamian religious creativity.

On the metaphysical level, the deity in Mesopotamia is experienced as an awesome and fear-inspiring phenomenon endowed with a unique, unearthly, and terrifying luminosity. Luminosity is considered a divine attribute and is shared in varying degrees of intensity by all things considered divine and holy, hence also by the king himself.[2] An impressive array of specific terms is constantly used in prayers and other texts to express this particular experience of the divine. Semantically, the Akkadian terminology used in striving for adequate formulation is linked intimately to terror and to a dreaded luminosity. As such it corresponds—though not etymologically—to certain expressions of the religious vocabulary of the entire Semitic ancient Near East. There we find again the same groping for the expression of the *ineffabile* in terms of a fearful supernatural

radiance emanating from the deity. In Akkadian the terminology is especially varied, in connotations that we can hardly
fathom.

The second group of texts to be examined contains myths and
mythologically embellished literary works. To state at the
outset my objection to the direct and indiscriminate utilization
of such texts, I submit that their contents have already unduly
encroached upon our concept of Mesopotamian religion.³ All
these stories about the gods and their doings, about this world
of ours and how it came into being, these moralizing as well as
entertaining stories geared to emotional responses represent the
most obvious and cherished topics for the literary creativeness
of a civilization such as that of Mesopotamia. They form something like a fantastic screen, enticing as they are in their immediate appeal, seductive in their far-reaching likeness to stories
told all over the ancient Near East and around the Mediterranean, but still a screen which one must penetrate to reach the
hard core of evidence that bears directly on the forms of religious experience of Mesopotamian man. By now, classical
scholars have learned how to bypass the screen created by
mythology—and even how to utilize what information it may
convey—but in our field we fall victim all too easily to its lure,
searching for deep insights and voices from the dawn of history,
which they allegedly convey. These literary formulations are,
in my opinion, the work of Sumerian court poets and of Old
Babylonian scribes imitating them, bent on exploiting the
artistic possibilities of a new literary language—apart from the
"Alexandrinian" elaborations of the late period (the Nineveh
version of the Epic of Gilgamesh) and the Epic of Creation with
its "archaic" and learned artificialities. All these works which
we are wont to call mythological should be studied by the
literary critic rather than by the historian of religion. What they
contain are adaptations, for a late public, of mythological
elements, unsophisticated and often primitive, dim reflections
of stories that circulated among certain groups of the population
of Mesopotamia as an inheritance of a distant past. Though the
myths in cuneiform (Sumerian and Akkadian) are undoubtedly
the oldest in terms of written evidence, they are by no means

"older" than those one finds elsewhere and at any time.

The third group of texts are the numerous descriptions of specific rituals to be performed by priests and priestly technicians in the sanctuary. These texts prescribe, often in considerable detail, the individual acts of a ritual, the prayers and formulae to be recited (given either in full or cited by incipit), and the offerings and the sacrificial apparatus required; in short, they succeed in conveying something of the activities in a Mesopotamian temple. This is especially true for the Babylon text on the "New Year's ritual," which details the ceremonies performed in Esagila from the second to the fifth day of the festival (the balance is lost), giving an unparalleled insight into the nature of this celebration which is only mentioned by name in other texts ever since the pre-Sargonic period.[4] Such essential and characteristic ceremonies as the reading of the Epic of Creation, the archaic "scapegoat ritual," and the execution and burning of two costly decorated figurines of wood are known to us solely from this description of the New Year's festival in Babylon, not to mention the strange ritual scene in which the king participated (see p. 122). How old these rites were is impossible to determine, because archaic features in a ritual do not bear direct witness to its age or its history. In order to illustrate this point and as a warning against our inclination to assume for religious practices a uniformity, a stability, or, at best, a unilinear development (meant primarily to fill the gaps which occur in our attestation) that is not warranted, I offer here a description of one specific ritual.[5]

The most potent tool of the Mesopotamian exorciser's craft was a copper kettledrum covered with the hide of a black bull. A number of rituals concern themselves with the ceremonies needed to provide the drum with a new drumhead. The texts come from Assur, from the library of Assurbanipal in Nineveh, and from the Uruk of the Seleucid period, and their close similarities show that they belong to the stream of the tradition, i.e., they go back to late Old-Babylonian or early Middle-Babylonian prototypes. This is also borne out by the use of the same Sumerian prayers and other features of ritual, although upon closer scrutiny deep-seated differences are apparent in certain formulations and in a transposition of emphasis. Basically, the procedure is concerned with the ritual preparation of the bull to be slaughtered, the tanning of the skin, and the mounting of the hide on the drum, all performed with appropriate ceremonies, prayers, and offerings. As in many religious ceremonies, there is a critical point, a sensitive area in which the reality of the act reaches with shocking immediacy into the dimension of the sacred. Here, the clash occurs when the carefully chosen and ritually prepared animal that has been an object of worship—into which divine powers have been transferred by magic means—is killed in order to transfer its potency and sacredness to the kettledrum. At this point, the late (Seleucid) Uruk text differs tellingly from the Assur fragment. The late ritual prescribes in a matter-of-fact way that the bull has to be killed, its heart burned in front of the drum, the hide and the tendon from its right shoulder removed, and the body buried facing west as if it were that of a human being, wrapped in a red blanket and sprinkled with oil. The Assur text, which is about six to eight hundred years older, enacts this scene in a quite different mood. After the bull has been killed and its heart burned, the exorciser assumes the position of a mourner and utters a solemn lamentation for the slain god, rejecting responsibility for the act with the enigmatic formula, "The totality-of-the-gods has done this deed; I did not do it!" whereupon preparation of the skin proceeds as described in the later text. The Assur text ends with the short but revealing remark, "The chief exorciser does not eat of the meat of this bull." Thus while the bull is buried with formal ceremony in Uruk, it is used to provide food for the priests in the older text (from Assur) as in the case of any other sacrificial animal, although its killing was there considered a terrible deed that had to be atoned for. Do we have here different local customs due to substratum influences, or are the differences in the interpretation of the ritual due to internal developments? No answer can be offered, but we should realize that rituals, *per se*, attest only indirectly to the religious life of which they form a special part. Consider what kind of information the codifications of the church rituals (for example, the *rituale Romanum*) would impart two or more millennia from now to scholars from a completely different culture who would be able to understand them linguistically only in the very imperfect way in which we understand cuneiform texts.

Where then shall we search for source materials that hold the promise of shedding light on Mesopotamian religion? The rather substantial number of texts which describe exorcism and other magic rituals reveals not more than that the ubiquitous practices of sympathetic and analogic magic were well known and often applied in Mesopotamia. They were meant to inflict evil on an enemy, to ward off attacks on oneself, and to cleanse persons and objects from the evil consequences of ominous encounters by transferring the "miasma" to carriers that could be easily and effectively destroyed. Nothing in these texts impresses one as being characteristically and uniquely Mesopotamian, or likely to grant insight into this civilization. Lists of deities, organized in several ways, or lists that enumerate the sacred animals of certain gods,[6] and other scribal attempts to speculate about the gods and their relationship—in short, what may be termed theology—lack that essential quality of *Sitz im Leben* and therefore bespeak the nature of Mesopotamian scholarship rather than the nature of Mesopotamian religiosity. An undue amount of attention has been given to the peripheral regions of the religious life—mainly to the priestly speculations concerned with the relationship between the several gods of the pantheon in terms of power, function, achievement, and kinship.[7]

The religion or, rather, the variety of religions that are imbedded in the millennial growth and decay, reinterpretation and fossilization that make up Mesopotamian civilization belongs, as the previous discussion has suggested, to a type that can hardly be dealt with in terms of a survey or a structural evaluation—if one desires to avoid generalizations. As a typical representative of a traditional and non-historical, i.e., non-revealed, religion, Mesopotamian religion presents itself as a complex, multilayered accumulation. Local developments under political pressure, stunted growth, and mutations of uncertain origin at any given moment in time yield what may be considered a clastic conglomerate, to use a geological term. In a diachronic view, such formations are of undreamt of, protean complexity, defying analysis and even identification of their components. Extant religions of comparable structure are very rare; most of them have disappeared under the impact of the historical religions. One might possibly compare the polymorphic complexities of Hinduism, and, from the past, Egyptian religion which, with regard to period, endurance, and the nature of the evidence, could well serve as a standard if it were better known. One purely technical feature, writing material, makes it nearly impossible to compare seriously these two religions of the first great Near Eastern civilizations. In Mesopotamia we have an abundance of texts from many periods and regions, all written on practically imperishable clay, but from Egypt nearly all the evidence on papyrus and leather has been wiped out, compelling the Egyptologist to rely predominantly on inscriptions on stone connected with the mortuary cult.

One principle might be singled out as a possible help in approaching Mesopotamian religious life and practice. This is its social stratification, which is more or less in evidence in the texts of all periods and regions. If one separates the royal religion from that of the common man, and both from that of the priest, one could possibly obtain something approaching an unobstructed vista. A large part of what we assume to be Mesopotamian religion has meaning only in relation to royal personages—and for this reason distorts our concepts. The religion of the priest was centered primarily on the image and temple; it was concerned with the service the image required—not only in sacrifices but also in hymns of praise—and with the apotropaic functions of these images for the community. In a later section of this chapter we shall discuss in detail how the practices that originally concerned only the king influenced successively the court and even, presumably, the common man in a process of diffusion that is well known to the student of the sociology of religion. The common man, lastly, remains an unknown, the most important unknown element in Mesopotamian religion. We have already pointed out that religion's claims on the private individual were extremely limited in Mesopotamia;

prayers, fasts, mortification, and taboos were apparently imposed only on the king.

A similar situation prevails with respect to divine communications. The king could receive divine messages of certain types, but it was not considered acceptable for a private person to approach the deity through dreams and visions. Such practices on the part of private persons are recorded in our sources, but only quite rarely, mostly from outside the Babylonian area (from Mari) and, later, from Assyria—possibly under Western influence. In both regions, certain types of priests make oracular utterances, a practice which is never attested for the Mesopotamian heartland. As already indicated, it can be asserted that communal religious experiences such as participation in cyclical festivals and mourning ceremonies, enacted in Mesopotamia always through the intermediary of the sanctuary, represent the only admitted avenue of communication with the deity. Manifestations of religious feelings, as far as the common man is concerned, were ceremonial and formalized rather than intense and personal.

This brings us to the conceptual difficulties of understanding a polytheistic religion as far removed in time and background as that of Mesopotamia. It may be stressed that neither the number of deities worshiped nor the absence or presence of definite (and carefully worded) answers to the eternal and unanswerable questions of man separate decisively a polytheistic from a monotheistic religion. Rather, it seems to be the criterion of a plurality of intellectual and spiritual dimensions that sets off most of the higher polytheistic religions from the narrowness, the one-dimensional pressure of revealed religions. Instead of the symbol of the path and the gate, which may be taken to be the "kenning" of monotheism, a primeval, inevitable, and unchanging design or order (dharma, ṛta, šimtu) organizes the multifaceted structures of polytheistic religions. They are characterized by the absence of any centrality and by a deep-seated tolerance to shifting stresses, making possible the adaptability that such religions need to achieve their millennial lifespan. It is open to serious doubt whether we will ever be able to cross the gap caused by the difference in "dimensions."

This conceptual barrier, in fact, is more serious an impediment than the reason usually given, the lack of data and specific information. Even if more material were preserved, and that in an ideal distribution in content, period, and locale, no real insight would be forthcoming—only more problems. Western man seems to be both unable and, ultimately, unwilling to understand such religions except from the distorting angle of antiquarian interest and apologetic pretenses. For nearly a century he has tried to fathom these alien dimensions with the yardsticks of animistic theories, nature worship, stellar mythologies, vegetation cycles, pre-logical thought, and kindred panaceas, to conjure them by means of the abracadabra of mana, taboo, and orenda. And the results have been, at best, lifeless and bookish syntheses and smoothly written systematizations decked out in a mass of all-too-ingenious comparisons and parallels obtained by zigzagging over the globe and through the known history of man.

The Care and Feeding of the Gods

It is typical of the Assyriologist's culture-conditioned approach to Mesopotamian religion that the role and the function of the divine image in that civilization have never been considered important enough to merit a systematic scholarly investigation. Only as far as the few known statues of gods or goddesses and other representations of the deity have been the concern of the Mesopotamian archeologist or the historian of art have they received a modicum of the attention they deserve.[7a] This neglect offers us a characteristic instance of the influence of subconscious associations on the selection of research topics. The aversion to accepting images as genuine and adequate realizations of the divine presence, manifested in a traditional human form ("the Sun in human limb array'd") has played an important role in the religious development of the Western world. The roots of the attitude of rejection stem not only from the Judeo-Christian heritage but existed, earlier and independently, in Greek thought.[8] In fact, pro- and anti-iconic tendencies have often been instrumental in shaping trends and releasing events in the history of our culture. And they are far from dead now. They still linger in the scholar's ambivalent attitude toward "idols" and taint his approach to all alien religions. This influence manifests itself, mainly, by subtly shifting emphasis from less acceptable manifestations of a foreign religiosity to those which we can more readily comprehend, or, at least, consider more acceptable in Western terms.

An additional impediment has contributed toward the neglect of the problems dealing with the role of images in Mesopotamian religion. They neither appeal to our esthetic prejudices nor do they provoke special curiosity due to any fantastic and irrational shapes or because of the number and size of their preserved remnants.

The role of the image was central in the cult as well as in private worship, as the wide distribution of cheap replicas of such images shows.

Fundamentally, the deity was considered present in its image if it showed certain specific features and paraphernalia and was cared for in the appropriate manner, both established and sanctified by the tradition of the sanctuary. The god moved with the image when the latter was carried off—expressing thus his anger against his city or the entire country. Only on the mythological level were the deities thought to reside in cosmic localities; the poetic diction of hymns and prayers either cleverly uses (for artistic purposes) or disregards this differentiation, which only matters to us.

What we know about these images from fragments, representations, and clay replicas is supplemented by literary evidence. We learn that most images were made of precious wood and where not covered with garments were plated with gold; that they had the characteristic staring eyes made of precious stones inset in a naturalistic way and were clad in sumptuous garments of characteristic style, crowned with tiaras and adorned with pectorals. The garments were changed in special ceremonies according to ritual requirements. Images always had human shape and proportions; exceptions occur, but only rarely and only for minor (the bull-shaped son of Šamaš) and peripheral figures of the pantheon (snake god), or for special reasons (Janus head, bull ears). On the other hand, monstrous combinations of human and animal shapes did command worship from the second millennium B.C. in certain regions of Mesopotamia—that is, they were admitted as adequate representations of numinous experiences. On Assyrian seals and reliefs that show the king and the god Aššur we often find both represented in identical attire and pose; this and the subscript of the bronze reliefs mounted on the gate of the New Year's Chapel in Assur, "the figure of Aššur going to battle against Tiamat is that of Sennacherib," seem to suggest that the image of the national god could reflect that of his priest, the king, rather than represent the heroic ideal. Other images portray the dignity of old age or the attractiveness or grace and majesty of femininity. The identity of the image, which alone guaranteed its functioning as adequate manifestation of the deity, seems to have been established less by means of facial expression than by the details of paraphernalia and divine attire. Nabonidus' attempt to change the tiara of the Sun god ran into strong opposition not only on the part of the priests of the sanctuary but also of the assembly of the citizens of Sippar.[9] Only Assyrian kings state that they had images made according to their own ideas, that is, in a novel way. They repeatedly make such statements, and often the images mentioned are those of important deities.

There are two distinct levels on which the image played a role within the cult life of the sanctuary: it served as the focal point for sacrificial activities, and it was carried in the internal and outdoor ceremonies that related the city to the deity. We shall discuss these functions presently.

The fact that the image was man-made constitutes a problem. To one's mind readily come the tirades of Old Testament prophets, pouring the acid of their derision on the idol and its maker. There were two arguments: first, that the human form carefully given to the image—no other but human representations seem referred to here—does not enable it to move, act, see, or hear as a god should; second, that the manufacturer of such an object foolishly worships what he himself has just fashioned. We know from Mesopotamian and Egyptian sources that images were fashioned and repaired in special workshops in the temple; they had to undergo an elaborate and highly secret ritual of consecration to transform the lifeless matter into a receptacle of the divine presence. During these nocturnal ceremonies they were endowed with "life," their eyes and mouths were "opened" so that the images could see and eat, and they were subject to the "washing of the mouth," a ritual thought to impart special sanctity. Similar practices were common in Egypt, where the image of the deity was invested with traditional capacities by means of magic acts and formulas.[10] All the same, the manufacture of images of the gods seems to create a certain malaise in all the religions in which they have a cultic or sacred function, as is indicated by the frequent legends and pious tales that stress a miraculous origin for the more famous of these representations.

As for the relationship of the image to the sanctuary in which it resided on its pedestal in the cella, it paralleled in all essential aspects that of the king in relation to his palace and, ultimately, to his city. The god lived in the sanctuary with his family and was served in courtly fashion by his officials, who relied on craftsmen and workers to provide them with the material setting needed to fulfil their functions in a way that befitted the status of the god and his city. In its cella, the image received the visits of lesser gods and the prayers of supplicants, although it remains a moot question to what degree and under what circumstances it was accessible, if at all, to the common man. We even know of Assyrian kings who came as conquerors and were allowed to worship the image only from outside the sanctuary in which it was enthroned. This practice may have differed according to regional traditions and the status of the deity. The image was lifted above the level of human activities by means of a pedestal, encased in the recessed niche of the cella, and shielded from the outside world by one or more antecellas, but still visible from the courtyard through several co-axially arranged doorways and within the frame of the monumental gates. In such cases, the common man was probably not permitted to enter the sanctuary; wherever architectural presentation prevents such a vista, we are at a loss to know whether the worshipers were admitted to or excluded from the sanctuary.

Like the king, the image could be seen when it was carried in solemn procession through the spacious yards of the temple compound or through certain streets of the city. In this characteristic way the cultic relationship between the city and its god was formalized, manifesting itself at cyclical festivals when the pageantry of the temple was displayed for the citizenry, such as at the New Year's festival, which seems to have been connected with a collective outing of the city and its god to an out-of-town sanctuary, and at the god's own festival (isinni ili), which was held in a mood of communal jubilation.

The relationship of the temple to the city is expressed in the concern for the social, economic, and legal spheres of life, shown by the role of the temple with regard to oath and ordeals as a means of establishing the truth in legal controversies or of insuring the validity of agreements, as well as in the endeavors to maintain the standards of weights and to control the rate of interest.[10a] All this tends to disappear after the Old Babylonian period in the continuous and progressive isolation of the temple as an institution in Mesopotamia. We have already pointed out the shrinking of the economic strength—and hence political importance—of the temple that followed the rise of the palace organization headed by the king. The fame, glamor, and size of the late temples of Mesopotamia—especially those of Babylon and Uruk—must not make us overlook this state of affairs.

The social and economic structure of the temple as one of the two "great organizations" in Mesopotamia has already been discussed. The best products of the agricultural holdings, fields, and gardens, and of the immense herds of cattle, sheep, and goats, were sent to the temple, to be used in three different ways: as food served to the image as required by the daily ceremonial of the sanctuary, as income or rations for the administrators and workers who supervised and prepared the food for the god's table, and, third, to be either stored for future use or converted into export goods and exchanged for raw materials the organization was in need of. We intend to concentrate here on the first use, which presents itself as the very *raison d'être* of the entire institution.

According to an explicit and detailed text of the Seleucid period, the images in the temple of Uruk were served two meals per day.[11] The first and principal meal was brought in the morning when the temple opened, and the other was served at night, apparently immediately before the closing of the doors of the sanctuary. There is only one reference to a noonday meal. Each repast consisted of two courses, called "main" and "second." They seem to have been differentiated by the quantities served rather than by their contents. The ceremonial and the nature and number of the dishes offered at the divine repast show the same human dimensions that characterized Mesopotamian images. We do not find here the Gargantuan quantities of Egyptian sacrificial repasts, which should not be compared to the Mesopotamian, since their function was to provide food on certain occasions for the entire staff of the sanctuary and sometimes even for the city. Nor can we discover any parallels to Old Testament sacrificial practices, except for the institution of the *tāmīd*, which seems to be late and possibly related to Mesopotamian practices.[12] The Mesopotamian image was served its meals in a style and manner befitting a king. We have every right to assume that the ceremonial of these meals reveals to us the practices of the Babylonian court, which otherwise remain completely unknown to us. Another important feature of these meals is revealed by an Uruk text, as we shall see presently.

From the several extant descriptions of divine repasts, the following sequence can be reconstructed. First, a table was brought in and placed before the image, then water for washing was offered in a bowl. A number of liquid and semiliquid dishes in appropriate serving vessels were placed on the table in a prescribed arrangement, and containers with beverages were likewise set out. Next, specific cuts of meat were served as a main dish. Finally, fruit was brought in in what one of the texts takes the trouble to describe as a beautiful arrangement, thus adding an esthetic touch comparable to the Egyptian use of flowers on such occasions. Musicians performed, and the cella was fumigated. Fumigation is not to be considered a religious act but rather a table custom to dispel the odor of food. Eventually, the table was cleared and removed and water in a bowl again offered to the image for the cleansing of the fingers.

Having been presented to the image, the dishes from the god's meal were sent to the king for his consumption. Clearly, the food offered to the deity was considered blessed by contact with the divine and capable of transferring that blessing to the person who was to eat it. This person was always the king. One exception, on a tablet from Uruk, mentions that the crown prince—this was Belshazzar—enjoyed the royal privilege.[13] The importance of the royal right to eat the food from Marduk's table is illustrated by Sargon II's remark, "the citizens of Babylon [and] Borsippa, the temple personnel, the scholars, [and] the administrators of the country who [formerly] looked upon him [Merodach-Baladan] as their master now brought the leftovers of Bel [and] Sarpanitu [of Babylon and] Nabu [and] Tašmetu [of Borsippa] to me at Dur-Ladinni and asked me to enter Babylon." Other Assyrian kings, too, prided themselves on having received the "leftovers" from the sacrificial meal in recognition of their royal status.[14] The custom of sprinkling the water from the bowl "touched" by the image's fingers upon the king and the priests present at certain of these repasts bespeaks the same concept: the water is blessed, and its blessing can be conferred. It remains uncertain whether the practice of sending the food to the king involved all the dishes or only certain ones, and whether it was repeated every day or only on special occasions. Perhaps the top officials of the sanctuary enjoyed the same privilege.

The large amounts of food, beer, bread, and sweets, and the great number of animals brought in every day from the pastures to be slaughtered, were destined for distribution among the personnel of the sanctuary. A complicated cultic terminology was used to characterize the nature, destination, and other characteristics of the incoming deliveries. What was not earmarked for the table of the main deity, his consort, children, and servant gods was distributed, again in a traditionally fixed ratio, to administrators and craftsmen.

We know of this from two substantial groups of legal texts from the Old Babylonian and the Neo-Babylonian periods.[15] Essential differences exist between these groups of texts. The practice of insuring adequate and timely delivery for the sacrificial needs of the sanctuary by means of assigning pertinent responsibilities to specific collegia of administrators, priests, and craftsmen seems to be as old as our documentation about the functioning of the organization. The services of these bodies were remunerated in various ways which show a certain development worthy of note, although the evidence is meager and may be misleading. Originally—so my proposed reconstruction assumes—fields were set aside for the support of the collegium (shared by its members in a ratio unknown to us); later, there seems to have evolved the practice of distributing shares of the incoming staples, foods, and animals to those responsible for their quantity, quality, and delivery. In either way, such officials changed from functionaries of the sanctuaries into groups who held, collectively in private ownership, either real estate or income from the sanctuary in return for the obligation to make deliveries at certain times.[15a] The practice of holding fields to insure these deliveries disappeared as early as the Old Babylonian period, while the distribution of income derived from the temple became a permanent and essential feature of the entire organization. The collective nature of the group organization made it necessary to divide the annual income among the members according to months, days, and even fractions of days. The rationale of the distribution among the group is unknown in the early period but may have been established originally by the casting of lots. At any rate, each member held his share in private ownership and was entitled to sell it, to give it as a dowry, or to leave it to his heirs. Such prebends were lucrative, and obviously their holders had every interest in keeping the sanctuary functioning according to the old rites, which insured them perpetual income.

As for the bill of fare, the following observations hint at certain essential religious concepts and also illustrate secular customs rarely mentioned in literary texts. Special blessings were to be pronounced when barley was ground for the sacrificial bread, when the baker was kneading the dough and taking the loaves from the oven, and when animals were slaughtered. There were restrictions on the kind of food to be offered to various deities, such as the prohibition against offering birds to chthonian goddesses. Such prohibitions give us a glimpse into the mythological background of divine figures, of which we know little or nothing. Wine, which was imported, was used for offerings, as was done in secular life by the king and his court, and the practice of serving milk (in alabaster containers) only at the morning meal probably reflects general custom.

There is no trace in Mesopotamia of that *communio* between the deity and its worshipers that finds expression in the several forms of commensality observed in the sacrificial practices of circum-Mediterranean civilizations, as shown by the Old Testament in certain early instances and observed in Hittite and Greek customs. The Mesopotamian deity remained aloof—yet its partaking of the ceremonial repast gave religious sanction, political status, and economic stability to the entire temple organism, which circulated products from fields and pastures across the sacrificial table to those who were either, so to speak, shareholders of the institution or received rations from it. At any rate, the image is the heart and the hub of the entire system. His attendant worshipers lived from the god's table, but they did not sit down with him.

Looking at the sacrifice from the religious point of view, we find coming into focus another critical point in that circulatory system, the consumption of the sacrificial repast by the deity, the transubstantiation of the physical offerings into that source of strength and power the deity was thought to need for effective functioning. Exactly as, in the existence of the image, the critical point was its physical manufacture, so was the act of consumption of food in the sacrificial repast. It represents the central *mysterium* that provided the effective *ratio essendi* for the cult practice of the daily meals and all that it entailed in economic, social, and political respects.

Several distinct ceremonial patterns externalized the nature of the transcendental concepts that underlay the feeding of the Mesopotamian gods. Food was placed in front of the image, which was apparently assumed to consume it by merely looking at it, and beverages were poured out before it for the same purpose. A variant of this pattern consisted of presenting the offered food with a solemn ritual gesture, passing it in a swinging motion before the staring eyes of the image. Both methods are also known from Egyptian religious texts and from the Old Testament.[16] But this should not make us overlook the deep-seated differences between the West—represented best by the Old Testament—and Mesopotamia with regard to the concept of the sacrifice. The Old Testament concept is best expressed by the burning of the offered food, a practice which had the purpose of transforming it from one dimension—that of physical existence—into another, in which the food became assimilable by the deity through its scent.[17] Another difference that separates the sacrificial rituals in the two cultures is the "blood consciousness" of the West, its awareness of the magic power of blood, which is not paralleled in Mesopotamia.[18]

A peculiar ritual pattern was evolved in Mesopotamia to underline the mysterious nature of the assimilation of the food by the image. The table on which the food was placed as well as the image itself were surrounded by linen curtains set up for that period when the god was supposed to be eating what was offered to him. After the meal was done, the curtains were removed; they were drawn again when the god was to wash his fingers—every contact between the world of physical reality and the world of the god was hidden from human eyes. To analyze this strange practice, which is quite often mentioned in our texts, one must differentiate between form and function. The form is clearly understandable: the curtain that hid the eater from the onlooker reflected a custom at court, as is well attested for the Persian court. Although there is no direct evidence that the Babylonian king ate behind curtains, that it was a feature of ritual suggests that the ceremony had its origin in Babylonia; that this practice was adopted by the Achaemenid court indicates that it could well have been a Babylonian court custom taken over as such. Its function as a court custom was to ward off evil magic that might possibly be wrought upon the king while he was eating and drinking. The transfer from court to cult ritual changed the function of the curtains: rather than to ward off the evil eye, they were to hide the deity as he was partaking of the repast in a way which was not to be seen even by the priest.[18a]

In other respects, the image lived the life of a king. One Uruk ritual describes in detail the ceremonial enacted on the morning of the eighth day of the New Year's festival.[19] Early in the morning the image of the servant god Papsukkal descends into the courtyard and takes up a position in front of the image of Anu; then, in groups according to rank, other images come from their cellas and take up their correct positions. A bowl of water is offered to Anu and his spouse for their morning toilette, and meat is served on a golden platter, first to Anu, then to the other images standing in the courtyard. Afterward, Papsukkal leads Anu ceremoniously to further activities. These *salutationes matutinae* reappear in the court ceremonials of Byzantium and Europe (the *lever du roi*) and hence must likewise have been practiced at the Babylonian court.[20]

There took place within the temple compound other cultic events—nocturnal ceremonies and marriage festivals in which the deity met his spouse. Other cultic occasions brought the images beyond the close into the processional road. From a Neo-Assyrian letter we learn that the image of Nabu went into the game park to hunt, which demonstrates charmingly how the life of the image in Assyria was patterned after that of the king.

Clearly, the preceding remarks cannot claim to characterize the cultic activities pertaining to all the temples of Mesopotamia. We have every reason to assume important differences in the scope, the nature, and the scale of these activities in each sanctuary. We know, from Sippar of the Neo-Babylonian period, that the horses of the sun god were attached to his chariot with a gold-studded harness, that they drank water from buckets made of precious metal, and that grass was cut for them with golden sickles.[21] And we know that prostitutes were permitted to live near the temple of Ištar in Uruk. These are only two indications of the varying practices in evidence in these temples. To characterize this variety, and to counteract the impression of uniformity, we terminate this section with a succinct and typologically oriented characterization of the pantheon.

Several circumstances contributed toward the complexity and size of the Mesopotamian pantheon. Apart from the basic dichotomy between Sumerian and Akkadian gods—not to speak of the composite substratum from which both the Sumerians and Akkadians borrowed to an undetermined extent—we have to deal with a millennial development which has given us layers upon layers of divine names. Although fusions created a number of hybrid figures, the names of the constituent deities were nevertheless preserved, yielding a plethora of local and minor deities despite the obvious identity or duplication of many of the names. A large number of them were preserved only in learned and theological texts such as lists of gods of two to three thousand names, and others were restricted to the countless personal names in and around Mesopotamia that contain the name of a deity.[22] The ever-changing preferences in personal names of this type mirror the fluctuations of the popularity of the individual deities, expose the gap between official and popular religion, and—if carefully studied—might help us to analyze the social texture of a given society and environment.

It is extremely difficult to penetrate to the individuality of the divine figures. The Sumerian custom of speaking of the deity as the lord or lady of the city rather than of mentioning it by name (only rarely was such an individualization of the city's patron and ruler admitted) presents a serious obstacle. The formalization of the god-man attitude and the narrow range of the hymnical terminology, which favored an extensive interchange of epithets among deities, blurs still more the individuality of all but the most outstanding and characteristic divine figures.[23] Seen typologically, they can be classified easily, though superficially, as old and young gods and astral deities, with a few unique and outstanding figures who remain unclassifiable. Old gods were such once-powerful deities as Anu the Sumerian sky god, and a Sumerianized substrate god Enlil (Illil), both of whom seem to have become more and more removed from the world of man and more misanthropic in character in the course of history. Both have a chthonian past, as is evident from Anu's relation to the world of demons and that of Enlil's temple, "Mountain House," in Nippur to the nether world. Only a few of their individual traits remain—Anu's relation to Ištar and to Uruk, Enlil's to the heroic Ninurta, and his position as the ruler of the gods. Even Marduk is to be classified among the old gods, because his original position as a young god, heroic and dynamic, although emphasized in late mythological texts, was replaced in the course of time (second half of the second millennium) by that of supreme god, because of the dominance of his city, Babylon. Ninurta, as Enlil's son, was a typical young god, without a city but appearing as a central figure in a cycle of myths that extol his prowess. Nabu, although said to be a son of Marduk, did not follow the same pattern. Only in the first millennium did he become the god of Borsippa, sister settlement of Babylon, and (replacing Nisaba) the patron deity of scribes. His popularity increased in the late period, but we cannot explain why this was so. Among the old gods of the pantheon, Ea (corresponding to Sumerian En.ki) occupied a special position. Originally the local deity of the southernmost city, Eridu, he shared, according to later speculation, the rule of the cosmos with Anu and Enlil inasmuch as his realm was the waters surrounding the world and those below it. Apart from having been the patron god of exorcists, Ea was a master craftsman, patron of all the arts and crafts, and endowed with a wisdom and cunning that myths and stories do not tire of extolling. He must have been thought of in certain respects as a "culture hero" until the late period, since an Ea figure seems to have been the prototype of the culture hero Oannes mentioned by Berossos.[24]

The foremost astral deities were, of course, Šamaš (Sumerian Utu) and Sin (originally Su'en, Sumerian Nanna), the sun god and the moon god. Each had two major centers in Mesopotamia, Šamaš in Larsa and in Sippar, where his temples were called "White House," and Sin in Ur and in far-off Harran. Both maintained their popularity throughout the entire history of Mesopotamian civilization, although Šamaš had a unique position. Not only was he the sun god but the judge of heaven and earth, and in this capacity he was concerned with the protection of the poor and the wronged and gave oracles intended to guide and protect mankind. He is not involved in crude mythological situations; even in myths he acts as judge and arbiter.

The figure of the storm god, Adad, stands apart. He had no center of his own in the alluvial plains but was worshiped under many, mostly foreign, names from Assyria westward to the Mediterranean and in the adjacent regions to the north and the south by Semites, Hittites, and Hurrians alike. For unknown reasons, Adad in later periods became linked to Šamaš in the role of the oracle-giver.[24a]

Aššur, as the city god of the capital of Assyria of the same name, was unique in many respects among the parochial gods of Mesopotamia. When his city rose to become the foremost political power in the ancient Near East, theologians provided him with all the trappings of the lord of the universe, creator and organizer of the cosmos, and father of the gods. Aššur's extraordinary relation to his priest, the king of Assyria, and the unique position of the latter, which we have mentioned (see p. 99), all point toward the composite nature of the background of this god. Quite in style for a deity of the region, Aššur was associated with a mountain sacred to him, Mt. Epih.

Among the lesser gods, Nergal and Tammuz (Dumuzi) should be mentioned as atypical. The former was not only the city god of Cutha in central Babylonia, but also considered, together with his spouse Ereškigal, "lady of the underworld," as the ruler of the realm of the dead and source of plague. Tammuz represents a divine figure *sui generis*—a god whose death and disappearance it was customary to mourn in solemn lamentations in certain strata of the early Mesopotamian population. His fate is the topic of an important body of Sumerian religious texts, and it remains a moot though often discussed point in what respect he should or can be related to certain divinities of later Semitic religions.[25]

The goddesses of the pantheon are either mother goddesses, such as Baba and Mama, or divine consorts without specific characterization, such as Sarpanitu and Tašmetu (probably foreign and Akkadianized), or among the figures associated with death and the nether world, like Ereškigal, its queen, or Gula, known as the Great Lady Physician, but originally—as her animal, the dog, indicates—a goddess of death. Ištar (Sumerianized substratum-name Innin and related designations) alone stands out, because of the dichotomy of her nature, associated with the planet Venus (as morning and evening star) and with divine qualities extremely difficult to characterize. This complex embraces the functions of Ištar as a battle-loving, armed goddess, who gives victory to the king she loves, at the same time it links her as driving force, protectress, and personification of sexual power in all its aspects. In all these roles she appears in Mesopotamian myths as well as in corresponding texts from the west, from Anatolia to Egypt, under similar or foreign names. In Mesopotamia her city was Uruk, where first she is reported as daughter, later as spouse, of Anu.

Remarkably little foreign influence can be detected in the Mesopotamian pantheon. There are occasional references to gods brought in by conquerors, such as Dagan, Amurru, Šumaliya, Šuriaš, and "Aramean Ištar," and a number of instances are known of foreign deities referred to under Sumerian and Akkadian names, just as Mesopotamian deities appear in peripheral and adjacent regions under foreign names (Tešup, Šauška).

One should draw attention, if only in passing, to those non-anthropomorphic objects of worship in which the presence of a specific deity was recognized. These are the symbols that commanded worship and sacrifice, substituting under certain circumstances for the traditional image or accompanying it. These symbols represent either cosmic phenomena, such as the sun disk, the crescent, and the eight-pointed star of Ištar, or are ceremonial weapons of specific shapes, such as lion-headed clubs and ram-headed staffs, or implements of daily life, such as the spade of Marduk, the stylus of Nabu, the plow, the lamp. Accompanying animals become such symbols: the dog of Gula, and the composite monsters mušhuššu (lion-snake-eagle) and suhurmašû (goat-fish), representing respectively Marduk and Ea. The bull standing for Adad belongs to a different religious level. Among the symbols is a small group of unidentified objects whose exact function and relationship to the images remain to be investigated.[26]

Mesopotamian "Psychology"

The relationship of the individual to the deity represents a crucial area of inquiry for any investigation of religious concepts. We have already seen (p. 75) that this relationship in Mesopotamia is conceived of, on a social level, as that between master and slave, or parent and child, although the latter is referred to rarely and only in certain contexts. The deity is sometimes felt to be the leader, patron, or protector of groups, be these families or professional and religious associations—but this again is rare and restricted to certain periods and situations.

To an overwhelming extent, the personal names from Mesopotamia, Sumerian and Akkadian alike, are theophorous, i.e., they relate the child or his parents to a specific deity, mostly in expressions of thanks and praise. Normally the name of a god forms part of a masculine name, the name of a goddess part of a feminine name. Because the deity named is not necessarily the same to appear in the names of the parents or the siblings of the child, we are not able to establish what consideration—pious or whatever—determined the selection. We remain equally in the dark with respect to the reason why, in the inscriptions on personal seals that date from the Old and Middle Babylonian periods giving the name and the parentage of the owner and his profession, he is, in addition, characterized as the servant (slave or slave girl) of a specific deity although not necessarily the one whose name he bears. Here, too, we do not know the basis of the association between the deity and the man or its consequences, cultic or otherwise. Clearly, reference is made here to an essential aspect of the god-man relationship so self-evident, so much taken for granted, that we can hardly hope to find any explanation to it in our text material.

Since the avenues of approach pointed out so far either fail to yield clear insight or cannot offer us sufficient material to elucidate the relationship between man and deity, I would like to present a new approach based on a study of the phraseology of prayer literature.

When one searches through the prayers to establish the topical range of the entreaties addressed to the deity, one discovers a substantial set of requests, each alluding to a specific and very personal experience. This experience is characterized by a feeling of strength and security that is taken to result from the immediate presence of a supernatural power. The experience is consistently described in terms of a pious and god-fearing individual surrounded and protected by one or more supernatural beings charged with that specific function. Thus, when feeling at his best, in full vigor, enjoying economic prosperity and spiritual peace, a man ascribes this enviable state of body and mind to the presence of supernatural powers that either fill his body or guard him. Conversely, a man readily blames his misfortunes, illnesses, and failures on the absence of such protection. Prayers and similar texts are filled with passages in which the sufferer demands from the great gods the assurance that these *daimons* will be near him, take care of him, and protect him from his enemies—men, sorcerers, and demons alike—to guarantee him physical well-being, success, and luck in all his dealings.

The prayers refer to these powers in mythological terms, i.e., they distinguish them by name, and assign specific functions to each. Thus, when only one such power is referred to, it is called *ilu* (god), but at times it is called *lamassu*, for which one may use—as a kenning rather than as a translation—the term angel. *Ilu* is masculine, *lamassu* is feminine. Both appear frequently with companion spirits, *ilu* with *ištaru* (goddess), *lamassu* with *šēdu*, who is masculine. At times, all four spirits are said to, or are requested to, protect their ward.

All this can readily be characterized as the expression of a psychological experience in mythological terms. To the student of comparative religion or the cultural anthropologist, the several "protective spirits" (to use the term customary in Assyriological literature) represent but another example of the widespread concept of multiple and external souls. The four protective "spirits" in Mesopotamia are individualized and mythologized carriers of certain specific psychological aspects of one basic phenomenon, the realization of the self, the personality, as it relates the ego to the outside world and, at the same time, separates one from the other. In order to establish the specific functions and basic meanings of the "souls" called *ilu*, *ištaru*, *lamassu*, and *šēdu*, it is necessary to discuss that terminology. These terms, seen philologically, are difficult to define, being fraught with connotations that bespeak their semantic instability and involved prehistory. The main purpose of this necessarily cursory discussion of the designations of the souls is to bring home to the reader the complex nature of the concept.[26a]

Two characteristics unite all four designations: they all have luck as an important shade of their range of meanings, and they all have some relationship to the world of the demons and the dead. To experience a lucky stroke, to escape a danger, to have an easy and complete success, is expressed in Akkadian by saying that such a person has a "spirit," i.e., an *ilu*, *ištaru*, *lamassu*, or *šēdu*. Most frequently mentioned in such assertions is *ilu*; one who has an *ilu* is what the Greeks term *eudaimon* (happy, lit. "having a good *daimon*") and is called *ilānû*, literally, "one who has an *ilu*," i.e., one who is lucky. It is more difficult to establish to what aspect of the experience of the ego the term *lamassu* refers. We know of several occurrences of that word in which it clearly refers to a likeness, a statue, and this may be taken as an indication that *lamassu* personifies in the guise of an external manifestation those essential aspects of individuality which comprise an assemblage of distinct and specific corporeal features. Through them the carrier of such features becomes an individual. In this function *lamassu* may be compared to the Greek *eidolon* (the term refers to a statue as well as to an apparition carrying the likeness of an individual) or to the term *angelos* in the specific sense in which that word is found in the New Testament (Acts 12:15). There, the "angel" of Petrus appears looking and speaking like him. The use of *lamassu* in Old Babylonian feminine personal names actually suggests the meaning "angel." The concept of an external soul manifested in the likeness of the individual reminds one of the Egyptian concept of the *ka*. In the present context, this comparison should be taken solely as an indication that the concept of multiple and external souls was also known in the ancient Near East outside Mesopotamia just as we have certain parallels to it in classical civilizations. These civilizations formulate the same experience differently, stressing certain aspects and functions and adding diverse elaborations which shift emphasis decisively. Nevertheless, such comparisons, bound as they are to be inexact, do contribute toward a better understanding of these old and tenacious creations of a doctrine of the soul—a non-Western "psychology."

The protective spirit called *šēdu* is linked as a male counterpart to *lamassu*. The term *šēdu* recurs in the Old Testament where it is used to refer to idols, while the Septuagint, interestingly enough, renders it by *daimon*. In Akkadian, too, *šēdu* is connected with the spirits of the dead. A demonic background is also evident for the soul manifestations *ilu* and *lamassu*, the latter being possibly related to the dangerous female demon Lamaštu. The function of *šēdu* may well have been to represent the vitality of the individual, his sexual potency. This is suggested by the fact that the Akkadian word *baštu*, which clearly has this specific meaning, at times replaces the designation *šēdu*. The Sumerian correspondence a l a d of the Akkadian *šēdu* corroborates such an interpretation: the term a l a d seems to be derived from the Semitic root meaning "to procreate" and thus invites comparison with the Latin term of similar etymological background which designates an external soul manifestation of comparable function: *genius*.[27]

It is much more difficult to determine the nature and function of the manifestation called *ištaru*, "goddess," corresponding to *ilu*, "god." I propose to take as a starting point for the short excursus needed to obtain some insight into *ištaru* the term *šimtu* which one finds at times, in contexts where one would expect *ištaru* in its meaning "protective goddess." Although it will lead us from our path, the investigation of the crucial and interesting *šimtu* can eventually help to suggest an interpretation for *ištaru* as the designation of an external manifestation of the soul.

Customarily, *šimtu* is translated by the Assyriologist as "destiny" or "fate," a translation that is inexact and misleading, since the two English words are endowed with connotations alien to the Akkadian term.[28] Quite generally speaking, *šimtu* denotes a disposition originating from an agency endowed with power to act and to dispose, such as the deity, the king, or any individual may do, acting under specific conditions and for specific purposes. Such a disposition confers in a mysterious way privileges, executive power, rights, and—when originating from a deity—even qualities (attributes), upon other gods, persons, and objects, deriving its effectiveness solely from the power and the right of disposition inherent in the acting agency. Thus the gods endow the king with strength, superior intelligence, good health, and success; thus the king assigns income and offerings to the sanctuaries, pastures to cities, and executive power to the administrators of his realm; and thus the private citizen disposes of his property to his sons and heirs. All this is done by making a *šimtu* (*šimta šâmu*). In certain religious contexts, however, the establishing of the *šimtu* refers typically to the specific act through which each man is allotted—evidently at birth, although this is nowhere stated explicitly—an individual and definite share of fortune and misfortune. This share determines the entire direction and temper of his life. Consequently, the length of his days and the nature and sequence of the events that are allotted to the individual are thought of as being determined by an act of an unnamed power that has established his *šimtu*. It is in the nature of the *šimtu*, the individual "share," that its realization is a necessity, not a possibility. A passage in the inscriptions of the king Aššurnaṣirpal II (883–859 B.C.) brings this out. The king says, after a succinct enumeration of his military achievements, "These are the *šimtu* pronounced [for me] by the great gods who made them come to realization as my own *šimtu*."[29] He speaks of his conquests and victories as part of his congenital "share," as much as is his entire life and, ultimately, his death. *Šimtu* thus unites in one term the two dimensions of human existence: personality as an endowment and death as a fulfilment, in a way which the translations "fate" or "destiny" fail to render adequately. It may perhaps help to turn to two Greek terms in order to better elucidate the Mesopotamian *šimtu* concept. These terms are *moira* and *physis*, each covering in part an essential aspect of *šimtu*. Where Hesiod, for example, says that the *moira* of Aphrodite is "love," referring thus to her divine function, power, and competence, we have the Akkadian Epic of Creation speaking of the primordial times "before the gods were given names and their respective *šimtu* [i.e., functions and assigned duties] were established." The incident of Hermes explaining to Odysseus the *physis* of the plant Moly—its particular nature and specific qualities—can be readily compared to the action of the god Ninurta in a Sumerian literary work, who establishes the *šimtu* (Sumerian n a m) of all precious stones by pronouncing upon each of them a sentence that enumerates—and thereby confers upon it—its characteristic qualities, the "attributes" determining its nature.[30] The *šimtu*, then, is the "nature" of these stones, and it is revealing that Latin *natura* renders Greek *physis*. But *šimtu* means, moreover, natural death as the consumption of one's share of life and luck. Fittingly enough, the announcer of death is called Namtar, the Sumerian equivalent of *šimtu* (Namtar, the "allotted n a m"). The final experience of man is here mythologized into the demonic doorkeeper of the nether world. To die means to encounter fate, one's own *šimtu*. There are two parallels to this interpretation of death: the pre-Islamic *Manaya* ("fate") was thought to be lying in wait for the encounter that spells death for the individual, and Greek sources speak of the demon *ker* who, invisible, follows everyone from birth to the moment of death, when it manifests itself for the first and last time, announcing, bringing, death.

We are dealing here with an existential contradiction. In every organized religion of ancient Near Eastern extraction there is posited a world order in which divine wisdom in foresighted planning, guided by divine justice in meting out punishment and rewards in terms of success or failure, determines the nature of the happenings that the individual encounters. There is no room here for the caprices of luck nor for the rigidity of destiny, and moreover, no possibility of provoking or changing events by magic means. In marked contrast, what we have said so far about *šimtu* and what we are to point out presently concerning kindred concepts, betrays the existence in the ancient

Near East, of a strong undercurrent which bespeaks the persistence of an age-old, pre-deistic, deterministic concept of life. It is far from homogeneous—concepts of this kind and age always show a variety of formulations—but it is tenacious, although often adapted to their purposes by zealous priests through superficial "theologizing." Let us survey Mesopotamia for such formulations. Here we have the *šimtu* referring to a supernatural act assigning attributes and properties to human beings, even to objects; and we also have the term *isqu*, which means literally "lot" and must refer—although this is nowhere explicitly stated—to the use of lots to determine fate. Just like *šimtu*, *isqu* has a wide semantic range, extending from lot, fortune, fate, to nature, quality, and even office (the Greek *kleros*). Other texts, mostly literary, use the term *uṣurtu* (Sumerian g i š . ḫ u r), which means drawing or plan, design, apparently referring to some kind of divinely predetermined—outlined, even "blueprinted"—course of events that determines all happenings. Again, we lack all detailed information; the term is used as if everyone were familiar with the underlying concept. We have some, but not clear, evidence for still another type of mythological determinism, from prayers and similar texts. A pair of supernatural beings, demons of some kind, are said to accompany man—quite different from the "protective spirits" discussed earlier. Their telltale names reveal their functions: one is called *mukīl rēš damiqti*, or *rābiṣ damiqti*, "he who offers good things," or "good demon"; the other is *mukīl rēš lemutti* or *rābiṣ lemutti* "he who offers misfortune," or "evil demon." Like their Greek counterparts, which produce the *eudaimonia* and *kakodaimonia*, they seem to have been in charge of the successes and failures of life, although we know nothing more of them than their names. Finally, one should point out that the imagery of deterministic thought is not less varied in the Old Testament; we have there several specific terms for "lot," "luck," and "share" and also the *topos* concerning man's portion served to him in a cup (Psalms 11:6, 16:5). A similar reference can be found in Greek literature—suffice it to mention here the scales of Zeus and his mixing of the "good and bad things" from the two jars (Iliad 24:527).

In view of what has been propounded above, I suggest that it was the function of the manifestation called *ištaru* and, sometimes, *šimtu*, to be the mythological, personified representation and the carrier of the *šimtu* of the individual that was to materialize in his "history" from his birth to his death. If this connection between *ištaru* and *šimtu* seems too feeble or too far-fetched, the proposed interpretation of *ištaru* as "fate" (to resort to a simplification) can be demonstrated in a different but equally interesting way.

From Sumerian and early Old Babylonian royal inscriptions we know that the relationship between the individual and his protective spirits corresponds to the relationship of the king to certain deities of the pantheon (often to Ištar) whom he considers especially charged with his personal protection. It remains a moot question whether we are to see in the formulation of the royal texts a secondary development induced by the wish to show the special position of the king or whether the later formulation, that of the prayers, represents another example of a transfer of religious concepts from the king to his subjects. Without offering any argumentation that would go beyond the aims of this section, I would like to state that the first possibility seems to me, at this moment, to be the more likely one. In the passages that refer to the king's relationship to Ištar, the goddess becomes the carrier, the fountainhead, of his power and prestige. In that role, Ištar is what the Greeks called the *tyche* of the king and the Romans the *fortuna imperatoris* (or *fortuna regia*). In Syriac, this Latin term is represented by *gadda de malkā*, "the luck of the king," an expression which provokes comparison with *ištaru* and *šimtu*.[31] In Mesopotamia, the kings speak of their relationship to Ištar, their *fortuna* (*tyche*, luck), in terms of human relations outside familial obligations but warranted to endure: Eannatum of Lagaš is loved by Innin, Sargon of Akkad by Ištar, and the Assyrian kings up to Esarhaddon intimate—as does Hattušili III—that their rise to power was due to Ištar's personal intervention. In such instances, Ištar is clearly the *Aphrodite nikephoros*, which again supports our explanation that the external manifestation called *ištaru* was the carrier of the *šimtu* of the individual. Consequently, we may see in the *ilu* some kind of spiritual endowment which is difficult to define but may well allude to the divine element in man; in *ištaru*, his fate; in *lamassu*, his individual characteristics; and in *šēdu*, his *élan vital*. All four external manifestations are intended to render the experience of the ego.

There is one final point to be made. The supernatural radiance which the Mesopotamian king shared with the gods and which represents the manifest expression of his unique status among men is called in Akkadian, as we have seen, *melammû*. In Old Persian *melammû* corresponds to *xvarena*, which in turn is represented in contemporary Aramaic texts by *gadia*, i.e., "luck." Following such converging developments—in which the concept of the divine nature of kingship and that of predetermined royal success meet—we obtain another glimpse into the complex and difficult nature of most of the religious *topoi* on which we have touched in this chapter.

The Arts of the Diviner

The importance of divination in Mesopotamian civilization is emphasized by the large number of omen collections and related cuneiform texts that have been preserved. These texts range in time from the late (post-Hammurapi) Old Babylonian period up to the time of the Seleucid kings, offering an abundance of material concerning various techniques of divination. Moreover, allusions to divination practices abound in historical and religious literature. There can be little doubt that Akkadian divination—all extant texts are written in that language—was considered a major intellectual achievement in Mesopotamia and surrounding countries.[31a] These texts were copied in Susa, the capital of Elam; in Nuzi; in Hattuša, the capital of the Hittites; and in such far-off places as Qatna and Hazor in Syria and Palestine. They were copied by local scribes trained in the writing and the languages of Mesopotamia; and translated into Elamite, Hittite, and Hurrian.[32] The disappearance of Mesopotamian civilization and its languages and system of writing did not impede the spread of certain methods of divination toward Palestine and Egypt—and from there into Europe. Influence toward the East is more difficult to evaluate, since the situation is more complex there. First, one has to realize that extispicy, i.e., prediction of the future from the appearances, deformation, and other peculiarities of the viscera of animals, has been practiced in China and Southeast Asia since time immemorial. In the West, the Etruscan art of divination (mainly haruspicy) is isolated and may have originated due to some contact with or stimulus from Asia Minor.[33] Then, one has to consider the fact that written evidence coming from the region east of Mesopotamia is late, in most instances later than the disappearance of Mesopotamian civilization. Mesopotamian astronomy of the first millennium B.C. is well known to have influenced India, but even if we cannot document Mesopotamian influence upon Eastern methods of divination, diffusion during earlier periods remains a distinct possibility. Through the medium of Islam which often drew on the practices of the ancient Near East via Hellenistic intermediaries, Mesopotamian divination methods—mainly astrology and the interpretation of dreams—experienced a renaissance in and around Mesopotamia long after the disappearance of the civilization in which they originated.

I plan to treat the topic of divination under three main headings: the nature and history of divination techniques, the text material as source of information, and the significance of divination, its *Sitz im Leben*.

Basically, divination represents a technique of communication with the supernatural forces that are supposed to shape the history of the individual as well as that of the group. It presupposes the belief that these powers are able and, at times, willing to communicate their intentions and that they are interested in the well-being of the individual or the group—in other words, that if evil is predicted or threatened, it can be averted through appropriate means. Contact or communication with these powers can be established in several ways. The deity can either answer questions put to it or of its own accord attempt to communicate in whatever medium is acceptable. Two-way communication requires a special technique; in fact, two techniques are known in Mesopotamia: operational and magical. In both instances the answer comes forth in two possible manners: one is binary, that is, a yes-or-no answer; the other is based on a code accepted by both the deity and the diviner.

The fact that Mesopotamian divination underwent a complex historical development should not be overlooked. Not only did emphasis and preferences change in the course of time, but the methods also differed from time to time and region to region. Equally important is a diversity of methods based on social status. There were practices for the king, others to which the poor resorted, native practices, and those that were imported.

Before we discuss these practices, the techniques must be characterized briefly. In operational divination, the diviner offers the deity the opportunity of directly affecting an object activated by the diviner, as is the case in the casting of lots, in the pouring of oil into water, or in producing smoke from a censer.[33a] The deity then manipulates the lots and affects the spreading of oil and the shape of the smoke in order to communicate. In what we have called magical technique, the deity produces changes in natural phenomena—wind, thunder, and the movement of the stars—or affects the behavior or the external or internal features of animals and even of human beings. Here again, there is a dichotomy: the acts of the deity can be provoked or unprovoked. To provoke the reply of the deity, a magical act of the diviner may single out certain areas in his ken in which he expects the deity to react in answer to his question— this is characteristic of Mesopotamian extispicy. The deity is here provided with a certain setting and a given time in which to communicate.

Of the three operational practices mentioned, the throwing of lots, the observation of oil in water (lecanomancy), and the observation of smoke from incense (libanomancy), the first had no cultic status in Mesopotamia. We know from legal documents that in the Old Babylonian period and in Susa lots were used to assign the shares of an estate to the sons.[34] We learn from later documents that shares of temple income were originally distributed by lot to certain officials of the sanctuary. In these instances the throwing of lots—marked sticks of wood—was to establish a sequence among persons of equal status that would be acceptable, as divinely ordained, to all participants. This is also

Illustrations

KING ASSURBANIPAL OF ASSYRIA (*R. D. Barnett*, Assyrian Palace Reliefs, *Paul Hamlyn, Ltd.*)

WINGED FIGURE CARRYING SACRIFICIAL ANIMAL (*R. D. Barnett*, Assyrian Palace Reliefs, *Paul Hamlyn, Ltd.*)

COURT MUSICIANS (*R. D. Barnett, Assyrian Palace Reliefs, Paul Hamlyn, Ltd.*)

CHARIOT IN ACTION (*E. A. Wallis Budge*, Assyrian Sculptures in the British Museum, *1914, courtesy British Museum Photographic Service*)

CONQUERED CITY (*Sidney Smith,* Assyrian Sculptures in the British Museum, *1938, courtesy British Museum Photographic Service*)

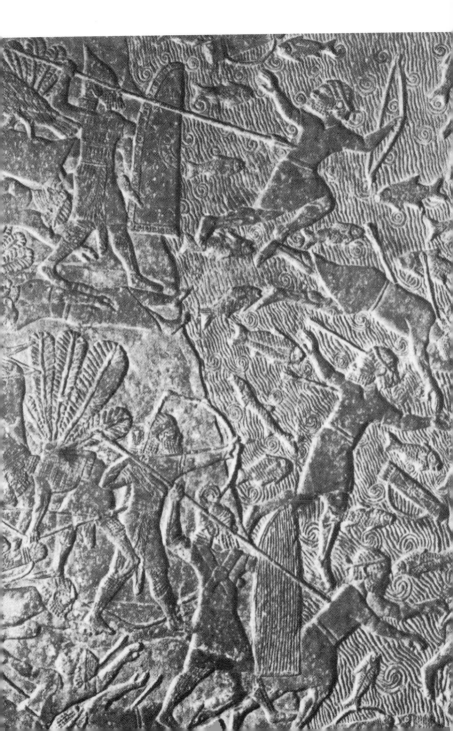

ROYAL CHARIOT (*Sidney Smith*, Assyrian Sculptures in the British Museum, *1938, courtesy British Museum Photographic Service*)

SCRIBES (*R. D. Barnett*, Assyrian Palace Reliefs, *Paul Hamlyn, Ltd.*)

FLOCKS (R. D. Barnett, *Assyrian Palace Reliefs, Paul Hamlyn, Ltd.*)

HUNTING WILD ASSES (*R. D. Barnett*, Assyrian Palace Reliefs, *Paul Hamlyn, Ltd.*)

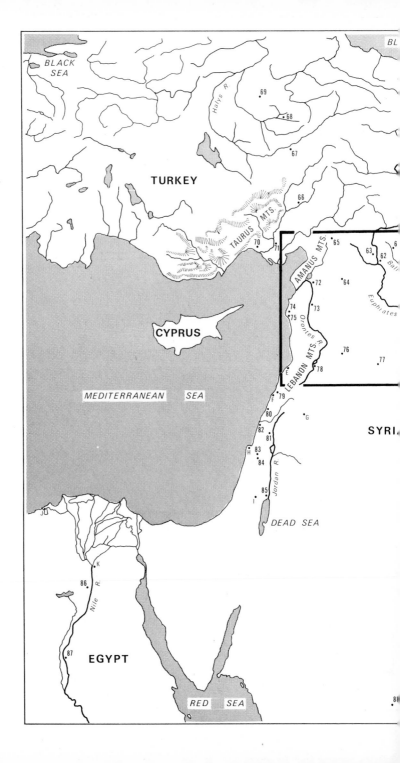

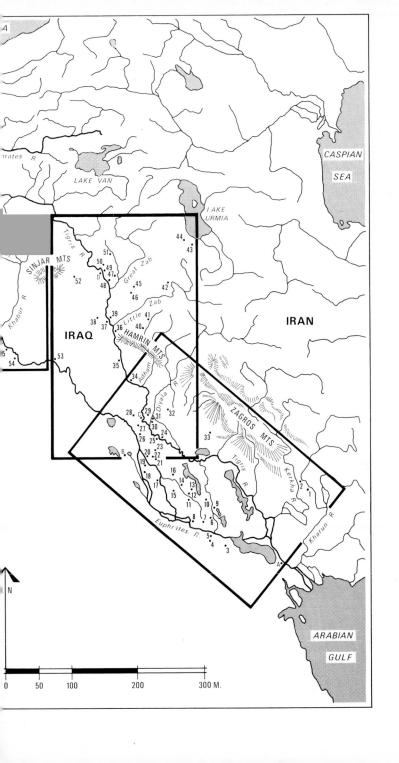

the case with the Assyrian custom used to select the official who was to give his name to the new year (see above, pp. 99 f.) by means of clay dice. The method of casting lots, however, is not mentioned in the compendia as a means of obtaining knowledge of the future. One exception comes from an isolated text from Assur, which speaks of the use of two stone lots, apparently furnishing positive or negative answers.[35] This indicates that the throwing of stone lots was used in Mesopotamia, but rarely and probably on an unofficial level. There is more evidence from Boghazkeui.[36] A small group of omen texts, written characteristically enough in Hittite, speak of divination by means of lots (written KIN, Hittite reading and meaning unknown).[36a] The Hittite and the Assyrian evidence suggest the possibility of a substratum influence in this type of divination; it is possible that the local practices of the northwestern periphery succeeded in reaching the level of literature in these isolated instances.

A practice for which we have no documentation in cuneiform texts is mentioned in Ezekiel 21:21, where it is said that the king of Babylon used arrows and examined the liver of a sacrificial animal to determine which direction to take "at the parting of the way, at the head of two ways."

A substratum influence also seems to underlie the preference in the same region (Asia Minor, Assyria, Syria to Palestine) for birds as oracle animals. The "bird observer" (dāgil iṣṣūri) as divination expert is well attested in Assyria, where we have native experts as well as Egyptians who were prisoners of war.[37] A king of Cyprus, in the Amarna period, once asked expressly for an Egyptian diviner who knew how to obtain answers from eagles—a very specialized augur indeed.[38] A person called "bird-keeper" is known from Hittite sources to have been an expert at divination, and we have a still earlier text from Alalakh that speaks of birds whose fighting was observed in order to predict the future.[39] Clearly, the West was as much the Kulturkreis of augury—literally, divination based on the behavior of birds—as Mesopotamia was for extispicy performed on lambs (in spite of Sum. m á š). Still, we do not know whether western augurs observed the behavior of captive or of wild birds, because this particular method of divination was not systematically recorded in scholarly compendia. In a strange cuneiform text excavated in Sultantepe, the old Harran, a late and provincial center of learning in Upper Mesopotamia, we find literary references to the observation of birds in flight, for which there are a few parallels in texts from Assur and an allusion in a tablet from Nineveh.[40] Unprovoked omens given by birds are rather frequently mentioned in cuneiform texts from Mesopotamia and are listed in the series *šumma ālu* (see below), which is often concerned with omens given through the medium of animals. From apotropaic rituals, the n a m b u r b i texts (see below), we know that encounters with certain kinds of birds were often thought to portend evil.

The remainder of this discussion of various methods of divination is based almost exclusively on a study of cuneiform omen collections, of which we have a substantial number. It seems appropriate to discuss first the nature and style of these texts.

Because of the belief that whatever happens within perception occurs not only due to specific if unknown causes, but also for the benefit of the observer to whom a supernatural agency is thereby revealing its intentions, the Akkadians of the Old Babylonian period began rather early to record such happenings. They first made reports on specific events, then assembled observations of each kind in small collections. The purpose was clearly to record experiences for future reference and for the benefit of coming generations. Thus, written records were made of unusual acts of animals, unusual happenings in the sky, and similar occurrences, and divination moved from the realm of folklore to the level of a scientific activity. The subsequent systematization of such collections represents high scholarly achievement. The collections take up an important part of the scholarly literature in cuneiform and represent an original product of the intellectual effort of the Semitic Akkadians. No Sumerian omen texts have been found, but—as we shall see— extispicy for the selection of a high priest was practiced by the Sumerians, or, perhaps more exactly, in Mesopotamia at a time when Sumerian was the language of all written documents. Each entry in these collections consists of a protasis that states the case, in exactly the same way as does a section of a law code, and of an apodosis that contains the prognostication. The wording of the "case" establishes the position and the sequence of the omens in each collection, with dividing lines often separating topical sub-sections. In well-written library texts, even the arrangement of individual signs within the protasis is used to organize the endless sequences of similar cases. The repertory of predictions in the apodoses contains elaborate phraseology that bears on times of prosperity, blessings, and victory and on times of famine, calamity, and desolation as far as the community and the country are concerned, on happiness in the family, success in business, and on disease, misfortune, and death for the individual.[40a] As for subject matter and style, the apodoses of the omen literature are closely linked to literary texts of the late periods that describe the blessings of peace and prosperity or the horrors of war, famine, and rebellion as well as elaborate blessings and curses similar to those found in certain Mesopotamian royal inscriptions and public legal documents. Older versions of omen collections give more specific and detailed predictions; these give way to greater standardization and the citing of alternate versions which the scribes collected from two or more slightly different originals at hand. Only exceptionally are we able to detect any logical relationship between portent and prediction, although often we find paronomastic associations and secondary computations based on changes in directions or numbers. In many instances, subconscious association seems to have been at work, provoked by certain words whose specific connotations imparted to them a favorable or an unfavorable character, which in turn determined the general nature of the prediction. From the point of view of literary history, one may note that the original practical purpose of such collections of omens was soon expanded, and even superseded, by theoretical aspirations. Instead of expressing general principles of interpretation in abstract terms, the scribes strove to cover the range of possibilities by means of systematic permutations in pairs (left-right, above-below, and so on) or in long rows.[41] The prediction contained in the apodosis, however specific and detailed in its wording, was considered solely a warning—which is exactly what the Latin *omen* means. If the correct apotropaic ritual was performed—and some omen collections are obliging enough to offer such rituals together with the pertinent omens—all evil consequences of the ominous event were considered obviated.

When the diviner, who was called *bārû*, poured oil into a bowl of water which he held in his lap, it was done to establish the will of the deity either with regard to the country or to an individual. The movements of the oil in the water, in relation to the surface or to the rim of the cup, could portend for the king peace and prosperity or war and rebellion; for the private citizen it might portend progeny, success in business, the recovery of health, and the right girl when he was about to marry—or the opposite. We have five Old Babylonian tablets that contain omens dealing with this type of divination, which apparently went out of use in a later period. These early tablets were not copied again; we have only a few excerpts on an Assur tablet.[42] We know less about the technique of divination that interprets the movements and forms of smoke rising from a censer held in the lap of the diviner. We have only an early Nippur text and a somewhat longer tablet of the Old Babylonian period.[43]

We turn now to those "communication techniques" devised for the deity to convey messages upon request through the medium of the body of an animal which was to be slaughtered for this purpose. The expert, called *bārû*, the diviner who interpreted the movement of oil and smoke, first addresses the oracle gods, Šamaš and Adad, with prayers and benedictions, requesting them to "write" their message upon the entrails of the sacrificial animal.[44] He then investigates, in traditional sequence, the animal's organs, such as the windpipe, the lungs, the liver, the gall bladder, and the coils in which the intestines are arranged, looking for deviations from normal state, shape, and coloring. Predictions are based on atrophy, hypertrophy, displacement, special markings, and other abnormal features of the organs. An exact description was made possible by an elaborate and complicated technical terminology which referred to their normal as well as to their abnormal features with scientific accuracy. Unfortunately, more often than not, we have been unable to interpret the technical terms used.

Some observations on the genesis of Mesopotamian extispicy are in order. They may help our understanding of the complex background of this type of divination. Two trends seem discernible, one that utilizes the liver (possibly together with the gall bladder), and another that includes nearly all the exta. In other words: hepatoscopy as against extispicy (literally, the observation of all the exta). There is reason to believe that the former is part of an earlier culture trait complex while the latter represents a characteristic Mesopotamian development. This proposed division into an older level—hepatoscopy—and a secondary, later level—extispicy—seems to be borne out by the following considerations: the later omen literature mentions specific historic events that had occurred in olden times after the observation of extraordinary formations of the exta. These observations always concern the liver of the sacrificial animal. In fact, such omens are expressly called "liver omens." That the training of the students of divination at that time was nearly always concerned with the same organ is shown by the numerous models of the liver made of clay. These come from Babylon proper, but more often from Mari,[44a] and from Asia Minor (Boghazkeui); recently, some were found in Hazor in Israel.[45] The political correspondence found in Mari provides us with further evidence of the importance of hepatoscopy.[46] This distribution pattern, combined with the general trans-Asiatic interest in the inspection of slaughtered animals and the Semitic belief in the importance of the liver as the seat of the emotions, is another indication that in Mesopotamia hepatoscopy was older than extispicy and much in the realm of folklore. The Sumerian practice of determining the e n priest of the city god by divination based on the observation of a sacrificial animal (see n. 6, chap. vi) suggests that early hepatoscopy was on a binary, yes-or-no level.[47] This is corroborated by a curious late text in which the scholarly Chaldean king Nabonidus describes in considerable detail how his own daughter was selected by the moon god for the highest priestly office of his cult. Nabonidus clearly imitates ancient methods as he narrows down the circle of eligible candidates through repeated yes-no decisions obtained by extispicy, and we may well assume that in the Sumerian period the e n -priest was selected in the same manner.

The method which we term here binary touches on another problem. In all extant omen collections referring to extispicy, the prognostication, always within two categories, favorable or unfavorable, is quite specific, often offering irrelevant details. Are we to assume two stages of internal development: one, the older, with yes-or-no answers, and a later one, with more specific apodoses? If so, is it possible that the contrast may correspond to one to be posited between folklore divination and divination as a sacred or scholarly lore requiring expert training, interpretation, and the study of written records? If both questions are answered in the affirmative, one may well posit a further contrast, that between a primary method, either native or introduced from the outside, and a secondary method that presents itself as the product of intellectual creativity, scholarly elaboration, and scientific activity. It will probably remain forever unknown how these contrasts relate to one another, that is, whether hepatoscopy, binary method, and folklore divination based on primitive and unwritten practices, and extispicy, with specific apodoses, and scholarly (and) written divination actually existed side by side or did so only in certain aspects, periods, or situations. Still, the preceding reflections should make clear to the reader the complexity of the problems involved and at the same time show divination in Mesopotamian civilization not only as an essential means of orientation in life but also as an arena for the display of intellectual endeavors and aspirations.

We do not know how the diviner proceeded when called upon to offer coherent expertise based upon inspection of all pertinent organs of the slaughtered lamb, each yielding a number of divergent and often explicit prognoses. It must have required considerable searching through the voluminous compendia arranged according to the ominous organs in order to interpret the message of the oracle gods. A drastic simplification can be observed in the late Assyrian period: in the royal archives of Nineveh has been excavated a substantial group of texts that contains queries addressed to the gods in matters of state.[48] The answer to each query consists solely of a list of the features of the exta observed by the diviner, who carefully quotes the pertinent predictions from the compendia. These predictions are considered to be of interest only insofar as they are favorable or unfavorable; the specific events predicted are disregarded. In short, the predictions are reduced to yes-or-no answers. The enumeration of answers relative to each query yields no more than a positive or a negative verdict, according to whether the majority of individual predictions are favorable or not. So we find again in the eighth century B.C. the yes-or-no method of divination, and the question cannot fail to arise whether this represents a new development or whether we have to assume that the method just described was used throughout Mesopotamian history. It is equally possible that the late evidence for the binary system is due to a Western or substratum influence lingering in Assyria or that the characteristic feature of Mesopotamian divination (the specific nature of the predictions) is only a vestige of a stage in our somewhat conjectural history of Mesopotamian divination. If so, the precisely arranged lists of omens with their elaborate predictions would have served no other purpose than to characterize a feature of the exta as being favorable or not. (For another indication pointing in this direction, see below, p. 217.)

The corpus of texts dealing with extispicy surpasses—as far as fragments are available—the number of texts on all other kinds of omens. No serious attempt has been made by the Assyriologists to organize the material on extispicy according to one or more main series, abridged editions (excerpt series), or annotated editions; nor has an attempt been made to trace the development of the compendia from the early and short Old Babylonian tablets to the extensive collections of the Seleucid period. Nor have local developments been identified. The tablets are arranged according to the parts of the exta to be inspected. It is no accident that tablets dealing with the liver are rare since they represent, as has been suggested (cf. above, p. 213), an earlier stage in the history of extispicy. The specific parts of each organ as well as markings and discolorations are denoted by an arcane technical terminology reminiscent of that of medieval alchemists.[49] There are such terms as "door of the palace," "path," "yoke," and "embankment" for the parts and "weapon" and "stand" for the markings. Certain tablets contain illustrations to explain difficult terms and diagrams—such as those of the coils of the intestines—to orient the reader. Some clay models of the liver and lungs are elaborate; others are rather crude. These models served several purposes, for instruction and illustration and also for reporting. The highly detailed Old Babylonian model of the liver now in the British Museum, and a number of other models,[49a] inscribed with one or more individual omens to illustrate a particular feature and the pertinent forecast, are clearly meant for instruction. The models found in Mari, the oldest in evidence (late Old Akkadian period), record the formation of a liver as it looked at the time of an important event. Their peculiar inscriptions and three-dimensional illustrations have the same function as the omens which appear in the compendia. The models seemed also to have served for reporting, e.g., to the king an actual observation together with the pertinent prediction. These "illustrated" reports are thus the forerunners of the later reports on ominous events (see below, p. 233).

Some omens offer instead of a prediction the statement that the features described in the protasis have reference to a specific event in the life of a historical ruler. These historical omens, by the way, provide us with several not unimportant bits of information dealing in the main with tragic and extraordinary events.[50] Such records, however, do not simply represent the empirical base of Mesopotamian extispicy, as is often asserted. This science predates writing. It is more reasonable to assume that the recording of omens in writing began with small collections, that is, lists assembled in some systematic way. Collections of this type were later enlarged and combined to form extensive series. The references to historical events in omen texts—in rare instances even outside of extispicy texts—seem to represent an intrusion into the "scientific" literature of the diviner. All the kings mentioned in the historical omens belong to the period before the first dynasty of Isin, i.e., they ruled many centuries before the process of the standardization of the omen literature began. We cannot say why and how this practice originated or why it was discontinued.

One more remark to illustrate how methods in Mesopotamian extispicy changed. Until the Middle Babylonian period, it was the custom for the diviner to write a special report on each inspection, listing in a specified order all the ominous features observed and ending with the statement that the omens were favorable or that a second extispicy was to be performed. Again, the question arises whether these reports represent only a passing technical (better: bureaucratic) variation, or whether they too, like the Mari reports (see note 46), have to be interpreted as an indication that a deviating "binary school" of divination was in evidence in Babylonia too. The practice of writing reports was not followed in the Neo-Babylonian period; in Assyria, however, it seems to have been replaced by "queries" (see pp. 214 f.). Queries contain divine answers (affirmative, as a rule) to questions that are quoted *in extenso* concerning the appointment of officials, the loyalty of generals, and the actions of the enemy, and end with the report of the features observed. Another kind of text concerned with extispicy disappeared with the Old Babylonian period. These were the prayers the diviner addressed to Šamaš before the extispicy asking for a reliable and positive answer. They enumerate in considerable detail all possible favorable features and markings the diviner hopes to find in the exta of the sacrificial animal. [50a]

Of the several ways in which animals served as a medium through which god and man might communicate by means of divination, extispicy represents only one, the one in which a two-way communication, query-and-answer, was possible. There are two other ways—both attested in numerous texts—in which the god made his intention known without being asked. The first of these ways of receiving communications was by observing malformed and monstrous newborn animals, and the second was by noting the behavior of animals either in general or under special circumstances.

In Mesopotamia the birth of malformed animals, and even of malformed children under certain circumstances, was considered highly ominous and often as bearing directly on the future of the state. Such omens were collected as early as the Old Babylonian period. They were copied in Hattuša and, at times, translated into Hittite; they were known also in Ugarit. In the course of time, they were assembled into a collection of which copies have been found in Assur, Nineveh, Calah, and at various sites in southern Babylonia.[51] The collection embraced at least twenty-four tablets and was called after its incipit *Šumma izbu*, "If a newborn animal . . ." and also "If a woman is pregnant and her fetus cries . . ." The collection clearly exhibits the process of growth by accretion, since the twenty-four tablets fall into three distinct groups. The central and oldest group forms the core; it refers exclusively to malformation in newborn lambs. To this were added four tablets dealing with multiple births and the birth of malformed children, strange beings, objects, and animals to human mothers as well as a number of tablets concerned with the offspring of ewes, mares, sows, bitches, goats, and cows. The importance of such teratological omens is illustrated by references to such incidents in private and royal letters and by a number of rituals designed to ward off the evil consequences caused by the birth of monstrosities. Scholarly interest in the series *Šumma izbu* is indicated by several short and one lengthy commentary found in many copies; they are, as is customary, mainly concerned with the explanation of rare and difficult words.

The behavior of animals could be accepted on three levels as conveying an expression of divine warning: it could be provoked, it could occur in an ominous location and at an ominous moment, and it could simply happen. None of these levels was important enough to stimulate scholarly interest, which would have led to the creation of pertinent compendia, though omens of this type do occur sporadically.

Provoked omens coming from animals are probably not genuinely Mesopotamian; an isolated instance is reported as a means of fortunetelling in a text from Sultantepe that speaks of the practice of sprinkling water on a bull after appropriate preparation and prayers to the oracle gods; the bull's reactions are then interpreted on a simple yes-no basis.[52] Typical ominous moments for the observation of animals were at the time an army marched out to war, during the course of a religious procession, and at the high point of a religious festival. The behavior of animals at the gates of a city or palace or within the temple was considered especially meaningful. Omens dealing with such situations occur in the series *Šumma ālu* (see below) but were never collected systematically.[53] With these belongs a small compendium of omens of a somewhat peculiar nature: due to an extension in time and in space of the numinous moment in which the oracle god Šamaš was supposed to inscribe his answer on the exta of the animals to be inspected by the diviner, the behavior of the sacrificial animal, from the moment it was brought into the presence of the diviner to its last convulsions, was considered ominous and predictions were derived from it.[54]

In connection with what has just been said concerning the ominous importance of certain moments and localities, we would like to mention here the techniques of magically creating both the time and the place when and wherein the deity was beseeched to communicate. Ultimately, extispicy was such a technique because the oracle god was asked to "write" his answer, then and there, upon the intestines of the animal. There existed two more divination practices which applied the same method. They are attested—again only on the fortunetelling level—in a tablet from Assur and in the curious tablet from Sultantepe already mentioned. The Assur tablet derives favorable omens from the passing of certain birds at a given moment before the observer from right to left; the tablet from Sultantepe, from the movements of shooting stars for which the observer was waiting. They are to move either from right to left—favorable—or from left to right—unfavorable.[55]

Attention should be drawn to the fact that all these rare—and un-Mesopotamian—divination practices appear solely in the texts of Western provenience, that is, Assur and Sultantepe. The practice of watching for a bird oracle which is to pass overhead in a certain direction at a specific time reminds one immediately of the Etruscan *templum*, the section of the sky in which the augur expected certain birds to give oracles by their behavior. This comparison should do no more than suggest that the practices of divination differ widely in the several civilizations of the ancient Near East and that the apparent preponderance and complexity of Mesopotamian techniques is due, in the main, to the practice of writing down these techniques upon material which has proved indestructible. Asia Minor, Syria, and probably Egypt doubtless evolved a like number of techniques, most of which have not come down to us.

We have already mentioned the omen series Šumma ālu as containing omens derived from the behavior of animals. It derives its name, "If a city is situated on a hill . . .," from the incipit of the first tablet. This series deserves more than cursory attention, being very long and of a rather complex composition, consisting of at least 107 tablets, and probably more.[56] Only one-fourth are preserved and often poorly, which makes it rather difficult to form an exact idea of the contents of the series. Yet some excerpt tablets, versions which contain on one tablet excerpts from several regular tablets of the series, and the fragments of a commentary as well as of catalogues of the incipits enable us to obtain more information and insight. Still, of more than thirty-five tablets only the first line is known, and nearly as many are completely unaccounted for.

The omen series represents a generous sampling of a motley of smaller omen collections which had been compiled into a large, catchall, series. Some of these collections are already attested in the Old Babylonian period, others only in later versions.[57] Since the series has not yet been adequately studied and published, not much can be said as to the time of its final redaction. Here is a succinct survey of its contents. The first two tablets refer to cities. The next tablets refer to houses and incidents happening in houses. More than twenty-five tablets (up to tablet 49, according to the numbering of the Assur version) deal with animals of all kinds. The behavior of insects, snakes, scorpions, lizards, ants, and several unidentified smaller animals is listed at length; domesticated animals, cattle, donkeys, and especially dogs are likewise dealt with. The three following tablets concern fire. Another contains political omens (tablet 53, "If the king respects the law . . ."), and eight deal in one way or another with agriculture. The balance—after tablet 60—is badly preserved; we may single out encounters with wild animals (tablet 67ff.) and human relations (tablet 94ff.) as making up the bulk of what is preserved.

The tablets of *Šumma ālu* concerned with "human relations" may be taken as a cue to shift our attention to omens concerned with human beings. We have pointed out that Mesopotamian civilization—only rarely and rather reluctantly—admits that the deity can use man as a vehicle for the expression of divine intentions. In this function man may act on several levels; he can become the mouthpiece of the deity, for which purpose he enters a specific psychological state, a prophetic ecstasis (of several kinds), or he can receive divine revelation in his sleep, or he can allow the deity to give "signs" through his physical person. Such signs may be meant for the entire group as in the case of specific deformations or the birth of malformed children, or they may be meant solely for their carrier, whose bodily features are taken to presage his fate.

Ecstasis as a means of communication between god and man did not occupy the important position in Mesopotamia that it did in Syria and Palestine. In fact, the few attested instances come mainly from the western outskirts of the Mesopotamian *Kulturkreis*, from Mari, Hittite Asia Minor, and from late Assyria, with its complex substratum and Aramaic influence. Certain designations for ecstatics are known, such as *eššebû*, *maḫḫû*, *zabbu*, *rag(g)imu*, referring either to physical characteristics or to the peculiar manner in which the divine commands were expressed. These persons are all of marginal importance, often connected with witchcraft—in short, of low social status. The only exceptions are the Assyrian prophetesses of the goddess Ištar (of Arbela and even of Assur)—men appear in this function quite rarely—who pronounced the will of the deity either as an edict, in the third person. or in the first person, identifying themselves with the deity who spoke through them. In Mari, the message was delivered verbatim but in a way that showed that the mouthpiece did not identify himself with the deity.[58] Both, the Western concept (Mari—and, of course, the Old Testament) as well as the native Assyrian (identification of

prophet and deity) are deeply alien to the eastern, Mesopotamian, attitude toward the god-man relationship. Noteworthy
is the absence of shamanistic concepts in Mesopotamia.

Normally, the dream offers nothing more than an "omen,"
which means that the dream is meaningful only when correctly
interpreted by an expert. Interpreters of dreams used for this
purpose collections of dream omens.[59] Fragments of one such
"dream book" have been found in Assurbanipal's library, and a
small number of earlier texts show that the text type was in the
stream of the tradition. Still, only fragments exist, and they are
by no means numerous; it is clear that this type of divination
was not in great favor. The series containing the dream omens
consists of eleven tablets of which the first and the last two are
dedicated to conjurations and the pertinent rituals for warding
off the consequences of bad dreams, those dreams predicting
disaster or other ills. Other rituals given in this collection were
to be used prophylactically, to protect the sleeping persons
against ominous dreams. The protean variety of dream contents
is organized rather pedantically in large and small sections that
refer to certain definite activities of the dreamer, such as eating
or drinking in one's dreams, traveling, and other activities of
daily life. In the section concerned with eating, cannibalism and
coprophagy are mentioned; in the tablet on traveling, dreams
of ascending to heaven and descending into the nether world
occur, as do dreams of flying. There are incestuous dreams,
dreams of losing one's teeth, of quarreling with members of the
family, of receiving gifts, of carrying objects. As may be expected
from other types of Mesopotamian omen texts, the associations
that link the dream to the prediction derived from it are rarely
understandable. Only a few omens bear out what has been said
above concerning man as carrier of "signs" through which the
deity addresses the entire community.

The first four tablets of the series Šumma izbu (see above,
p. 218) list omens derived from malformed children and other
accidents at birth as well as from multiple births, and a section
of the first tablet of Šumma ālu relates the physical features of
certain citizens to the fate of the community when speaking of a
city in which there are many crippled, deaf, and blind; also

mentioned are cities in which there are many merchants, diviners, or cooks—and one city in which the women have beards.

Furthermore, man is thought to carry on his own body signs which—when correctly interpreted—refer to his fate, at times even to his own "nature." The interpretation of these signs is contained in collections called physiognomic omens by Assyriologists.[60] The color of the hair, the shape of the nails, the size of specific parts of the body, the nature and location of moles and discolorations on the skin—to mention only a few of the topics— are treated more or less extensively in a number of series, the most important of which contains ten or more tablets. The composition of the series shows the typical growth by accretion which we have seen with respect to birth omens (*Šumma izbu*). The earliest texts of the Old Babylonian period refer mainly to moles, while the later—from the library of Assurbanipal and also from the Neo-Babylonian south—include other features of the body, personal peculiarities and mannerisms in speech and gait, and even moral qualities.

A very special situation is dealt with in an important collection of omens, *Enūma ana bīt marṣi āšipu illiku*, meaning "[If] the exorcist is going to the house of a patient. . . ." The forty tablets incorporate a number of smaller collections of varied nature, all concerned with the prospects of the patient. The series seems to present a late compilation,[61] although certain of its components have parallels in earlier texts; we have a Hittite text clearly translated from a lost Old Babylonian original and a Middle Babylonian tablet from Nippur,[62] both indicative of the existence of kindred texts for these periods. The series does not prescribe any treatment of the patient; it informs the physician concerning the diseases of his patient in the form of diagnoses— and often offers prognoses as to the outcome by such terse statements as "He will get well," "He will die," sometimes qualified as to time and other circumstances. The form used is that of an omen collection. The protases refer exclusively to the appearance of the patient's body, his behavior, and other objective symptoms. They are listed systematically, beginning with the skull and ending with the toes (see also p. 246).

Whenever a treatment is prescribed—and that is only rarely the case—it is not medical but exclusively magical. Even the names of the diseases mentioned are not medical but point as a rule to the deity or demon that has caused them. Only the first two tablets fit the title of the series inasmuch as they concern themselves with the ominous happenings the exorcist may encounter on his way to the house of the patient who called for him. These signs refer to the prospects of recovery or death for the sick person. After the main section (tablets 3–35), four tablets refer to pregnant women and predict the fate of the child, its sex, and the difficulty of the labor from the discoloration of the skin and the formation of the nipples of the expectant mother. At the end there is a tablet dealing with sick infants similar to the tablets of the main section of the series. (For further discussion of this series, see pp. 290f.)[63]

A number of these tablets utilize the established pattern of the omen (protasis-apodosis) as a form of presentation of medical lore. The same discrepancy between form and purpose can be observed in other omen collections, which are, in fact, literary compositions offering political tenets or other wisdom of a moral nature. The former can be found in a text containing advice to a king (rather like the medieval *speculum principis*),[64] the latter in a text which stresses the importance of rational behavior.[65]

The royal art of astrology is the method of divination for which Mesopotamia is famed. Study of the rise of astrology in Mesopotamian civilization has hardly begun. The pertinent evidence is preserved on a few Old Babylonian tablets with astrological omens of a rather primitive type, mainly among texts found at the periphery of Mesopotamian influence—in Boghazkeui, Qatna, Mari, and Elam.[66] They testify to the existence of an astrological tradition already diversified at the crucial Old Babylonian period. This is borne out by references, in a late text, to observations of the planet Venus made at the time of the Old Babylonian king Ammiṣaduqa.[67] The fact that astrological texts were imported to Susa and Hattuša and translated into Elamite and Hittite emphasizes the readiness with which this type of divination was accepted outside Babylonia proper, even before the rise of astrology.

The bulk of astrological omen texts comes from the library of Assurbanipal. Some were written in Assur and Calah, and others were found in the south, the latter dating mainly from the later period and coming from Babylon, Borsippa, Uruk, Kish, and Nippur. A Middle Babylonian fragment found in Nippur and another found in Nuzi indicate the continuity of the tradition.[68] The "canonical" series, consisting of at least seventy tablets, apart from excerpt texts and tablets with commentaries, is called *Enūma Anu Enlil* ("When Anu and Enlil . . .") after the first words of its solemn bilingual introit. The moon is treated in twenty-three tablets, then the sun, meteorological phenomena, the planets, and the fixed stars.[69] The time and other circumstances of the disappearance of the old moon, its reappearance, its relation to the sun, and other data on eclipses, offer the "signs" which the series describes and interprets in detail. Less extensive treatment is given halos, strange cloud formations, and the movements of the planets (mainly the planet Venus) among the fixed stars. Meteorological phenomena—thunder, rain, hail, earthquakes—are believed to have ominous validity in matters of state and predict peace and war, harvest, and flood. In the archives in Nineveh have been preserved hundreds of reports of astrologers sent to the Assyrian kings in answer to queries occasioned by such phenomena.

A different level of astrology is revealed in texts that date from the fifth (410) and third centuries B.C. These are horoscopes which mention the date of birth—in an isolated instance, the date of conception—followed by an astronomical report, concluding with predictions of the future of the child.[70] The important fact about these texts is that their dates prove this type of astrology to be a late development in Mesopotamia, or better, in Babylonia, rather than under the stimulus of Greece, as was previously assumed. These horoscopes have to be connected with a Seleucid tablet which relates the future of a child to certain astronomical conditions, the rising and the movements of planets, eclipses, and other phenomena that occurred at his birth.

In the omen texts there are only a few indications of the ideological background of Mesopotamian divination. The basic problems, in theological terms, are related to the motives for divine communication and to its accuracy and inevitability. An additional complication is the conflict between superstition and religion, that is, between the pre-deistic world view and that of the theologians.

Divine interest in the well-being of the individual or the group for which a sign is given is bound to center on the person of the king. In fact, it is the king's duty and privilege to receive such signs and to act according to their message. Only very rarely do we find the king averse. The concept of the king's personal responsibility toward the deity and the concomitant sentiment of intimacy in this relationship intensified the omen-consciousness of the Assyrian king and of his entire court. There it engendered speculations that reflect concern with theological problems and led not only to refinement of the methods of interpreting omens but also to constant changes in techniques of divination.

The common man, of whose moral and intellectual problems we know nothing, used divination in a naïve, ego-centered way that corresponded only to a limited degree to the techniques used by the king. This contrast is paralleled by a similar one in the realm of magic, where the common man and the court differed mainly in regard to theological elaboration and scholarly refinement. The complex purification rituals (n a m b u r b i) evolved to ward off the evil predicted by ominous happenings are geared to the repertory of the omen collections. Their specific purpose was to counteract and to nullify the evil predicted in the apodoses of these collections. The n a m b u r b i' s seem thus to have been the answer of the theologians to the diviners. They represent the reaction of the purification priests to the transfer of the pre-deistic folklore tradition of divination to the level of the king or other persons who had recourse to the ministrations of purification experts. To protect the belief in the efficiency of their magic, the inevitability of the diviner's predictions had to be abandoned.[70a]

Any overtly skeptical reaction to those ubiquitous omens of evil is only rarely discovered. Still, the fact that such instances occurred in portent-ridden Mesopotamia—and, moreover, that they originated from the person of the king—makes it worthwhile to mention them.[71] One of the several Naram-Sin legends which we find attested in an Old Babylonian version and in later texts from Nineveh and Harran describes the anger of the king when the gods refused him oracles. The king asks "Has a lion ever performed extispicy, has a wolf ever asked [advice] from a female dream-interpreter? Like a robber I shall proceed according to my own will!" He soon repented his sacrilegious outburst and was granted the unique privilege of hearing Ištar as evening star speak to him from the sky. Although announcing his own intentions in a moment of *hubris*, Naram-Sin clearly relates to animals and outlaws the way of living and acting without constant watching for signs of divine approval or disapproval. Civilized existence, as epitomized in a king's way of life, relied on omens, and only a king of such mythical fame as Naram-Sin could be allowed to venture a criticism, but even then only in a form and context that canceled the gesture.[72] Nevertheless, even those kings reputed to be very superstitious did not always give credence to the predictions of diviners. This we know from a revealing passage in a letter addressed to Esarhaddon: "This is what it [the text] says about that eclipse that [occurred in] the month of Nisan: 'If the planet Jupiter is present during an eclipse, it is good for the king [because] in his stead an important person [at court] will die,' but the king closed his ears—and see, a full month has not yet elapsed and the chief justice is dead!"[73]

At times the distrust of omens is formulated as distrust in the professional honesty of the diviners. And when one reads through their reports to the Assyrian kings, one can be amused at their efforts to interpret bad omens in a favorable sense by means of complicated reasoning. We have evidence of awareness of this practice when Sennacherib separates the diviners into groups in order to obtain a reliable report in an important question without collusion among the experts.[74]

Nowhere in Mesopotamia do we come across the attitude that speaks so forcefully in Isaiah 47:13: "Let now the astrologers, the stargazers, the monthly prognosticators, stand up, and save thee from these things that shall come upon thee."

V

Laterculis coctilibus

THE MEANING OF WRITING

THE SCRIBES

THE CREATIVE EFFORT

PATTERNS IN NON-LITERARY TEXTS

Writing constitutes a characteristic feature of the early civilizations of the southwest Asia complex. From the Indus to the
Nile, systems of writing are found as early as the beginning of
the third millennium. Although the existence of a single
primary impulse must be posited within that complex, several
different systems of writing established themselves, permanently
in most instances, within the cultural traditions. Since the region
eventually became an important center of diffusion, writing
spread throughout the entire Eurasian continent. Systems were
borrowed by some cultures, new systems derived or re-created
under stimulus by others.

The Meaning of Writing

The most important writing systems in this area are: the
cuneiform system and its affiliates in and around Mesopotamia;

the hieroglyphic system of Egypt; and the family of writing systems based on an alphabetic script which originated on the shores of the Mediterranean Sea. Marginal, undeciphered, or badly attested systems shall remain outside this discussion. Among the latter are: the system customarily called hiero-glyphic Hittite, the Old Persian system of alphabetic cuneiform, the only partly intelligible system or systems of Crete, the undeciphered Proto-Elamite script, and that of the Indus valley, and the few traces of other writings.[1]

The three main systems evolved their own characteristic writing techniques, that is, the use of specific materials and tools, and these techniques in turn had a direct influence on the chances of survival of the texts and thus upon the extent and even the nature of our knowledge concerning the uses of writing in these civilizations. Clay, which was used for the several cuneiform systems, happens to represent, especially when fired, the best—that is, the cheapest and most durable—writing material yet utilized by man, while papyrus, parchment, leather, wood, metal, and stone survive mainly by chance. Climatic conditions, the nature of the soil, and the ever-present human factor often wiped out such materials completely. Where the system of writing changed from one using clay to one for which more perishable materials were used, entire periods are blacked out for us. The disappearance of the last phases of Mesopotamian civilization is a good example of such a situation.

The complete loss of all documentary evidence on leather or parchment pertaining to the development which led to the formation of the corpus now called the Old Testament compels modern scholars to rely on reconstructions for essential phases of the history of these texts. Egypt presents a special case because inscriptions on stone and metal in most instances differ widely in content and style from those utilizing papyri or leather rolls. The disappearance of the latter creates a hiatus that will always seriously complicate the Egyptologist's efforts to reconstruct the literature of that important civilization. In comparison with such difficulties, those faced by the Assyriologist seem relatively minor. The soil of Mesopotamia will continue to yield more and more of the tablets that it preserves so well.

Three typical uses of writing can be found in the civilizations of the ancient Near East: the recording of data for future use; the communication of data on a synchronic level; and what I would like to term ceremonial use—a term that seems vague only to us of the late Western world where such a use has become rare. In individual civilizations, the three main uses are attested in specific patterns of distribution. The emphasis reflected in these preferences varies not only from civilization to civilization but also, historically, within each civilization. Each use is outlined here in necessarily general terms but with special consideration given to its attestation in specific civilizations. We begin with the best attested use, that of writing for the recording of data.

Five purposes are singled out here and listed in a sequence of diminishing frequency: recording for administrative purposes, for the codification of laws, for the formulation of a sacred tradition, for annals, and, eventually, for scholarly purposes. Such a listing, of course, cannot be expected to correspond adequately to the gamut of practices which have acquired special meanings and functions in each of these civilizations.

The use of writing for administrative purposes evolves readily wherever personnel and goods (staples, materials, or finished products) move through the channels of a bureaucracy under the supervision of personally responsible officials who serve for definite terms of office. In redistribution systems such as those centered in the Mesopotamian palaces and temples, these officials recorded incoming taxes, tributes, and the yield of the royal or priestly domain and workshops as well as the distribution of materials and rations to craftsmen and workers. This type of recording, strictly formalized and astutely co-ordinated, is very much in evidence in Mesopotamia and wherever, under Mesopotamian influence, officials in similar economic situations have resorted to writing on clay. Corresponding evidence from Egypt has nearly completely disappeared; the few papyri and ostraca which have chanced to survive make us feel the loss only more keenly. It should be kept in mind, however, that the use of writing is not absolutely necessary for recording and controlling complex bureaucratic transactions. Where writing is not used, operational methods of bookkeeping can be effectively applied. Their existence and utilization is well known from outside our complex of civilizations, and we do have indications of the use of operational devices (such as tallies and counters) even in Mesopotamia.[2]

In Mesopotamia as well as in Egypt the total acceptance of bureaucracy as a social phenomenon, or rather as a technique of social integration, found a curious echo on tne speculative level. In certain cuneiform texts describing the nether world, mention is made of the scribe of the ruler of the dead who keeps lists with the names of all those who are to die each day.[3] It is this reference to some kind of divine bookkeeping rather than the role of Nabu, the divine scribe and patron deity of the scribes that can be related to the famous passage in Psalm 139 which speaks of God's book in which man's deeds are entered before they happen. Later eschatological speculation deftly changed this imagery from the realm of bureaucracy, where the wise administrator takes care of his clients and dependents, to that of deterministic apprehension and the submission of man to the inscrutable fate fixed by the deity.[4]

The recording of law collections is well known in the ancient Near East, and a number of such collections from Mesopotamia and other civilizations are extant. Several Sumerian,[4a] Akkadian,[4b] and Hittite[4c] codes, and several codifications incorporated into the Old Testament are available, and indications exist that Egypt, too, had law collections on papyrus.[5] Two immediate purposes for such writings are evident, that of superseding oral tradition and practices, and the aim of bringing the law into line with changed social, economic, or political conditions. As we have already pointed out (see p. 158), Mesopotamian codifications under these circumstances become the repository of aspirations to change such situations or to emphasize the king's or the god's interest in the welfare of his subjects. To what extent these laws actually became effective and under what circumstances the letter of the law prevailed over the realities of life need not concern us here. And yet it needs to be said that the fateful concept that reality should adjust to the requirements of a written corpus remains unknown to Mesopotamia—

and probably to the entire ancient Near East. Only in a late and definitely peripheral development that sprang from the desire to create, for ideological reasons, a specific social context did Judaism succeed in creating such a pattern of behavior.

Not only laws but also sacred lore have been preserved in writings in the civilizations with which we are concerned. By "sacred lore" we should understand a record of the "story" of a deity, of a religious figure, or of an ethnic or otherwise coherent unit, inasmuch as such a story is incorporated into the ideology that sustains the circle of worshipers and the congregation of believers. Records of this type are written down for the purpose of maintaining a corpus of traditions, beliefs, and precepts under changing social conditions or under outside pressure. Writing, then, is used here for a reason basically different from that which prompted the codification of the laws of the region. It was to "freeze" a tradition, not to adapt and adjust it to reality. Such written formulations were meant to prevent hypertrophic growth of the corpus under inside pressure, especially to restrain the theologian from reinterpreting the story, elaborating it, embellishing, and thus distorting it. Under such circumstances, several rather typical situations may evolve. Thus, a text may come into being which reflects in its wording both the influence of the pressure toward change and the tendency to resist. The text of the Old Testament as it is preserved shows clearly the imprint of such conflicts. Or the text may remain basically unchanged but coexist with a different tradition, overtly or covertly. A special situation seems to have evolved in Mesopotamia with respect to the Epic of Creation. As to topic and style of presentation, one is tempted to see in it the formulation of theological tenets valid for an entire civilization, somehow comparable with the Egyptian "theology of Memphis."[6] Such a view—suggested by the situation that speaks out of Old Testament writings—is not acceptable for the *Enūma eliš*. It was written relatively late, though probably influenced by earlier texts and traditions, primarily for the Marduk cult of Babylon. It represents a transformation to a literary level of earlier and perhaps locally restricted practices such as, for example, a mimic performance or the like that took place at a New Year's ritual. Thus, even though the *Enūma eliš* offers the story of Marduk as creator and formulates a theological interpretation of this world, it was not used to communicate to the believers a testimonial of the deity's achievements but as a vehicle for the expression of the priest-god relationship: it was read to the god himself in the sacred seclusion of the temple. It is a hymn in praise of Marduk by which the priest extols his god.

Although there is no scarcity of documents bearing on history in ancient Near Eastern sources, annals that record contemporary events systematically appear only rarely and rather late. Many of the documents that claim to be historiographic record events for different purposes. Even such a famous and unique monument as the Egyptian Palermo Stone seems simply a list, in the form of annals, of the donations of the Pharaohs to temples, just as the lost Book of the Wars of Yahveh and certain Babylonian chronicles or histories record victories and defeats only in theological terms.[7] Still, these documents do presuppose a tradition of annual recording that may have grown out of bureaucratic practices maintained in temples and palaces. Records containing data of such basic historiographic relevance as the Old Babylonian date lists and lists of the Assyrian eponyms were intended for practical purposes. For political, but at times also for scholarly purposes, such materials were incorporated or used in literary compositions.

The use of writing to record what we term today scholarly data is old in Mesopotamia and was maintained there up to the latest period. As early as the Old Babylonian period, we come across objective and standardized reports on extispicies performed by the diviners. The observation of specific features was clearly separated from interpretation, which was based on precedent, either directly or through deductive reasoning. About a millennium later, the movements of the planets among the constellations and the rising and setting of the sun and the moon are described with adequate precision. Although no textual evidence is available, we may safely assume that the data of these observers enabled later Mesopotamian astronomers to state certain events in the movements of the heavenly bodies in mathematical terms and eventually provided the Greek astronomers of Alexandria with an important corpus of information.

Writing was also used to communicate information on a synchronic level, such as in letters, royal edicts, and public announcements. The durable nature of the writing material has put in our hands literally thousands of Mesopotamian letters (see pp. 23 f.). Inscriptions of a public nature are used for political and legal purposes. They appear on stone stelae of a characteristic shape (Egypt, Syria, Mesopotamia) and on the *kudurru* stones which represent a special development in Babylonia. One specific use of this type of communication is conspicuously absent in Mesopotamia: the funerary inscriptions so important in circum-Mediterranean civilizations. These texts address themselves to the passer-by, naming the deceased and protecting the safety of his monument.[7a] The only text of this kind found in Mesopotamia proper concerns the mother of the Babylonian king, Nabonidus, who speaks to us in the first person—as is typical in funerary inscriptions—of her life; then her royal son reports on her burial in a postscript.[8] Form, function, and style are at cross-purposes in this late and unique document and characterize it as an oddity.

The considerable body of texts that existed both in Egypt and Mesopotamia for the purpose of training the scribes and of thus assuring the continuity of the craft and its tradition will occupy us in the next section of this chapter.

Under "ceremonial uses of writing" one should place more texts than one might expect to be listed under such a heading. Here belong all those numerous inscriptions from Egypt and Mesopotamia that were not intended to be read by human eyes—or at least were not written for that specific purpose. All the Egyptian mortuary texts, from the Pyramid texts to the Book of the Dead, fall into this category, as do the innumerable foundation documents in cuneiform from Babylonia and Assyria—cones, prisms, barrels, and tablets. None of these texts address living persons. These "ceremonial" inscriptions give us most of the information we have on Egypt and Mesopotamia. This is also true of the inscriptions carved beside cataracts, on mountain slopes, and in gorges. Their primary purpose was to relate the king to his gods in a magic way. Ceremonial writing is in evidence also on other levels, where its magic function is obvious. The numerous amulet-shaped tablets with cuneiform inscriptions and the phylacteries meant to assure the well-being of children are examples.[9] The inscriptions on Mesopotamian amulets range from spells against demons to an entire literary opus (the Epic of Irra) meant to protect a house against the plague. Outright magic is in evidence in Egyptian "execration texts,"[10] intended to destroy the enemies whose names are written on them, as well as in the rarely attested symbolic act of breaking a cuneiform tablet (evidently inscribed with a list of cultic sins) to purify and to heal an afflicted person.[11]

The Scribes

The cuneiform source material is such that in it we have the unique opportunity of observing the evolution of a writing system. Nearly all but the very first stages are discernible, and enough, if not too much, material is available to allow an extensive discussion of the paleography and the history of the system, the dynamics of its development, diversifying as well as standardizing tendencies, several adjustments of the system to internal changes, and its adaptation to foreign demands—to mention at random some of the many aspects of this problem.

In the early, Sumerian, stage of the cuneiform system of writing, we are able to observe better than in similar systems the change from a "logographic" to a "phonographic" technique of writing. In a bureaucracy in which officials had to account periodically for the movements of goods, staples, and animals belonging to an authority, the use of word signs (logograms) for these items and for a number of typical transactions was as essential and probably as natural to the scribes as the use of signs to render numbers and measures. Once the practice of keeping written records became established, such symbols were freely used to record quantities, qualities, and types of objects as well as types of transactions. When, thereafter, the need arose to refer to new objects, to new materials, to proper names (personal or geographical), the inventors of this system made ingenious use of the accepted word signs, combining them as signs for syllables to write the new terms—in short, used them as "phonograms." The syllables (normally monosyllables) were read without regard to the meaning content which they had when used as logograms. The result was a fateful mixture, for the scribes neither discarded the use of a sign as a logogram when elsewhere in the text it might appear as a phonogram nor differentiated graphically or in any other way between logograms and phonograms. This mixed system, employing signs in two different functions, led to a number of complications which made it necessary for scribes to undergo a long and difficult training and brought about, in the long run, the disappearance of the entire system. But one should stress that this innate handicap must not be connected with the collapse of the Mesopotamian system of writing because of the competition with much simpler alphabetic systems. This would represent an unwarranted simplification.

Alphabetic systems as such go back to a prototype which represents an adaptation of the Mesopotamian technique of writing, in the sense that the earliest known alphabetic signs were written in wedges on clay.[12] Whether the later technique of writing alphabetic signs with ink on parchment and wood represents a direct development from the clay writing prototype, or whether the latter should be assumed a locally restricted transfer from a still earlier ink writing to the use of clay, is immaterial. The alphabetic systems did succeed, from the last third of the second millennium B.C. onward, in crowding out the cuneiform system, restricting it more and more to its home territory, and they eventually invaded the latter. In Babylonia proper, it was the replacement of the Akkadian language by the Aramaic, not the competition with the more efficient and easier system of alphabetic writing, that reduced the use of the cuneiform system to an ever-dwindling number of text categories.

As a curiosum in this context should be mentioned the rise of a late cuneiform system used by the Achaemenid rulers (from the sixth to the fourth century B.C.) and attested in southern Persia and Susa. The system presents a complex hybrid containing logographic, syllabic, and alphabetic elements and seems to owe its origin to the desire of the Persian kings to have a "national" system of writing beside the systems used for Babylonian and Elamite.[13] We may well say that the Persian system owed its existence to considerations of prestige rather than to the needs of a bureaucracy.

It is fairly certain that the principle of logographic writing was invented by the non-Sumerian predecessors of those Mesopotamians who wrote the earliest intelligible records on clay in Sumerian. The relationship between the posited proto-Sumerian writing and the somewhat younger and still un-deciphered writing system which we dub proto-Elamite—because it has been found so far only in Elamite sites—remains obscure. Equally problematic is the connection of this with the Indus valley script. The decipherment of these writings would shed light on the earliest stages of Mesopotamian writing, but there is very little hope that the extant evidence will be sufficient for decipherment. The Egyptian hieroglyphic system is customarily assumed to have developed independently yet under the stimulus of the cuneiform system. The concept of writing spreads rather easily when a social organization has reached a certain level and is still ready to react positively to stimuli from the outside.

More valuable than to speculate about diffusion and relationships is to investigate the characteristic uses made in several civilizations of the technique as such. It seems that the transfer from logographic to phonographic values was facilitated in Mesopotamia by the polysynthetic character of the Sumerian language as well as by the frequency of nouns composed with a classifying element (in initial position) in that language. As I have indicated, the development of Sumerian writing from logographic to phonographic was never carried through to completion. The slowly increasing practice of rendering spoken relators—pre-, in-, and suffixed short syllables—in writing and adding them to the logogram for the word itself further complicated the system. The entire system was then transferred from Sumerian to the Akkadian language. The phonograms were simply taken over even though their inventory falls far short of the phonetic requirements of the first Akkadian dialects (Tigrido-Akkadian, see p. 54) which utilized it. This resulted in the appearance of a number of ambiguous writings caused by the differences in the phonological systems of the two languages. Certain logograms were taken over in order to render roughly corresponding Akkadian nouns and adjectives—and even verbs. To resolve doubts in identifying such words, it became customary to add phonograms (mainly after the logogram) in order to indicate explicitly what Akkadian word was meant and in which grammatical form it was to be read. This entire development was accompanied by a paleographic evolution which tended toward simplification and standardization of sign forms as well as toward their reduction in number.

With the subsequent shift that brought early Old Babylonian dialects (Euphrato-Akkadian, see p. 54) to dominance, paleography and the system of writing changed even more decidedly. Although the entire complicated and cumbersome system was never completely abandoned wherever Akkadian was written in cuneiform, the use of word signs was greatly reduced in the Old Babylonian period. Word signs were restricted to certain often-occurring nouns, such as "god," "king," "silver," and "city." Only slowly a small number of new signs came into use, and other practices were evolved to render phonetic differences that were significant for Akkadian. Even so, a number of signs remained phonetically—and phonologically—ambiguous both with respect to the contrast between voiced and voiceless consonants and those with the so-called emphatic articulation. This and the inherited polyvalence of certain signs—telltale indications of the transfer from a non-Sumerian language to Sumerian—made the task of the scribes still more difficult and compelled them to study an extensive set of reference works for a prolonged period. The scribes became thus, of necessity, a group of highly trained experts (schooling methods will be discussed presently). This explains the stagnation and regression that soon after the transfers described enveloped the cuneiform system of writing. No meaningful changes toward simplification or increased efficiency occur, although complicated signs were discarded here and there, and in texts on very technical subjects certain frequently used logograms appear in abbreviated form. A strange reversal, to be noticed in the late Old Babylonian period and appearing full-fledged in the Assyrian text collections of the first half of the first millennium, expresses itself in a sharp increase in the use of logograms. This practice is restricted to scholarly texts of a technical nature, mainly omen texts. Logograms appear for nouns as well as for verbs and are provided with the minimum of phonetic complements necessary to establish syntactic relations. Their use permits the scribe to evolve a quasimathematical conciseness and formulaic brevity of presentation which makes the texts of this type nearly unintelligible to the uninitiated.

In spite of its obvious shortcomings and its cumbersomeness, the writing system was elastic enough to be used for rendering such foreign languages as Hittite, Elamite, Hurrian, and Urartian. Only in a few instances did diacritical variations and specific practices have to be invented to handle the alien phoneme inventory without much distortion.[14]

Paleographically speaking, periods, regions, and text types became distinct as did certain physical features, the shape of the clay tablets, the arrangement of lines and columns. Certain over-all trends become obvious, especially differentiations between cursive and monumental writing styles and between Assyrian and Babylonian sign forms and scribal practices. Schools of scribes are in evidence from the earlier periods; training was not restricted to the use of the stylus, the teaching of sign values and uses, and whatever knowledge of Sumerian was considered necessary but included strict rules as to the shape and physical preparation of the tablets and the arrangement of the writing.

The smooth and plastic surface of wet clay can be easily impressed with appropriate tools, and these impressions become permanent whether the clay is kiln-fired or sun-dried. It is sensitive enough to retain the finest lines of the stylus and all the minute details of a cylinder seal rolled over the tablet or of a stamp seal impressed on it. For writing purposes, clay was used in three main forms: in tags or bullae which protected the knots made in the strings that safeguarded the contents of bags and baskets; in tablets of a large variety of forms and sizes; and in a number of ceremonial forms, such as prisms, cylinders, and barrels, which hold many more lines than can tablets and are less apt to break.

The wedges were impressed with a stylus, usually of reed but sometimes of wood or other material. The stylus was also used to make rulings; vertical lines, marking the columns, sometimes were made by means of a thread pulled over the soft tablet. Certain tablets are covered with a slip of finer clay that made writing in small characters easier. The shapes of the tablets differ widely, from thin squares the size of a postage stamp, larger cushion-shaped forms with narrow or thick rims, to beautiful large tablets measuring in a few instances up to a yard; some are square, others oblong. Most of the tablets are inscribed parallel to the short side. Each period and region show characteristic preferences; the content of the tablet, moreover, whether it is a legal tablet, a letter, or an administrative text, influences its shape and size. One can often classify a clay tablet without reading it. Frequently, tablets were imitated in stone or metal, especially when used for important transactions or as foundation deposits.

In the earliest period, individual words were written in the form of vertically arranged signs within boxes placed in bands side by side from right to left, as is best illustrated by the text of the Codex Hammurapi, which is inscribed in this (at that time already antiquated) way. Soon, a change of direction took place: On small, hand-size tablets the writing was turned 90° to the left, so that the first word of a text written originally downward with its syllable signs one under the other in the first box at the right end of the tablet now appears in the first box or line of the first column in the left upper corner. To inscribe the reverse, the tablet was normally turned to bring its lower edge to the top. Larger tablets were utilized in carefully laid-out parallel columns in which the scribe wrote, proceeding from left to right on the obverse and in the opposite direction on the reverse. Certain important accounting tablets and all literary texts reserve space in their last column for either a summing up or the title of the composition. This section, called the colophon, contains, in a literary tablet, the information which a modern book presents on its title page. It gives the title of the text—usually the incipit or first line—the names of the owner and the scribe, often the date, and pertinent remarks referring to the original which the scribe had copied. Sometimes a text is declared secret or curses are added against those who would remove the tablet from its location without authorization or keep it overnight. If a given literary or scholarly composition is too extensive to be copied on one tablet, the colophon refers expressly to this fact and indicates the first line of the tablet on which the text is continued. Normally the tablets of such a series are numbered, at times with double numberings referring to sub-series. In libraries, the tablets of such a series seem to have been stored on shelves or clay banks in bundles fastened by strings with tags attached indicating the contents.[15] Some of these tags have been preserved, as well as catalogs which list such series by titles and often give the number of the tablets that make up the series.[16] Clay jars held private archives; the extensive records of the Ur III administration were kept in baskets provided with appropriate labels of which we have found quite a number. To facilitate the identification of a specific tablet among those of a larger administrative archive, short remarks were written on the rim of the tablet (Ur III); later, Aramaic dockets were added to Neo-Babylonian business documents for the scribes who apparently could not read easily the cuneiform writing.[16a]

Two technologically interesting inventions were made to replace hand writing by more efficient techniques but were utilized very rarely by Mesopotamian scribes. The custom of inscribing bricks for palaces, temples, and other buildings with the name of the king and the building led to the invention of clay stamps. Some of these stamps even made use of ingenious interchangeable sign units, rather like movable type.[17] Equally noteworthy as an example of technological achievement was the practice of the scribes in Elamite Susa, who resorted to the use of cylinders on which were engraved curses that could be transferred to the soft clay surface by rolling the cylinder over it in order to save themselves the bother of writing these tiresome formulas by hand.[18]

In the early first millennium B.C., scribes began to use long, narrow wooden tablets provided with a thin layer of wax on which they impressed the cuneiform signs. It is not quite clear whether this was done in imitation of an alien technique of writing or was an invention of the scribes for the purpose of display. A set of such tablets was recently found. It consists of a number of oblong ivory plates hinged end to end by means of leather straps and opening like a screen.[19] Clearly, it was more convenient to carry such a "book" than a set of heavy and bulky—and breakable—clay tablets. All the same, we would have lost most of the literary and scholarly texts in cuneiform had the practice of using these books been generally adopted. There are indications that such books made of precious wood panels were a luxury item. It is likely that Aramaic was written in this way before the Akkadian scribes began to use it for cuneiform and that with the loss of these fragile books an entire literature in Aramaic may have perished in Mesopotamia.[20]

In contrast to Sumerian and especially Egyptian literature, Akkadian texts only rarely extol the craft of the scribe and his importance in society. We know next to nothing about the social position, background, and political influence of Mesopotamian scribes. The patrons of the craft were at first the goddess Nisaba and, later, the god Nabu, in whose temple and chapels, called Ezida, scribes used to deposit, as votive offerings, beautifully written tablets. It is not known what the relationship between these deities and the scribes implied. In a number of instances one can observe that the lore of the scribe was handed down in families. In general, education and training prepared the apprentice to deal with every kind of text, as we know from the bilingual compositions that describe the wide variety of topics which made up the curriculum.[21] There are only a few indications of specialization in evidence; there were scribes called *ṭupšar-enūma-Anu-Enlil* because they were dealing with astrological and astronomical tablets, and others who appear as administrators among the officials of the court of Nebuchadnezzar II as well as the "city scribes" who are mentioned among the top administrative officials in Middle Assyrian and Neo-Assyrian texts.

The characteristic method of training has left us countless "school tablets"—mostly small, lentil-shaped disks—with a sign, a word, or a short sentence in the teacher's writing on one side (or above a line), and on the reverse (or on the line below) the pupil's efforts to copy the example. Other tablets—often rather poorly written—contain excerpts from several literary works copied by the students.

Beginning with simple signs and sign groups, and progressing to more complex and difficult arrangements, the student had to copy and to learn by rote the pronunciation and the reading of a wide variety of sequences of such signs and combinations of signs. A well-established curriculum apparently had to be followed not only with regard to the more elementary lists but also with regard to the study of literary works. The very fact that the first tablets of important series are preserved in many more copies than the following tablets—which, by the way, leaves us much too often in doubt concerning the last tablets of such compositions—illustrates this point. The apprentice scribe was apparently not required to complete his copy of the series before moving on to the next text of the prescribed curriculum.

The student copied these tablets not only for practice purposes but, at times, also to reproduce the original for his master's or his own use, this being the usual way of building up a collection. Individual and most probably all scholarly-minded scribes succeeded in accumulating through the work of their pupils a personal collection of tablets. Scribes and scribal schools attached to palaces and especially to temples enjoyed an amount of economic security and leisure that was bound to lead to an increase of interest in specialized topics. This, in turn, created such an accumulation of tablets dealing with scholarly pursuits that Assyriologists like to call them libraries. Such libraries have been found in Assur and in Sultantepe as well as in many of the sites in southern Mesopotamia which have not been excavated by professionals but were plundered toward the end of the nineteenth century. But one should stress that a library in our sense, a systematic collecting of texts copied for the purpose of being included in such a collection, existed in Mesopotamia solely in Nineveh. Here, at the instance of Assurbanipal, king of Assyria, such a library was assembled, and large sections of it have been preserved. From his own letters, we know that the king was eager to assemble the tablets, that he sent emissaries to Babylonia to look for certain texts, and that he showed so much interest in this project that he himself decided which tablets were to be put into the library and which to be omitted.[22] Many texts were copied for the library in a standardized form, with great care and scholarly accuracy; their colophons mention the name of Assurbanipal and contain allusions to his interest in literature and scholarship. We have estimated above (pp. 16 f.) the number of tablets kept in the collection; here attention should be drawn to the fact that no systematic study has yet been undertaken to establish the contents of the library of Assurbanipal or the provenience of tablets and text groups. Nevertheless, there are indications that substantial parts came from the old capital of Calah where Tiglath-Pileser I (1115–1077 B.C.) seems to have brought together much earlier Babylonian originals after his conquest of Babylon.[23] And private collections were apparently incorporated in the library of Assurbanipal. An investigation of the original contents of the Kuyundjik Collection is bound to yield important information on the intellectual history of Assyria.

Primarily intended for teaching purposes but eventually changing into the only accepted method of scholarly presentation, a text type of a special nature was created by Mesopotamian scribes. These are texts containing nothing but lists of signs, sign groups, or words arranged in narrow vertical columns. This list of signs originally had the purposes of teaching the scribe how to write a sign while memorizing its pronunciation; if one sign had several readings, the sign was repeated as often as necessary. From a purely mnemotechnic device, these lists developed into a complex apparatus for the higher training of the scribes and assumed several specific forms which a presentation of Mesopotamian civilization cannot afford to omit. Their very number imposes upon us the obligation to study these "syllabaries" or "vocabularies." These ancient lists have contributed greatly

toward the decipherment of cuneiform writing and the establishment of the basic facts of the Akkadian lexicon and grammar
from the earliest days of Assyriology. After the publication
of larger sections of these syllabaries before World War I, only a
few attempts were made to organize the texts and to investigate their form and function. For thirty years, Benno Landsberger gave much of his time to the task of preparing these texts
for publication. By now a substantial part of the material has
appeared.[24]

The following is a succinct presentation of these lists, arranged
typologically. We shall deal first with the sign lists. Three types
of sign lists seem to have existed in the early Old Babylonian
period. One type contains syllable-signs grouped according to
the vowel sequence u-a-i (e.g., bu-ba-bi); another arranges the
signs according to their forms in larger and smaller groups.
There is a third type, which Assyriologists call "Ea" after its
first sign. The first two types of sign lists were used in primary
education outside of Nippur, the third in Nippur itself. The first
group remained unchanged, but the second (called "Syllabary
a," S^a, in the early days of Assyriology) developed in a manner
worth discussing. The signs—written carefully one underneath
the other—were eventually provided on the left with their
reading in Sumerian (expressed in simple syllable signs) and, on
the right, with their Akkadian names. Thus three-column
syllabaries came into being in which vertical lines neatly
separated the individual columns (pronunciation : sign : sign
name).

The Nippur syllabary—the Ea type—proved an arrangement
that produced a complex chain of related lists. Originally, it
contained signs essential for reading and writing Sumerian on
an elementary level; it offered not only the signs but all the
specific readings they had due to the polyphonic nature of the
writing system. The prototype (now conventionally termed
Proto-Ea) was soon enlarged and enriched; an exhaustive series
comprising forty tablets was thus created which added to the
original arrangement, which was like that of S^a, a fourth column
(at the extreme right) with the Akkadian translation of each
Sumerian logogram, often giving several Akkadian translations

for one Sumerian sign. The Akkadians called it after its first line á A= *nâqu* (literally, "a" is the pronunciation of the sign A in the meaning "to complain"). In some versions, the column with the sign names was omitted. For practical purposes, excerpts were made of the full text; one such excerpt, on eight tablets, is called ea A= *nâqu*. From the latter derives a two-tablet compendium for elementary training ("Syllabary b," Sᵇ) with only the most common signs and meanings.

An acrophonic list of signs and their compounds was used in Nippur for the higher training of the scribes. The original Sumerian list (now called Proto-Izi) was later enlarged, and provided with Akkadian translations, into the series i z i= *išātu* ("i z i means fire"). It comprised at least sixteen tablets. Another Nippur series served similar purposes: this is the originally bilingual series diri ᴅɪʀɪ *siāku*= *watru* ("diri is the pronunciation of the sign ᴅɪʀɪ called *siāku* literally [si-plus-a] in the meaning "excessive"). In an acrographic arrangement, it restricts itself to groups of signs whose Sumerian readings differ from that of the individual components. It comprises seven tablets.

The trend toward bilingual lists ("vocabularies") increased from the Middle Babylonian period on. The new crop of lists is arranged in groups of synonyms usually comprising three words. One such list of more than ten tablets is called a n . t a . g á l= *šaqû*; another, of more than six, e r i m . ḫ u š= *anantu*. Here also belongs a topically arranged series a l a n= *lānu*, and one (sɪɢ₄ + ᴀʟᴀᴍ= *nabnītu*) that contains, on more than thirty tablets, Sumerian and Akkadian equations in which the principle of arrangement is carried by the Akkadian column. It lists parts of the human body, and verbs referring to their activities, in a sequence which starts with the head and ends with the feet.

Special traditions in different periods and schools have left us their traces in a number of fragmentary word and sign lists, not to speak of fragments that may or may not belong to the collections mentioned, many of which are only imperfectly preserved.

We now turn to topically arranged word lists. They are attested at a very early period and became increasingly important later on. They are composed exclusively of nouns and are organized in large groupings. Originally they consisted of sequences of composite Sumerian nouns, that is, of nouns with a classifying element in initial position (g i š . m e s= mes-tree, g i š . g i š i m m a r= palm-tree, etc.) which served as a criterion for the arrangement of the entries. Only later were they provided with Akkadian translations, the reliability of which is in some instances impaired by the time lag. We thus have word lists offering us the names of trees, of wooden objects, of stars, of garments, and of many more classes of objects. From Sumerian prototypes thus developed in the late Old Babylonian period a famous bilingual series of twenty-two tablets (tablets 3–24) called ḪAR.ra= ḫubullu. It deals with the following topics: trees, wooden objects, reeds and reed objects, earthenware, leather objects, metals and metal objects, domestic animals, wild animals, parts of the human and animal body, stone and stone objects, plants, fish and birds, wool and garments, localities of all description, and beer, honey, barley, and other foodstuffs. Each left-hand column contains a Sumerian term beginning with the essential classifier, and the right-hand column translates either the entire Sumerian word or an important section of it. Eventually, many of the Akkadian words became rare or even obsolete, and, in a new series, a second Akkadian column with an explanation was added which supplemented the old by a new word. This new series, collecting all the commented terms in a three-column arrangement, was called ḪAR.GUD= imrû= ballu, i.e., "m u r-fodder for oxen= fattener= (new term) mixture (of fodder)." On four tablets, another series of the topical type deals with designations of human beings such as officials, craftsmen, cripples, and social classes. It is obvious that these lists represent unique material not only for the lexicographer but for the student of technology. In fact, they have not begun to yield all the information they contain.

Since the list was accepted as the characteristic tool for teaching and philological research, other works pertaining to these activities were cast in the same form. A number of grammatical texts designed to teach Sumerian morphology to Akkadian scribes are preserved in list form dating from the Old as well as from the Neo-Babylonian period. To illustrate the dialectal differences within Sumerian, a series was created which lists first the dialectal (e m e . SAL), then the main dialect word, and gives the Akkadian translation in its third column (the series is called: d i m m e r= d i n g i r= *ilu*).[25] An Old Babylonian compendium from Nippur, called *ana ittišu*, that contains legal formulas to train the scribes for the correct phrasing of deeds and contracts, is preserved.[26] Excerpts thereof form, for unknown reasons, the first two tablets of the series ḪAR.ra= *ḫubullu*, which thus differ completely from the balance of this work as described above. What appears to represent a kind of pharmacopoeia (Ú uru.an.na= Ú *maštakal*)[27] is likewise styled as a list and so are, quite naturally, enumerations of gods and goddesses and catalogs of stars. Also to be mentioned are synonym lists which explain rare and obsolete or dialectal Akkadian words by more common terms and therefore have Akkadian in both columns. They are of late origin. To a still higher level of scribal training belong those specialized list arrangements that are, in fact, reference books. Thus we have texts which describe in detail the appearance of stones and plants, giving their names in each instance. Their functional use cannot be established, but they should not be adduced as evidence of scientific interest in mineralogy or botany.[28]

The preceding presentation has stressed, and in certain instances possibly even overstressed, the operational element in the rise and development of the numerous lists we have been discussing. The operational interpretation seems to me to be simpler and to fit the essential features of the lists more adequately than to invoke such a quasi-mythological concept as *Ordnungswille*, according to which the scribes who made these lists aimed at "organizing" the universe around them by listing what they saw of it in word signs written in narrow columns on clay.[29] Equally unwarranted seem to me to be the claims that the word lists with names of plants, animals, and stones, are the beginnings of botany, zöology, and mineralogy, respectively. Such claims originate in the climate of today's opinion in which achievements in what we choose to term "science" are considered essential in an alien civilization if it is to be worthy of study. What we have to see in these numerous and diversified lists is much the same process of growth by accretion, the same preference for additive elaboration and amplification (rather than structural changes) which we can observe in Mesopotamian legal practices, in the evolution of the votive inscriptions, in the layout of a temple, to mention some few examples. A formally very simple and short pattern is utilized by the scribes to render a large variety of complex and elaborate contents. In this way the form as such does not exercise any tyranny, nor does it coerce the content, but serves as vehicle; in fact, it forms a matrix for a progressive development. The results of such an attitude can be judged adequately only from the angle which is indicated by the basic form pattern; from any other point of view a confused and blurred picture results.

We have already discussed the evidence for "political" bilinguality without reference to the scholarly side of this phenomenon. The traditional bilinguality of the Mesopotamian scribe was maintained by the training in which a great deal of Sumerian material was used. Interest in Sumerian grammar and lexicography was effectively kept alive by the use of Sumerian in certain religious contexts, and the "stream of tradition" which included a number of Sumerian texts with interlinear Akkadian translation contributed toward maintaining this bilinguality. The translations of Sumerian texts were first written as glosses (in smaller characters) below the Sumerian or in the free spaces left on the line, then on separate and indented lines below the Sumerian text, very rarely only on the reverse of a tablet that carried the Sumerian on its obverse. The reliability of these translations varies greatly, but their importance for the investigation of Sumerian was discovered early. Again, we are still without systematic investigation of these text categories that represent an important and very early linguistic achievement of the scribes of Mesopotamia. These texts are either religious in nature and function or "magic," e.g., the extensive series *utukkē lemnūti* ("Evil demons") and similar compositions. Only quite rarely was Sumerian poetry translated (the works called Lugale u₄ melambi nergal and Angimdimma) or were some of the very extensive proverb collections of the Sumerians provided with an added translation in Akkadian.

The Creative Effort

It is difficult to discuss the creative effort of an alien literature for the benefit of a reader who is, at best, familiar with only a small number of well-known and often translated texts. By refusing to escape into a listing of the various types of literary forms evolved in Mesopotamia and to offer translations of selected passages, I will have to steer a difficult course between a discussion of poetic forms of expression and an inventory of poetic topics. This will leave the basic question of the nature and goal of the creative effort largely unanswered but may allow the reader to form an idea of the nature of this effort, if only in an indirect way.

When one applies the characterization "literary" to all cuneiform texts that are not concerned with the direct communication of information, two basic form patterns can be discerned. One is patently "poetic" inasmuch as tenor, range, and means of expression are restricted and formalized; the other is more difficult to grasp because the restrictions are less obvious and act on a more subtle level.

We begin with a discussion of texts of the first type. They are diversified in their background, mood, and function but are united by such features as the rhythmic organization of their sentence units and sub-units, the structural organization linking these "verses"—sentence units, to be exact—into smaller (distichs) or larger groups (strophes, stanzas), and by their vocabulary and distinctive topical range. The rhythmic organization articulates the entire sentence structure into sub-units of four to six or seven words; the particular stress features of these words are utilized in a pattern of two half-verses separated by a caesura, which the scribes often carefully indicate by leaving a blank space. It still remains uncertain—but is not relevant at this point—whether this verse pattern utilizes stress or syllable length, or both, to arrange the words or word groups within the sentence. Neither alliteration nor rhyming devices are used to link the half-verses across the caesura or the distichs within the carefully maintained external verse arrangement. All interrelation is done on the level of meaning. The meaning content of each verse appears normally in two parallel formulations separated by the mentioned caesura—a pattern that is termed *parallelismus membrorum.* While in such instances the first member formulates a subsection of the sentence in some "rhythmic" manner, the second echoes it in a slightly different wording, preferably in an even more "poetic" diction, i.e., with the use of words less well known or words endowed with more refined connotations. This rather primitive arrangement can be replaced by one that embraces the half-verses of the entire distich, and even more lines if special effects are looked for. All this is meant to link together verses with meaning patterns which make use of the poetic tension evolving from the parallel formulations of the same or of opposite statements. Here are two examples:

> When above : the heaven had not been named [yet]
> below the earth : had not been called by name—

> *or*

> Even the gods   became afraid of the flood,
> they retreated, they went off   to the heaven of Anu;
> [there] they are lying at the outside [of heaven]   cowering like dogs.
> Ištar screams   like a woman in labor,
> the Lady-of-the-Gods moans—she whose voice is [so] lovely.

The poetic impression is conveyed by a number of factors—the careful segmentation of the information into small meaning units, the elaborate echoing, repeating and counterpointing, of these units by means of the skeleton of the over-all verse arrangement. Texture is added through the selection of words that are subtly distinguished either through semantic nuances or through rare or artificial morphological features. Much still escapes us of the poetry inherent in certain modifications of the verbal stem, the choice of noun formation, the application of a sophisticated synonymy which weighs not only words but syllables. Both the dynamics of the meaning distribution and the charm conveyed by the variety and breadth of the vocabulary are fused into a poetic unit by the organizing principle of the over-all rhythmization of the poem. As said above, we are unable to analyze the elements that carry the rhythm, but it is clearly applied in two stages: the individual verses are held together by a pattern that allows more weight (and words) to the second half, and the strophic structure which links the sequence of verses in groups of two or more uses the same metric device to accentuate that grouping. In this respect we often come across apparent irregularities which cannot be described in rational terms but which may well have contributed in keeping the attention of the listener. Whether these and other irregularities in the rhythmic structure were purposely applied, simply tolerated, or to be corrected when the poem was recited in the appropriate way, we cannot tell. Questions of this sort are linked to the phonemic role of stress and vowel quantity within the spoken language and to the history of the poetic genre under discussion. Was it meant to be recited or was it to be sung, alone, to the accompaniment of musical instruments or with a choir? Additional complications are brought in if there existed a dichotomy in the poetic tradition of Mesopotamia, the Sumerian poetic form and content contrasting with the Akkadian and even general Semitic background. It is in view of such problems that we must concentrate our interest on the descriptive rather than the historical aspects of Mesopotamian poetry.

It is evident that poetry of this form is best fitted to deal with descriptions and with orations and hymnic addresses, all easily subdivided into short statements which the poet uses to shape a poem. The slow and stately pace that such poetry achieves is not suited to the presentation of dramatic incidents. Hence a restriction of topics; only certain situations were considered suitable material for poetry; others had to be transformed or transposed for this purpose. When one reads the description of Marduk's fight against Tiamat (see p. 264), the passages of the Epic of Gilgamesh which deal with the events leading up to the great Flood that destroyed nearly all mankind, or such short pieces as the story of Adapa (see p. 267), one cannot fail to notice the effects of this specific poetic style. The poet shows his interest in solemn speeches, in the description of objects and of preparations and the effects of certain acts and situations, with an abundance of verses intended to entertain the reader or listener rather than to advance the story. Crucial events and decisive changes in fortune are stated in a minimum of verses. The resulting impression is that of a sequence of static situations connected by a few succinct lines in which the story progresses. All this in combination with the patent lack of interest in dealing with the setting of the events in relation to either the realities of life or to the background against which the events take place account for the curious lifelessness of much of the epic literature in cuneiform. Of course, an ingenious poet can make sophisticated use of the same features, and the late version of the Epic of Gilgamesh bears evidence in several instances to such artistry.

Having discussed what we have termed the first type of literary creations, i.e., that which is poetic and cast in well-established forms, we turn to the second type. The poetic aspirations of the latter manifest themselves on a more subtle level, and form and content requirements are more difficult to establish. Into this category I would like to place royal inscriptions from Babylonia and Assyria insofar as they contain more than the minimal wording necessary for this text type and do not represent schematized reports on campaigns. Whenever these texts turn to descriptions of the locale, deserts or mountains, forests or swamps, or to descriptions of the heroic achievements of the king and the intervention of the deities in battles or other emergencies, they shift perceptibly from the wearisome patter of official diction into a style that can only be described as poetic. In vividness of expression, these passages in royal inscriptions are usually far more poetic than verse in meter. Nothing better illustrates this than a comparison of Sennacherib's report on the battle of Halule with that crucial mythological, or cosmological, contest between Marduk and Tiamat described in the fourth tablet of the *Enūma eliš*, the Creation story.[30] In the latter, after preparations and cumbersome deliberations are rendered at length, only twelve verses are dedicated to the battle itself. The victory of Marduk is not very thrilling, based as it is on a primitive stratagem, a trick encountered often enough in folklore.[31] The form is poetic but neither the mood of the incident nor the style of the presentation deserves this characterization. Quite different is the way in which the battle of Sennacherib is presented. It is told in fifty long lines and exhibits such *brio*, such patent delight in the furor and the joys of the fight, that one forgets it is—formally—written in prose. The imagery is vivid and novel and judiciously mixes crass naturalism with a hectic flight of religious imagination. In short, it mirrors the existence of an established literary tradition that well knew how to utilize the formal and lexical possibilities of the language, that dared to be inventive in its similes and did not refuse to see the realities of the battlefield amid the description of the gory triumph. This battle account and the descriptions of the landscape in Sargon's report on his campaign through the mountains and forests of Armenia, the fantastic account of Esarhaddon's travels through the deserts of Arabia, and Assurbanipal's redundant but intense report on the defeat of the rebellious Arabs, are easily superior to contemporary Assyrian compositions intended as poetry. The description of Nebuchadnezzar I in the fight against Elam shows a kindred spirit, although transposed to a Babylonian "key."[32] Even if one links the emergence of this new style in historical inscriptions at the beginning of the first millennium to certain literary works in the poetic style of Mesopotamia (see below), one wonders why two poetic traditions, one in historical texts, the other in the traditional literary genres, coexisted in Mesopotamia. Even if it was stylistically not acceptable to have royal inscriptions written in poetic form, a genetic relationship seems to have existed between Sumerian royal hymns and texts of our type as is borne out by the exalted, hymnic diction of certain sections of Assyrian royal inscriptions.

In discussing the problem of poetic form, we have been dealing with that of poetic content as well. We have suggested that the description of static situations, of the features of objects and the rendering of speeches was preferred to the narration of dramatic happenings. Only rarely—as in the isolated Old Babylonian Gilgamesh fragments (see below, p. 261)—is some attention granted to the realities of a scene, an attempt made to render a non-mythological locale, or the personal reaction of the individual to the world around him.[33] There is no scarcity of passages that do credit to the power of observation of the poet and his readiness to make use of such observations in his imagery; still, the marvels of the cosmos, the magic of symbolic dreams, and, above all, the solemn speeches of the protagonists take up much of the text of the known epics.

We turn now to a presentation of content and a discussion of the individual style and of the state of our knowledge concerning the most important literary texts. In order not to let this presentation degenerate into an enumeration of literary works or an inventory of extant fragments, we shall restrict the area of our interest. The literary history of Mesopotamia cannot be more than outlined, and it is open to serious doubt—and I am inclined to side here with the skeptics—whether enough material is available to embark on the venture of writing such a history.

In the creativity of Mesopotamia we have at hand a unique opportunity to observe the extent of the reinterpretation of the Sumerian legacy. This legacy was either maintained or elaborated upon as in the realms of the other arts and the realm of technology or was left far behind, as in divination and the sciences; the situation in respect to literature is far more complex. In astonishing richness and variety, Babylonian literary production had soared into pre-eminence when the Sumerian formulation of Mesopotamian civilization was still very much in evidence, albeit in decline. Nevertheless, a wide range of Sumerian topical inventory and of literary techniques, in modified form, was accepted as the basis of Babylonian literature. As far as our present knowledge goes, this represents a unique phenomenon in Mesopotamian cultural history, although one day a broader and deeper understanding of the development of religious concepts may show parallel instances.

Foremost among Mesopotamian epics in Akkadian—and not only in size and state of preservation—is the Epic of Gilgamesh. An idea of Mesopotamian literary achievement at its best—its literary trends and topical composition—may be gained from a study of what is known of this important work. The latest version of the epic is preserved in the library of Assurbanipal on twelve tablets containing more than 3,000 lines and on a number of small fragments dating from the Neo-Babylonian period. The earlier material is available in Sumerian versions, in a few Old Babylonian tablets, and in a small number of copies found further west, one in Boghazkeui, one in Megiddo,[33a] and one, quite recently, in Ugarit.[34] Both Hittite and Hurrian translations come from Boghazkeui.[35] In spite of the relative abundance of material, it is still not possible to restore the entire story without gaps, which occur at crucial junctures. Before we turn to a discussion of the epic, the often repeated assertion must be refuted that it is to be considered a literary work of such essential and representative nature as to be termed a "national" epic. Apart from the fact that all so-called national epics from Vergil's Aeneid on are patent imitations of Homeric epics, the imposition of such a time-bound pattern on Mesopotamian literary history should be rejected a priori. Moreover, there is no evidence in cuneiform texts that the Epic of Gilgamesh, or ša naqba īmuru as the Akkadians also called it (after its incipit), had any special position in their literary tradition. On the contrary, there are indications that the entire epic, which so much appeals to us, was little known in Mesopotamia proper.

For all its sweep, the variety of its adventures, its human appeal and often exquisite poetry, the epic failed to interest the Mesopotamian scribes. The few extant fragments as yet cannot be linked, even provisionally, in a textual history. The version from the royal library in Nineveh is still the most important; without the information it contains we could hardly make sense of the several earlier fragments. The lack of response to the epic is evident in the absence of quotations from it in literary texts or in texts from outside the stream of tradition. These same texts, however, contain a number of direct quotations and paraphrased segments of the Epic of Irra, which shows that this composition had much wider currency than that of Gilgamesh in the same period. More important still is that none of the striking personalities and the memorable events and achievements which the Epic of Gilgamesh offers so abundantly are more than alluded to in the rest of the literature. Nor has the fantastic world of the epic left any clear traces in Mesopotamian iconography.[36] This is in contrast to the numerous, obvious, and fascinating parallels the story offers to Old Testament, Ugaritic, and Greek mythological motifs and figures and the popularity it enjoyed outside of Mesopotamia. A Greek writer even offers us a somewhat different version of the Epic of Gilgamesh.[37]

Gilgamesh's life and his adventures during his unsuccessful quest for immortality are told on eleven of the twelve tablets.[38] The poet uses with skill two parallel scenes, one at the beginning of the first and the other at the end of the eleventh tablet as a frame to round out the story and to emphasize the futility of the quest by returning to the starting point. It shows a sense for drama that the starting point of the epic is the only work of the hero that promised, even guaranteed, his immortality—the walls of his city, Uruk which he had built. Moreover, the poet uses twice the lines which describe these walls for two entirely different purposes: first he himself, speaking in the introit and addressing the reader, presents the walls and their fateful connection with the hero of the story; then, at the end, he has Gilgamesh repeat the description to Uršanabi as he points out with pride his city and its walls to his guest; but Gilgamesh does not refer to the walls as being intimately linked to the story of his own life. The restraint of the poet in this respect is remarkable and difficult to understand. The drive for immortality as the primary motif of the epic is elaborated, in the main, on the rather crude level of a desire for eternal youth with a secondary stress on a wish for fame derived from extraordinary deeds as a vehicle for the extension of the personality beyond the grave. Two closely related *topoi* are omitted, the immortality which children, especially a son, provide for the father, and the enduring fame which a building of outstanding size confers on its maker. The latter kind of immortality is alluded to distinctly, though not expressly, in the frame of the epic, and suggested in certain details included in the description of the oppression of the citizens of Uruk who must do *corvée* work for their king. A direct reference to the descendants of Gilgamesh is carefully and pointedly avoided. Two explanations may be suggested for this reticence: either the literary tradition knew of no son of Gilgamesh (in spite of the Sumerian king list) or the poet who composed the latest version did so at the court of a king who had no son and heir. There the topic would be taboo, and the artistry of the court poet strives to treat with delicacy the story of Gilgamesh in order to mirror the tragic fate of his king, holding out to him at the same time the hope that is implicit in the twelfth and last tablet of the final version. This hope is contained in a description of the nether world, in which Gilgamesh rules after his death as divine judge over the shades, guiding and advising them as Šamaš serves the living. The rationale for linking the description of the nether world—a typically Sumerian literary topic—to the story of Gilgamesh is more apt to have been a desire to please a living ruler than a wish of the poet to offset the alleged pessimism of the futile quest for immortality told in the first eleven tablets.[39] Of course, this reasoning is based on arguments *e silentio*, since the Old Babylonian Gilgamesh fragments do not indicate that the last tablet had been incorporated at that time. In view of the fact that another, clearly extraneous story—that of the Flood— also has been fused, with more or less cogency, into the main story, the suggestion of the connection between the last tablet and the bulk of the epic gains in plausibility.

The introit raises further questions. Having extolled Gilgamesh as wise and widely traveled, the poet mentions as his final achievement a stela on which the hero had inscribed a report of his travels. From that source, supposedly, comes the information which the poet used in the epic. The suggested derivation of the epic from the text of the stela is a literary *topos*, and its use presupposes a reader who is sophisticated enough to accept it as a literary fiction and not as proof of the authenticity of the text or, worse, an imposition on his critical sense.

The term "reader" is used here in order to register my exception to the theory, sometimes voiced, that bardic poetry existed in Mesopotamia and influenced the growth and development of the epic tradition. The theory is based on the unwarranted assumption that the same conditions as in Greece existed in Mesopotamia. Literary life did not necessarily follow such a pattern in Mesopotamia. Sumerian epics (for example, the Enmerkar story) are at times as patently a product of the royal court as those written in Akkadian; one may admit, however, that the early Akkadian versions of the Epic of Gilgamesh, with their distinct poetic structure, suggest the influence of a background of popular poetry. One should seek to discover as sources of Mesopotamian epic literature all types of literary production, including popular poetry, court poetry, and learned, that is, written poetry.

The second part of the introit of the epic bears out rather convincingly that the work was meant to be read rather than recited. When speaking of Gilgamesh as the builder of the walls of Uruk and of the temple of Eanna, the poet turns to those he addresses, exhorting them to behold these structures, to touch them, to enter the temple, to mount the wall. In short, these verses establish a relationship between author and his readers on the level of pure imagination. No bard can thus address his audience, nor can allocutions in this style originate in a literary genre which has a rhapsodic past. The passage is meant to be read, hence this part, at least, of the poem addresses itself to a public that either can read or lives in a social context that makes it possible to hear the epic read.

Upon the conclusion of the introit, the story of Gilgamesh proceeds from episode to episode in a cleverly calculated sequence, following the fate of the hero but moving to other localities when essential developments originate there. Thus, the home of Enkidu and his *éducation sentimentale* are presented, the mood and apprehensions of the mother of Gilgamesh are described, and we are given Ištar's dialogue with Anu. Persons come and go, but Gilgamesh remains the center of attention as the all-powerful and famous king who at first achieves his goals and then, suddenly, is reminded of his mortality by the death of his friend Enkidu. The appearance of Enkidu is occasioned by the *hubris* of Gilgamesh, who forces all the inhabitants of his city to work for him, building the very walls and temples, which at first we are asked to admire and which are eventually to secure him lasting fame; enraged, the gods create Enkidu in order to check Gilgamesh. That the gods react so promptly to the complaints of the citizens of Uruk, whose civic liberties have been disregarded by their king, could be taken to date the milieu of the poet as the late Kassite period when the *kidinnu* concept became a powerful political factor (cf. above, p. 124).[40] With a fine feeling for the necessity of dramatic motivation, the poet thus relates the appearance of Enkidu, presaged by wondrous dreams, to the sin of Gilgamesh.

To the story of Gilgamesh's achievements, first as the builder of Uruk, then as the somewhat reluctant victor over the giant monster Humbaba and as the killer of the Bull of Heaven sent against him by the goddess whom he had wantonly offended, the story of Enkidu is skilfully added. Enkidu, introduced first as a subhuman, demonic being from the wilderness, accompanies Gilgamesh to the Cedar Mountain where Humbaba lives and thereafter helps him in his fight against the miraculous bull. The text dealing with adventures on the Cedar Mountain is poorly preserved, and neither of the earlier versions—the Sumerian and the Akkadian—sheds light on this episode. This much, however, is certain: Enkidu is somehow connected with that mysterious mountain and has committed a grave sin, either by leading Gilgamesh to the mountain or by instigating his friend to the act that brought about the death of the guardian, Humbaba. For this he pays with his life; and it is Enkidu's death at the height of triumph that makes Gilgamesh turn from his quest for fame to a quest for eternal life.

The importance of this crucial adventure is stressed by the extensive preparations which are made for it; its dangerous nature is pointed out time and again, as is the ambiguous response of the gods. The allusion to Enkidu's relationship to Humbaba, the tantalizing and diverse hints of Enkidu's role in the adventure contained in numerous fragments indicate that without sufficient knowledge of what happened on the Cedar Mountain, much of the artistry of the poet's composition, much of the meaning he intended to convey through the structure of his poem, is lost to us. Our comprehension of the epic hinges on this adventure of the two friends.

We cannot do more than mention here the careful elaboration with which the poet has embellished the structural organization of the epic. The appearance of Enkidu living among the wild animals, his taming by the hierodule from Uruk, his transformation into a human being, nay, a civilized human being, are described with loving care, with the poet exhibiting a discreetly stressed pride in his own sophistication. One can easily detect in the praise of the joys of civilized living in Uruk and the idyllic descriptions of the shepherds and their way of life the expression of a relationship between city and open country that is unique in Mesopotamia. In lieu of emphasis on the customary contrasts that separate these ways of life, politically, socially, and in other respects, we find a sentimental interest in rusticity. The poet characterizes Enkidu as a "noble savage." Since early Old Babylonian versions of the epic show the same attitude, and elaborate on it, the later poet is following tradition. Possibly his praise of Uruk and his praise of rustic activities are reflections of the earliest Akkadian versions of the epic.[41]

Other descriptions of nature in the epic are pervaded by a quite different spirit. The marvels of the Cedar Mountain are conceived as those of a garden kept with great care and provided with wonderful shade trees. It is apparent that the poet was a city-dweller who can conceive of nature's wonders solely in well-kept gardens.

As has been said, the death of Enkidu provides the turning point of the story. It is separated from the adventure on the Cedar Mountain by the Ištar episode, which the poet adroitly links to the triumphant return of Gilgamesh. This episode is not integrated in the version of the story we have; it apparently had to find a place because it was known to belong to the Gilgamesh cycle.

In contrast to the Sumerian version, where the fear of death comes upon Gilgamesh at the sight of people dying, the death of Enkidu serves the same purpose more effectively and dramatically. The mingling of the themes of friendship and of the horrors of death achieve an intense human appeal and justify the change in style, tenor, and content in the second half of the epic. The death of Enkidu is carefully staged. In an elaborate curse, Enkidu reviews the persons connected with the history of his life, an interesting device of the poet to recapitulate the story. His death is presaged by a complex dream in which

Enkidu is shown the nether world—duplicating and anticipating curiously the last tablet of the epic, and the death occurs with a suddenness that explains the deep shock felt by Gilgamesh.

The lamentation of Gilgamesh fills the eighth tablet; together with the space given on the seventh tablet to the death of his friend, two of the eleven tablets are concerned with matter that is not directly relevant to the forward surge of the poem, elsewhere continuously maintained. I have no interpretation to suggest for this slackening of pace.

Mood and subject matter change abruptly when Gilgamesh sets out—as if fleeing, rather than pursuing a goal—on the quest for a means to escape death. Gone is his concern for lasting fame and heroic deeds, gone his kingly or heroic status. Stripped of insignia, naked as Everyman, he doggedly searches the earth for a magic remedy against death. And magic he encounters again and again, but he always fails to recognize it or to keep and use it. Within the two tablets, Gilgamesh wanders all over the earth and penetrates into regions inaccessible to man, where magic is offered to save him from death and always cunningly withdrawn.[42]

The quest is embellished with sundry episodes. There is the story of a passage through the mountain at the rim of the world, guarded by monsters, half-scorpion, half-human, where the sun appears and disappears. There is a description of a jewel garden—unfortunately, in fragments—and of a meeting with a strange veiled female, Siduri, the tavernkeeper on the shore where no human being passes, a Mesopotamian Sybill, who knows so much about mankind and the gods. She gives Gilgamesh fair warning that his quest is futile and then offers directions on how to reach the only human being who achieved what Gilgamesh is striving for, escape from death. This is Utnapištim, the Mesopotamian Noah. After crossing the Waters of Death, with the assistance of the skipper of the ark which weathered the Flood, Gilgamesh meets Utnapištim on the island of the blessed. Upon being challenged by Gilgamesh, Utnapištim tells the story of the Flood. In less than two hundred lines we have a gem of Mesopotamian epic poetry. There is a fluid ease in description, interspersed with those incidents that

Mesopotamian poets like to present in a minimum of words. There are speeches and responses not without verve, and there is an admirable description of the Flood and the building of the ark. So rich is the diction of the story within the story that one wonders whether the preceding tablets were intended in contrast. Again and again, Gilgamesh is asked, "Why are you wandering?" and he unfailingly replies with an identical account of his woes and fears. There seems to be an awkward break in the continuity when Utnapištim abruptly shifts from his account of the Flood and resumes his dialogue with Gilgamesh, a dialogue interrupted when Gilgamesh challenges him to explain how he escaped death. Utnapištim answers, as did Siduri, that nothing is permanent and that man must die when the gods so ordain. But Gilgamesh might escape—so Utnapištim intimates—if he were able to stay awake for six full days. It is sleep, the semblance of death, that marks the difference between man and the immortal gods. Gilgamesh fails.

Next, Utnapištim urges Gilgamesh to bathe in a fountain which seems to have been the Fountain of Youth, the source of his own eternal vigor, and once again Gilgamesh fails to take advantage of this promise of immortality. He is then given a "magic" against death—the Plant of Life—by Utnapištim, who is moved by the plea of his wife who takes pity on the twice-defeated Gilgamesh, but a snake steals this "magic" and is rejuvenated. The sudden reversals serve as peripety, a dramatic device used to foreshadow the final failure of Gilgamesh, but they also suggest that there were a number of independent episodes in the cycle of Gilgamesh.

Before turning to short characterizations of other epic works, it should be pointed out that the tablets which contain their texts appear with considerable frequency outside of Mesopotamia. The epics of Zu and of Etana come from Susa; the Adapa story and that of Nergal and Eriškigal were found in Amarna. Chance alone may explain these discoveries, and chance alone may explain why no Old Babylonian version of Ištar's Descent to the Nether World has been found—but the distribution of fragments corroborates the observation made above (p. 256) concerning the Gilgamesh Epic.

Shorter than the Epic of Gilgamesh, the Creation story (*Enūma eliš*) has seven tablets, each containing between 115 and 170 lines. This work represents something of a "sacred book," inasmuch as it was to be recited at the New Year's festival in Babylon, and thus occupies a special position among the mythological texts; but the *Enūma eliš* is, as a literary work, much inferior to the Epic of Gilgamesh. In the stilted hymnic style of the Kassite period, it tells the story of the theogony,[42a] the sequence of the generations of the primeval deities up to the birth of Marduk who will assume the role of organizer of the universe. Replete with obscure mythological allusions and decked out with some "pre-philosophical" concepts of a speculative nature, the text recounts, with many long and cumbersome repetitions, the conflict of the *di superi* with the powers of the abyss. Compared with that of Gilgamesh, the plot of the story is primitive; it follows a pattern common in many mythologies, the story of a young god, in this case Marduk, who intervenes in a difficult situation to save the elder gods. When Ea, the wise god full of wiles and stratagems, fails, Marduk acts as savior and defeats the evil powers in a battle against Tiamat, the monstrous personification of the primeval ocean. The poet musters little enthusiasm for that epoch-making event, although he carefully describes—with the usual interpolated episodes—the incidents and battle preparations leading up to it. The battle itself is decidedly not a heroic encounter but rather a contest of magic powers, in which Marduk, quite in style, wins by trickery.[42b] The duel between Marduk and Tiamat seems to have contributed an important motif to Assyrian iconography. We not only have cylinder seals which refer to it, but also a description of the bronze relief from the gate of the New Year's chapel in Assur, which is expressly said to represent it.[43] The contrast in mood between the account of the battle in the epic itself and the description of its representation on the relief is of interest, for the relief makes the encounter a more heroic event. We also have textual evidence to suggest the custom of mimetic presentation at certain sanctuaries, mirroring that mythic battle. Indications of the cultic role of the epic and the audience for which it was intended are so meager that we cannot compare or relate in any convincing way the three levels— literary, inconographic, and mimetic—of the fight between the two antagonists of the creation drama.[44]

With patent interest and poetic emphasis, the poet describes on tablet 5 the organization of heaven and earth and the assignment of duties and functions to gods and stellar bodies by Marduk, who has now become the supreme deity. It is somewhat hard for us to accept the fact that his rule and power.is based as much on his victory over Tiamat as it is on the clever stipulations that insured him, before the battle, the submission of all the other gods as the price for their deliverance from Tiamat's wrath. The story of the creation of man from the blood of a "fallen" god (on tablet 6) is obviously transferred from an earlier story about Ea and ascribed here to Marduk. Ea's former role is echoed in the curious and highly compressed *doublette* to Marduk's victorious battle against Tiamat in which is described Ea's fight against Apsu, the male personification of subterranean waters. This episode appears as an overture at the beginning of tablet 1. Skilfully used as a literary device, it also serves the theological purpose of establishing that Marduk is *porphyrogenetos*, i.e., born where the ruler of the universe should be born, in the palace called "Apsu," and sired by a father who was the supreme god. The final scene of the story of creation shows us the gods assembled in their newly built heavenly mansions solemnly affirming the supremacy of Marduk. The epic ends with the enumeration of Marduk's fifty honorific names together with highly contrived explanations of each—playful and pious etymologies which the poet believes so important that he asks scholars to study them and fathers to teach them to their sons. That a special commentary deals only with the last tablet underlines the importance attributed to this type of theological reasoning. Copies discovered at Nineveh, Assur, and Sultantepe in Assyria, and at various Babylonian sites differ very little; they all seem to go back to one prototype. The strange epilogue (lines 149–62) attached to the epic, apparently in praise of the pious king of Babylon under whom the scribe wrote the canonical version, does not mention a royal name. This is atypical and prevents us from dating the composition by other than secondary considerations.

Another long epical text concerned with the primeval period is called *inūma ilū awīlum,* "When the gods were men" and is preserved on a set of three Old Babylonian tablets (originally containing 1245 lines) and in a number of other copies. The story tells of the creation of mankind by the goddess Mama in order to relieve the gods of the necessity to toil. Its main topic is the Flood and what caused it and the escape of the Noah figure, Atrahasis.[45] The structure of the poem is loose; secondary motifs are introduced, and circumstantially described calamities are given much space. Although obviously dependent on this epic or on similar texts, the poet who wrote the concise and poignant Flood story of the Gilgamesh Epic had the creative power to use his raw material in a more sovereign and inspired way.

Substantial fragments are preserved of a poem dealing with a mythical king whose name, Etana, appears in the Sumerian king list, as does that of Gilgamesh. It is a dynastic story, preserved on two Old Babylonian, a Middle Assyrian, and a Nineveh fragment, into which the poet has woven the fable of an eagle and a snake living together in a tree. The dynastic story has as central motif the king without offspring searching for the Plant of Birth. Merciful Šamaš has advised the king to seek the help of the eagle in obtaining the magic plant, which seems to grow only in heaven. The eagle, having broken his oath of friendship with his neighbor, the snake, has been tricked by the latter into a pit, again on the advice of Šamaš who thus stages the meeting between the king and the eagle. When Etana frees the eagle, the thankful bird carries him on his back to the heaven of Anu. Though the text fails us from that point, we may assume that Etana obtained the plant and subsequently a son and heir. We may also assume that the clever son of the eagle, always admonishing his rash father with pious speeches, had his share in the adventure. The idyllic symbiosis of the two animals reflects, on the level of a fairy tale, a Sumerian myth called "Gilgamesh and the huluppu-tree" in which an eagle and a snake live in a willow tree.[45a]

Adapa, the principal figure of another story, is a mortal of divine extraction, comparable to a Greek hero. Like Gilgamesh, he narrowly misses immortality by a trick of the gods, and—again like Gilgamesh—he receives compensation: he becomes the wisest of men.[46] The story is preserved on a tablet used in the Egypt of the Amarna period for training scribes in Akkadian, and it appears on some fragments found in the library of Assurbanipal. When Adapa, caretaker of the city of Eridu, the protégé of Ea, breaks the wings of the south wind which had overturned his fishing boat, he is called before Anu to account for this crime. Ea, the god of Eridu, advises Adapa not to partake of any food or drink offered him in heaven, although Ea knows that the food of the gods imparts immortality; with this ruse he prevents Adapa from becoming immortal. The end of the story is lost, but Anu seems to have compensated Adapa by granting him and his disciples, the exorcists of Eridu, special magic powers to fight demons and disease. One of the fragments from Nineveh ends abruptly with the remark "And so forth ..." and continues with a conjuration, which suggests that the poem was copied in abridged form for apotropaic purposes and that its content was to be recited in order to prove to the demons the divinely ordained function and effectiveness of Adapa, said to have been the exorciser (āšipu) among the apkallu, the seven famous sages. The use of literary compositions for such purposes is also attested in the case of the Epic of Irra. It was thought to ward off pestilence and often appears on amulet-shaped clay tablets that were hung on the walls of houses to protect the inhabitants.

The Epic of Irra is a late and poetic concoction in a number of partly preserved copies which yield about two-thirds of the text originally contained on five tablets.[47] The poet's interest is more than usually concentrated on descriptions, especially on those of the ravages of war and pestilence and of the blessings of peace and prosperity. These themes were always dear to the Mesopotamian artistic tradition; suffice it to mention here the "Standard of Ur," which presents in its colored inlays elaborate

scenes characteristic of war and peace. We find in the Epic of Irra
an effective use of these contrasts. Pestilence and war are the
work of Irra, but the god Marduk brings about those happy
times which the poet describes and presents as assured for Babylon by the presence of the city god. A rather thin thread of a plot
links these descriptions into some logical sequence: Babylon
was ravaged by Irra, that is, by pestilence and enemy attack,
solely because Marduk was tricked by Irra into descending into
the lower world of Ea in order to obtain in the nether world the
precious materials and craftsmen needed to repair or replace
his godly attire. His departure released Irra's rage against
the city and all of Babylonia. Having been appeased by
his good vizier Išum—just how is not clear—Irra pronounced
blessings on Babylonia and predicted its return to wealth and
happiness. The long lament over the destruction of Babylon
in the fourth tablet, a lament in which even Marduk joins,
takes up an old Sumerian literary tradition, the lamentations
over destroyed temples and cities.[48] It is possible that the sack
of Babylon by the Elamite king Šutruk-Nahhunte inspired the
poet and that the opus was composed, in a dark period, to
promise the city a brighter future. This may also explain the
unique epilogue, in which the poet unequivocally asserts that
the entire work was revealed to him—Kabti-ilāni-Marduk—in
a dream; he alone was the spokesman for the deity who offered
this revelation, and not a single line had been added or omitted.[48a]

The Epic of Irra belongs to a new phase of literary activity
which manifests itself in an extensive but poorly preserved
group of texts coming from Assyria as well as from Babylonia.
Prominent among them is a group of Babylonian tablets once
called "Kedorlaomer Texts" by Bible-conscious Assyriologists,
and documents related to them. Preserved in a few copies is
the ambitious epical composition which glorifies the Assyrian
king Tukulti-Ninurta I (1244–1208 B.C.). And there are a number
of smaller compositions, of which isolated fragments are
contained in the collections of Assur and of Nineveh. The extent
and the internal history of this *dolce stil nuovo* have not been
evaluated as yet. To its foremost creations belong such gems as
the royal prayers of Aššurnaṣirpal I (1050–1032 B.C.), Tiglath-

Pileser I (1115–1077), and the hymnic sections of the *kudurru* of Nebuchadnezzar I (1124–1103). The royal prayers of this period are taken up in those of the last Assyrian kings, especially of Assurbanipal. It is quite possible that those phases of Mesopotamian literary history to which belong the poets or compilers of the Epic of Creation form part of this development, which deserves special attention. Unfortunately, the scarcity of preserved texts will always hamper our search for the nature, scope, and literary merits of a phase of Mesopotamian literature which flourished apart from and, probably, in contrast to the stream of tradition.

To return to the epical texts, the story of the mythological bird Anzu (formerly read as Zu) is the most important of those not yet discussed.[49] A considerable number of tablets and fragments from Susa and the library of Assurbanipal—not to speak of several Sumerian versions—contain the story of this bird-shaped son of Anu. Neither in content nor in style and diction does this epic excel others we know. The *topoi* are typical: the rebellious contender to supreme power robs the legitimate holder of the symbol and magic charm of supremacy and threatens the very existence of the gods, who have to search for a savior. The chosen savior defeats the usurper in heroic combat and thus obtains fame and power. The entire text is clearly in praise of a victorious god, whose name in some texts is Ningirsu, in others Lugalbanda, or Ninurta. The only interesting feature of this work is the nature and function of the charm, the mere possession of which assures its holder supreme power over the gods and the world. Its designation—*ṭup-šīmāti*, "tablet of office" or "official tablet," just as *kunuk šīmāti* means "official" or "state seal"—represents only a secondary rationalization of the very early concept of magic.

Two shorter works should be considered here, both dealing with the nether world: the story of Nergal and Ereškigal, which tells how Nergal became king of the nether world, and that of Ištar's descent into the nether world. The former, known from Amarna and Sultantepe, is a lively account, with the charm of genre literature, of the life of the gods; to this has been added a description of the nether world of Sumerian extraction.[50] The second story is unfortunately incomplete—only 150 lines are preserved on Assur and Nineveh tablets—but what is extant seems to show a poem of wider ambition and artistic sophistication. Evidently patterned after a well-known Sumerian prototype, the poem describes with a diction of elegant ease how— not why—Ištar entered the nether world, how she was imprisoned there, and how she was saved by a ruse of Ea. As ceremoniously as she entered, the goddess left the realm of the dead through the gates of its seven concentric walls. The story as well as the main incidents and the entire background are alluded to in a minimum of words and seem to differ essentially from those of the Sumerian version, in which the name of the goddess is Innin and the descent is the main incident in a story of much greater complexity.[51] Ea's ruse to save Ištar appears to have been the creation of a being neither man nor woman— a eunuch—in order to circumvent a curse of the queen of the nether world who apparently prohibited everyone, male and female, from coming to the relief of Ištar whom she kept imprisoned. Ištar had been afflicted with all the diseases of the nether world, thus bringing all sexual activity among men and beasts to an end. The last thirteen lines of the Assur and Nineveh versions of Ištar's descent seem to come from poems of kindred content and mood, just as the entire Akkadian version gives the impression of being only an episode selected from a larger body of literature concerned with the cult of the god Tammuz and written mainly in Sumerian.[52]

In this connection a late Assur tablet should be mentioned, a poetic description of a vision of the nether world and its inhabitants and rulers, which seems to have political implications.[53]

With the exception of the tablets concerned with ritual instructions, nearly all religious texts for cultic use are in the form of prayers and make use of poetic devices. The text recited as an act of worship (in the wider sense of this term) is called in Akkadian a "conjuration" and, to be considered a valid cultic act, was accompanied by a ritual (see above, p. 175). Among these prayers, the type named š u . i l a, "uplifted hands," is the best attested. These texts have not been collected in a compendium but have been utilized in several series of rituals. The individual prayers follow a given sequence: an invocation praising the deity, followed by a middle section of varying length devoted to the complaints or entreaties of the worshiper, succeeded by expressions of anticipatory thanks and renewed praise at the close. Only in a few instances do these compilations of stock phrases, epithets, and hymnical quotations achieve a fusion into a literary structure, as is the case in a lengthy prayer to Ištar and in the poem in praise of Šamaš. In the two hundred lines of this well-attested text (Nineveh, Assur, and late Sippar) one finds many new formulations of the traditional *topoi* of the Šamaš prayers: the exultation over the sun's rising and its course, over the blessing it bestows on gods and men (at times paralleling the mood of Egyptian hymns to the sun), and praise of the god's role in dispensing social justice, often with passages that suggest social criticism. Diction and tenor vary, in other prayers, depending on the nature of the deity addressed or the special use to which the prayer ritual is put. These uses vary from those intended to impart magical effectiveness to sacred objects, materials, and paraphernalia to those intended to ward off the evil effects of eclipses and untoward dreams. There are, as well, special prayers such as the *šigû*-prayer, comprised of lamentatory complaints, and the *ikribu*-prayer, intended to convey blessings and benedictions.

Stylistically, these prayers are all rather poor in spite of the elaborate embellishments provided in individual instances. This characterization is confirmed by the contrast evident in the prayers used outside the cult and its textbooks. The various prayers added to Neo-Assyrian and Neo-Babylonian royal inscriptions show more genuine feeling, verve, and poetic inspiration than those composed for use in the cult. This is especially true in respect to the very elaborate and often moving royal prayers which began to appear toward the end of the second millennium (see above, pp. 268 f.). Even earlier, hymnic texts which expressly relate a deity to a named king had been composed in praise of specific deities.[54] We thus find that the poetic tradition at court, which first produced royal hymns and then elaborate and recondite royal inscriptions, concerned itself likewise with religious topics (see p. 149). In contrast, the cult showed little interest in literary creativeness. The compendia for priests specializing in exorcism and related practices, to whom the suffering individual turned for assistance, contain prayers of a different nature. In two sister series called *Šurpu* and *Maqlû*, we find conjurations addressed either to deities famed for their exorcistic faculties or to the means—fire, for example—used to destroy the figurines (made of wax and other combustibles) representing the enemies of the sufferer.[55] These prayers vary greatly in style, content, and literary value. Side by side with the justly praised "Prayer to the Gods of the Night," we find the hackneyed repetition of customary phrases and senseless, abracadabra-like sequences of words.[56] Often, however, these prayers contain allusions to mythological incidents and fresh imagery taken from folklore, suggesting that under certain circumstances the background or history of the genre influenced the literary formulation of the prayer.

Among the few works of Mesopotamian literature directly concerned with the expression of religious feelings but not intended for cultic use, the poem called *Ludlul bēl nēmeqi* occupies a pre-eminent position.[57] A princely sufferer describes with considerable elaboration and display of unusual words the afflictions which caused his fall from grace and his ensuing ill health. These complaints, wordy and repetitious as they are at times, offer interesting insights into the social climate, the psychological frame of reference, and certain aspects of the god-man relationship, and they deserve extensive study. They fill the first tablet (apart from a hymnic dedication to Marduk as introit) and the second and spill over into the third, which contains the turning point: three dreams that are harbingers of divine pardon and return to grace. Much less space is given to the results of divine intervention; in fact, the distichs which proclaim the miraculous cure are largely given over to a pointed contrast with earlier misery, with emphasis on the latter. The fourth and probably final tablet is not well preserved. It resumes the hymnic praise of Marduk as savior and describes the rehabilitation of the sufferer as a demonstration of the power of the god. Technically the composition is primitive. No attempt is made to structure the overlong complaints or to prepare for the denouement with transitional passages or suggestions of the inner development of the sufferer, which might well be expressed in a prayer addressed to Marduk. Of course, passages of this sort may have been part of fragments now lost to us.

Although the poem Ludlul bēl nēmeqi has been rather inadequately dubbed a Babylonian equivalent of the Book of Job, its verses contain only few vague references to theodicy. This topic is taken up in full in another poem distinguished by several rare features. This text, conventionally termed the Babylonian Theodicy, probably was composed later than the Ludlul—written toward the end of the Kassite period—and was equally popular in the first millennium B.C.[58] Copies of both poems come from Babylonia as well as from Assyria, and a commentary is attested for each, suggesting the interest such texts evoked among Mesopotamian scribes. The Theodicy consists of a dialogue written as an acrostic poem (the acrostic gives the name of the poet in a pious phrase)[58a] in stanzas of eleven lines each (of unusual metric structure) in which a skeptic and a pious man alternately present their views in a polite and ceremonious fashion, complete with learned abstrusities and far-fetched expressions. The topic of the misfortunes and the bad luck of the pious contrasted with the success of the ungodly is brought up again and again by the skeptic; with similar repetitiousness his adversary extols the virtues of piety and devotion to the gods, whose wisdom in distributing success and failure remains beyond human understanding. The argument is without vigor and cogency, the end contrived and lame. The skeptic puts himself at the mercy of the gods, but one fails to see why he should do so, save for the reason that the acrostic has reached its natural end.

Since the form of the Theodicy is that of a dialogue, we may mention a similar text, the poetic work called the "Dialogue of Pessimism." It presents a master and his servant engaged in an obviously comic dialogue. The master gives order after order, to which the servant responds with a number of proverbial sayings that are meant to prove the wisdom of the master's wish. When the master abruptly changes his mind and revokes

each order, the servant has no difficulty in finding other proverbs to support the latest orders. The purpose—other than to
amuse the reader—seems to have been a demonstration that the
wisdom of proverbs is no reliable guide. To enliven the presentation, the servant is shown as much brighter than his master,
whom he patently attempts to please and to appease.[59] The
servant is given the final word—a curse against his master, who
has threatened to kill him: "[I wish] then that my lord survive
me by only three days!" thus saving his own neck and
confounding his master.

A similar instance of implied social criticism in a literary
work, is furnished by the rogue's tale known as "The Poor Man
of Nippur."[60] The pranks of a poor man are told in a poetic text
from Sultantepe, which is paralleled on a small fragment in
Assurbanipal's library. The locale is Old Babylonian Nippur
but in fact we are in a fairyland where anyone can enter the
king's palace and ask the king that a chariot be put at his
disposal for a day upon payment of one mina of gold. A poor
man, cheated of his last possession, a goat, by the mayor of
Nippur, takes threefold revenge by playing tricks on the dis-
honest official, tricks which always result in his giving the mayor
a sound beating. The story is told with great freshness and gives
us much precious information about everyday speech, the
mores of the citizens of Nippur, and a number of facts about
workaday life not to be found in the usual type of documentation. The three beatings are cleverly connected: first, the rogue,
appearing in state in the borrowed royal chariot and acting as
if he were a person of importance, pretends that gold he was
carrying was stolen in the mayor's house and uses this pretense
to beat the mayor; next, as a physician, he comes to treat the
mayor's wounds, which allows him to inflict additional pain:
lastly, he uses a lie to lure the mayor from his house and beat
him outside the city wall. The text is concise and direct, with a
minimum of repetition. In fact, some of the details are lost in the
onward rush of the tale. One is under the impression that
rendered here in poetic form is a well-known story, since the
listener is expected to supply from memory what is passed over
all too quickly. If this explanation is correct, the poem repre-

sents a court version of a popular tale. Note that the satire is directed solely at the official and that the king is addressed ceremoniously and with recondite phrases, a situation which reminds one of the Egyptian story of "The Eloquent Peasant."[61]

A Sumerian literary genre, the disputation, seems to have had only limited appeal for later scribes, who were interested in maintaining the Sumerian literary tradition and in elaborating and expanding it in their own language. In these poetic texts, two opponents plead their case in highly stylized form before a divine tribunal. At stake are their respective merits in terms of usefulness to society. Thus Winter and Summer, Silver and Bronze, the Ax and the Plow, and many others, argue in the numerous Sumerian texts of this genre.[62] In Akkadian literature we have only a few fragments concerning plants and animals—the Tamarisk and the Palm, the Grain and the Wheat, the Ox and the Horse. The same antagonists also appear in fables. We have few fragments in Akkadian, most in an unsatisfactory state of preservation. The story of the Willow Tree, for example, is lost but for a mention in a catalogue of tablets; the story of the Fox, the Dog, and the Wolf is preserved in a number of fragments which stimulate our curiosity but cannot yet be organized in an intelligible way. A small number of short beast fables, or extended proverbs with animals as actors, have survived. However, either lack of scribal interest or the accidents of preservation have reduced the number of examples available.

We must also mention proverbial sayings, proverbs, and similar utterances. Here again, the Sumerian scribes assembled several large collections, of which we have only scanty parallels in Akkadian, mostly in bilingual form.[63] The imagery of these proverbs is based on the daily life and daily worries of Mesopotamian man. They often contain pointed contrasts, rhetorical questions, and riddles, and they are expressed with pungent cynicism devoid of sentimentality or self-pity. The practical wisdom summed up in these proverbs is nowhere contrasted with a pattern for ideal behavior, but good advice—without normative aspiration—is presented in a small group of texts containing admonitions and prohibitions.

Patterns in Non-Literary Texts

The training of the scribes, as I have said, involved instruction in form patterns to be applied to specific text categories. Letters and legal documents of all descriptions had to be written in accordance with certain requirements as to the use of words, the sequence of phrases, the arrangement of the lines, and even the size and shape of the clay tablet.

Sumerian bureaucracy has left us a staggering number of texts; we are unable even to venture a guess as to how many tablets beyond the far more than 100,000 now in museums may be buried in southern Mesopotamia. They range from the nearly pictographic tablets of Ur, Djemdet-Nasr, and Uruk to the vast administrative archives of the empire of the third dynasty of Ur. The latter, coming mainly from the two mounds, Drehem and Djokha, from the city-complex of Telloh, and—to a much smaller extent—from the capital of the empire, Ur, are extremely well written. All tablets are dated, and they are often indexed at their rims so that they may be easily found in the tablet baskets in which they were stored. The extant labels of these baskets show their well-organized contents. One may observe that content, size, and shape are carefully correlated, a practice which warrants special study. In all transactions, the object as well as the names of the persons who delivered and received it are carefully indicated and the responsible official is named. The same practices continued, with certain text types disappearing and others coming into use, in subsequent periods when tablets from Ur, Larsa, Isin, and Sippar record the transactions of the Old Babylonian palace and temple administrations. Changes occur, of course, such as a preference for a ledger-like arrangement with entries organized in columns with appropriate headings, and in the early Old Babylonian period, unlike the Ur III period, circular tablets appear again, as was the case among the pre-Sargonic texts. Eventually, however, a certain carelessness is to be noted in the paleography, the look, and the arrangement of the texts. More decisive changes can be observed when, after the Dark Age, administrative documents inform us of the activities in the palace administration of the Kassite kings (Nippur, Dur-Kurigalzu) and, later, of the administration of large Babylonian sanctuaries, including the Ebabbar in Sippar, the Eanna in Uruk, and—in Assyria—palace administrations in Assur, Calah, and Nineveh.

Similar texts appear in all those administrative centers outside of Babylonia proper where characteristic Mesopotamian bureaucratic techniques were accepted, modified, and adapted for the use of the palace—in Mari, Chagar Bazar, Susa, Alalakh, and Nuzi, to mention only the main sources.[64]

The style of a letter or a message took one of two forms. One form is that of an administrative order given to a messenger, instructing him to recite the order verbatim ("Say to PN . . .") to the addressee named in the heading of the letter. The order is always in the imperative and concerns administrative matters, normally the delivery of goods or animals. This type of letter is found from the Sumerian up to the Neo-Babylonian period.[65] For reports to higher authorities, or for more complex administrative dispositions, a second and slightly different heading ("Thus [says] PN: say to PN₂ . . .") was retained through the Kassite period, until replaced by the laconic Neo-Babylonian formula "Letter of PN . . .." This second form, from the Old Babylonian period onward, has more or less elaborate blessings and greetings inserted after the heading—according to the social relationship between writer and addressee—and uses certain stereotyped locutions to bring home the urgency of a request. In letters issued by the central authority, the chancellery of the kings of the Hammurapi dynasty adopted the practice of quoting in the answer to an official application, complaint, or report the wording of the original document. This is a great boon to us, who find these official letters, administrative decisions, requests for assignments and instruction, and claims often difficult to understand.

Commercial activities are rarely reflected in Old Babylonian letters. However, the correspondence of the Old Assyrian traders in Anatolia deals predominantly with overland trade and matters of disposition and execution, accounting, and intricate transactions. Still, certain extraneous affairs are touched upon which are occasionally of historical and cultural interest. Private letters are the exception and as a rule were written only in the Old Babylonian period; all Neo-Babylonian letters, that is, letters from the South, deal with the administrative affairs of the temples, while those found in the royal archives of Nineveh are concerned with affairs of state.

Letters, at times, were used in international diplomatic correspondence. The exchange of letters in Sumerian between Ibbi-Sin, the last king of the third dynasty of Ur, and Išbi-Irra, the first of the rulers of Isin, and other kings of the period, has been preserved in a collection assembled by some history-conscious scribe.[66] This composition is of value both from a historical and a literary point of view, the literary surpassing the historical in importance. Of historical relevance are the letters exchanged between Hammurapi and Zimrilim of Mari, between Iasmah-Addu of Mari, the son of Šamši-Adad I, and the lesser kings with whom he was in contact, and—above all—the archive found in the new capital of the Pharaoh Akhnaton, the Amarna letters. Here we have copies of letters sent by the Egyptian king as well as the original correspondence addressed to various pharaohs by the kings and rulers of the entire Near East. They come from Babylonia and Assyria, from the kingdoms of Mitanni and the Hittites, from Cyprus and, the greatest number, from the rulers and Egyptian officials of Upper Syria and Palestine. Apart from a letter in Hurrian and two in Hittite, all are written in the barbarized Akkadian used at that period as the diplomatic language outside Mesopotamia—with the exception, of course, of the few texts coming from Babylon and Assur. According to their provenience, the political situation, and the literacy of the scribes at the ruler's service, style, diction, and orthography of these documents vary greatly. A good indicator of the political relationship between the writer and the addressee are the introductory formulas which often take up a substantial section of the epistle. The imagery of hectic adulation used in the letters from Syria and Palestine is characteristic, contrasting with the ceremonial dignity of the letters written by more powerful kings. Although these letters have been known for more than half a century and have been the topic of a number of scholarly investigations, much more is to be learned of their style, the provenience and literacy of the scribes and scribal schools (to teach Akkadian to foreigners) that flourished all over the Near East at that period, and the linguistic features of their several vernaculars. Moreover, the documents from Alalakh, and especially those from Ugarit—legal, administrative, and, above all, letters—will have to be compared to the archive at Amarna and to the correspondence and other pertinent documents found in the Hittite capital.

Another find deserving to be called a royal archive was made at Kuyundjik, the site of Nineveh. Of its far more than two thousand letters and letter fragments, only about two hundred concern the royal correspondence. They cover the period from Sargon II to Assurbanipal. Due to the accidents of discovery, most of the letters found are written by or to Assurbanipal; there are many addressed to Sargon and Esarhaddon but none to Sennacherib.[67] The Assyrian kings of the late period introduced a change of style: their official letters begin with the words "Order of the king." The archive contains, furthermore, a new epistolary type, reports made to the king by divination experts who interpreted ominous happenings. These texts, of which about four hundred are known, are answers to specific questions asked by the king. The style is characteristic: the scholar omits the usual introductory formula and begins by quoting the omen passage or passages he considers applicable to the case put before him in the query. In astrological matters, as a rule, he adds some explanation for the benefit of the king, often in order to twist a bad omen into one of good portent. At times, personal requests and all sorts of incidentals are added. The scholar ends the report with his name, in the same abrupt and matter-of-fact way he began.[68]

The letter form is also used for communications of a special nature: letters written to the gods. We have a number of examples, a few in Sumerian and more in Akkadian, dating from the Old Babylonian and Mari periods up to the Neo-Assyrian and Neo-Babylonian periods.[69] Letters to gods were written as an expression of piety by private persons and rulers; at times they accompanied the dedication of votive offerings. Possibly they were deposited in the sanctuary of the deity addressed, but it is more likely that they represent stylistic exercises of pious scribes.

In a special category fall here the letters written by the Assyrian kings Shalmaneser IV, Sargon II, and Esarhaddon to their god Aššur and to all the other deities of Assur, as well as to all its citizens.[70] They contain reports on victorious campaigns, written in a lively and poetic style and evidently intended to be read to the priesthood of the god and the assembled citizenry of the city sacred to his name. Some of their stylistic peculiarities can only be explained by this assumption. Two curious letters should be pointed out: one, "from" the god Ninurta and addressed to an Assyrian king, expresses the god's discontent (only the beginning is preserved in a copy from Nineveh); the second, found in Assur, purports to have been written by the god of the city to the king, Šamši-Adad V. What is extant of this fragment seems to indicate displeasure at the skepticism toward divine utterances shown by the king. If my interpretation of these "divine" letters is correct, they represent admonitions from the clergy revealed through the medium of god-sent letters rather than by the voice of a prophet.

The Sumerian scribal schools appreciated the art of letter writing, as a number of practice letters, and even a letter writer, show.[71] The letters are congratulatory messages, long-winded, obscure, and abstruse, characteristic of court style, addressed to the king.

Legal documents in Mesopotamia, whether Sumerian or Akkadian, are drawn up on a rigorous pattern:[72] first the object of the transaction is mentioned and duly identified—whether a house to be rented, a field to be sold, a girl to be married, or a child to be adopted; then listed are the names of the persons engaged in the transaction, with care taken to establish the ownership of the object to be sold or exchanged, or given in marriage. The relationship between the owner and the person who acquires rights or privileges is expressed in a characteristic phrase, a formula which specifies the nature of the transaction: "He has bought [from] ..." or "He has hired [from] ..." or "He has received as a loan [from] ...." Thus one phrase establishes all the essentials of the transaction and represents the minimum requirement in recording it by relating the acting persons to each other. Additional clauses follow, referring to value given or specifying the obligation assumed as to amounts and date due as well as further declarations of the parties involved concerning secondary arrangements. These clauses are formulated in an accepted way, terse and condensed. Such a strict and consistent formalism in recording at times made it necessary to subdivide a complex transaction into several simple ones for which formulas existed. Such formulas are listed in the series *ana ittišu*, composed in the Nippur of the Old Babylonian period for the training of the scribes; it is bilingual, with Sumerian formulations and their Akkadian translations. In the Neo-Babylonian period, practice texts were used to familiarize the apprentice scribe with the strict requirements of legal documents.[73]

The formulary varies, of course, in time and region with respect to technical terms and the style of the key phrases, just as do the shape of the tablet and other external peculiarities, including the sealing and the dating. Certain features remain constant or predominant, such as the use of witnesses whose presence at the transaction is noted and whose names are given at the end of the document. Sometimes these witnesses affix their seals in order to demonstrate their presence; at times they are given a small fee for their services. The name of the scribe is nearly always added after the names of the witnesses, but it should be stressed that he did not have the function of a notary. At the end, the date and the place of the transaction are often added, the exceptions being transactions from peripheral areas, such as Kaniš, Susa, Nuzi, and Ugarit. Radical changes in style occur rarely and only in marginal or late text groups. Thus, a number of legal documents from Nuzi take a more personal form, with the person who makes the disposition speaking in the first-person singular.[74] A group of late Neo-Babylonian documents are styled in dialogue form: one party expresses in formal manner his intention to buy, rent, or marry and is answered in the same formal manner by the one who accepts the offer.[74a]

As indispensable as the presence of witnesses was the practice of having the person who assumes the obligation indicate this responsibility on the tablet by rolling his cylinder seal over the soft clay, or by impressing the seal of his ring, or—at certain periods in certain regions—making an impression with his fingernails in a prescribed way, or even by pressing to the clay the hem of his garment. The purpose in all these instances is to indicate his presence, and thus his consent, during the transaction. It was not a method of identification, although the scribe might write underneath an anepigraphic seal that the imprint was made by the ring of the person named, even when the seal bears his name. It was permissible to use another person's seal if this was stated in the document.

In order to protect the wording of a legal document against fraudulent alterations, two practices are attested. In Babylonia, until the middle of the second millennium, and in Assyria for almost the entire period under discussion, the inscribed document was placed in a thin clay envelope (a "case") on which its content was repeated verbatim; the wording of the case could be easily checked against that of the tablet when the case was removed by the judge. In the Neo-Babylonian period, protection was achieved by making a copy of the original so that each party was provided with a document, and this fact had to be duly mentioned in the document. The characteristic features of pre-Dark Age legal documents, the use of seals and the casing of tablets, originated in the administrative practices of the bureaucracy of the Ur III period. The use of seals on tablets for the purpose of establishing the responsibility of an official was first practised in Ur III, as was the placing of tablets in cases to protect them. In earlier periods, seals were used only on tags and bullae. Seals were used on legal texts only from the Old Babylonian period on, when this practice was transferred from administrative texts.

The earliest known legal documents concern the sale of slaves (even before the Akkad period, much more frequently in the Ur III period). The sale of fields and houses, although attested in isolated texts before the Ur III period, became a common practice only from the early Old Babylonian period on. Sales of animals, boats, and other items are only sporadically contracted for in writing, in spite of a provision of the Codex Hammurapi requiring this practice. Sales of temple incomes (see above, p. 190) appear early in the Old Babylonian period and are also among the last cuneiform legal tablets attested in Uruk (at the time of the Seleucid kings), where they represent the most frequently occurring text type. Transactions styled as loans record obligations to deliver goods or to render services, or sales on credit, a practice made necessary by the strict formalism of Mesopotamian legal practices. The payment of rent for houses, fields, boats, animals, and wages for services are well attested throughout the entire period of Mesopotamian civilization. Here, as is true of equally well-attested court settlements, loans, and warranty contracts, one comes across a wide variety of specific stipulations in response to special situations, regional practices, and developing and changing institutions. Equally complicated is the picture of Mesopotamian family law as seen in the mirror of the legal documents available for study. Marriage and adoption contracts, well attested for the earlier, were rare in the late periods, as were divorce settlements and wills, that is, texts regulating the division of property among survivors. Certain text types disappear, such as contracts dealing with the nursing and upbringing of children (only in the Old Babylonian period); others appear late, such as apprenticeship contracts (almost exclusively from the Neo-Babylonian period).[75] In peripheral regions, Susa, Nuzi, Alalakh, and Ugarit, transactions are recorded in Akkadian and in imitation of Mesopotamian patterns, although patterned for alien social and economic situations.

Only exceptionally is the specific setting of the recorded transaction indicated in the strict sequence of the legal phraseology. A Nuzi text depicts a touching scene: "My father, PN, was sick, and lying in bed, holding my hand, my father said to me: 'These older sons of mine have taken wives, but you have not taken a wife, so I give you the slave girl PN as your wife!' "[76] A group of Neo-Babylonian documents relates a strange situation in Nippur, where, under duress created by a siege, parents sold their children to persons who could support them.[77]

Criminal proceedings were apparently not recorded on

tablets; a Sumerian text from Nippur describing a murder trial and the execution of the murderer may well represent a literary exercise.[78] Old Babylonian reports on a strangled slave and a kidnaped baby, Mari references to political murder and to the discovery of the mutilated body of an infant, as well as several incidents concerning murdered merchants in the West, a political criminal executed in Alalakh, a case of high treason under Nebuchadnezzar II, represent all we know of such events. Recorded cases of theft or burglary are rare and late.[79]

Contractual arrangements between rulers or cities to terminate a state of war are also known in Mesopotamia. They are rare in early periods. The Sumerian Stela of the Vultures, which proclaims the new boundaries established by the victorious Ennatum of the city of Lagaš and the ruler of Umma, is an isolated instance. A treaty written in Old Elamite and mentioning Naram-Sin of Akkad cannot be understood.[80] Yet, there are allusions to international treaties in the texts from Mari, and such an agreement has been found in the old layers of Alalakh.[81] Of the several peace treaties concluded between Assyria and Babylonia during their protracted conflicts, we have only one, and that in a fragmentary state: between Šamši-Adad V (823–811 B.C.) and Marduk-zakir-šumi (854–819 B.C.). A summary of such agreements appears in the "Synchronistic History." Assyrian treaties (but see below for a qualification) with Western rulers are twice attested—between Aššur-nirari V (754–745 B.C.) and an Aramean ruler of Syria (Matiʾilu), and between Esarhaddon and a king of Tyre. Most of the treaties written in Akkadian come from the Hittite capital and are much earlier than the texts just mentioned. The most famous international agreement found in Boghazkeui is the treaty between Hattušili III and the Pharaoh Ramses II, preserved in a Hittite version, in a badly preserved Akkadian copy, and in an Egyptian version, carved on the walls of buildings erected by Ramses II. The treaties between the Hittite kings and their vassals describe carefully and in set form the duties and obligations of the vassals and what they are entitled to expect from their Hittite overlord. They end with a solemn invocation to the gods of both parties who are to serve as witnesses and

contain elaborate curses and blessings to insure the keeping of
the agreement.

The documents which show how the Assyrian kings assured
the loyalty of foreign vassals reveal primitive and ritualistic
practices. Those of Aššur-nirari V describe symbolic manipulations to illustrate, in a crude way, the fate of any offender
who breaks the treaty: ". . . this head is not the [cut off] head of
a ram but the head of Matiʾilu . . . should Matiʾilu break these
agreements, his head should be cut off just as this head of the
ram has been cut off."[82] They thus correspond pointedly to
certain magic practices applied for evil purposes described so
elaborately in a number of religious texts. It remains a moot
question whether the Assyrians had to accept the barbaric
customs of their neighbors in order to impress upon them the
seriousness of the consequences of a broken agreement, or
whether the attitude expressed illustrates a change in cultural
level that might have taken place between the time of the
Hittite treaties, with their supernatural sanctions, and that of
the last Assyrian kings, with their magic practices. These practices are mentioned in an Aramaic treaty between Matiʾilu and
his vassals inscribed on a stela, and they are paralleled by comparable primitive practices in evidence in Mari and mentioned
in the Old Testament.[83] The oath of loyalty imposed upon
the Median chieftains by Esarhaddon in order to secure their
allegiance to his son and successor Assurbanipal is insured by
similar magic rituals. We do not know whether the oath of
loyalty taken by high Assyrian officials was reinforced by ritual
acts, but it is very likely. We learn about this means of securing
the allegiance of the officials from the royal correspondence
found in Nineveh; some fragments survive containing that part
of the oath in which special stress is put on the duty of the
officials to report everything they saw or heard to the
king.[83a]

As an isolated instance of an agreement established in writing
between an Assyrian king and his subjects, one should refer to
the charters of the free cities. Only one such charter is attested,
that in which Sargon granted the inhabitants of Assur special
tax exemptions which his predecessor had abolished, obviously

in return for services rendered to Sargon during his fight for the throne.[84]

Normally, the king depended upon edicts to regulate the duties of his officials and the obligations of his subjects. Edicts concerning officials and their obligations are frequent in Hittite; in Mesopotamia they appear only in and around Assyria.[85] The chief representative of this text type is a Middle Assyrian collection of royal edicts through which nine kings of the post-Amarna period attempted to regulate in great detail the duties of the officials in charge of or otherwise connected with the royal harem.[86] Another document of a similar kind, from Nuzi, determines the responsibilities of the mayor of the city.[87] Babylonian edicts are represented by two important decrees, one issued by Samsuiluna and one by Ammiṣaduqa, both of the Hammurapi dynasty.[88] They are concerned with the lifting of certain debts in order to bring relief to specific sections of the population. Although references to such social acts (seisachtheia) by the kings of that period are found in texts and in the names of certain years, this tablet is the only representative of a text category that must have been fairly common. Its content is highly important in a study of Old Babylonian economic and social life because it defines rather precisely the extent of the royal act and the details of the exceptions permitted, and it offers unique insight into the economic structure of the population.[88a]

Royal grants during the Middle and the Neo-Babylonian periods generally were written on oval or pillar-shaped stone boundary markers, the kudurru's.[89] Over eighty such monuments are extant, covering the period from Kadašman-Enlil I (ca. 1380 B.C.) to Šamaš-šum-ukin (668–648 B.C.), the brother of Assurbanipal. Only thirteen of these texts can be dated precisely, and a few of the later exemplaries do not contain royal grants. These stones were used to publicize the grant; they were set up in fields or larger agricultural holdings which the king thus granted to private citizens. Exceptionally, grants to temples are recorded in the same manner; copies of these kudurru's on clay tablets were deposited in temples to insure their preservation. An integral part of the inscription were the designs

engraved on these stones; they show divine symbols corresponding to the major deities of the pantheon and at times
are provided with identifying inscriptions. The text calls these
symbols by a variety of names, such as "gods," "standards,"
"weapons," "drawings," and even "seats," because the symbols
often are placed on stands such as are used in representations of
enthroned deities. Their function is clearly stated; they were
meant to protect the monument. Reliefs carved upon the
kudurru's may have served the same purpose; they represent
the king, alone or with the recipient of the grant, or the recipient
in worship before the deity. Additional protection was insured
by the elaborate curses and blessings inscribed on the kudurru's
to prevent their removal or destruction, since it was their
presence that guaranteed the validity of the royal grant. Because
the period in which these monuments were erected is poorly
documented, the language of these inscriptions, the legal and
social practices they mention, the names they contain of kings,
officials, and others offer precious information. Nor must we
neglect to mention the importance of their decorations for the
historian of Mesopotamian art.

Last but not least, the Codex Hammurapi is to be mentioned
as a royal decree in the form of a decorated stela. At least three
such stelae were in existence, as fragments excavated in Susa
show.[90] The stelae were brought to Susa as spoils by victorious
Elamite raiders.

CHAPTER **VI** *There are many strange wonders, but nothing more wonderful than man*

(SOPHOCLES)

MEDICINE AND PHYSICIANS

MATHEMATICS AND ASTRONOMY

CRAFTSMEN AND ARTISTS

The material presented in this chapter is not included in the preceding one largely for the convenience of the reader. Everything we know today of Mesopotamian science and a large portion of what we have come to learn about Mesopotamian technology comes from cuneiform texts and should therefore have been treated in the fifth chapter. The texts which furnish data on Mesopotamian science and technology fall into such different categories as astronomical ephemerides, receipts of working materials handed over to craftsmen, collections of medical prescriptions, descriptions of works of art, including statues and reliefs, inventories enumerating precious objects, word lists, multiplication tables, omens derived from the movement of the planets, and allusions in literary and legal documents. Artifacts, ruins of buildings, statuary, metal objects, and cylinder seals convey information—but only to a limited extent—about the technology which created them; this is especially true in regard to metallurgy and the manufacture of glass and glazes and pottery. Even rarer are the instances in which one is fortunate enough to be able to link extant objects to textual material, or techniques used to contemporary techniques described or alluded to on clay tablets. In fact, archaeological evidence and written documents are less apt to be complementary in Mesopotamia than they are in Egypt. Archaeological evidence is much more profuse in those early periods of Mesopotamian history for which documents are either rare or irrelevant. Nearly all the extant documents which could shed light on the history of early technology deal with textile and metals, i.e., they pertain to techniques of which we have no or only few artifacts—no examples of weaving, only a few pieces of metallurgy.[1] There are, as well, certain techniques which have no written tradition—architecture, pottery, agriculture.[2]

Medicine and Physicians

Instead of presenting medical, mathematical, and astronomical texts as literature and discussing their formal structure, vocabulary, and textual history, I prefer to present at this point a discussion of a limited number of problems concerned with science as well as with technology in order to show the efforts of Mesopotamian man to deal in a rational manner with the world of reality within his ken.

Our knowledge of the nature and the extent of Mesopotamian medicine is based on medical texts, consisting of handbooks and collections of prescriptions, supplemented by letters, references in the law codes, and allusions in literary texts. The former show us the lore of the physician; the latter illustrate his relationship to the patient and the physician's social position.

The texts bearing on medical lore belong to a very large extent to two clearly separated traditions. To differentiate them is essential for an understanding of Mesopotamian medicine as a science. Both traditions originated in the Old Babylonian period and are attested on a number of clay tablets coming, in the main, from the two large sources of documentation, the collections found in Assur and those in the library in Nineveh.[3] There is, as well, enough evidence in scattered tablets from Nippur, Boghazkeui, Sultantepe, and several late sites in southern Mesopotamia to demonstrate that both traditions were part of what we call the stream of tradition.

I propose to label the two medical traditions, or schools, the "scientific" and the "practical." The scientific school of Mesopotamian medicine has left us a large body of tablets, already mentioned in the last section of the fourth chapter (p. 224), where they were somewhat summarily characterized as prognostic omens. The principal document of this school is the series called after its incipit, "If the conjurer, when he goes to the house of a sick person . . ." Its form, as one can easily see, is that of the omen collections and need not be discussed here; we shall come back to its utilization and to the scientific attitude underlying it after describing the form of the texts of the second school, that of the practitioners of medicine. Most of the texts of this type, termed by Assyriologists "medical texts," follow a specific pattern, as is characteristic of Mesopotamian scribal practice. They resemble formally omen texts and also are arranged in collections. Each tablet is composed of sequences of identically organized units, beginning, as a rule, with "If a man is sick (and has the following symptoms) . . ." or "If a man suffers from (such and such) pain in his head (or other part of the body) . . ." The enumeration of specific symptoms is detailed, using a more or less consistent terminology to describe subjective sensations as well as observable symptoms. It is followed by detailed instructions to the physician concerning the *materia medica* indicated and its preparation, timing, and application, all described in a wide range of technical terms.

Normally, each unit concludes with the assurance "He will get well . . ."—but sometimes the physician is warned that the patient will not survive the disease. Needless to say, a number of variations and special formulations are to be noted in these texts. There are tablets which present a diagnosis naming the disease; others refer to the causes—mostly evil magic, or sins—of the suffering. No detailed investigation of the text types and their distribution in time and region has yet been made, although the results promise to be interesting. Whatever variants and deviations are observed, the unit structure is consistently maintained and is used, typically, to build long sequences arranged according to the wording of the initial statement—that is, tablets contain prescriptions listed either according to the nature of the symptoms or according to the parts of the body affected. The value of "handbooks" of this sort for the practicing physician is evident.

We have texts dating from the middle of the second millennium, from the Hittite capital, Hattuša, where Hittite scribes copied, either directly or through some still unknown intermediaries, Old Babylonian originals. Next in time come the tablets found in the two Assyrian capitals, Assur and Nineveh, dating from about 1000 B.C. to 612 B.C. Those from Assur contain a number of, as yet unpublished, early Middle Assyrian versions, which in turn go back to Old Babylonian originals or to their descendants. The Old Babylonian text group is extant in a number of copies, which still await publication. To the same source can be traced the few Middle Babylonian fragments and a small group of Neo-Babylonian medical texts. Since essential sections of this corpus are not yet available, the historian of medicine will have to wait until some Assyriologist offers a translation of these medical texts before attempting to trace the chain of tradition to establish the changes which occurred during a period of more than a millennium.

It is already apparent that all extant tablets of this type, whatever their date or provenience reflect only the medical practice and the state of medical knowledge in the Old Babylonian period. The later copies, as well as those found outside of Mesopotamia proper, show that the physicians who wrote them were interested solely in maintaining the tradition.

Insofar as these texts reveal the nature and the extent of the medical lore of the period in which they were composed, Mesopotamian medicine is shown to be a typical folk medicine on the level of the lore described in early English leech books. The *materia medica* consists mainly of native herbs of many kinds, animal products, such as fat, tallow, blood, milk, and bones, and a small number of mineral substances. Nothing of notable rarity or expense imported from far-off regions is mentioned, nor are there any outspoken preferences for specific medication or types of application. The herbs—roots, stems, leaves, fruits— were used either dry or fresh, ground and sifted or soaked and boiled. They were mixed with such carriers as beer, vinegar, honey, and tallow. Some were to be swallowed or introduced into the patient's body by means of enemas and suppositories; others were to be used on the body directly or in lotions or as salves. As might be expected, among the herbs are a number of laxatives, diuretics, and cough remedies. At times their use shows clearly that the qualities and effects of such herbs were known. All too often, however, their use seems to have been dictated by reasons other than positive knowledge. It will require much detailed research on the part of philologists, and the co-operation of experts in the history of pharmacology as well as of botanists thoroughly at home in the flora of Iraq to detect the principles underlying the use of such herbs, alone or in combination.

Efforts to identify diseases out of the welter of symptoms and other indications in terms we understand will have to be related to an investigation of the herbal, which represents the main source of our knowledge of Mesopotamian medication. In fact, the term *šammū*, "herbs," seems often to be an equivalent for "medicine." In this respect, an essential source of information is the long composition (three tablets) called *Uruanna: maštakal*, with its listing of hundreds of herbs, parts of animals, and other, not always identifiable, materials. The text is arranged in two columns which pair remedies in a way and for a purpose not yet understood.[4] It offers a revealing insight into the Mesopotamian pharmacopoeia, listing vegetal matter (leaves, roots, seeds, and other parts of plants) beside minerals (salts, alum, crushed stones) and parts of animals. The nomenclature is deliberately cryptic and therefore obscure.

Medical instruments are rarely mentioned in the text group we are discussing. Spatulas and metal tubes appear as well as the lancet, which, perhaps revealingly, is called the "barber's knife." It was used to produce fontanels and other scarifications; pertinent references are extremely rare. Syringes are not mentioned, although enemas are prescribed. It is possible that a number of simple tools and instruments were used which the texts do not mention because their names and their manner of application were self-evident. In view of the primitive nature of this medical lore, one is not surprised that surgery was the resort solely in desperate cases—in fact, no medical text or any other passage referring to the activities of physicians mentions what we would term surgery.[5] The Caesarian section referred to in a matter-of-fact way in a legal text of the Old Babylonian period does not contradict this statement, since it was performed after the death of the patient.[6] Such operations are known from Greek and Roman sources, as well as from the Babylonian Talmud, which attests them for Mesopotamia proper. They are also known to occur among peoples whose medical knowledge is extremely primitive. Magico-medical practices, such as excision of teeth, trepanation, and circumcision, are not attested for Mesopotamia. Midwifery was even then in the hands of women; pertinent references in secular texts are rare.[7]

In popular books on Mesopotamian civilization and medicine, one often finds the statement that operations for cataract are referred to in the Codex Hammurapi. This is not the case. The activities of a physician mentioned in this law code as possibly endangering a person's life concern scarification meant to offer relief in certain diseases of the eye, a common practice in Alexandrian medicine.

The patient-physician relationship in Mesopotamia has two aspects which one must distinguish if one is to understand the medical science of this civilization. As a member of the "practical school" of medicine, the practitioner is not expected to examine the body of his patient or to investigate his symptoms objectively. The physician identifies the disease with the help of the lists of symptoms arranged for that very purpose and applies the specific treatment indicated for each case.

Members of the "scientific school" exhibit an entirely different approach to the patient and his disease. The symptoms are not considered an indication of what remedies to apply but rather as "signs" which bear on the outcome of the disease, and at times help to identify it, so that the expert can apply the appropriate magic countermeasures. This double aspect has consequences. The interest of the "diviner physician" in symptoms is far more immediate, and he is given to an exact and minute observation of the body of the patient, which is not the concern of the "practitioner," for whom symptoms have only heuristic value. The interest of the former is strictly "scientific" inasmuch as he carefully examines the body of the patient, notes the temperature of the skin, which he tests in several places, and observes the blood vessels—their coloring as well as the movement of the bloodstream. Thus he discovers the pulse, but not as an indication of the physiological state of the sick man; but rather as a "sign" intended for the trained observer and bearing on the fate of the patient.[8] Much of what we know of Akkadian anatomic nomenclature, the terminology of the healthy and the morbid body and its functions, comes from texts we have termed omen texts or, to be exact, prognostic omens. The expert who carefully searches for revealing signs is not called a physician (asû) but an āšipu, which we translate traditionally as "conjurer." The signs observed tell him whether the patient will live or die, how long the illness is to last, and whether it is serious or passing.[8a]

Exactly as the diviner does not content himself with observing the exta of the sheep slaughtered but to derive additional signs extends his observation to the behavior of the animal before it is killed, so does the āšipu in his treatment of the patient. Not only do the symptoms of the sick man convey information but the situation in which he is observed is taken into account. The time of day or night, the date are observed and signs interpreted. But what is the nature of the countermeasures taken by the *āšipu*? In view of what we know of Mesopotamian divination, there is every reason to assume that magic acts—conjurations and rituals—are indicated. Yet we have no pertinent information.

This question takes us to another problem intimately connected with Mesopotamian medicine. There are many indications that the Mesopotamians believed in the effectiveness of two media, two fronts of action, in the treatment of disease: the application of medication and the use of magic. These two media were not kept rigidly apart; medical treatment as a rule shows only minor admixtures of magic practices, while magic measures against diseases make use of the traditional pharmacopoeia, although the reasons for this are usually not obvious. Magic elements used by the practitioner consist of short conjurations, reliance on the magic of numbers (such as seven drops of liquid), symbolic acts (the tying of knots), requests for special timing of certain tasks in the preparation of the medication or the assistance during treatment of special persons (a child, a virgin). We should not attempt to explain away or overstress such practices. It will require much research and patient investigation to establish a typology of situations in which medical or magical treatments, separately or together, were thought to be indicated. In this respect it is essential to establish the dividing line between Mesopotamian concepts of diseases and those familiar to us—thus, for instance, prescriptions against graying hair are medical, not magical. Ineradicable infections of the eye, annually recurring epidemics, pulmonary and intestinal disorders, mental disturbances—to mention here only the most frequent complaints discussed in our texts—lay within the provinces of both practitioners and scientists. To emphasize the importance of the dichotomy in Mesopotamian medicine which I have tried to characterize by the use of these two key words, their relationship should be examined before we return to Mesopotamian medical lore as such.

Although both traditions (see above, p. 290) originated in the Old Babylonian period and were maintained with little change by the scribes until the second half of the first millennium B.C., a shift can be observed at that time in the position of the physician (*asû*) as practitioner. He clearly loses importance in the face of the experts in divination and conjuration. Definite indications of this development are to be found in the letters which deal with patients and treatment. The letters of the Old Babylonian period and those coming from provincial Mari frequently mention physicians and their activities; letters from Nippur of the Middle Babylonian period speak at length of patients and symptoms and give interesting details on medical treatments in a way that suggests the existence of a clinical institution. Yet, the latter do not use the term *asû* any more. This is also true of the royal correspondence from the Assyrian court which offers us most of the information we possess on the care of the sick and medical practices—including references to dentistry.[9] The persons who report in these late letters on illnesses in the royal household and the health of the king himself, and who issue prescriptions—in short, those who act as one expects a physician to act—are all scholars and experts in divination, exorcists, conjurers, or whatever other designations Assyriologists choose to use. From the Mesopotamian point of view, however, they are all representatives of the "scientific school" of medicine. All the evidence concerning the "practitioner" physician and the "scientific" physician seems to point out that the practitioner lost status and importance in the course of the millennium which separates the Old Babylonian from the Neo-Assyrian period, while the "scientific" physician grew in status and joined the royal court. To what extent they offered actual medical treatment cannot be established, but it is safe to assume that they took over the practitioner's methods.[9a]

It is much too pretentious to call this summary a history of Mesopotamian medicine; it is sufficient to point to the shift in attitude which brought prestige to what we consider unscientific medical speculations, to the detriment of a sober, although hardly very efficient, folk-type medicine based on whatever positive knowledge of plants and the human body the experienced practitioner had been able to assemble and digest. A similar change of emphasis seems to have taken place in Egyptian medicine. There the great papyri with their startling achievements unparalleled in medical history until the time of Hippocrates, come from a period even earlier than the Old

Babylonian. Still we read in Horapollo's *Hieroglyphica*, a curious fourth century (A.D.) concoction on the marvels of Egypt, that Egyptian physicians had a book, called *Ambres*, which enabled them to recognize whether a given disease was fatal or not. In view of the Mesopotamian opus on medical divination, one might well suggest that the book *Ambres*—if Horapollo's reference happens to be more reliable than what he elsewhere says about Egypt—corresponded in function (although certainly not in outlook and approach) to our series "If, when the conjurer is on his way to the house of a patient . . . ."

To characterize Mesopotamian medical lore one must look first at the situation under which the codification of the Old Babylonian texts took place. We certainly cannot tell when the scribes attempted to transfer to writing the oral traditions of the physicians based on the practices of their own and the preceding period. Even if the as yet unpublished Old Babylonian medical texts were available, they would not be likely to shed any light on that crucial period of incipient medical writing. But there are other indications; first, an early (Ur III) pharmaceutical text written in Sumerian and mentioning the mainstays of the Mesopotamian pharmacopoeia, and, second, a small group of fragments found in Boghazkeui containing medical texts of the type we are discussing but written in Sumerian rather than in Akkadian.[10] This suggests that in the Old Babylonian period medical texts in Sumerian existed in sufficient number to find their way to the Hittite capital. Since Old Babylonian texts concerned with divination are never written in Sumerian and Sumerian as well as Akkadian is used in writing mathematical problem texts, one may suggest that the writing of mathematical and medical material preceded the collecting of omen texts (dealing with extispicy, teratology, and divination from oil and smoke). This sequence, however, is not necessarily due to time differential; a regional distribution could well have had the same effect. Possibly medical and mathematical texts were put in writing in scholarly centers where the Sumerian tradition was more effectively maintained than in those localities in which divination practices shifted from the folklore level to that of scholarly pursuits based on written texts. Since we have few

scholarly and literary texts from the critical period of Mesopotamian creativity—the few centuries around and after the
middle of the second millennium B.C.—and, moreover, much
may be lost for the excavating archeologist under the rising water
table of the region in which this creativity seems to have
flourished, we may never have at our disposal any but indirect
evidence of this essential intellectual development.

A word of warning in this connection: the language in which
a given category of cuneiform texts (that is, a given field of
intellectual endeavor) was first transferred to writing does not
bear direct witness to the ethnic background or linguistic
affiliation of those who wrote them. Thus one cannot say that
divination is Akkadian and mathematics and medicine
Sumerian. All are the fruition of long processes through which
Mesopotamian civilization realized itself, using—quite broadly
speaking—first the Sumerian language and then the Akkadian
as its vehicle. All the same, this sequence did not materialize
everywhere and seems to have been affected locally by still
undetermined political and social factors.

Once the scribes of that formative period characterized by the
constant enlargement of the repertory of their craft admitted
medical observations and prescriptions to the corpus of written
documents, these were copied by successive generations. Thus
they were kept from oblivion. This raises a question: did Mesopotamian medical knowledge and pertinent techniques continue to develop independently from the corpus of traditional
texts, allowing a gap to develop between written formulations
and changing practices? I am inclined to assume that the
tradition in Mesopotamia had the same paralyzing effect as any
written tradition is bound to have on the development of a
discipline. The history of medicine all over the world demonstrates this phenomenon. Furthermore, there exists no textual
evidence to indicate that anyone in Mesopotamia was aware of a
discrepancy between tradition and practice. It is possible, of
course, that a minute analysis of the medical texts would bring
out traces of changes in methods and medication which the
scribes added to the texts they copied. Still, the conservativism
exhibited in, for example, mathematical literature speaks

against such a possibility. New applications of existing scientific methods have to create their own pattern, as did those texts which give us information on mathematical astronomy.

Mesopotamian medicine remained always at a low state of development. Herodotus (III, 1) makes his opinion clear when he speaks of Babylonians bringing their sick to the market in order to inquire of passers-by what remedies they would suggest. Although Assyriologists find it convenient to disbelieve this remark of Herodotus, it is quite plain that the Greek traveler did not show the same admiration he felt for Egyptian medicine and Egyptian physicians when speaking of Babylonia. It would be a mistake to blame the traditionalism of the medical literature in cuneiform for the low standing of medicine in Mesopotamia. Even interest in the copying of medical texts decreased in the course of time, which seems to indicate a change in attitude toward the medical tradition. After the collapse of Assyria, the centers of learning in Babylonia produced large numbers of lexical texts, omen collections, and literary and religious tablets, but copies of medical texts of the "practitioner school" are rare. This is in contrast to the larger number of such texts found in Assur and (to a lesser degree) in the library of Assurbanipal in Nineveh.

Several explanations come to mind, yet none of them is sufficient to clarify an apparently extremely complex situation. It could be that the "scientific school" was favored in the learned circles of the south, or that special interests caused the unusual accumulation of medical texts especially in Assur and in Nineveh. We shall probably never know to what extent intellectual trends in Mesopotamian scholarship were stimulated by court fashions and royal preferences. Medicine is susceptible to such influences. There can be little doubt that both Mesopotamian medicine and divination were greatly influenced by internal developments as well as external pressures. These texts do not show the same monolithic uniformity which links mathematical texts across the millennium or more separating their main text groups.

Furthermore, one should not rule out the possibility that ideological considerations may have affected the physician's craft. It has certainly been recognized by the historians of medicine that the attitude toward the physician, the trust placed in his ability to help, represents a culture-conditioned behavior, highly characteristic for any civilization. Paradoxically, one's attitude toward death seems to condition one's attitude toward physicians. Two contrasting examples bear out this link. The intense interest in medicine shown by Egyptians, the purposeful and scientific approach one can observe in medical papyri, the specialization within the profession which so impressed Herodotus, the rich and complex pharmacopoeia admired in the Odyssey (IV, 229, 231), all assume significance when one views them against the background of the existential concern with death of the Egyptians. Death was to be vanquished by a new kind of "life" which was to continue beyond the barrier of death by means of the preservation of the body, the care bestowed upon the mummy, and whatever this entailed in social, religious, and economic customs. Nevertheless, death and disease are combatted by the consummate skill of the physician. Conversely, we come across in the Old Testament a few eloquent passages (cf. especially ". . . in his disease he sought not to the Lord but to the physicians . . ." in II Chron. 16:12) which express aversion to the services of a physician. This reluctance to accept any other healer but the Lord at times seems to have been virulent; this may explain why Jesus Sirach had to plead so sincerely for a physician, as he does in his book, 38:2: "It is from God that the physician getteth wisdom." And in the fourth verse: "God hath created medicines out of the earth and let not a discerning man reject them." The attitude of resignation in the Old Testament seems to be related to the concept of death as the end of individual existence, without the promise of an afterlife. Revealingly enough, when the promise of apocalyptic bliss and the expectation of heavenly mansions were accepted throughout the region, the attitude toward the physician changed; his knowledge and help were in demand and appreciated.

It is possible that the status of Mesopotamian medicine was due to a concept of death akin to that of the Old Testament. Mesopotamian determinism, pointed out in the chapter on religion, may have been a contributing factor, mitigated though it was by the belief in divination and apotropaic magic.

To round out our picture of Mesopotamian medicine, it is necessary to characterize, however sketchily, the social status, the functions, and the mores of the physician. Pertinent evidence has been rather meager until recently and shed little light on this topic, but the already mentioned text found not so long ago in Sultantepe and named by its editor "The Tale of the Poor Man of Nippur" has proven to be more revealing than all the medical texts found to date. This should remind us once again of the chief shortcoming of nearly all the documentation we have in cuneiform—its remoteness from the realities of everyday life.

The tablet contains the story I summarized in the preceding chapter (see pp. 274 f.). Even more valuable than its literary merit is the insight it gives us into the living habits of the ordinary man. The pertinent passages allow us to observe the social texture in a direct way which the formalism inherent in most literary media rarely allows. Of the three episodes, each dealing with a prank played by the poor man on the avaricious mayor of Nippur, the second one is of importance in the present context. It deals with the prankster disguised as a physician. In a number of difficult, broken lines, the text tells us that the prankster had his hair shaved off and that he provided himself with a libation jar and a censer. Made unrecognizable by this change in his appearance, holding the two insignia of his calling (libation jar and censer), the poor man must be assumed to have been clad only in a loincloth or the like, since the text makes no reference to a costume as it did expressly when the rogue disguised himself as an official. He appears at the mayor's house and presents himself in the following way: "I am a doctor, a native of the town of Isin, one who understands . . ."—and here the tablet is broken. We may assume that it contained the customary self-recommendations of a physician of the period. The introduction was effective, and the false doctor was admitted and shown the patient and his wounds. He examined them so professionally and made such a good impression that the mayor praised him as an expert doctor. This may be taken to indicate that the practitioner was usually not held in high esteem. The prankster reacted promptly to the compliment by saying, "My lord, my medication is only effective in darkness." Once alone with his patient, the "doctor" made use of the tools he was carrying in a way which the text does not describe. I suggest that he poured water from his libation jar upon the glowing ember to fill the room with smoke. He then tied the mayor hand and foot and beat him. Neither the request of the prankster, nor the binding of the patient, his screams, or the smoke seem to have aroused the suspicions of the mayor's attendants.

Before we analyze the incident in its bearing on the physician, we have to realize that the events told are much older than the text we have on a seventh-century copy from Upper Syria and a parallel, attested in a tiny fragment, from the library of Assurbanipal. Locale, personal names, and diction place the tale clearly in the middle or early second half of the second millennium; it is thus likely to be some centuries younger than the period in which the medical texts were first written down.

The physician in this tale was clean-shaven—an old Sumerian requirement of a man who was supposed to approach the deity —and probably only scantily clad, but hardly naked as Sumerian priests are represented. According to references in vocabularies and an unpublished fragment from Nineveh, the physician carried a bag, probably containing herbs and bandages. Another indication comes from a religious text which contains a self-presentation of the goddess Gula as physician and runs, "I am a physician, I know how to heal, I carry with me all the herbs . . ." "I am provided with a bag full of effective conjurations, I carry texts for healing, I effect cures for all."[11] The physician of the story carries a libation jar instead of a bag—a characteristic of the Sumerian officiant often shown on early seal cylinders— and a censer. His appearance endows him with some of the characteristics of the medicine man. This is by no means a "primitive" trait; not long ago doctors wore special garb even in daily life, and they are still expected to wear a uniform of a sort when treating a patient. We have no way of knowing whether Mesopotamian diviners, conjurers, and priests had to wear a characteristic dress when performing their duties or appearing in public. There are indications that certain persons connected with the sanctuary wore linen garments, but this is all that is known.

The rogue disguised as doctor is most likely acting quite in style when he advertises his services with immodest references to his effectiveness. This was apparently as acceptable as his offering his help when someone was in need of a physician. The fact that the prankster announces that he is a native of the learned city of Isin in order to impress his prospective patient is interesting, because the same claim is made by a diviner (bārû) on a seal inscribed with his name.[12] Since it is not customary to indicate one's native city on a seal, the diviner may be assumed to have added this information for exactly the same purpose as the rogue in the tale of the poor man of Nippur.

Another passage in cuneiform literature places diviner and physician on the same level, together with two other professions, that of the innkeeper and the baker.[13] We refer to a conjuration said to be effective in providing these four experts with a brisk trade. We can learn from this passage that the physician and the diviner depended on their patients for a living. Both were technicians, more or less well trained, since not every physician and diviner came from the famous "university" of Isin.

The constellation of experts who made use of conjurations to increase their clientele is startling only to us. It represents faithfully the earliest nucleus of free professional experts on the village level. With urbanization, the diviner and the physician moved to the capital. The innkeeper, as the first industrialist, continued to sell his beer to the villagers and townspeople—on credit during hard times—, acted as money lender in the Old Babylonian period, and made his establishment a social center. The baker represents the first shopkeeper, providing the townspeople with daily bread and baked goods. The street of the bakers in Jerusalem (Jer. 37:21) illustrates tellingly this situation. The mention of these four occupations shows that this conjuration stems from an early period.

Physicians, under these circumstances, must have realized that it was highly advantageous for their economic and social welfare to attach themselves to the palace rather than to rely on conjurations. Indeed, most references to physicians until the second third of the second millennium show them connected with the palace. These references are in texts from peripheral regions—from Mari, the Amarna letters, and the tablets found in Hattuša. There are also scattered references referring to the same situation until the middle of the first millennium. In most of these passages, physicians are sent by the king to assist his servants and officials, and write reports to the king about the health of their patients. At times the court physicians are sent to foreign countries to give assistance to their rulers, thus increasing the king's prestige by impressing his allies with the skill of the doctors under his rule. Equally important was the role of the physician at court for the health of the king, his family, and his harem. From a Middle Assyrian collection of royal ordinances (see above, p. 286) concerning the harem, we learn that a physician attended the women sheltered there. Private physicians are rare throughout the entire history of Mesopotamia, but they are mentioned in Ur III and Old Babylonian texts. There is an isolated reference to a woman physician at the palace in an Old Babylonian text from Larsa and to an eye doctor (asû īnī), a unique reference to a specialized physician in Neo-Babylonian texts.[14] As pointed out, medical treatment at the Assyrian court and in important cases was under the direction of "scientists" who were not called asû. They were mašmāšu and āšipu experts, trained in the lore of Eridu, far in the south, rather than of Isin. They predicted the course of the disease from signs observed on the patient's body, and they offered incantations and other magic as well as the remedies indicated by the diagnosis.

The profession of the practitioner, asû, was neither lucrative nor endowed with any special status; at least, there is nothing in extant references to suggest any favored position. The absence of a special divine patron for this profession—except for Ea, who is the patron of all the crafts—is taken as corroboration of their relative unimportance. There are no references in the Mesopotamian pantheon to such deified physicians as the Egyptian Imhotep and the Greek Aesculapius. Though the Mesopotamian goddess Gula is often called the "Great Lady Physician," she is a deity of death and healing (see p. 197) and belongs to the religious life, and has no function as a patron deity.

The word lists name the *asû* among divination experts and conjurers, with the *asû* the last to be mentioned. It may be assumed that the learned members of the profession copied the handbooks of their craft, but only one text is known which, as the subscription tells us, was copied by an apprentice physician (*asû agašgû*).[15]

The study of Mesopotamian medicine is nearly a century old, but Assyriology still has to show that its results are important for the history of medicine, let alone the history of science. A handicap has been the zeal of enthusiasts who hoped to impress students of the history of science with a Mesopotamian medicine of high achievement devoid of the practice of magic. The groping of two generations of scholars for an understanding of the technical vocabularies of the old physicians and pharmacists has not been too successful. Progress in this respect will not come simply from a corpus comprising all medical texts—although such a work would expedite matters—but rather from an understanding of the function and nature of the several text types in evidence and from an approach to the history of medicine which judges past achievements within their own frame of reference without striving to integrate them into an over-all evolutionary scheme.

Mathematics and Astronomy

It is to be regretted that such an essential aspect of Mesopotamian science as the topics of the present section, mathematics and mathematical astronomy, cannot be utilized more directly in the presentation of Mesopotamian civilization. Throughout this book it has been my aim not to step beyond the limits given by texts and documents which I have read myself and judged relevant for the "portrait" toward which I have been striving. In the case of mathematics and astronomy, I have to restrict myself to a short report based on the presentation of experts who have treated these texts firsthand and have written extensively on them (see the Bibliographical Note to this chapter).

Non-mathematical cuneiform texts refer only rarely to mathematics, and when they do, they speak of mathematics in more or less general terms. So does Assurbanipal in the self-praise which introduces one of his inscriptions. He mentions that he learned how to find the "complicated reciprocals and the products (of multiplication)," in the same context in which he speaks of his knowledge of Sumerian and his ability to read old tablets, all part of his elaborate "liberal" education.[16] The literary compositions in which the learned scribes speak of their training offer another reference to the teaching of mathematics. They boast that they have been taught "multiplication, reciprocals, coefficients, balancing of accounts, administrative accounting, how to make all kinds of pay allotments, and how to divide property and delimit shares of fields."[17] Many of these topics recur in the text type called "problem texts," important for our understanding of the teaching of mathematics in the scribal schools, although the enumeration just cited does not offer an adequate picture of the intellectual achievement, the elegance of execution, and the sophisticated use of tools of ingenious simplicity of which the Mesopotamian mathematicians had every reason to be proud. Their mathematical methods can well stand comparison with the accomplishments of all other civilizations up to the middle of the second millennium A.D., i.e., for more than three thousand years.

Most of what we know of Mesopotamian mathematics comes from two types of cuneiform mathematical texts: the tables used for multiplication, and other purposes, and the problem texts. Both types are attested for the Old Babylonian and the Seleucid periods. No previous stages of the historical development which led to the Old Babylonian texts nor any evidence for the continuation of the tradition across the millennium which separates the two text groups are known, except for a third, small group of mathematical texts, the "coefficient texts," which serve basically practical purposes.[18] As for content, mathematical method, and presentation, the texts of the last three centuries differ only in minor points from those of the Hammurapi period.

The mathematical tables are designed for multiplication and

division; they also list squares and cubes and the pertinent roots, and lists of figures, "exponential functions," needed to compute compound interest. The problem texts address the reader in the second person and are written in Akkadian and, in a few instances, in Sumerian. They either state a problem by giving the basic facts and figures, prescribing then step by step the way to the solution of the problem, or list large numbers of problems without indicating any solution. The sequence in which these problems, amounting at times to two hundred or more, are listed in maximal condensation, progresses from simple to complex and elaborate relations. They convey the procedure as such without the elaboration of the numerical results, using measurements and other given numbers solely to illustrate the operations described. Mathematically speaking, one might say that the problems which most interested Meso-potamian mathematicians—such as quadratic equations and related operations—are algebraic in nature although formulated in geometrical terms.

The same sudden development which brought Mesopotamian mathematics from the level of a practice developed and main-tained for administrative reasons and utilitarian purposes to that of a vehicle of scientific creativity occurs in astronomy more than a millennium later. After the middle of the first millennium B.C. in southern Mesopotamia, a change took place in the interests and the methods of scribes and scholars concerned with the phenomena to be observed in the sky, especially the move-ments of the planets and the moon, and the changes in the length of day and night. We are completely at a loss as to the nature of this development and the factors which contributed to it; we may state only that it occurred contemporaneously with the rise of Greek mathematics initiated by Euclid. One may suggest the possibility that it was the genius of one Meso-potamian scholar who first applied well-known mathematical methods to express the variations observable in the movements of the moon with respect to a fixed point and took note of other recurrent irregularities in order to compute those happenings in the sky which were considered important. The introduction of mathematics into astronomy was a crucial step forward in the history of Mesopotamian science—and equally important for the neighbors of Mesopotamia to the west and also to the east.

As early as the Sumerian word lists and their bilingual successors, the names of stars and constellations appear. In prayers addressing Sin, Šamaš, and Ištar there are references to certain facts concerning the moon, the sun, and the planet Venus. There are, as well, a number of prayers that speak of stars and constellations as early as the Old Babylonian period. The Big Dipper and the Pleiades seem to have been favored, and among the larger stars, Sirius. The fifth tablet of the Creation Epic uses only a few lines to describe the marvels of the cosmos, the course of the sun and the moon, the arrangement of the stars, and the calendar.[19] Still, the relative unimportance of any cult accorded the stars and constellations should be noted. A certain amount of basic astronomical knowledge must have accumulated and was formulated in some way which eventually led to the formation of a three-tablet series called MUL.APIN.[20] Preserved in the library of Assurbanipal, it contains not only a list of stars organized in three parallel "roads" (the central one following the equator) but also references to the planets and to the complexities of the calendar. In connection with early astronomical lore should be mentioned the observations of the disappearance and reappearance of Venus behind the sun, preserved in astrological omens expressly said to have been made during the rule of the Old Babylonian king Ammisaduqa, the fourth king after Hammurapi. Their real or imaginary importance for second-millennium chronology notwithstanding, they are testimony of special interest in what happens in the sky, especially at the moment when day changes to night.[21]

This interest also speaks out of the few preserved astrological omens of the early period.[22] Under still unknown circumstances, a number of small omen series grew in the subsequent five to six centuries into an impressive body of material (see above, p. 225) which was maintained in Assyria up to the fall of the empire and in Babylonia into the Seleucid period. The omens refer to the heliacal rising of planets, to eclipses, the timing of the new moon, the length of the day, and the path of the planets among the stars in order to obtain predictions concerning the king and his country. Astrology became important at the Assyrian court of the Sargonids, surpassing even extispicy, as we learn from royal letters and other texts. Its role in Babylonia cannot be judged, since no such text material is in evidence. At any rate, astrology neither precluded the rise of mathematical astronomy nor was there a loss of interest when, for example, the regularity of eclipses was recognized and they could no longer presage dire events—at least, we are inclined to assume this, today. Astrology and mathematical astronomy moved in different social and intellectual circles, and yet, curiously enough, both exercised considerable influence on Egypt and the Hellenistic West, either directly or through intermediaries. Astrology established the reputation of "Chaldean" science, which spread through all of Europe, while the Hellenistic astronomers utilized the achievements of Mesopotamian astronomy and thus preserved them and saved them from oblivion. The stages of this process are still under investigation, an investigation which will range from the east coast of the Indian Ocean to the records that remain of the astrologers of Rome and Byzantium. Although the role of Hellenism as the originator, transformer, and carrier of ideas hardly can be overestimated, one must keep in mind that another "international" movement preceded it. This is the still incompletely known network of Aramaic-speaking-and-writing groups which covered approximately the same territory and must have represented not only international trade but also a measure of intellectual contacts.

Like the mathematical texts, most of those bearing on astronomical matters fall into two categories. They are either "procedure texts," establishing the rules for computing specific events (positions of the planets and the moon, eclipses) or the results of these computations, i.e., "ephemerides." The ephemerides list full and new moons for periods up to two years and eclipses for periods up to more than fifty years. Other tables list lunar velocity, daily solar and lunar motions, and positions. In order to establish a system to measure the progress of the sun and the planets, a zodiac was determined and utilized and rules for exact lunisolar intercalations were evolved. The practical value of all this in making a calendar is evident. The interest of the Babylonian astronomer in the planets was governed by similar, more or less practical considerations; he was interested in predicting specific events such as heliacal risings and settings and oppositions. The planets studied are Jupiter, Venus, Mercury, Mars, and Saturn.

Craftsmen and Artists

Any investigation of the state of Mesopotamian technology antedating written sources is hampered by a number of difficulties. To describe the fundus of the native technological traditions is made difficult by the loss of most of the artifacts except for the more or less accidental survival of objects made of stone, shells, bones, clay, and metals, in addition to the foundations of some buildings. Pictographic records showing men and animals, buildings, and boats are meager. The paucity of evidence and its specific nature induce us to turn to the techniques applied by other civilizations in hope of finding contemporary parallels to the situation as it was in Mesopotamia. Here Egypt occupies a key position because of the amount and the variety of the pertinent objects found. No less revealing in this respect is the information contained in documents and to be adduced from artifacts found in Syria, Anatolia, and Palestine. These, combined with Egyptian material, should offer enough variety to enable us to reconstruct Mesopotamian arts and crafts.

A "comparative technology" presents itself as the only adequate way of handling the data available to us. It is more promising to compare specific techniques in several civilizations than to make a separate inventory of each civilization and then compare what data are available. In this respect such topics as metallurgy, weaving methods, the construction of houses, boats, and complex appliances such as plows, chariots, and musical instruments readily offer themselves. Comparisons concerned with specific artifacts should embrace not only form, function, and execution, but should go beyond this purely descriptive approach and study the challenge and response between the maker and his materials and between his tools and the demands made on them. Equally important are the advantages and ecological limitations which often determine the technology and, above all, the influence of ideological contexts. The latter create both inhibitions and specific demands; they may cause stagnation, which in turn fossilizes technology, or they may stimulate creative innovations. Finally, one has to account for the influence of the social structure on technology; its stratification may foster the coexistence of separate levels of technology, such as sacred and secular, prestige and subsistence, and native and imported or imposed. In short, comparative technology may well be considered as important for an understanding of one civilization within the framework of others as are comparative philology and comparative religion. What makes comparative technology outstanding in this august company of recognized and institutionalized disciplines is its reach in time and area, greatly surpassing anything the other two approaches have yielded thus far. Not only do techniques spread farther and more easily than religious concepts and languages, but they sometimes leave us tangible proofs, artifacts, and pictorial representations where comparative religion evokes only mirages based on the theories of the day and where comparative philology resorts to complex and fragile systems of dead reckoning.

From the wide range of techniques known in Mesopotamia, the technology of minerals shall be discussed more fully than, for instance, the complex of problems connected with the domestication of plants and animals. Within these three vistas (plants—animals—minerals) most aspects of Mesopotamian technology will come under scrutiny.

The domesticated plants cultivated by Mesopotamians were grown from the earliest known period in gardens and in fields; additional vegetable food may have been gathered from wild or ruderal plants. Essential differences separate the garden from the field. In gardens were planted slips, shoots, and certain seeds, plants which demanded, as a rule, special care while growing and produced bulbs, roots, or tubers whose harvests could be spaced throughout the year to assure an adequate and steady supply. Field-grown domesticated grasses, on the other hand, required intense seasonal work and some kind of machinery, yielded a harvest, as a rule, only once a year and in a quantity which necessitated the organization of laborers, storage, and some kind of budgeting. The garden as a source of food is much older than the field. Its products were those which could be utilized without preparation over a fire, by drying, salting, and maceration. The plow and harrow are as characteristic for the field as the dibbling stick is for the garden; moreover, the hoe is much less effective in the field than in the garden. Fields can easily be enlarged; gardens, however, require a stable amount of continuously available manpower, which in turn determines their size. All this deeply affected the social structure of the community, its density, the distribution of the population over the arable territory, and the division of labor. If we knew about the relationship between the acreage used for fields and gardens in Mesopotamia, we would have better insight into the economic and social texture than that offered us by many hundreds of documents. We know that both fields and gardens were cultivated and that garden produce was auxiliary to the domesticated grasses and sesame grown in the fields, but we do not know to what extent. Only in groves of date palms did the garden play an important economic role in Mesopotamia. The date palm was the only essential fruit tree in the region. The domestication of the date palm seems to have taken place on the eastern shores of the Indian Ocean, spreading west toward the Persian Gulf, the Mediterranean, and the Nile valley.[23] The tolerance of the date palm to the salty and brackish water and alkaline soil of southern Mesopotamia, its crop, of great nutritional value, which could be preserved and stored, its numerous by-products (leaves, fiber, timber) gave the tree a unique importance. The date palm requires little manpower but expert care in planting, artificial pollination, and in special treatment of its fruit. All these techniques, for the acquisition of which Mesopotamian man had every reason to be thankful, were the results of the experiment and methodical searching of generations long past. No other fruit tree has received similar attention; the date palm occupies in Mesopotamia the position of the olive tree around the Mediterranean.

Less spectacular but no less impressive were the efforts of those early "scientists" who domesticated and evolved those numerous and diversified plants that filled the Mesopotamian gardens. The representatives of the lily family (among them, onions and leeks) or those of the parsley family (coriander and fennel) and the Brassica (cabbage plants, mustard, and radishes) are characterized by their pungent taste and odor which attracted early man's attention and stimulated domestication. To these early agriculturists and their protracted endeavors, Mesopotamia likewise owed the leguminous plants whose protein richness could be easily stored in their seeds (lentils, peas, chick-peas) and utilized in many ways. If Assyriologists were able to define more exactly the nature of the garden plants mentioned so frequently in early Sumerian texts, we could trace —with the help of botanists and other specialists—the history of their cultivation and the lines of their diffusion far beyond the limits of our region.

In the fields of Mesopotamia we meet a similar display of outstanding agricultural achievements. Apart from the grasses, sesame and flax were cultivated. A special terminology, differing from that of the cereals, arose with the culture of sesame. Sesame represents only one phase in early man's quest for essential fats; they were also found in the seeds of certain turnips, especially rape, and flax and hemp. Eventually, other properties of these plants, such as the uses to which the fiber of flax and, perhaps, of hemp, could be put, were recognized.

The domestication of the grasses illustrates that care given to plants increases their yield, and cases of endemism (locally restricted forms) or spontaneous mutations occur and are preserved. A process of selection takes place, and the less productive or slower maturing plants are automatically crowded out by superior forms. A fertile source for changes which often deeply affect the development of domestic grasses is the transportation of seeds to new soils and to different climates. Thus the subtropical flax with large blossoms, many twigs, and oleïferous seeds on low stalks is assumed to have changed in cooler climates to a plant with few seeds and long, twigless stalks yielding a fiber of great economic importance. On the other hand, weeds associated with certain grasses can replace them under such circumstances, as oats and rye replaced barley and wheat when the latter were moved by man to different climates and soil conditions. The essential step in the domestication of barley—for whatever reason it came about—was the toughening of the axis which keeps the seed on the spike and allows man to harvest the full stalks in order to obtain the kernels. Harvesting became a process which required effective methods but offered high yield. When the planting was "mechanized," the growing of barley and such early cereals as emmer and emmer wheat brought about far-reaching changes in population density and in seasonal working patterns, and encouraged the rise of a storage economy. The key to the mechanization of planting was the plow, a tool of great complexity and difficult development, which had to be adapted to the nature of the soil and its state at the plowing season. The Mesopotamian plow was a supreme technological achievement. Cattle were used to draw it, and a seeding attachment dropped the seeds into the furrow. The seeding apparatus had its only parallel in the Far East.[24]

Mesopotamian farmers used no manure on their fields, although there is evidence that rubble from ruined settlements was used to improve the fertility of the soil.[25] This practice is still well known all over the Near East and continues to work havoc on ancient sites.

The tangled history of the cereals within the mountain triangle formed by the Zagros-Taurus-Abyssinia highlands cannot be our concern here; and yet something should be said of the technological consequences of the cultivation of barley and wheat. Since barley can be grown in poor and alkaline soil, it was preferred to wheat in Mesopotamia; Egypt became the wheat land, and the regions in between used the cereal which best responded to local conditions. Once harvested, barley has to be threshed, winnowed, washed, and dried before it can be safely placed in storehouses, as it was in the Old Babylonian period, or stored in communal piles covered with mats, as in the Neo-Babylonian period.[26] For consumption, the kernels may be husked by singeing ("parched grain"), soaked, or beaten with pestles into coarse groats. Groats can be used in porridge-like dishes (or baked as a bread substitute). The kernels were sifted, pounded, or milled on a push quern, since no rotary quern was used before the Hellenistic period. Barley flour was made into flat bread cakes for immediate consumption. Wheat flour required yeasts obtained from plants or through fermentation. The dough was baked in a chamber oven and made a finer bread than did barley flour.

The fermentation process, used in the preparation and preservation of other vegetable products, was applied to barley, which was allowed to sprout. From sprouted malt was produced an alcoholic drink which seems to have been an essential part of the daily fare. The technology of Mesopotamian beer production was complex, and a rich vocabulary naming ingredients, beer types, and by-products can be traced down to the last half of the second millennium.[27] As a rare example of an innovation in Mesopotamian food technology, we discover in Neo-Babylonian texts references to a beer, or better, an alcoholic drink, made of dates, a practice not mentioned before this period. As to other procedures—the preparation of dishes from cereals, agricultural methods—no essential changes occurred throughout the whole documented period. No new plants were domesticated or introduced from the outside, and no new techniques seem to have been applied to plowing and harvesting. Mesopotamian agricultural technology seems to have remained at a standstill. This statement may have to be qualified when the exact meanings of a number of difficult technical terms are at last clearly established. Only the economic nature of the transactions recorded in the texts dealing with agriculture and its products differ sharply across the gap of two millennia that separates the documents of the early period from those of the late period.

Man's relationship to animals differs considerably from civilization to civilization. The incentive of having supplies of fresh meat at hand is not always a major reason for keeping certain animals in captivity. Some animals have utilitarian uses;

others are kept for purposes of display; some few become pets; others can be tamed and used for hunting and fighting. The mungo, or mongoose, and the chameleon were lived with; other animals were lived on, as were the herds of buffalo, reindeer, and sheep that were followed by migrating groups in a more or less sophisticated form of symbiosis.

The success of domestication is not assured until the animals breed in captivity. Once the animal has reached this stage, a process of degeneration begins, the result of new feeding habits, special care, inbreeding, and changed living conditions. Endemic changes work with or against the disposition of the animal, its adaptability or tolerance to changed conditions, and the place assigned to it in the ideological framework of the group of humans with whom the animal lives. Thus cows were brought to yield milk not only when their calves needed it but the year round; similarly, the chicken became what the Egyptians called a "bird which gives birth every day."

There is Mesopotamian evidence of experiments in domestication which we also find in Egyptian sources. There was a time when sheep had no wool, which developed from down. The artistic motif of the cow licking her calf, found throughout the region, takes us a step farther back in time; it goes back to a phase of the domestication of cattle when it was necessary to keep the calf near its mother during milking just as the Cyclops in the *Odyssey* (IX, 245) put a lamb to each of the ewes when he milked them.

In a survey of the animals domesticated in the ancient Near East or introduced there by diffusion, we should consider animals of economic importance and those whose products require special techniques to be of use to man. Such domesticated animals as the donkey (of probably western origin in Mesopotamia), the dog, the duck and goose, and the pig (of uncertain origin) do not stimulate technological advance nor do they need special and advanced techniques to be useful to man. As for goats, sheep, and dairy cattle, they all require a certain amount of care. They must be fed, watered, and protected. They yield meat to be prepared or stored (dried, salted) and skins to be tanned in different ways, and they provide a regular supply of young animals. Sheep, goats, and cows give milk which can be churned to butter or made into cheese. Here one has also to mention the hair of goats and the wool of sheep and what these two important raw materials entail in special techniques such as felting, spinning, weaving, and dyeing. Harnesses were developed so that cattle could be used to pull plows, wagons, and sledges. When the horse came into use, only minor changes occurred; the speed possible with a horse necessitated a lighter vehicle, the anatomy of the horse a different harness.

Of course, fishing, hunting, and trapping evolved necessarily pertinent technologies which often produce tools and apparatus that attest to the ingenuity of their designers, but of all that only a list of Sumerian and Akkadian words for nets, traps, and so on, which remain without much meaning, are left to us.

The technological inventory related to domesticated animals showed no marked extension in and around Mesopotamia throughout the entire historical period, as was the case with regard to domesticated plants. Certain enlargements of the inventory did indeed occur, such as the increased use of the camel (perhaps even its actual domestication), although this did not affect Mesopotamia in any important way;[28] both the peacock and the chicken passed through on their way westward—the Sumerians called the chicken the "bird from Meluhha" and the Syrians called it the "Akkadian [bird]." The over-all picture does not show the development of more effective methods to utilize these animals and the products to be had from them. There is no reason to assume that wagons and chariots improved or that methods of weaving and tanning changed for the better. In the late periods donkeys are still carrying their burdens, ducks and geese are still fattened with dough, sheep and cattle move from winter to summer pasture, horse and bull are still pulling the swift chariot and the clumsy wagon, the pig has all but disappeared.

In order to characterize the level of Mesopotamian technology concerned with the utilization of animal products, I would like to discuss here, somewhat cursorily, two important crafts: tanning and weaving.

About the process of tanning in Mesopotamia we happen to

be better informed than we are about many other crafts. Two especially explicit ritual texts describe how, in one instance, the hide of a black bull was to be prepared to cover the sacred kettledrum, and in the other, how the hide of a kid was to be tanned. Both texts prescribe a variety of liquids, some composed of fats, oils, and flour, others containing all sorts of vegetable matter; solutions made with alum imported from Asia Minor are also mentioned. The hide, after having been treated by soaking in these liquids and rubbing with fats and oils, was considered adequately tanned. Each of the methods mentioned (i.e., the use of alum, of fats, of materials containing tannic acid) would alone have sufficed to produce the desired effects. Hides can be tanned by using a fat treatment, preferably vegetal fat (as is illustrated in the *Iliad*, XVII, 389ff.), or salt and alum, which stop decay and make the leather last (English: tawing), or by applying vegetable matter (such as oak bark, gall nuts, and certain roots and leaves) in solution to act as an astringent (English: tanning). In short, Mesopotamian technology was not aware of the effectiveness of each of the individual processes for the preservation of animal skins, but used them all, not yet applying special methods for specific materials and purposes. It is possible, of course, that techniques which were out of date were required for ritual reasons but were not used by professional tanners. If correct, our assumption would only transfer this technological problem to an earlier period.

Although a wealth of technical terms refer to parts of the Mesopotamian loom or to loom types, to the craft and the products of the weaver, next to nothing can be ascertained concerning the nature of the loom—whether it was horizontal or vertical—and its construction and functioning. For an appreciation of the Mesopotamian technology of weaving, in the absence of exact information, one can only speculate and rely on analogies and contrasts supplied by our information about weaving in Egypt. One immediate contrast: Egyptian weavers used vegetable fibers, the weavers of Mesopotamia used wool from animals. Egypt rejected wool.

Whereas vegetable fiber when moistened always curls in one direction and can therefore easily be spun, animal fiber does not have such a tendency and requires more manual work and a heavier whorl to produce a thread from a strip of roving. The spinning of wool seems to have developed in imitation of the spinning of vegetable material.

The Egyptians evolved a weaving technique for linen which was clearly under the influence of mat weaving; the linen fiber was used only for plain cloth weaving. No technical elaborations were admitted, nor did they utilize any of the possibilities offered by the fine and even structure of the linen fiber and its tensile strength. Those relatively simple technical devices which so easily pattern the structure of the web by arranging the warp through the use of heddles were also disregarded.

Mesopotamian weaving developed under different circumstances. The natural use for the fine and fluffy hair plucked or combed from the sheep is to beat it into a matting by means of sticks and, by using moisture and pressure, to produce out of this matting a pliable, water-resistant, warm material. The resulting wool product is felt. I would like to propose that felt was the prototype of Mesopotamian wool weaving exactly as the reed mat was that of Egyptian linen weaving. In Mesopotamia the weaver was not concerned with the structure of the woven fabric. He used grating, teaseling, and surface felting to obliterate any visible structure and to present a smooth, felt-like surface. Rather than using different colors in the warp and weft, he liked to decorate the finished product with surface appliqué, looping, and fringes. Since the finished piece of material was used as a garment as it came from the loom, without cutting or sewing, multicolored decorative strips could be added to brighten the fabric.

The Mesopotamians seem to have been aware that the technical level of their textile products was below that of the West. The Assyrian kings in their reports on booty taken in the continuous warfare against their western neighbors refer as often to multicolored garments as they do to silver, gold, and other precious objects so that it becomes obvious that they prized these textiles highly. In the second millennium the region beyond the Euphrates to the borders of Egypt developed a textile technology surpassing that of both Egypt and Mesopotamia especially in the use of brilliantly colored fibers and other decorative techniques, probably using a primitive type of pattern weaving which produced narrow bands. The famous Phoenician purple industry must have been built on a long tradition. Due to the paucity of literary evidence, this entire development can only be guessed from extant Egyptian and Mesopotamian descriptions. As a matter of fact, the weaver's art was not the only domain of technology in which the West excelled; its jewelry and other products of its metallurgy and its glass work may be mentioned in this context.

The entire ancient Near East never seems to have progressed beyond the one-heddle pattern which developed in Egypt and Mesopotamia from quite distinct technological sources, as we have tried to show here. It was the Chinese multiheddle technique—which allows pattern weaving—that swept westward from India to the Mediterranean in the last centuries of the first millennium and crowded out the archaic methods of the first great civilizations.

To round out this somewhat sketchy picture of Mesopotamian technology, one should include such topics as the construction of houses, furniture, chariots, and boats. I may only point out that such a complex artifact as, for instance, a river boat reveals much about the technological aspiration of its builders. The history that lies behind the planning of a boat and the style in which it is constructed reveals the eternal struggle between creative intention and the characteristics of the given material to be shaped and transformed. A boat represents an achievement of its designer equally important to our understanding of the past as a relief in stone or a statue. In fact, a boat can often yield more substantial evidence of the sophistication of its builder and insight into the conflict between tradition and invention.

In his unending quest for the ideal working material for his innate creativeness, man turned quite early to minerals, earlier perhaps than to the plastic clay which can be fashioned so easily. The wide variety of stones, their durability and attractiveness, even their colors and textures, have always excited man's curiosity. Some can be shaped and polished relatively easily; some are translucent and soft, others are very hard, but the hard stone yields a keen edge under expert flaking. Still other "stones"—such as native copper—can be hammered and stretched into required shapes. Again we have to forgo listing the manifold uses to which stones have been put in the technological inventory to which Mesopotamian man fell heir. There is preserved a galaxy of fashioned and polished beads, stone vases and other stone objects (weights, lamps, spindle-whorls) and, above all, cylinder seals made of stone and decorated with incised patterns (see below, pp. 329f.)

The development of the chamber oven allowed the melting of certain "stones" (Lat. *metallum*= stone) and made it feasible to shape and form them in molds. The furnace for the smith's crucible, the kiln for the potter, and the oven in which wheat bread was baked are all the results of a crucial "revolution," from the use of fire for food preparation to its utilization for technical purposes. The utilization of fire made not only metallurgy possible but also the firing of clay and the permanent coloring, i.e., glazing, of stones, which eventually led to the making of glass. In all these instances, mineral materials are transformed by fire.

It is not our purpose to speculate here upon the internal development within metallurgy, the techniques applied and the metals and alloys used. Suffice it to say that Mesopotamian man made use of the chamber oven, even though the baking of wheat bread in such an oven was not practised in this region; barley cakes do not require this. Copper, bronze, silver, and gold were used by the Mesopotamian smith who worked with some kind of bellows, and probably also with charcoal, to produce the temperatures required. The metal work of the earliest period is technically excellent but hardly outstanding compared to the general level of the ancient Near East. In contrast to that of Egypt, most of the metal work created in Mesopotamia during the second and first millennium B.C. has been lost. Still, there are some chance survivals and, above all, a considerable amount of evidence in written documents as to such work, evidence which, by the way, is still to be collected and studied systematically.

The use of iron in Mesopotamia is of considerable interest. It was slow to appear in the ancient Near East, but it spread across the entire region around the turn of the second millennium. Early metallurgists, who succeeded in changing beautiful green and blue minerals into a new material which, when cast hot into molds, could be made to assume nearly every form and shape, certainly tried time and again to apply this technique to red-colored minerals. Although iron ore can be reduced at a lower temperature than copper ore, the product obtained could not be used in the same way as copper and bronze; it could not be cast. This has to be done at high temperature, a technique first practiced by European metallurgists in the fourteenth century. On the other hand, iron when hot can be hammered into a desired form relatively easily. It can be changed into a kind of steel when repeatedly heated (to induce carbonization) and quenched in cold water. The point to be made here is that while the technique of cold-hammering copper and other metals was well known in the ancient Near East, that of hammering hot metal was applied only late. It seems that a "block" in technological reasoning caused the retardation, and its removal brought about the diffusion of the use of iron.

The changeover from copper and bronze to iron was gradual, and traces of the early use of iron have all but disappeared. It was only a technological change and not a revolution with any direct military, economic, or social consequences, as has often been suggested. In the ancient Near East iron was both a new-comer to be excluded in certain ideological contexts and a metal known from of old, a metal that could fall from heaven and was therefore considered endowed with magical properties. With the coming of iron, there were certain dislocations in the trade routes that brought ores and metals to Mesopotamia and in the position of the smith of whom the working of iron demanded a much higher technical knowledge. The desire to preserve the lore of their craft created secrecy, seclusion, and, necessarily, defamation for the smith.

Mesopotamian man's fascination with colored and precious stones seems to have given rise to a highly complex development linked again—as was the case with the colored ores (malachite, haematite)—to the use of fire technology. It is still far from clear whence came the impetus which gave rise to glass making.

The scarcity of imported precious stones led to the manufacture of artificial stones or to the decoration of cheap native stones to increase their attractiveness. In Egypt, defective pieces and chippings of the coveted lapis lazuli were pounded, ground up, and compressed into beads, using some alkaline substance of low fusibility as a binder. In Mesopotamia quartz pebbles were painted with mineralic blue and green colors which under heat changed into vitreous colored glazes of high and permanent gloss. The indispensable prerequisite for success in this technique was the use of a carrier of the glaze which contained silica (quartz pebbles, for example) and steatite, which for many reasons was a favored material. Steatite is soft enough to be easily carved, has a fine and even grain and, above all, hardens when heated. Another stone treated with fire was the carnelian. It can be bleached in fire by means of alkaline substances placed on it, and it can be decorated with red mineral dyes, a technique practised quite early from India to Egypt.

It is apparent that the chemists of the fourth and third millennia B.C. were at work experimenting with such chemicals as lime, soda, and silicates (sand of quartzite) in combination with mineral substances in vivid colors to produce glazes, frits, and glass of many compositions, some durable, others quickly deteriorating, some opaque, others translucent, some to be used on carriers ("cores"), others to be formed in molds (like cast metal objects) and eventually treated in a special technique suitable to the nature of this wonderfully plastic material—glass.

I cannot discuss here the history of ancient glazes and glass in the Near East—how they came into being and developed in a constant interchange of ideas and techniques from Mesopotamia via Syria to Egypt and back again. Much technical sophistication and ingenuity was spent on the quest for these artificial stones in which man succeeded in imitating nature and of which the Mesopotamian chemist was rightly proud. Technologically speaking, it would be interesting to trace the course of this development in its accidental or conscious fusion and transfer of specific techniques, in its trials and errors, new departures and dead ends. Such questions as to when, where, and for what reason the glaze was divorced from its core and changed into a new raw material, when and where the techniques were evolved to treat this new material in such a way that its technical and aesthetic possibilities were best utilized are still open. These and other questions will be answered only when extant glass objects have been analyzed and related to the cuneiform texts in which Mesopotamian craftsmen handed down their methods in writing. Such texts are unique in cuneiform literature: only the perfume makers[29] and the glass makers[30] thought highly enough of their professional work to seek to preserve in writing the traditions of their crafts.

The last aspect of the technology of mineral materials to be mentioned here is concerned with clay, that versatile, durable, and nearly ubiquitous "plastic." Of the three main uses of clay in Mesopotamia—pottery, clay tablets, and bricks—only for the first was firing indispensable; tablets and bricks were sun-dried as well as kiln-fired. From the point of view of our interest in comparative technology, the clay tablet, as important as it be for our knowledge about Mesopotamia, represents an oddity, and the products of the Mesopotamian potters, at times exquisite and impressive, do not justify more than a passing mention here. This is not to imply that the potter's art does not require much technical expertise in the selection of the clay and its admixtures, the use of certain kinds of wheels and pertinent tools, the throwing and decorating of the pot, the construction of the kiln (air access, temperatures), in the firing itself, and the decorating and burnishing of the finished object. All these are worthy topics for technological investigation and are likely to yield insight into the technological thinking of ancient craftsmen.[31]

For the purpose of the present discussion, however, the brick is a more suitable subject. The Mesopotamian brick wall on which is based most of the sacral architecture of that civilization is as characteristic a means of artistic expression as the wall and column combination by means of which the Greek builder articulated his intentions. This brick wall developed from the terre-pisée wall construction (murus terreus) and was, technologically speaking, never able to evolve beyond this initial handicap. From the *terre-pisée* technique it inherited the dimensional limitations, i.e., the relationship between thickness and height which for a wall of stamped earth is determined by the laws of gravity and the quality of the work (foundation, ramming technique). Although a batter on the outside could increase the height, it was rarely resorted to because such a structure could not be expected to dry properly and evenly throughout. The use of pre-dried and standardized units—bricks—proved a great boon; they made the walls lighter, and hence these could rise higher. They added stability because points and lines of stress could be treated with special care. Yet these advantages were not adequately utilized due to certain technological inhibitions of the Mesopotamian builders.

The only technical possibility of overcoming the impasse created by the *terre-pisée* technology is the use of mortar combined with that of fired bricks; but mortar was not applied, although it was known, as were kiln-fired bricks. The Mesopotamian architect, who used bricks profusely, was always hiding them behind the thick mud facing applied to all walls. He failed to realize that the use of a different type of mortar to set bricks would permit him to increase the height of his walls without making them so thick as to endanger their durability. Eventually, under western influence, mortar was used in combination with fired bricks, and the technology of arches and domes was transposed from the level of stone block architecture to that of brick architecture. The width of the rooms, hitherto restricted by the span of the roof timbers, or expanded by means of a forest of columns, then increased. A new technique was created, based on the interplay of weight and support, stress and counter-stress, structure and fill, and the heavy mud-faced and gaudily painted walls and the massive, piled-up temple towers were replaced, after a little more than a millennium, by scintillating walls in enameled and intricately patterned bricks, and by slender towers and graceful domes. But even before this development the builders of Mesopotamian temples and palaces achieved a measure of success in planning, layout, and execution. These architects and builders eventually produced monumental works of art, surpassing in many respects the creations of the artists in sculpture and relief. Bound as the builders were by the conventions of their craft and the limitations imposed by their techniques, they strove to break the monotony of the endless and ubiquitous mud-coated walls. In non-secular buildings, they articulated these walls with rhythmically distributed stepped recesses and buttresses. We do not know the functional origin of these recesses, nor can we tell why this distinctive ornamentation was restricted to temples. Special techniques were often applied to decorate the layer of mud over the brick walls. White and colored plaster was used to produce designs which were soon made more permanent in Babylonia by executing them in mosaics consisting of clay cones driven in the mud with only their colored heads visible. Murals are known from a very early period (Tepe Gawra); in secular buildings they were later replaced by glazed brick panels (in Assyria, and in the palace of Nebuchadnezzar II in Babylon), and by stone slabs incised with relief. This was done in Assyria, where adequate stone is available and where orthostats placed at the foot of the brick walls were used either structurally or for prestige purposes. As a strange and obviously imported technique we find in a temple in Middle Babylonian Uruk stone reliefs—as such an un-Babylonian feature—imitated in premolded bricks. The temple was built by a king of the Kassite dynasty (Karaindaš, beginning of the fourteenth century B.C.). The same technique, further enhanced by polychromatic glazes, is again encountered on the well-known Ištar gate of Babylon erected by Nebuchadnezzar and on the walls of the Achaemenian palace in Susa. Assyrian examples offer abundant evidence that secular buildings, especially palaces, are always susceptible to foreign influence.

Apart from the recessing of brick walls and the use of terraces which lift the entire building—or a significant part of it—above the level of the daily life,[31a] Mesopotamian architectural structures serving gods and kings are also distinguished by a characteristic layout. We can observe an impressive trend toward a well-organized configuration of the rooms, corridors, and courtyards which make up the Mesopotamian temple.[32] At times, the larger and more famous sanctuaries show a lack of "grand design," probably due to the accretion of structures over the centuries of building activity. In smaller sanctuaries, however, a harmonious arrangement seems to have been achieved more often.

Buttressed towers accentuate the entrance which leads the pious into one or more spacious paved yards without allowing him to look directly from one unit into the next, be it another yard, corridor, or the sanctuary itself. An altar and well in the main yard served functions which we can only guess. Intricately recessed walls stress the importance of the cella itself. Here again, one or more antecellas separated the image from immediate contact with the outside world. On a slightly elevated platform, the carefully sheltered image, framed by a recessed niche, could be served in dignity and splendor by the officiating priests.

The number of variables in the general arrangement of a Mesopotamian temple cannot be discussed at length here, but two variations may be mentioned. The first is a symmetrical arrangement in which the image was visible from the yard, in the background of the broad and shallow cella, and the second, an asymmetrical one, which permitted the person who was allowed to enter the cella itself to face the deity enthroned on a dais at the far end of long and narrow room, only after making a ninety-degree turn. With a few exceptions the asymmetrical arrangement seems to have been preferred in Assyria, the symmetrical in Babylonia.

Beginning with the Third Dynasty of Ur, a tower became an essential part of a Mesopotamian temple. These strange, multistaged accumulations of stamped earth and brick revetments coated with colored plaster (later, with enameled bricks), wound about with steep outside stairways, and rising high above the whitewashed temples, were uniquely Mesopotamian. They are even mentioned in the Old Testament, which makes no reference to the pyramids. In the south, these imposing structures were placed in separate *enceintes* and provided with monumental stairways. In Assyria, the temple tower was placed near the sanctuary; at times the sanctuary extended into the core of the tower structure so that the niche with the image was located within the base of a temple tower, which was, so it seems, without external stairways. The purpose and function of these ziqqurratu's, as the Mesopotamians called them, are as yet unknown, although they are mentioned by name and spoken of in general terms in literary and historical texts. Herodotus (I, 182) was told that the priestess of Bel passed a night atop the temple tower to wait for the deity to alight; this can neither be confirmed nor denied from cuneiform texts, although it sounds very much like a tale told by a dragoman.[32a]

The temple tower distinguished the sanctuary from the palace in Mesopotamia. The similarities in the layout of temple and palace are striking. Moreover, they serve to illustrate what was said above (pp. 95 f.) on the nature and function of the temple as the abode of the deity. The most important part of the palace was the throne room, where the king ceremoniously received ambassadors and tribute-bearing vassals. It corresponded to the cella of the temple where the deity was enthroned; even the placement of the throne seems to be patterned upon the placement of the dais in the cella. The throne faced the entrance in Nebuchadnezzar's palace in Babylon; in Assyrian palaces, entering visitors had to make a ninety-degree turn to face the king enthroned at the end of the long room. Almost as important as the throne room itself was the courtyard in front of it, linked with it by the same kind of monumental, towered gate which framed the entrance to the cella in the temple. Extensive living quarters were a part of the palace, and there was also a large hall, which may have been used for those large-scale banquets reported in historical and religious texts.[33] Near the dais on which the Assyrian king sat was a set of smaller rooms, one of which was used for the ritual cleansing and lustration of the king.

One more distinctive characteristic of the Assyrian palace should be noted: mural decorations representing the king as the protegé of the gods, as ever-victorious warrior and successful hunter. They also contain battle scenes, the bringing in of tribute and presents, and the slaughter of the defeated, all meant to impress those who came to do homage to the king. These representations, originally on painted walls and, later, on shallow-cut and painted orthostats, lined the throne room, the entrances, and other important parts of the palace. The reliefs are in evidence from the time of Tukulti-Ninurta I on and thus cover a period of about half a millennium (thirteenth century to seventh century). Their artistic development is characterized by the inclusion of landscape and other settings as background to the action portrayed and by the increasing attention given to anecdotic happenings, a tendency which is underlined by the subscriptions added in a number of instances. Animal represent-ations exhibit an impressive interest in realism, but the battle scenes are enacted by an ever-increasing number of stereotyped figures, often organized to tell a story. Individually, these figures are badly schematized and confined to a limited variety of gestures and positions. The composition of some is more successful than others; one day we shall be able to discern here style patterns and not rely mainly on inventories of details and motifs.

The artists who produced these reliefs, the stelae, the sculp-tures, the statues of kings cast in copper and in precious metals, and whatever other works of art which may be lost, remain completely unknown. The few designations for seal cutter and stone mason we have been able to identify nearly all come from lexical texts. References to their activities are confined to statements in royal inscriptions that the king had a stela erected with his own likeness on it, or that of certain deities; that he ordered the colossi that decorated and guarded the entrances to palaces and temples; and that he also provided costly votive offerings, furnishings for the temple, divine symbols, and a host of objects of which we know nothing but their designation and of what they were made. References to artists and their work are rare even in letters; in the royal correspondence of the Sargonids there is mention of statues to be made of the king and his family, of the transportation of the heavy, human-faced bull statues, of gold and precious stones to be assigned to the craftsmen; and we gather some data concerning works of art and their manufacture (size, techniques, alloys, and even descriptions) from royal inscriptions. The personality of the artist, however, remains completely beyond our reach.

Of the few Mesopotamian works of art preserved—apart from the reliefs and the seal cylinders—only a very small number appeals to our aesthetic conventions and is genuinely interesting to us on other than antiquarian and technological grounds. Even in the works which we admire, one has to realize that the marble face of a Sumerian goddess, which now is so remote in its melancholy, may have looked much less dignified with naturalistic, set-in, staring eyes, and that the head of a king of the Akkad period, made of bronze and endowed with a sweep of forceful elegance, may have looked quite different atop the statue to which it belonged. Still, under their smooth dignity and in their dimensional concentration, the several well-known statues of Gudea of Lagaš (ca. 2200 B.C.) show how well-contained the inner pressure had become which seems to characterize the Sumerian statuary of the preceding periods. Of all that, Babylonian art was only able to maintain a smooth and external formalism. The later stelae and statues, and expecially all those reliefs which do not strive to mirror reality, emanate only the boredom of extreme traditionalism. But the host of monstrous creatures which Mesopotamian artists endowed with startling persuasiveness shows these artists at their best, free of the conventions that govern so tyrannically the representation of gods and kings and their activities.

Within the extreme dimensional limitations of the seal cylinder and the circle of style restrictions imposed by its function, the Mesopotamian artists often showed themselves at their best. They enlivened the confines of these seals with a world of enthroned deities, monsters, and animals heraldically displayed or graced with charming realism, with battling heroes and the depiction of a host of ornaments and objects to fill in the gaps in the frieze-like impression of the seal cylinder. The iconographic inventory changes repeatedly and so does the style of presentation—shifting from geometrically accentuated abstractions to a petty realism, from teeming surfaces to the dignity of sophisticatedly displayed empty spaces; also changing are the engraving techniques and the use and content of inscriptions. These changes characterize certain periods and regions and make of the seals a sensitive barometer, registering foreign influence, the impact of artistic creativeness, and the handiwork of individual artists and schools, none of which ever succeeded in breaking through the heavy crust of ingrained traditionalism which hampered artistic expression in other media of Mesopotamian art.

Thus, to mention an obvious example, without the small body of extant Middle Assyrian seals and seal impressions, we would have missed the startling vitality and appealing immediacy of the art of that period which its monuments hardly reflect. This *élan* and the superb technique which was its vehicle live on in the animals represented fighting and dying on the wall reliefs of Neo-Assyrian palaces. They also evoke a comparison with the much earlier Old Akkadian art which had its impact on the Babylonian artistic tradition in the representation of human beings. The millennia of tired but polished conventionality which followed in Babylonia were emulated in Assyria, which saw in its southern sister civilization a prototype. The fine arts demonstrate the effects of the same conflict between creativeness and traditionalism which characterizes Mesopotamian *belles lettres*. And the coexistence of two artistic traditions in Assyria—that concerned with the representation of human beings in its dependency on the southern prototype and that concerned with animals in which an entirely different attitude toward reality is exhibited—illustrate the same internal conflict in Assyria.

Epilogue

Although this book nowhere makes pretense of aiming toward an inclusive, or balanced, presentation of Mesopotamian civilization, the author feels that he should bow out with a confession of his more glaring omissions.

The injustice committed by treating the languages of Mesopotamia—Sumerian and Akkadian—solely as a tool and not as an expression of that civilization which permits immediate approach to it can be defended on the ground that it would not only have made the book replete with philological discussions but would have yielded as distorted a picture as, for instance, presentations which restrict themselves to archeological and iconographic evidence.

More serious is the distortion caused by restricting the presentation of Mesopotamian law to the textbooks rather than delving into the fountainhead of primary information offered by the tablets which report actual legal practices. In their immediacy and their variety in period, region, and topic, the tablets would have added much to just these co-ordinates of our "Portrait." The fundamental dilemma inherent in the cuneiform source material—textbook evidence borne by the tradition versus the protean variability of all other records—has caused me, in the case of Mesopotamian law, to turn toward the former as an expedient refuge from the superabundance of detailed information. To follow my personal inclination and to concentrate on legal practices would have destroyed the already precarious correlation between the chapters of this book.

My discussion of Mesopotamian religion represents a frankly polemic shift of emphasis from the tepid climate of sentimental and patronizing interest in which it is customarily treated. Purposely, the subject matter has not been set forth in what may be called its "best light"—if light indeed can be called the frame of reference provided by our built-in Old and New Testament "guidance system." A de-westernization of the topic is aimed at, although I fully realize that the aim is utopian and that work in this direction will have to wait for a generation of Assyriologists free from emotional and institutionalized interests in the religions of the ancient Near East.

I shall offer the same excuse for not making full use of the textual evidence to present the several Mesopotamian concepts of the divine, ranging from the great celestial figures to the fallen gods, demons, and evil spirits.

It would have been desirable to dedicate a section to the Mespotamian concept of death, not so much because our own religious and social patterning assigns it, consciously or unconsciously, such importance, but because that very importance is conspicuously absent in Mesopotamia. However, a monographic study seems to offer a better way to sort out and to study the conflicting concepts. Moreover, archeological evidence may need to have its say with respect to burial practices.

If the degree of abstraction and projection in my attempt to co-ordinate the several societal systems of Mesopotamia at a given period and region would seem excessive, it is because reconstructions in specific settings cannot yet be supported by sufficient and unequivocal textual evidence. Still, although Mesopotamian civilization evolved in several discrete phases and formulations—to whatever qualifications this statement has to be subjected—its primary articulation as brought out in my reconstruction seems justifiable.

A word of explanation may be in order concerning my over-all attitude to the study of Mesopotamian civilization. Even at the price of being accused of a new kind of pan-Babylonism, I have placed Mesopotamia in the center of the picture. The terms used for its neighbors, such as "satellite civilizations," the "Barbaric West," stress this approach which is as defensible as that which uses the evidence from Mesopotamia solely as a contrasting background for other studies, or as an illustration for dogmatic tenets, be they concerned with religious, ethical, or economic evolutions. I was quite determined—perhaps imprudently—to pay more than lip service to the *Eigenbegrifflichkeit* theorem which was advanced more than thirty years ago by B. Landsberger, but has found only a very few adherents.

In one respect I finish this book with an acute sense of frustration. Many areas in the interwoven spheres of Mesopotamian civilization can be singled out for which intelligible information on specific scientific and technological achievements, on ingenious social adaptations, and on well-defined artistic formulations is preserved. This material usually covers only a restricted area and period, permitting but an occasional insight into a perhaps unique situation whose relationship to the over-all picture can well be likened to an accumulation of irregular blotches and short lines meandering from nowhere to nowhere, suddenly disappearing, leaving wide empty spaces on the grid of time and locale. To deal with these topics would have demanded a selective and purely subjective classification bound to result in a presentation comparable to the interpretation of the ink blots used in tests—where only the creative associations of the viewer distribute accent and import and thus produce a picture that mirrors only the viewer's mind.

Moreover, it would have yielded a book twice the size of the present one.

Appendix: Mesopotamian Chronology of the Historical Period

BY J. A. BRINKMAN

The following tables present the chronology of the principal rulers of Mesopotamia from the twenty-fourth century B.C. to the seventh century A.D. As with most chronologies of the ancient Near East, the picture here is continually shifting as new evidence is brought to bear on old problems. The schema offered below seems the best presentation available as of November 1975.

As a general rule, the dates given are approximate; but probable maximum limits of variation may be set down. For dates before 1500 B.C., it is unlikely that they will ever be raised or lowered much more than 64 years. For dates from 1500 to 900 B.C., an eventual deviation of more than two decades need not be expected. After 900, an error of more than one or two years (in most cases) cannot be foreseen, with the exception of the Parthian Dynasty where the evidence is still very scanty.

1. DYNASTY OF AKKAD [1]

1. Sargon	2334–2279 [2]	(56)
2. Rimuš	2278–2270	(9)
3. Maništušu	2269–2255	(15)
4. Naram-Sin	2254–2218	(37)
5. Šar-kali-šarri	2217–2193	(25)
6. Igigi		
7. Nanijum		
	2192–2190	(3)
8. Imi		
9. Elulu		

10. Dudu	2189–2169	(21)
11. Šu-Turul	2168–2154	(15)

2. Third Dynasty of Ur

1. Ur-Nammû	2112–2095	(18)
2. Šulgi	2094–2047	(48)
3. Amar-Suen (Amar-Sin)	2046–2038	(9)
4. Šu-Sin	2037–2029	(9)
5. Ibbi-Sin	2028–2004	(25)[3]

3. First Dynasty of Isin

1. Išbi-Irra	2017–1985	(33)
2. Šu-ilišu	1984–1975	(10)
3. Iddin-Dagan	1974–1954	(21)
4. Išme-Dagan	1953–1935	(19)
5. Lipit-Ištar	1934–1924	(11)
6. Ur-Ninurta	1923–1896	(28)
7. Bur-Sin	1895–1874	(22)
8. Lipit-Enlil	1873–1869	(5)
9. Irra-imitti	1868–1861	(8)
10. Enlil-bani	1860–1837	(24)
11. Zambija	1836–1834	(3)
12. Iter-piša	1833–1831	(3)
13. Urdukuga	1830–1828	(3)
14. Sin-magir	1827–1817	(11)
15. Damiq-ilišu	1816–1794	(23)

4. Larsa Dynasty

1. Naplanum	2025–2005	(21)
2. Emişum	2004–1977	(28)
3. Samium	1976–1942	(35)
4. Zabaja	1941–1933	(9)
5. Gungunum	1932–1906	(27)
6. Abisare	1905–1895	(11)
7. Sumuel	1894–1866	(29)
8. Nur-Adad	1865–1850	(16)
9. Sin-iddinam	1849–1843	(7)
10. Sin-eribam	1842–1841	(2)
11. Sin-iqišam	1840–1836	(5)
12. Şilli-Adad	1835	(1)

13. Warad-Sin   1834–1823   (12)
14. Rim-Sin (I)   1822–1763   (60)

5. First Dynasty of Babylon (Hammurapi Dynasty)[4]

1. Sumuabum   1894–1881   (14)
2. Sumulael   1880–1845   (36)
3. Sabium   1844–1831   (14)
4. Apil-Sin   1830–1813   (18)
5. Sin-muballiṭ   1812–1793   (20)
6. Hammurapi   1792–1750   (43)
7. Samsuiluna   1749–1712   (38)
8. Abi-ešuh   1711–1684   (28)
9. Ammiditana   1683–1647   (37)
10. Ammiṣaduqa   1646–1626   (21)
11. Samsuditana   1625–1595   (31)

6. First Dynasty of the Sealand

1. Ilumael (Iluma-ilum?)   (60)[5]
2. Itti-ili-nibi   (56?)[6]
3. Damiq-ilišu   (26?)[7]
4. Iškibal   (15)
5. Šušši   (24)
6. Gulkišar   (55)
6a. ᵐGÍŠ-EN   (12)[8]
7. Pešgaldaramaš   (50)
8. Adarakalamma   (28)
9. Ekurduanna   (26)
10. Melamkurkurra   (7)
11. Ea-gamil   (9)

7. Kassite Dynasty[9]

1. Gandaš   (26)[10]
2. Agum I   (22)
3. Kaštiliašu I   (22)
4–5. (uncertain)
6. Urzigurumaš
7. Harba-x
8–9. (uncertain)
10. Burnaburiaš I

11–14. (uncertain)
15. Karaindaš[11]
16. Kadašman-Harbe I
17. Kurigalzu I

18. Kadašman-Enlil I	(1374)–1360	(15)[12]
19. Burnaburiaš II	1359–1333	(27)
20. Kara-hardaš	1333	
21. Nazi-Bugaš	1333	
22. Kurigalzu II	1332–1308	(25)
23. Nazi-Maruttaš	1307–1282	(26)
24. Kadašman-Turgu	1281–1264	(18)
25. Kadašman-Enlil II	1263–1255	(9)
26. Kudur-Enlil	1254–1246	(9)
27. Šagarakti-Šuriaš	1245–1233	(13)
28. Kaštiliašu (IV)	1232–1225	(8)
29. Enlil-nadin-šumi	1224	(1)
30. Kadašman-Harbe II	1223	(1?)
31. Adad-šuma-iddina	1222–1217	(6)
32. Adad-šuma-uṣur	1216–1187	(30)
33. Meli-Šipak	1186–1172	(15)
34. Merodach-Baladan I	1171–1159	(13)
35. Zababa-šuma-iddina	1158	(1)
36. Enlil-nadin-ahi[13]	1157–1155	(3)

8. SECOND DYNASTY OF ISIN[14]

1. Marduk-kabit-ahhešu	1157–1140	(18)
2. Itti-Marduk-balaṭu	1139–1132	(8)
3. Ninurta-nadin-šumi	1131–1126	(6)
4. Nebuchadnezzar I	1125–1104	(22)
5. Enlil-nadin-apli	1103–1100	(4)
6. Marduk-nadin-ahhe	1099–1082	(18)
7. Marduk-šapik-zeri	1081–1069	(13)
8. Adad-apla-iddina	1068–1047	(22)
9. Marduk-ahhe-eriba	1046	(1)
10. Marduk-zer-x	1045–1034	(12)
11. Nabu-šumu-libur	1033–1026	(8)

9. SECOND DYNASTY OF THE SEALAND

1. Simbar-Šipak	1025–1008	(18)
2. Ea-mukin-zeri	1008	(5 mos.)
3. Kaššu-nadin-ahhe	1007–1005	(3)

10. Bazi Dynasty

1. Eulmaš-šakin-šumi	1004–988	(17)
2. Ninurta-kudurri-uṣur I	987–985	(3)
3. Širikti-Šuqamuna	985	(3 mos.)

11. Elamite Dynasty

1. Mar-biti-apla-uṣur	984–979	(6)

12. Undetermined or Mixed Dynasties

1. Nabu-mukin-apli	978–943	(36)
2. Ninurta-kudurri-uṣur II	943	(8 mos.)
3. Mar-biti-ahhe-iddina	942–	
4. Šamaš-mudammiq		
5. Nabu-šuma-ukin I		
6. Nabu-apla-iddina		
7. Marduk-zakir-šumi I		
8. Marduk-balassu-iqbi	–813	
9. Baba-aha-iddina	812–	
(interregnum)		
10. Ninurta-apl?-[x][15]		
11. Marduk-bel-zeri		
12. Marduk-apla-uṣur		
13. Eriba-Marduk		
14. Nabu-šuma-iškun	(760)–748	(13)[16]
15. Nabu-naṣir	747–734	(14)
16. Nabu-nadin-zeri	733–732	(2)
17. Nabu-šuma-ukin II	732	(1 mo.)
18. Nabu-mukin-zeri	731–729	(3)
19. Tiglath-pileser[17]/Pulu	728–727	(2)
20. Shalmaneser[18]/Ululaju	726–722	(5)
21. Merodach-Baladan II	721–710	(12)
22. Sargon II	709–705	(5)
23. Sennacherib	704–703	(2)
24. Marduk-zakir-šumi II	703	(1 mo.)
25. Merodach-Baladan II	703	(9 mos.)
26. Bel-ibni	702–700	(3)
27. Aššur-nadin-šumi	699–694	(6)
28. Nergal-ušezib	693	(1)
29. Mušezib-Marduk	692–689	(4)

30. Sennacherib	688–681	(8)
31. Esarhaddon	680–669	(12)
31a. Ashurbanipal	668	(1)[19]
32. Šamaš-šum-ukin	667–648	(21)
33. Kandalanu	647–627	(21)[20]
(interregnum)	626	(1)

13. NEO-BABYLONIAN (OR "CHALDEAN") DYNASTY

1. Nabopolassar	625–605	(21)
2. Nebuchadnezzar II	604–562	(43)
3. Evil-Merodach	561–560	(2)
4. Neriglissar	559–556	(4)
5. Labaši-Marduk	556	(3 mos.)
6. Nabonidus	555–539	(17)

14. PERSIAN RULERS

1. Cyrus II	538–530	(9)[21]
2. Cambyses II	529–522	(8)
3. Bardija	522	(6 mos.)
4. Nebuchadnezzar III	522	(2 mos.)
5. Nebuchadnezzar IV	521	(3 mos.)
6. Darius I[22]	521–486	(36)
7. Xerxes I	485–465	(21)
8. Bel-šimanni	482	
9. Šamaš-eriba	482	
10. Artaxerxes I	464–424	(41)
11. Xerxes II	424	(1½ mos.)
12. Darius II	423–405	(19)
13. Artaxerxes II Memnon	404–359	(46)
14. Artaxerxes III Ochus	358–338	(21)
15. Arses	337–336	(2)
16. Darius III	335–331	(5)

15. MACEDONIAN RULERS

1. Alexander III	330–323	(8)[23]
2. Philip Arrhidaeus	323–316	(8)
3. Alexander IV	316–307	(10)[24]

16. SELEUCID DYNASTY

(year 1, Seleucid Era = 311 B.C.)

1.	Seleucus I Nicator	305–281 [25]
2.	Antiochus I Soter	281–261
3.	Antiochus II Theos	261–246
4.	Seleucus II Callinicus	246–226
5.	Seleucus III Soter	225–223
6.	Antiochus III (the Great)	222–187
7.	Seleucus IV Philopator	187–175
8.	Antiochus IV Epiphanes	175–164
9.	Antiochus V Eupator	164–162
10.	Demetrius I Soter	162–150
11.	Alexander Balas	150–145
12.	Demetrius II Nicator	145–139
13.	Antiochus VI Epiphanes	145–142
14.	Antiochus VII Sidetes	139–129
15.	Demetrius II Nicator	129–125
16.	Alexander II Zabinas	128–123
17.	Antiochus VIII Gryphus	126–96
18.	Seleucus V	125
19.	Antiochus IX Cyzicenus	115–95
20.	Seleucus VI Epiphanes Nicator	96–95
21.	Antiochus X Eusebes	95–83
22.	Demetrius III Eukairos	95–88
23.	Antiochus XI Epiphanes Philadelphus	92
24.	Philip I	92–83
25.	Antiochus XII Dionysus	87–84
26.	Antiochus XIII Asiaticus	69–64
27.	Philip II	65–64

17. PARTHIAN OR ARSACID DYNASTY

(year 1, Arsacid Era = 247 B.C.)

1.	Arsaces I	250–248 [26]
2.	Arsaces II (Tiridates I)	248–211
3.	Artabanus I	211–191
4.	Priapatius	191–176
5.	Phraates I	176–171
6.	Mithradates I	171–138

7.	Phraates II	138–128
8.	Artabanus II	128–124
9.	Mithradates II	123–88
10.	Gotarzes I	91–81
11.	Orodes I	80–76
12.	Sinatruces	76–70
13.	Phraates III	70–58
14.	Mithradates III	58–55
15.	Orodes II	57–37
16.	Phraates IV	37–2
17.	Tiridates II	30–25
18.	Phraataces	2 B.C.–4 A.D.
19.	Orodes III	4–6
20.	Vonones I	7–11
21.	Artabanus III	12–38
22.	Tiridates III	36
23.	Cinnamus	37
24.	Gotarzes II	38–51
25.	Vardanes	39–47
26.	Vonones II	51
27.	Vologases I	51–77
28.	Pacorus II	78–109
29.	Artabanus IV	79–80
30.	Osroes	109–128
31.	Parthamaspates	117
32.	Vologases II	105–147
33.	Mithradates IV	128–147
34.	Vologases III	148–192
35.	Vologases IV	191–207
36.	Vologases V	207–222
37.	Artabanus V	213–224[27]

18. Sassanian Dynasty

1.	Ardashir I	224–241
2.	Shapur I	241–272
3.	Hormizd I	272–273
4.	Bahram I	273–276
5.	Bahram II	276–293
6.	Bahram III	293
7.	Narses	293–302
8.	Hormizd II	302–309

9.	Shapur II	309–379
10.	Ardashir II	379–383
11.	Shapur III	383–388
12.	Bahram IV	388–399
13.	Yazdegerd I	399–420
14.	Bahram V	420–438
15.	Yazdegerd II	438–457
16.	Hormizd III	(457–459)
17.	Firuz	457–484
18.	Balash	484–488
19.	Kavadh I	488–496
20.	Jamasb	496–499
21.	Kavadh I	499–531
22.	Chosroes I	531–579
23.	Hormizd IV	579–590
24.	Chosroes II	590–628
25.	Bahram VI	590–591
26.	Bistam	591–596
27.	Kavadh II	627–628
28.	Ardashir III	628–630
29.	Purandokht	629–631
30.	Shahrbaraz	630
31.	Hormizd V	631–632
32.	Chosroes III	632–633
33.	Yazdegerd III	633–651

19. KINGS OF ASSYRIA

1. Ṭudija
2. Adamu
3. Janqi
4. Sahlamu
5. Harharu
6. Mandaru
7. Imṣu
8. HARṣu
9. Didanu
10. Hanu
11. Zuabu
12. Nuabu
13. Abazu
14. Belu

15. Azarah
16. Ušpija
17. Apiašal
18. Hale
19. Samanu
20. Hajanu
21. Ilu-Mer
22. Jakmesi
23. Jakmeni
24. Jazkur-ilu
25. Ila-kabkabi
26. Aminu
27. Sulili
28. Kikkija
29. Akija
30. Puzur-Aššur I
31. Šalim-ahum
32. Ilušuma
33. Erišum I
34. Ikunum
35. Sargon I
36. Puzur-Aššur II
37. Naram-Sin
38. Erišum II
39. Šamši-Adad I   1813–1781   (33)
40. Išme-Dagan I   (40)
40a. Mut-Aškur
40b. Rimu-x
40c. Asinum
41. Aššur-dugul   (6)
42. Aššur-apla-idi
43. Naṣir-Sin
44. Sin-namir
45. Ipqi-Ištar
46. Adad-ṣalulu
47. Adasi
48. Belu-bani   (10)
49. Libaja   (17)
50. Šarma-Adad I   (12)
51. IB.TAR-Sin   (12)
52. Bazaja   (28)
53. Lullaja   (6)

54. Šu-Ninua[28]		(14)
55. Šarma-Adad II		(3)
56. Erišum III		(13)
57. Šamši-Adad II		(6)
58. Išme-Dagan II		(16)
59. Šamši-Adad III		(16)
60. Aššur-nirari I		(26)
61. Puzur-Aššur III		(24)[29]
62. Enlil-naṣir I		(13)
63. Nur-ili		(12)
64. Aššur-šaduni		(1 mo.)
65. Aššur-rabi I		
66. Aššur-nadin-ahhe I		
67. Enlil-naṣir II	1430–1425	(6)[30]
68. Aššur-nirari II	1424–1418	(7)
69. Aššur-bel-nišešu	1417–1409	(9)
70. Aššur-rim-nišešu	1408–1401	(8)
71. Aššur-nadin-ahhe II	1400–1391	(10)
72. Eriba-Adad I	1390–1364	(27)
73. Aššur-uballiṭ I	1363–1328	(36)
74. Enlil-nirari	1327–1318	(10)
75. Arik-den-ili	1317–1306	(12)
76. Adad-nirari I	1305–1274	(32)
77. Shalmaneser I	1273–1244	(30)
78. Tukulti-Ninurta I	1243–1207	(37)
79. Aššur-nadin-apli	1206–1203	(4)[31]
80. Aššur-nirari III	1202–1197	(6)
81. Enlil-kudurri-uṣur	1196–1192	(5)
82. Ninurta-apil-Ekur	1191–1179	(13)[32]
83. Aššur-dan I	1178–1133	(46)
84. Ninurta-tukulti-Aššur		
85. Mutakkil-Nusku		
86. Aššur-reš-iši I	1132–1115	(18)
87. Tiglath-pileser I	1114–1076	(39)
88. Ašarid-apil-Ekur	1075–1074	(2)
89. Aššur-bel-kala	1073–1056	(18)
90. Eriba-Adad II	1055–1054	(2)
91. Šamši-Adad IV	1053–1050	(4)
92. Aššurnaṣirpal I	1049–1031	(19)
93. Shalmaneser II	1030–1019	(12)
94. Aššur-nirari IV	1018–1013	(6)
95. Aššur-rabi II	1012–972	(41)

96. Aššur-reš-iši II	971–967	(5)
97. Tiglath-pileser II	966–935	(32)
98. Aššur-dan II	934–912	(23)
99. Adad-nirari II	911–891	(21)
100. Tukulti-Ninurta II	890–884	(7)
101. Aššurnaṣirpal II	883–859	(25)
102. Shalmaneser III	858–824	(35)
103. Šamši-Adad V	823–811	(13)
104. Adad-nirari III	810–783	(28)
105. Shalmaneser IV	782–773	(10)
106. Aššur-dan III	772–755	(18)
107. Aššur-nirari V	754–745	(10)
108. Tiglath-pileser III	744–727	(18)
109. Shalmaneser V	726–722	(5)
110. Sargon II	721–705	(17)
111. Sennacherib	704–681	(24)
112. Esarhaddon	680–669	(12)
113. Assurbanipal	668–627	(42)
114. Aššur-etel-ilani		
115. Sin-šumu-lišir		
116. Sin-šar-iškun	–612	
117. Aššur-uballiṭ II	611–609	(3)

Notes to the Appendix

1. M. B. Rowton in *The Cambridge Ancient History* (third edition) I/1 219–20 dates this dynasty ca. 2370–2190. W. W. Hallo in the *Reallexikon der Assyriologie* III 713–14 presents evidence that only about forty years may have elapsed between the death of Šar-kali-šarri (the fifth ruler of the Dynasty of Akkad) and the rise of Ur-Nammu (first monarch of the Third Dynasty of Ur); if this position should prove correct, the Dynasty of Akkad would have to be dated ca. 2293–2113.

2. This may include a period during which he was a dependent prince before his final victory over Lugalzagesi.

3. Possibly (24).

4. The dates listed here for the First Dynasty of Babylon are those according to the so-called "middle chronology." If one would wish to adjust to the corresponding "high chronology," all dates for the first five dynasties in these tables would have to be raised by fifty-six years (e.g., Hammurapi, 1848–1806); for the "low chronology," the shift would be downward by sixty-four years (e.g., Hammurapi, 1728–1686).

5. The figures given here for the lengths of reign for this dynasty are taken from the only available king list data (that of King List A). These are difficult to place within any coherent scheme of chronology; and it is possible that some of these numbers, especially the longer reigns, should be reduced.

6. Grayson in *Alter Orient und Altes Testament* I 107 states that his collation of King List A shows that the number in question might be read as 45, 46, 55, or 56.

7. Grayson, *ibid.*, says the number is "probably 26." It is certainly at least 16.

8. This ruler is not listed in either King List A or King List B, but is inserted in the Assyrian synchronistic King List A. 117 before Pešgaldaramaš (reading of the inserted name is based on a collation of the tablet which I made in 1971). The existence of a missing king is not unexpected because in King List A the total number of years given in the dynastic summary exceeds the figure obtained by adding up the individual reigns.

A reign of twelve years is not listed in any text, but is obtained by subtracting the total of the other reigns (356 years) from the total given for the dynasty (368 years) in King List A. If the figures for some of the other reigns are adjusted (see nn. 6–7 above), corresponding adjustments must be made in the length of the reign of this king.

9. Detailed evidence for this revised Kassite chronology may be found in my *Materials and Studies for Kassite History*, I (Chicago: Oriental Institute, 1976). The chief difference between the table presented here and the material in the book just cited is that some Kassite royal names whose separate elements are hyphenated in the book (e.g., Burna-Buriaš, Kara-indaš) continue to be written unhyphenated here so as not to conflict with forms found elsewhere in this volume.

10. If one accepts the total length of reign given for this dynasty in King List A, the reign of Gandaš would begin about 1729.

11. The numbering of kings 15–20 of this dynasty is uncertain because there is some doubt as to whether Nazi-Bugaš (21) was included in the royal canon. If Nazi-Bugaš was omitted, then Karaindaš through Kara-hardaš should be numbered 16–21; and the name of king 15 would be unknown.

12. This king ruled at least 15 years.

13. The attested writings of this name are ambiguous. It may be read either as given or as Enlil-šuma-uṣur.

14. The dates for the Babylonian monarchs from the Second Dynasty of Isin down to 722 B.C. are those established in Brinkman, *A Political History of Post-Kassite Babylonia, 1158–722 B.C.* (Rome: Pontificium Institutum Biblicum, 1968), pp. 37–77, with a one-year adjustment downward for the earlier kings as required by newly discovered Assyrian evidence (*Orientalia* n.s. XLII [1973] 310 and n. 20).

15. The reading of even the first element of this king's name may be uncertain. See Grayson, *Alter Orient und Altes Testament* I 114.

16. Reigned at least 13 years.

17. Identical with Assyrian king 108, Tiglath-pileser III.

18. Identical with Assyrian king 109, Shalmaneser V.

19. This reign is not listed in any Babylonian king list; but texts are dated in Babylonia in the accession year (669) of Assurbanipal and 668 was reckoned as the accession year of Šamaš-šum-ukin.

20. Though Kandalanu died in 627, in certain parts of Babylonia documents continued to be dated under his name in 626.

21. His reign in Iran began in 559.

22. Ascended the throne in the last months of 522 (=accession year). Rulers 3–5 were all usurpers, as were also rulers 8–9.

23. His reign in Macedonia began in 336. From this time on, the custom of "accession years" is seldom observed, hence the inconsistency in the numbering of total regnal years. Alexander is assigned a reign of 7 years in some Babylonian chronological documents.

24. Probably murdered in 310, but his official reign was prolonged by a legal fiction.

25. After his conquest of Babylon in 312, his first year of reign commenced in 311; but the fiction of the royal house of Alexander was continued for the first several years. Later king lists sometimes give his reign as 311–281 (31).

26. Dates for this dynasty are often highly uncertain.

27. Vologases V and Artavasdes, a son of Artabanus V, seem to have exercised independence in Mesopotamia in 228 and perhaps even later.

28. The reading of this name is uncertain. See the recent discussion in *Orientalia* n.s. XLII (1973) 318–19.

29. Variant: (14).

30. For the revision of dates between 1430 and 935 B.C., see *Orientalia* n.s. XLII (1973) 310–11 and especially nn. 20 and 29.

31. Variant: (3). If this variant is accepted, all dates from 1430 to 1206 as listed here should be lowered by one year.

32. Variant: (3). If this variant is accepted, all dates from 1430–1191 as listed here should be lowered ten years. (The effect would be cumulative for the variants noted for rulers 79 and 82.)

The variants listed in nn. 31 and 32 would also require comparable adjustments in the chronology of the Kassite dynasty, which is calculated on the basis of Assyro-Babylonian royal synchronisms.

CORRIGENDUM: On page 342, king no. 15a, Pacorus I (died 38 B.C.), has been omitted after Orodes II.

Notes

Throughout the Notes of this book, references to books or articles which may be of interest to the outsider have been given with full title or, at least, abbreviated in a way which makes it possible to identify the publication. References to cuneiform texts, however, are given in the abbreviated form familiar to the Assyriologist. Therefore no list of abbreviations is given here.

The Notes themselves represent a compromise between the need to offer a modicum of information and the desire to exhibit the riches of the material. As is to be expected under such circumstances, they must remain incomplete and unsatisfactory in both respects.

Chapter I (pp. 31–73)

1. For information and literature on the "village" see R. J. Braidwood and B. Howe, *Prehistoric Investigations in Iraqi Kurdistan* (Chicago, 1960), pp. 1ff.; for chronology, *ibid.*, pp. 147ff.; for literature, *ibid.*, pp. xiiiff.

2. On the history and typology of domesticated plants and animals (paleoethnobotany and -zoology) see H. von Weissmann, "Ursprungsherde und ihre Abhängigkeit von der Klimageschichte," *Erdkunde*, 11 (1957), 81–94 and 175–93; also R. H. Dyson, Jr., "Archaeology and the Domestication of Animals in the Old World," *American Anthropologist*, 55 (1953), 661–73; F. Hançar, "Zur Frage der Herdentier-Domestikation," *Saeculum*, 10 (1959), 21–37; B. Brentjes, "Wildtier und Haustier im Alten Orient," *Lebendiges Altertum*, 11 (Berlin, 1962); *idem, Die Haustierwerdung im Orient* (Wittenberg, 1965); W. Herre, "The Science and History of Domestic Animals," in *Science in Archaeology*, ed. D. Brothwell, E. Higgs, and G. Clark (New York, 1963), pp. 235–49; H. Helbæk, "Paleoethnobotany," *ibid.*, pp. 177–85; F. E. Zeuner, *A History of Domesticated Animals* (London, 1963); W. Nagel, "Frühe Tierwelt in Südwestasien," *ZA*, 55 (1962), 169–222; R. Berger and R. Protsch, "The

Domestication of Plants and Animals in Europe and the Near East," *Orientalia*, n.s. 42 (1973), 214-27.

3. See A. L. Oppenheim, "Seafaring Merchants of Ur," *JAOS*, 74 (1954), 16f.; and, for an opposing view, T. Jacobsen, *Iraq*, 22 (1960), 184, n. 18. See, however, Falkenstein, *ZA*, 55 (1963), 252f., and 56 (1964), 66f.; for the knowledge of the Egyptians about the connection between the Red Sea and the Persian Gulf, see E. Otto, *Ägypten* (Stuttgart, 1953), p. 186.

For the widening of our knowledge of the early contacts of Southern Mesopotamia with the regions around the Persian Gulf, see G. Bibby, *Looking for Dilmun* (New York, 1969); M. E. L. Mallowan, "The Mechanics of Ancient Trade in Western Asia, Reflections on the Location of Magan and Meluhha," *Iran*, 3 (1965), 1-7; Elisabeth C. L. During Caspers, "Further Evidence for Cultural Relations Between India, Beluchistan, and Iran and Mesopotamia in Early Dynastic Times," *JNES*, 24 (1965), 53-56; idem, "Some Motifs as Evidence for Maritime Contact Between Sumer and the Indus Valley," *Persica*, 5 (1970-71), 107-18; idem, "New Archaeological Evidence for Maritime Trade in the Persian Gulf During the Late Protoliterate Period," *East and West*, 21 (1971), 21-44; I. J. Gelb, "Makkan and Meluḫḫa in Early Mesopotamian Sources," *RA*, 64 (1970), 1-8; M. Tosi, "Dilmun," *Antiquity*, 45, no. 177 (1971), 21-25.

4. The term "nomad" is used here in the indefinite and conventional way which is customary among the philologists dealing with the ancient Near East. See J.-R. Kupper, *Les nomades en Mésopotamie au temps des rois de Mari* (Paris, 1957); also, idem, "Le rôle des nomades dans l'histoire de la Mésopotamie ancienne," *JESHO*, 2 (1959), 114-27; also, H. Klengel, "Halbnomaden am mittleren Euphrat," *Das Altertum*, 5 (1959), 195-205, and "Zu einigen Problemen des altvorderasiatischen Nomadentums," *ArOr*, 30 (1962), 585-96; also, K.-H. Bernhardt, "Nomadentum und Ackerbaukultur in der frühstaatlichen Zeit Israels," in *Das Verhältnis von Bodenbauern und Viehzüchtern in historischer Sicht* (Berlin, 1968), pp. 31-40; H. Klengel, "Halbnomadischer Bodenbau im Königreich von Mari," *ibid.*, pp. 75-82; idem, *Zwischen Zelt und Palast* (Leipzig-Vienna, 1972); and a series of articles by M. B. Rowton, "Autonomy and Nomadism in Western Asia," *Orientalia*, n.s. 42 (1973), 247-58; "Urban Autonomy in a Nomadic Environment," *JNES*, 32 (1973), 201-15; "Enclosed Nomadism," *JESHO*, 17 (1974), 1-30.

5. For the designations of Mesopotamia and their Akkadian correspondences see J. J. Finkelstein, "Mesopotamia," *JNES*, 21 (1962), 73-92.

6. On irrigation in Mesopotamia see M. G. Ionides, *The Régime of the Rivers Euphrates and Tigris* (London, 1937); H. Neumann, "Die physischgeographischen Grundlagen der künstlichen Bewässerung des Iran und Iraq," *Wissenschaftliche Veröffentlichungen des Deutschen Instituts für Landeskunde*, Neue Folge, 12 (1953); also, R. McC. Adams, "Developmental Stages in Ancient Mesopotamia," in *Irrigation Civilizations, a Comparative Study*, J. H. Stewart, ed. (Social Science Monographs, Social Science Section I, Washington, 1955), I, 6-18.

7. For a map see T. Jacobsen, "The Waters of Ur," *Iraq*, 22 (1960), pl.

xxviii; also R. McC. Adams, "Survey of Ancient Water Courses and Settlements in Central Iraq," *Sumer*, 14 (1958), 101–3.

8. On the problem of salinization see Jacobsen and Adams, "Progressive Changes in Soil Salinity and Sedimentation Contributed to the Breakup of Past Civilizations," *Science*, 128, no. 3334 (1958), 1251–58.

9. On the tectonic problem see G. M. Lees and N. L. Falcon, "The Geographical History of the Mediterranean Plains," *Geographical Journal*, 118 (1952), 24–39, and subsequent discussion there. See also R. C. Mitchell, "Instability of the Mesopotamian Plains," *Bulletin de la Société de Géographie d'Egypte*, 31 (1958), 127–40.

10. For the latest presentation see Sigrid Westphal-Hellbusch and Heinz Westphal, *Die Maʿdan. Kultur und Geschichte der Marschenbewohner im Süd-Iraq* (Berlin, 1962), and W. Thesiger, *The Marsh Arabs* (London, 1964).

10a. As the seeds of sesame (*Sesamum indicum*) are conspicuously absent from Mesopotamian soil, we cannot establish to what oleoferous seed the Akkadian *šamaššammū* refers. For the problems involved, see F. R. Kraus, "Sesam im Alten Mesopotamien," *JAOS*, 88 (1968), 112–19.

11. This refers to the fattening of stags. See also B. Brentjes, "Cervinae (Hirsch als Haustier, Hirschformen des Nahen Orients, Hirschhaltung des Alten Orients, Hirsch und Religion)," *Mitteilungen Anthrop. Gesellschaft Wien*, 92 (1962), 34–46; and C. Gaillard, "Les tâtonnements des Egyptiens de l'ancien empire à la recherche des animaux à domestiquer," *Revue d'ethnographie et de sociologie*, 3 (1912), 329–48.

12. For the onager, see R. H. Dyson, Jr., "A Note on Queen Shub-Ad's 'Onagers'," *Iraq*, 22 (1960), 102–4; B. Brentjes, "Onager und Esel im Alten Orient," in *In memoriam Eckhard Unger: Beiträge zu Geschichte, Kultur und Religion des Alten Orients*, ed. M. Lurker (Baden-Baden, 1971), pp. 131–45.

13. The problems related to the domesticated birds have found hardly any attention although there is evidence that they may reflect contacts between Mesopotamia and the East (India) as exemplified by the much later turkey and peacock. See K. Sethe, "Die älteste Erwähnung des Haushuhns in einem ägyptischen Text," in *F. C. Andreas Festschrift* (Leipzig, 1916), pp. 109–16, referring to the region east of the Lebanon. For a Sumerian description of the rooster (wearing a red "beard") see A. Falkenstein, *ZA*, 55 (1962), 253.

13a. There was a "street of the fowlers" in Nuzi; see A. Salonen, *Vögel und Vogelfang im alten Mesopotamien* (Helsinki, 1973), p. 27. Fattened ducks are mentioned sporadically in texts from the Neo-Babylonian period.

13b. The topic of the royal hunt would well deserve a systematic investigation based on literary and iconographic evidence. See provisionally W. Dostal, "Über Jagdbrauchtum in Vorderasien," *Paedeuma*, 8 (1962), 85–97; R. L. Alexander, "The Royal Hunt," *Archaeology*, 16 (1963), 243–50; A. K. Grayson, "New Evidence on an Assyrian Hunting Practice," in *Essays on the Ancient Semitic World* (= Toronto Semitic Texts and Studies I [Toronto, 1970]), ed. J. W. Wevers and D. B. Redford, pp. 3–5; W. Helck, *Jagd und Wild im alten Vorderasien* (Hamburg-Berlin, 1968).

14. For the elephant, see A. J. B. Wace, "Obsidian and Ivory," in *Bulletin*

of the Faculty of Arts, Farouk I University (Cairo, 1943), p. 8; see also R. Koldewey, *MDOG*, 38 (1908), 19; H. G. Güterbock, *ZA*, 42 (1934), 29; R. D. Barnett, *A Catalogue of the Nimrud Ivories with Other Examples of Ancient Near Eastern Ivories in the British Museum* (London, 1957), p. 164 n. 3; B. Brentjes, "Der Elefant im Alten Orient," *Klio*, 39 (1961), 8–30; *idem*, "Der syrische Elefant als Südform des Mammuts?" *Säugetierkundliche Mitteilungen*, 17 (1969), 211–14; W. Krebs, "Zur Rolle des Elefanten in der Antike," *Forschungen und Fortschritte*, 41 (1967), 85–87; and H. Schmökel, "Bemerkungen zur Grossfauna Altmesopotamiens," *Jahrbuch für Kleinasiatische Forschung*, 2 (1965), 433–43. For the ostrich see B. Laufer, "Ostrich Egg-Shell Cups of Mesopotamia and the Ostrich in Ancient and Modern Times" (Field Museum of Natural History, Department of Anthropology, leaflet 23; Chicago, 1926).

15. See, apart from the text translated by E. Ebeling, *AfO*, 16 (1952), 68, CT 22, 56, and YOS 7, 19. See also note 79 in chap. v.

15a. For the complex history of these animals see B. Brentjes, "Das Kamel im Alten Orient," *Klio*, 38 (1960), 23–52; K. Schauenburg, "Die Kameliden im Altertum," *Bonner Jahrbücher*, 155–56 (1955–56), 59–94; *idem*, "Neue antike Kameliden," *ibid.*, 162 (1962), 98–106; R. Bulliet, "Le chameau et la roue au Moyen Orient," *Annales: Economies, sociétés, civilisations*, 24 (1969), 1092–103.

16. This is the letter EA 10, written by Burnaburiaš.

17. See A. Falkenstein, *Archaische Keilschrifttexte aus Uruk* (Berlin, 1936); E. Burrows, *Archaic Texts* (*UET*, 2); A. Deimel, *Die Inschriften von Fara* (*WVDOG*, 40, 43, and 45); S. Langdon, *The Herbert Weld Collection in the Ashmolean Museum Inscriptions from Jemdet Nasr* (*OECT*, 7); and R. D. Biggs, *Inscriptions from Tell Abū Ṣalābikh* (*OIP*, 99, Chicago and London, 1974). For a survey of the problems involved see E. Sollberger, ed., *Aspects du contact suméro-akkadien* (*Genava*, n.s. 18 [1960], 241–314), with contributions by P. Amiet, D. O. Edzard, A. Falkenstein, I. J. Gelb, S. N. Kramer, and F. R. Kraus; F. R. Kraus, *Sumerer und Akkader: Ein Problem der altmesopotamischen Geschichte* (Amsterdam, 1970); and J. S. Cooper, "Sumerian and Akkadian in Sumer and Akkad," *Orientalia*, n.s. 42 (1973), 239–46.

17a. From a recent investigation of bilingual texts by J. S. Cooper only the section dealing with such texts for Boghazkeui was published, "Bilinguals from Boghazköi, I and II," *ZA*, 61 (1971), 1–22, and *ZA*, 62 (1972), 62–81. Multilingual texts are attested only from Boghazkeui, such as E. Laroche, "Un hymne trilingue à Iškur-Adad," *RA*, 58 (1964), 69–78, and the "Message of Lú-dingir-ra to his mother," a Sumerian literary composition provided with both an Akkadian and a Hittite translation in Boghazkeui; see M. Civil, "The 'Message of Lú-dingir-ra to his Mother' and a Group of Akkado-Hittite 'Proverbs'," *JNES*, 23 (1964), 1–11, and, for the fragment found in Ugarit, J. Nougayrol, *Ugaritica*, vol. 5 (Paris, 1968), pp. 310–19 and E. Laroche, *ibid.*, p. 773 no. 2.

18. See F. R. Kraus, "Provinzen des neusumerischen Reiches von Ur," *ZA*, 51 (1955), 45–75.

19. For an interesting exception see P. Dhorme, "Les tablettes baby-loniennes de Neirab," *RA*, 25 (1928), 53–82, with 27 texts from Syria, from Nebuchadnezzar II to Darius I.

20. See J. J. Finkelstein, "Assyrian Contracts from Sultantepe," *AnSt.*, 7 (1957), 137–45, and for contemporary texts from Tell Billa, *idem, JCS*, 7 (1953), 137–41, 169–76. For the texts from Calah see D. J. Wiseman, *Iraq*, 12 (1950), 184–200; D. J. Wiseman and J. V. Kinnier Wilson, *Iraq*, 13 (1951), 102–22; Wiseman, *Iraq*, 15 (1953), 135–60; Barbara Parker, *Iraq*, 16 (1954), 29–58, *Iraq*, 19 (1957), 125–38, and *Iraq*, 23 (1960), 15–67; H. W. F. Saggs, *Iraq*, 17 (1955), 21–50, 126–54, *Iraq*, 18 (1956), 40–56, *Iraq*, 20 (1958), 182–212, *Iraq*, 21 (1959), 158–79, *Iraq*, 25 (1963), 70–80, *Iraq*, 27 (1965), 17–32, *Iraq*, 28 (1966), 177–91, *Iraq*, 36 (1974), 199–221; J. V. Kinnier Wilson, *The Nimrud Wine Lists: A Study of Men and Administration at the Assyrian Capital in the Eighth Century B.C.* (London, 1972); J. N. Postgate, *Taxation and Conscription in the Assyrian Empire* (Rome, 1974); and *idem, The Governor's Palace Archive* (London, 1973).

21. On the problem of the Amorites see the summing up of previous research by I. J. Gelb, "The Early History of the West Semitic Peoples," *JCS*, 15 (1961), 27–47; also W. von Soden, *WZKM*, 56 (1960), 186ff. Cf. also G. Buccellati, *The Amorites of the Ur III Period* (Naples, 1966); and A. Haldar, *Who Were the Amorites?* (Leiden, 1971). The literature available on the enigmatic "Habiru" has been increased recently by R. Borger, "Das Problem der ᶜapiru ('Ḫabiru')," *Zeitschrift des Deutschen Palästina-Vereins*, 74 (1958), 121–32. A very handy survey on what is known about the Kassites is offered by K. Jaritz, "Die Kulturreste der Kassiten," *Anthropos*, 55 (1960), 17–84.

22. See the bibliography of J. J. Koopman in *JEOL*, 15 (1957f.), 125–32, and a convenient resumé by B. Mazar, "The Aramean Empire and its Relations with Israel," *The Biblical Archaeologist*, 25/4 (1962), 98–120.

23. See E. Sollberger, "Graeco-Babyloniaca," *Iraq*, 24 (1962), 63–72, with a discussion of the entire evidence known, mostly lexical texts and a few incantations, also J. Oelsner, "Zur Bedeutung der 'Graeco-Babyloniaca' für die Überlieferung des Sumerischen und Akkadischen," *MIO*, 17 (1972), 356–64.

24. The seal is published in *Collection De Clercq, Catalogue méthodique et raisonné* (Paris, 1888), vol. 1, pl. 9, no. 83, and designates its bearer as a person who translated from his native language into a foreign one (eme.bal), in this case, the language of Meluhha. See also W. von Soden, "Dolmetscher," *Reallexikon für Antike und Christentum*, vol. 2 (1958), 138–40; and I. J. Gelb, "The Word for Dragoman in the Ancient Near East," *Glossa*, A Journal of Linguistics, 2 (1968), 127–28.

25. See L. le Breton, "The Early Periods at Susa, Mesopotamian Relations," *Iraq*, 19 (1957), 79–124; R. Meyer, "Die Bedeutung Elams in der Geschichte des alten Orients," *Saeculum*, 9 (1959), 198–220; R. Labat, "Elam (c. 1600–1200 B.C.)," *The Cambridge Ancient History*, II/pt. 2 (3d ed.; Cambridge, 1975), chap. 29; W. Hinz, *Das Reich Elam* (Stuttgart, 1964); P. Amiet, *Elam* (Auvers-sur-Oise, 1966).

25a. See I. J. Gelb, "New Light on Hurrians and Subarians," in *Studi Orientalistici in onore di Giorgio Levi Della Vida*, vol. 1 (Rome, 1956), pp. 378–92.

26. See R. D. Barnett, "Ancient Oriental Influences on Archaic Greece in the Aegean and the near East," in *Studies Presented to Hettie Goldman* (Locust Valley, N.Y., 1956), pp. 212–38; also T. J. Dundabin, *The Greeks and their Eastern Neighbors: Studies to the Relations Between Greece and the Countries of the Near East in the Eighth and Seventh Centuries B.C.* (London, 1957); W. Helck, *Die Beziehungen Ägyptens zu Vorderasien im 3. und 2. Jahrtausend v. Chr.* (Ägyptische Abhandlungen no. 5, Wiesbaden, 1962; 2d ed., 1971); Helene J. Kantor, *The Aegean and the Orient in the second millennium B.C.* (Bloomington, Ind., 1947); R. Labat, "Le rayonnement de la langue et de l'écriture akkadiennes au deuxième millénaire avant notre ère," *Syria*, 39 (1962), 1–27; J. Nougayrol, "L'influence babylonienne à Ugarit d'après les textes en cunéiformes classiques," *ibid.*, 28–35; R. Borger, "Ausstrahlungen des Zweistromlandes," *JEOL*, 18 (1965), 317–30.

27. See C. Virolleaud, *JA*, 238 (1950), 481–82; R. Dussaud, *Syria*, 27 (1950), 376; also Frank Moore Cross, Jr., and Th. O. Lambdin, "A Ugaritic Abecedary and the Origins of the Proto-Canaanite Alphabet," *BASOR*, 160 (1960), 21–26.

Chapter II (pp. 74–142)

1. Such a slave was to be marked on his forehead with the words, "A runaway—seize him!" (Ai. II, iv, 13).

2. See the text VAT 8722, published in *AfO*, 13 (1939–41), pl. 7, dealing with the sale of a slave girl described as *um-za- < ar >-ḫu EME Aš-šu-ra-i-[t]e*, "free (born), with Assyrian as mother tongue."

2a. See M. O. Dandamayev, "The Economic and Legal Character of the Slaves' Peculium in the Neo-Babylonian and Achaemenid Periods," in *Gesellschaftsklassen im Alten Zweistromland und in den angrenzenden Gebieten*, ed. D. O. Edzard, XVIIIᵉ Rencontre Assyriologique Internationale (Bayerische Akademie der Wissenschaften, Phil.-historische Klasse, Abhandlungen, Neue Folge Heft 75; München, 1972), pp. 35–39.

3. On "family names" see A. Ungnad, "Babylonische Familiennamen," *Analecta Orientalia*, 12 (1935), 319–26; idem, "Das Haus Egibi," *AfO*, 14 (1941–44), 57–64.

3a. Special arrangements existed for Assyrian traders in Asia Minor to take an Anatolian wife in addition to a spouse in Assur; see J. Lewy, *HUCA*, 27 (1956), 3–10.

4. On this type of adoption see P. Koschaker, "Fratriarchat, Hausgemeinschaft und Mutterrecht in Keilschriftrechten," *ZA*, 41 (1933), 1–89.

4a. For the problems here involved see M. Liverani, "Il fuoruscitismo in Siria nella tarda età del bronzo," *Rivista Storica Italiana*, 77 (1965), 315–36, and J. Renger, "Flucht als soziales Problem in der altbabylonischen Gesellschaft," in *Gesellschaftsklassen im Alten Zweistromland*, ed. Edzard, pp. 167–82.

4b. The problem of aliens in the social context of Mesopotamia has been given scant attention. Aliens are often referred to by gentilicia (*amurrû, sutû, ḫattû, gutû, marḫašû, ḫāpiru, ḫumaja* ["man from Cilicia"]), which imply either status or occupation, or by terms which express contempt by stressing that the aliens are outsiders (*aḫû, nakru*), fugitives (*munnarbu, munnabtu,* see note 4a), prisoners of war, or displaced persons (*nasīḫu, ālānû*). For a recent discussion see H. Limet, "L'étranger dans la société sumérienne," in *Gesellschaftsklassen im Alten Zweitsromland,* ed. Edzard, pp. 123–38.

5. See MRS 9 p. 159 RS 18.115:22.

5a. On cultic associations in Ugarit, called *mrzḥ* in Ugaritic, see O. Eissfeldt, "Kultvereine in Ugarit," *Ugaritica,* vol. 6 (1969), pp. 187–95, and P. D. Miller, Jr., in *The Claremont Ras Shamra Tablets,* ed. L. R. Fisher (Rome, 1971), pp. 37–48. See also E. von Schuler, "Hethitische Kultbräuche in dem Brief eines ugaritischen Gesandten," *Revue Hittite et Asianique,* fasc. 72 (1963), 43–46.

6. On the role of the merchant see W. F. Leemans, *The Old-Babylonian Merchant, His Business and His Social Position* (Leiden, 1950), which has only a limited scope in time, region, and penetration. The problem of the role and functioning of the "merchant" in ancient Near Eastern civilization is still far from being studied objectively. It always was and still is under the bane of conflicting emotional attitudes and social preconceptions grown out of the OT tradition, its transformation on a Marxist key, and the reactions these have created. Witness the striking juxtaposition of the articles by E. A. Speiser, "The Word SHR in Genesis and Early Hebrew Movements," and by W. F. Albright, "Some Remarks on the Meaning of the Word SHR in Genesis," *BASOR,* 164 (1961), 23–28 and p. 28, respectively. See also H. W. F. Saggs, *Iraq,* 22 (1960), 202ff. The following literature deals with the merchants and their activities in Mesopotamia proper and adjacent regions: J. B. Curtis and W. W. Hallo, "Money and Merchants in Ur III," *HUCA,* 30 (1959), 103–39; W. F. Leemans, *Foreign Trade in the Old Babylonian Period as Revealed by Texts from Southern Babylonia* (Leiden, 1960); *idem,* "Old Babylonian Letters and Economic History. A Review-Article with a Digression on Foreign Trade," *JESHO,* 11 (1968), 171–226; A. L. Oppenheim, "Trade in the Ancient Near East" (a paper prepared for the Fifth International Congress of Economic History, Leningrad, 10–14 August 1970); M. O. Dandamayev, "Die Rolle des *tamkārum* in Babylonien im 2. and 1. Jahrtausend v.u.Z.," in *Beiträge zur sozialen Struktur des alten Vorderasiens,* ed. H. Klengel (Berlin, 1971), pp. 69–78; I. Nakata, "Mesopotamian Merchants and their Ethos," *ANES,* 3/2 (1971), 90–101; R. McC. Adams, "Anthropological Perspectives on Ancient Trade," *Current Anthropology,* 15 (1974), 239–58. For overland and overseas trade see note 15a, chap. ii.

7. On "Staatskapitalismus" see the decisive investigation of Anna Schneider, *Die Anfänge der Kulturwirtschaft: Die sumerische Tempelstadt* (Essen a.d. Ruhr, 1920); and a recent summing up by A. Falkenstein, "La cité-temple sumérienne," *Journal of World History,* 1 (1953–54), 784–814; and F. R. Kraus, "Le Rôle des temples depuis la troisième dynastie d'Ur jusqu'à la première dynastie de Babylone," *ibid.,* pp. 522–36.

8. On this "banking house" see G. Cardascia, *Les archives des Murašu, une famille d'hommes d'affaires babyloniens à l'Epoque perse (455-403 av. J.-C.)* (Paris, 1951). Here one should refer to R. Bogaert, *Les origines antiques de la banque de dépôt: Une mise au point accompagnée d'une esquisse des opérations de banque en Mésopotamie* (Leiden, 1966), as well as to the caveat expressed in my review in *JESHO*, 12 (1969), 198-99.

9. Everything of the Nippur find that has been published is presented and discussed by H. Torczyner, *Altbabylonische Tempelrechnungen aus Nippur* (Vienna, 1913), but so many unpublished texts are kept in the Archeological Museum, Istanbul, and the University Museum, University of Pennsylvania, that a complete re-study of the archive has to be made in order to evaluate the importance of the material. This is now being done by J. A. Brinkman, who is collecting a large corpus of such texts and investigating them with regard to their historic and socioeconomic importance. A small group of similar texts coming from Ur are published by O. R. Gurney in the series *UET* as volume 7.

10. See *CAD* sub *istatirru*. Certain texts even refer to the elephant struck on Seleucid coins. Cf. CT 49 105:1f., 106:1f.

11. See *CAD* sub *ze'pu.*

12. The letter is published by J. Nougayrol, MRS 6 p. 19 RS 15, 11:23.

13. Note also the remarks directed against Tyre and Sidon in Isaiah 23:3 and passim in this chapter, while the passage in Nahum 3:16 about merchants as numerous as the stars is directed against Assyria; see as well the references to the Midianites and Ishmaelites in Gen. 37:25 and 28, etc., apart from allusions to the Canaanites which appear, however, in a different context. These refer to peddling and retail trade, for which see also the references to Išbi-Irra as peddler of nuluḫḫa spice, meant to be an invective; cf. D. O. Edzard, *Die "zweite Zwischenzeit" Babyloniens* (Wiesbaden, 1957), n. 275 on A. Falkenstein, *ZA*, 49 (1950), 61:18. I have discussed the early evidence for food peddlers in Sumerian texts in my presentation, "Trade in the Ancient Near East" (see n. 6, above), which is not easily accessible. The passages cited there speak of persons (lú.še.sa.sa) selling roasted barley (there was low esteem for these people) and of the beer maker visiting harvesters at work to offer beer for their thirst. Early dynastic lists mention other peddlers selling salt and alkali (used for soap), cf. MSL 12 19:179ff. This practice reappears in first millennium texts when salt, firewood, spices, etc. are huckstered by persons called *ša ṭābtišu, ša gaṣṣātešu*, etc. See also B. Landsberger, "Akkadisch-hebräische Wortgleichungen," in *Festschrift zum 80. Geburtstag von Walter Baumgartner* (Leiden, 1967), p. 179 n. 1.

14. Apart from Kultepe, these tablets have been found in Alishar (see I. J. Gelb, *Inscriptions from Alishar and Vicinity* [Chicago, 1935], with a discussion on pp. 7f.); in Boghazkeui (H. Otten, "Die altassyrischen Texte aus Boğazköy," *MDOG*, 89 [1957], 68-80). From outside of Asia Minor come the texts from Gasur (later Nuzi) (see T. J. Meek, *Old Akkadian, Sumerian, and Cappadocian Texts from Nuzi* [HSS, 10] Cambridge, Mass., 1935, nos. 223-27);

from Tell ed-Dēr (see IM 46309, in W. F. Leemans, *Foreign Trade in the Old Babylonian Period* [Leiden, 1960], p. 101). Note also I. J. Gelb in *JNES*, 1 (1942), 219–26, and I. J. Gelb and E. Sollberger in *JNES*, 16 (1957), 163–75.

On the organization of the Anatolian trade see P. Garelli, *Les Assyriens en Cappadoce* (Paris, 1963); M. T. Larsen, *Old Assyrian Caravan Procedures* (Istanbul, 1967); L. L. Orlin, *Assyrian Colonies in Cappadocia* (The Hague, 1970), and the important review by M. T. Larsen, *JAOS*, 94 (1974), 468–75; K. R. Veenhof, *Aspects of Old Assyrian Trade and its Terminology* (Leiden, 1972); and M. T. Larsen, *The Old Assyrian City-State and Its Colonies* (Copenhagen, 1976).

14a. The term *mandattu*, used in this acceptation only in the Akkadian texts from Ugarit (see *CAD maddattu* mng. 3), could possibly refer to the capital entrusted to the merchant (corresponding to *ḫarrānu* used in Mesopotamia proper). For the problems of trade in Ugarit and the twofold aspect of trade (overseas and overland), see the following literature: A. F. Rainey, "Business Agents at Ugarit," *IEJ*, 13 (1964), 313–21; J. M. Sasson, "A Sketch of North Syrian Economic Relations in the Middle Bronze Age," *JESHO*, 9 (1966), 161–81; idem., "Canaanite Maritime Involvement in the Second Millennium B.C.," *JAOS*, 86 (1966), 126–38; F. C. Fensham, "Shipwreck in Ugarit and Ancient Near Eastern Law Codes," *Oriens Antiquus*, 6 (1967), 221–24; R. D. Barnett, "Ezekiel and Tyre," *Eretz Israel*, 9 (1969), 6–13; R. Yaron, "Foreign Merchants of Ugarit," *Israel Law Review*, 4 (1969), 70–79; W. Helck, "Ein Indiz früher Kauffahrten syrischer Kaufleute," *UF*, 2 (1970), 35–37; M. C. Astour, "Maʾhadu, the Harbor of Ugarit," *JESHO*, 13 (1970), 113–27; idem, "The Merchant Class of Ugarit," in *Gesellschaftsklassen im Alten Zweistromland*, ed. Edzard, pp. 11–26; G. Kestemont, "Le commerce phénicien et l'expansion assyrienne du IXe-VIIIe siècle," *Oriens Antiquus*, 11 (1972), 137–44.

15. For merchants killed en route according to the Hittite texts see A. Goetze, *Kleinasien* (München, 1957), pp. 114f.; for a reflection in literature see H. A. Hoffner, Jr., "A Hittite Text in Epic Style about Merchants," *JCS*, 22 (1968), 34–45; for a case of boycott for political reasons see F. Sommer, *Die Aḫḫijavā Urkunden* (München, 1932), pp. 325–27.

15a. The continuing role of Assyria in the textile trade is illuminated by a Middle Babylonian text from Dūr-Kurigalzu to which Prof. J. A. Brinkman drew my attention. It speaks of preparing textiles for the Assyrian merchants who supposedly are coming to Babylonia to obtain this merchandise for distribution to their customers in their empire, exactly as the Old Assyrian merchants did with the garments they called "Akkadian." Evidence for overland trade in the first millennium has been assembled in my paper, A. Leo Oppenheim, "Essay on Overland Trade in the First Millennium B.C.," *JCS*, 21 (1967, published 1969), 236–54.

16. See the Calah text published by C. J. Gadd, *Iraq*, 16 (1954), 179.

16a. For the problematic earlier trade contacts between Mesopotamia and Egypt see D. O. Edzard, "Die Beziehungen Babyloniens und Ägyptens in der mittelbabylonischen Zeit und der Gold," *JESHO*, 3 (1960), 38–55, and

W. F. Leemans, "The Trade Relations of Babylonia and the Question of Relations with Egypt in the Old Babylonian Period," *ibid.*, 21–37.

17. See R. Borger, *Die Inschriften Asarhaddons, Königs von Assyrien* (abbreviated below as Esarhaddon; Graz, 1956), pp. 25f.

18. See E. Unger, *Babylon, die heilige Stadt* (Berlin and Leipzig, 1931), p. 290. From unpublished tablets of the archives of the Šamaš temple in Sippar, we learn the name of the king's merçhant, who has the good Akkadian name Sin-aḫa-iddin, while his father is called I-ni-da-a-a-ʾ (82–7–14,1357 and 1694) or In-nu-da-i-na-ʾ (82–7–14,83). All texts deal with barley loans; the two first cited describe the barley as *ša ḫarrān* PN, which seems to mean that it was imported from abroad.

18a. These persons received food allowances for their sustenance, for which see I. J. Gelb, "The Ancient Mesopotamian Ration System," *JNES*, 24 (1965), 230–43. Whether they disposed of other means (from small land holdings, etc.) is still a moot question. (For a short but pertinent discussion see I. J. Gelb and I. M. Diakonoff in *Gesellschaftsklassen im Alten Zweistromland*, ed. Edzard, pp. 41–52 and 81–92.)

19. See H. Limet, in *Actes de la XVIIᵉ Rencontre Assyriologique Internationale*, ed. A. Finet (Ham-sur-Heure, 1970), p. 68, and G. Wilhelm, "Eine neusumerische Urkunde zur Beopferung verstorbener Könige," *JCS*, 24 (1972), 83. For a striking instance of traditionalism see the passages in Neo-Babylonian texts which refer to the veneration given to the image of Sargon of Akkad, Strassmaier Cyr. 256:9, and Camb. 150:4.

20. On the topic *melammu* see A. L. Oppenheim's partly obsolete presentation, "Akkadian *pul(u)ḫ(t)u* and *melammu*," *JAOS*, 63 (1943), 31–34, and Elena Cassin, *La splendeur divine: Introduction à l'étude de la mentalité mésopotamienne* (Paris, 1968).

21. See Oppenheim, "The Golden Garments of the Gods," *JNES*, 8 (1949), 172–93.

22. See A. Falkenstein, *Journal of World History*, 1 (1953–54), 796ff.; T. Jacobsen, *JNES*, 12 (1953), 179, n. 41, and *ZA*, 52 (1957), 107, n. 32.

23. See F. Thureau-Dangin, *Syria*, 12 (1931), 254, n. 1; H. L. Ginsberg and B. Maisler, *JPOS*, 14 (1934), 250f.; H. G. Güterbock, *ZA*, 44 (1938), 82f.; W. von Brandenstein, *AfO*, 13 (1939–1941), 58, and *ZDMG*, 91 (1937), 572, n. 1.

24. For the inscription on the die YOS 9 73 see E. F. Weidner, *AfO*, 13 (1939–1941), 308.

25. On the *šar pūḫi* ritual see R. Labat, "Le sort des substituts royaux en Assyrie au temps des sargonides," *RA*, 40 (1945), 123–42; also W. von Soden, "Beiträge zum Verständnis der neuassyrischen Briefe über die Ersatzkönigsriten," in *Christian Festschrift* (Vienna, 1956), pp. 100–107; and W. G. Lambert, "A Part of the Ritual for the Substitute King," *AfO*, 18 (1957–1958), 109–12; H. M. Kümmel, *Ersatzrituale für den hethitischen König* (Studien zu den Boğazköy-Texten, Heft 3; Wiesbaden, 1967). The celestial omens sometimes predict, "There will be a king ruling one hundred days in Babylonia" (e.g., R. C. Thompson, *The Reports of the Magicians and Astrologers of Nineveh and Babylon in the British Museum*, 2 vols. [London, 1900], no. 269).

26. For a presentation of some of the numerous Assyrian royal rituals see K. F. Müller, *Das assyriche Ritual, Teil I, Texte zum assyrischen Königsritual* (Leipzig, 1937) (=MVAG 41/3); and R. Frankena, *Tākultu de sacrale maaltijd in het assyrische ritueel* (Leiden, 1954), also, *idem, BiOr,* 18 (1961), 199–207.

27. See n. 4, chap. iii, for the designation *rab ummâni.*

28. TCL 17 76.

29. See Oppenheim, "The City of Assur in 741 B.C.," *JNES,* 19 (1960), 133–47. For Idrimi see M. Liverani, "Partire sul carro, per il deserto," *Annali dell' Istituto Orientale di Napoli,* 32 (n.s. 22) (1972), 403–15.

30. Reference is made here to the intricate problem of the early references to the *hieros gamos* ritual, for which see Falkenstein in A. Falkenstein and W. von Soden, *Sumerische und akkadische Hymnen und Gebete* (Zürich and Stuttgart, 1953), pp. 90ff., no. 18; see also S. N. Kramer, "The Sumerian Sacred Marriage Texts," *Proceedings Am. Philosophical Society,* 107 (1963), 485–527; also, *idem, The Sacred Marriage Rite: Aspects of Faith, Myth, and Ritual in Ancient Sumer* (Bloomington, 1969).

31. Price regulations appear in the law codes (Codex Hammurapi, Laws of Eshnunna, and the Hittite laws), in historical inscriptions (Šamši-Adad I, Sin-kašid, and Assurbanipal [Piepkorn AS no. 5, pp. 30f.]), on a late stela (BBSt. no. 37), in the Neo-Assyrian letter in *Iraq,* 21 (1959), 162 no. 52, and in a prayer of Assurbanipal (LKA 31; see E. F. Weidner, *AfO,* 13 (1939–41), 210ff.). Note also the Hittite instructions to a market overseer in KUB 29 39 (communication of H. G. Güterbock). For prices see LBAT 1487, col. iii'; see A. Sachs, "A Classification of the Babylonian Astronomical Tablets of the Seleucid Period," *JCS,* 2 (1948), 286; also B. Meissner, *Warenpreise in Babylonien* (Berlin, 1936); W. H. Dubberstein, "Comparative Prices in Later Babylonia (625–400)," *American Journal of Semitic Languages and Literatures,* 56 (1938), 21–72. On the remission of debts through a royal edict see F. R. Kraus, *Ein Edikt des Königs Ammi-Ṣaduqa von Babylon* (Leiden, 1958); see also, *idem, BiOr,* 16 (1959), pp. 96–97.

32. See the passages in Edzard, *Zwischenzeit,* pp. 31f., which describe the MAR.TU-people and their reflection in the royal inscriptions of Sargon II and other Neo-Assyrian kings referring to uncivilized tribes. Similar remarks about nomads occur in the "Instructions for King Meri-ka-re," see J. A. Wilson in *ANET*[2] p. 416:93f.

33. The best attested instances come from the Old Testament and from the Hittite records; see H. Donner, "Art und Herkunft des Amtes der Königinmutter im Alten Testament," in *J. Friedrich Festschrift,* pp. 104–45. It does seem possible that we have to deal in the Assyrian court with a "Western" custom.

34. The mention of Queen Stratonike in an inscription of Antiochus Soter (280–262/1 B.C.) in one of the latest historical inscriptions in cuneiform and the dating of the much later astronomical tablet ACT 194c (see O. Neugebauer, *ACT,* 1, 23, sub Zkc) after Arsaces, the king, and his wife [P]iriustanā, the queen (68/67 A.D., see ACT 1, 182), are atypical and reflect non-Mesopo-

tamian practices. For another mention of Arsaces and his mother in a date, see BRM 2 53:28.

For Semiramis see H. Goossens, "La reine Sémiramis. De l'histoire à la légende" (=Mededeelingen, *Ex Oriente Lux*, no. 13; Leiden, 1947); W. Eilers, *Semiramis: Entstehung und Nachhall einer altorientalischen Sage* (Wien, 1971).

34a. For the problems involved see F. R. Kraus, "Le rôle des temples depuis la troisième dynastie d'Ur jusqu'à la première dynastie de Babylone," *Journal of World History*, 1 (1953–54), 518–45; I. J. Gelb, "On the Alleged Temple and State Economies in Ancient Mesopotamia," in *Studi in onore di Edoardo Volterra*, vol. 6 (Milan, 1971), pp. 137–54; J. N. Postgate, "The Role of the Temple in the Mesopotamian Secular Community," in *Man, Settlement and Urbanism*, ed. P. J. Ucko, R. Tringham, and G. M. Dimbledy (London, 1972), pp. 811–25.

35. See Oppenheim, "A Fiscal Practice in the Ancient Near East," *JNES*, 6 (1947), 116–20.

36. See Rivkah Harris, "Old Babylonian Temple Loans," *JCS*, 14 (1960), 126–37.

37. See YOS 6 154 and, referring to special circumstances, Oppenheim, "'Siege-Documents' from Nippur," *Iraq*, 17 (1955), 71ff.

38. BA 6/1 p. 136 v 4ff.

39. VAB 4 pp. 263ff. (Nabonidus no. 7).

40. Cf. W. L. Westerman, "Concerning Urbanism and Anti-Urbanism in Antiquity," *Bulletin of the Faculty of Arts*, 5, Farouk I University (Cairo, 1949), 81–96.

41. On the Rehabites in the Old Testament see W. R. Jeremia, *Handbuch zum Alten Testament* I/12 (Tübingen, 1958), pp. 207ff. and M. Y. Ben-gavriel, "Das nomadische Ideal in der Bibel," *Stimmen der Zeit*, 88/171 (1962–63), 253–63.

42. See Oppenheim, *JNES*, 19 (1960), 146f.

43. See TCL 16 No. 64, translated by H. G. Güterbock, *ZA*, 42 (1934), 28ff.

44. For the assembly in Mesopotamia and the meager evidence available see Oppenheim, *Orientalia*, n.s. 5 (1936), 224–28; T. Jacobsen, "Primitive Democracy in Ancient Mesopotamia," *JNES*, 2 (1943), 159–72; G. Evans, "Ancient Mesopotamian Assemblies," *JAOS*, 78 (1958), 1–11; Addendum, *ibid.*, 114–15; E. Szlechter, "Les assemblées en Mésopotamie ancienne," in *Liber Memorialis Georges de Lagarde* (Louvain and Paris, 1970), pp. 3–21.

Proceeding westward, one finds indications that the social structure of the city differed markedly from that of Mesopotamia proper. Thus, according to the prism of Sennacherib (OIP 2 31f. ii 73 and iii 8), the citizens of Ekron in Palestine fall into two or perhaps three classes: military leaders (called *šakkanakkē*), nobles (*rubê*), and common people (*nišē* or *mārē āli*). Even the first-millennium texts from Assur show similar distinctions (cf. ABL 1238, but see also ABL 815). Note in this context J. A. Wilson, "The Assembly of a Phoenician City," *JNES*, 4 (1945), 245, and H. Reviv, "On Urban Representative Institutions and Self-Government in Syria-Palestine in the Second Half of the Second Millennium B.C.," *JESHO*, 12 (1969), 283–97.

45. The terms used to refer to this body (called *ālum, puḫrum*, and *šibūtum*) vary, and their mutual relationship is still to be established. For a discussion with special reference to the Old Assyrian evidence see M. T. Larsen, *The Old Assyrian City-State and Its Colonies* (Copenhagen, 1976), pp. 160ff.

45a. See J. N. Postgate, *AfO*, 24 (1973), 77.

46. SIL.DAGAL LÚ MEŠ *Ì-si-in-na*[ki] in BE 6/1 105:10.

47. Cf. the passage in an inscription of Utuḫegal, *RA*, 9 (1912), 111ff. ii 14–15, kaskal.kalam.ma.ke₄ ú.gíd.da bí.in.mú "tall grass grew on the roads of the country," and parallel gú.má.[gíd].da.i₇.da.ba ú.gíd.da ba.an.mú ḫar.ra. an giš.gigir.ra ba.gar.ra.ba ú.a.nir ba.an.mú "on its banks, along which boats used to be towed, grew tall grass; on its roads, made for chariots, ... grew," A. Falkenstein, "Fluch über Akkade," *ZA*, 57 (1956), 64 lines 275–76, and see the remarks of Falkenstein, *ibid.*, p. 122. For the similar topos of temple ruins covered with weeds see the Nabonidus inscription YOS 1 45 (especially col. i 39–42) and the parallel on a stela of Tutᶜankhamen, (A. Gardiner, *The Egypt of the Pharaohs* [Oxford, 1961], p. 236f.).

48. See A. Falkenstein, *ZA*, 50 (1952), 64 and 80f.; also Edzard, *Zwischenzeit*, n. 250 and 492.

48a. For the problems connected with the status and function of such persons see I. J. Gelb, "From Freedom to Slavery," in *Gesellschaftsklassen im Alten Zweistromland*, ed. Edzard, pp. 81–92, especially p. 87. For the Old Babylonian period see the more recent discussions on persons called *muškēnu* by W. von Soden, "*muškēnum* und die Mawāli des frühen Islam," in *ZA*, 56 (1964), 133–41; H. Wohl, "Towards a definition of *muškēnum*," *ANES*, 1/1 (1968), 5–10; and B. Kienast, "Zu *muškēnum* = *maulā*," in *Gesellschaftsklassen im Alten Zweistromland*, ed. Edzard, pp. 99–103. For the Hittite empire, see H. G. Güterbock, "Bemerkungen zu den Ausdrücken *ellum, wardum* und *asīrum* in hethitischen Texten," *ibid.*, pp. 93–97.

49. See Edzard, *Zwischenzeit*, pp. 80ff.

50. Cf. I. Mendelsohn, "Samuel's Denunciation of Kingship in the Light of the Akkadian Documents from Ugarit," *BASOR*, 143 (1956), 17–22; M. C. Astour, "The Amarna Age Forerunners of Biblical Anti-Royalism," in *For Max Weinreich on His Seventieth Birthday* (The Hague, 1964), pp. 6–17.

51. Cf. W. F. Leemans, "*Kidinnu*, un Symbole de Droit divin babylonien," in *Van Oven Festschrift*, pp. 39–61.

52. ABL 878:9ff.

53. See F. Thureau-Dangin, *Rituels accadiens* (Paris, 1921), p. 144.

54. See R. Borger, *Esarh.* p. 42, i 43.

55. See the inscription of Shalmaneser III from Calah, published in Layard 76f., iii 1 and 8.

56. A brick found in Susa (MDP 28, p. 5, no. 3), which comes apparently from the base of a stela, refers to an inscription exhibited on the market place which is said to contain information as to the "just price" of commodities.

57. Streck Asb. 76 ix 49, and parallels.

58. The term *bīt maḫirim* denotes a shop or stall in the Old Babylonian period (mainly in texts from Sippar) and even earlier (A. Falkenstein, *Gerichtsurkunden*, vol. 2, 110). See now *CAD* sub *maḫiru* in *bīt maḫīri*. In spite of the claims of archaeologists, no parallel to the Arabic *sūq* "market" is attested in Mesopotamia; in Neo-Babylonian texts only *sūqu* "street" occurs; for the etymological relation between the two words see B. Landsberger, *Hebräische Wortforschung, Festschrift zum 80. Geburtstag von Walter Baumgartner* (Leiden, 1967), pp. 184f.

59. Reference is made here to the inscription *RA*, 7 (1910), pl. 5f. (see W. von Soden, *Orientalia*, n.s. 22 [1953], 257), and to the conquest of Carchemish by Šuppiluliuma I. For the citadel in the kingdom of Mari see G. Dossin, "Adaššum et kirḫum dans les textes de Mari," *RA*, 66 (1972), 111–30. For the Hittite term for citadel see A. Goetze, *BASOR*, 79 (1940), 33.

60. We also know from the Old Testament that the kings demanded a participation in the use of the temple, a claim which was vigorously and successfully opposed by the prophets.

61. For Aramaic inscriptions coming from Assur and Hatra, mentioning such Assyrian and Babylonian gods as Aššur, Bēl, Šerūa, Nabû, Nergal, Nanai, and Nansi, see W. Andrae and P. Jensen, "Aramäische Inschriften aus Assur und Hatra aus der Partherzeit," *MDOG*, 60 (1920), 1–51; also A. Caquot, *Syria*, 29 (1952), 89–118 and *passim* in *Syria*, 30, 31, and 32; and H. Ingholt, *Parthian Sculptures from Hatra* (*Memoirs of the Connecticut Academy of Arts and Sciences*, 12, 1954).

62. See Taha Baqir, "Tell Harmal, a Preliminary Report," *Sumer*, 11 (1946), 22–30 (with map).

62a. See J. Schmidt, "Strassen in altorientalischen Wohngebieten. Eine Studie zur Geschichte des Städtebaues in Mesopotamien und Syrien," *Baghdader Mitteilungen*, 3 (1964), 125–47. For plans of residential areas, see also A. Parrot, *Temple d'Ishtar* (Paris, 1956), pl. IX; and E. J. Wein and R. Opificius, *7000 Jahre Byblos* (Nürnberg, 1963), Plan D.

63. See C. A. Burney, "Urartian Fortresses and Towns in the Van Region," *AnSt*, 7 (1957), 37–53. See also M. N. van Loon, *Urartian Art, its Distinctive Traits in the Light of New Excavations* (Istanbul, 1966), p. 59.

64. See D. Stanislawski, "The Origin and Spread of the Grid-Pattern Town," *The Geographical Review*, 36 (1946), 103–20.

65. See D. D. Luckenbill, OIP 2, 152f.; and for border stelae from Egypt (Amarna period) see G. Daressy, *RT*, 15 (1893), 50–62.

66. See H. T. Bossert, *Altanatolien* (Berlin, 1942), no. 115:2–4; note for Egypt, R. Engelbach, *Annales du Service des Antiquités*, 31, 129–31 and pl. 3; and D. Krenker, *Forschungen und Fortschritte*, 12 (1936), 29–30.

67. For an excellent rendering see Eva Strommenger, *Fünf Jahrtausende Mesopotamien* (München, 1962), pl. 236 (with a different caption).

68. The absence of references to beggars in cuneiform texts is worth noting; the term *pisnuqu* is purely literary, very rare, and does not mean simply "beggar."

69. For prostitutes leaning out of windows see H. Zimmern, "Die baby-

Ionische Göttin im Fenster," *OLZ*, 31 (1928), pp. 1–3; and R. Herbig, "Aphrodite Parakyptusa," *OLZ*, 30 (1927), pp. 917–22.

70. See Oppenheim, "A New Prayer to the 'Gods of the Night'," *Analecta Biblica*, 12 (1959), 282–301, especially pp. 289ff.

Chapter III (pp. 143–170)

1. On Akkadian historiography one may quote A. T. E. Olmstead, *Assyrian Historiography* (Columbia, Mo., 1916); J. J. Finkelstein, "Mesopotamian Historiography," *Proceedings Am. Philosophical Society*, 107 (1963), 461–72; and J. Krecher and H.-P. Müller, "Vergangenheitsinteresse in Mesopotamien und Israel," *Saeculum*, 26 (1975), 13–44. Nothing comparable in scope and presentation corresponds in our field to Anneliese Kammenhuber, "Die hethitische Geschichtsschreibung," *Saeculum*, 9 (1958), 136–55. When *Einleitung in die assyrischen Königsinschriften, Handbuch der Orientalistik*, 1. Abteilung, Ergänzungsband V, 1. Abschnitt (Leiden and Köln, 1961–) (1. Teil: R. Borger, "Das zweite Jahrtausend vor Chr.," 1964; 2. Teil: W. Schramm, "934–722 v. Chr.," 1973) has been completed and provided with indexes, it may become a useful tool for the historian.

2. For these "diary" texts see A. J. Sachs, "A Classification of Babylonian Astronomical Tablets of the Seleucid Period," *JCS*, 2 (1948), 271–90, especially pp. 285f.; also Sachs, in T. G. Pinches and J. N. Strassmaier, *Late Babylonian Astronomical and Related Texts* (Providence, 1955), pp. xiiff.

3. For the Sumerian king list see T. Jacobsen, *The Sumerian King List* (Chicago, 1939); J. J. Finkelstein, "The Antediluvian Kings. A University of California Tablet," *JCS*, 17 (1963), 39–51; W. W. Hallo, "Beginning and End of the Sumerian King List in the Nippur Recension," *ibid.*, 52–57; H. J. Nissen, "Eine neue Version der Sumerischen Königsliste," *ZA*, 57 (1965), 1–5; and for the latest king lists see A. J. Sachs and D. J. Wiseman, "A Babylonian King List of the Hellenistic Period," *Iraq*, 16 (1954), 202–11, and the tablet from Warka discussed by J. van Dijk, *UVB*, 18 (1962), 53–60, and pl. 28a. See also J. J. Finkelstein, "The Genealogy of the Hammurapi Dynasty," *JCS*, 20 (1966), 95–118; A. Malamat, "King Lists of the Old Babylonian Period and Biblical Genealogies," *JAOS*, 88 (1968), 163–73; W. Röllig, "Zur Typologie und Entstehung der babylonischen und assyrischen Königslisten," in *Festschrift Wolfram Freiherr von Soden zum 19.VI.1968 gewidmet von Schülern und Mitarbeitern* (= *AOAT* 1; Neukirchen-Vluyn, 1969), pp. 265–77.

4. The official mentioned beside the king is his *ummânu*, probably his secretary-in-chief or his chief of chancelry rather than a vizier in the function in which such an official occurs in the Egyptian texts.

5. No study or even systematic presentation of the Old Babylonian and earlier date lists has yet been offered, although N. Schneider, *Die Zeitbestimmungen der Wirtschaftsurkunden von Ur III* (Rome, 1939), and A. Ungnad's article "Datenlisten" in *Reallexikon der Assyriologie* (Berlin and Leipzig, 1933), 2, 131–94, offer a handy listing for practical purposes. For Mari see n. 6 below. For Sultantepe see O. R. Gurney, "The Sultantepe Tablets; the Eponym Lists," *AnSt*, 3 (1953), 15–21.

6. A complete survey of all known types of eponym lists is given by Ungnad, *RLA*, 2, 412–57, supplemented by Margaret Falkner, "Die Eponymen der spätassyrischen Zeit," *AfO*, 17 (1954), 100–120; cf. also E. F. Weidner, *AfO*, 16 (1952), 213–15. For an Old Assyrian list see K. Balkan, *Studies in Honor of Benno Landsberger on His 75th Birthday* (= *AS* 16, 1965), p. 166; N. B. Jankowska, "A System of Rotation of Eponyms of the Commercial Associations at Kaniš," *ArOr*, 35 (1967), 524–48; and M. T. Larsen, *The Old Assyrian City-State and Its Colonies* (Copenhagen, 1976), pp. 360ff. For Mari see G. Dossin, "Les noms d'années et d'éponymes dans les 'Archives de Mari'," *Studia Mariana* (Leiden, 1950), pp. 51–61.

7. The latest historical inscription in the traditional style is that of this king (see *ANET*², p. 317) who ruled from 280 to 262/1 B.C. (note also YOS 1 52 [244 B.C.]), while inscriptions found in Uruk date as late as 152 B.C. See A. Falkenstein, *Topographie von Uruk* (Leipzig, 1941), pp. 9, 34. The inscription ascribed to Cyrus (538–530 B.C.) is quite atypical in content, tenor, and style. See W. Eilers, "Der Keilschrifttext des Kyros-Zylinders," in *Festgabe deutscher Iranisten zur 2500 Jahrfeier Irans* (Stuttgart, 1971), pp. 156–66 with photo; C. B. F. Walker, "A Recently Identified Fragment of the Cyrus Cylinder," *Iran*, 10 (1972), 185–59; and P.-R. Berger, "Der Kyros-Zylinder mit dem Zusatzfragment BIN II Nr. 32 und akkadischen Personennamen im Danielbuch," *ZA*, 64 (1975), 192–234.

8. On the literary problem involved see provisionally S. Mowinckel, "Die vorderasiatischen Königs- und Fürsteninschriften, Eine stilistische Studie," in *Eucharisterion H. Gunkel* (Göttingen, 1923), pp. 278–322; W. Baumgartner, "Zur Form der assyrischen Königsinschriften," *OLZ*, 27 (1924), pp. 313–17. Even though most of these inscribed objects are lost, their historic information was preserved for us by those Mesopotamian scribes who were interested in history. From the second and the first millennia we have a number of tablets on which are copied individual inscriptions (at times paleographically exact) or collections of those bearing the name of a certain ruler, with added remarks about the nature of the object and even the emplacement of the original. For the early texts of that kind see F. R. Kraus, "Altbabylonische Quellensammlungen zur altmesopotamischen Geschichte," *AfO*, 20 (1963), 153–55; D. O. Edzard, "Neue Inschriften zur Geschichte von Ur III unter Šūsuen," *AfO*, 19 (1959–60), 1–32. On a first millennium tablet we even find a reference to the circumstances of the scribe's discovery, in the ruins of the palace of Narām-Sin, of an inscription of Šar-kali-šarri; see A. T. Clay, "An Ancient Antiquary," *Museum Journal*, 3 (1912), 23–25.

9. See D. J. Wiseman, *Iraq*, 14 (1957), 24–44.

10. See the text VAB 4 no. 8, pp. 271ff. in *ANET*², pp. 308–11.

11. See E. Unger, *Babylon, Die heilige Stadt* (Berlin, 1931), pp. 282–94 and pl. 52–56.

11a. See G. R. Castellino, *Two Šulgi Hymns* (Rome, 1972); W. W. Hallo, "Royal Hymns and Mesopotamian Unity," *JCS*, 17 (1963), 112–18; J. Klein, "Šulgi D, A Neo-Sumerian Royal Hymn" (Ph.D. diss., University of Pennsylvania, 1968 [Ann Arbor, Mich., 1969]); D. D. Reisman, "Two Neo-Sumerian Royal Hymns" (Ph.D. diss., University of Pennsylvania, 1969 [Ann Arbor, Mich., 1970]); W. H. Ph. Römer, *Sumerische "Königshymnen" der Isin-Zeit* (Leiden, 1965); Å. W. Sjöberg, "Hymns to Meslamtaea, Lugalgirra and Nanna-Suen in Honour of King Ibbīsuen (Ibbīsîn) of Ur," *Orientalia Suecana*, 19–20 (1972), 140–78.

12. See YOS 9, no. 35; and L. C. Watelin, *Excavations at Kish* (Paris, 1930), III, pl. xii.

13. An alleged inscription of Šagarakti-Šuriaš is cited verbatim by Nabonidus in CT 34 34 iii 44–63.

14. For the text cf. E. Sollberger, "The Tummal Inscription," *JCS*, 16 (1962), 40–47; see also M. B. Rowton, *The Cambridge Ancient History*, I, pt. 1 (3rd ed.; Cambridge, 1970), chap. 6, pp. 201f.

15. For such a proverbial saying see E. I. Gordon, "Mesilim and Mesannipadda—Are They Identical," *BASOR*, 132 (1953), 27–30; for chronicles and similar evidence see H. G. Güterbock, *ZA*, 42 (1934), 22–24. For the omen passages see J. Nougayrol, "Note sur la place des 'présages historiques' dans l'extispicine babylonienne," Ecole Pratique des Hautes Etudes, *Annuaire* 1944–45, pp. 5–41; A. Goetze, "Historical Allusions in Old Babylonian Omen Texts," *JCS*, 1 (1947), 253–65; Erica Reiner, "New Light on Some Historical Omens," in *Anatolian Studies Presented to Hans Gustav Güterbock on the Occasion of his 65th Birthday* (Istanbul, 1974), pp. 257–61; and H. Hunger, "Ein 'neues' historisches Omen," *RA*, 66 (1972), 180–81. For later kings mentioned in omen texts see E. F. Weidner, *AfO*, 14 (1941–44), 176. See also the article of J. J. Finkelstein cited above, n. 1.

16. See H. G. Güterbock, "Die historische Tradition und ihre literarische Gestaltung bei Babyloniern und Hethitern bis 1200," *ZA*, 42 (1934), 1–91, and *ZA*, 44 (1938), 45–149; for the *šar tamḫari* see *idem*, *ZA*, 42 (1934), 86ff. Note also J. Nougayrol, "Un chef-d'oeuvre inédit de la littérature babylonienne," *RA*, 45 (1951), 169–83; W. G. Lambert, "A New Fragment of The King of Battle," *AfO*, 20 (1963), 161–62. See also Å. W. Sjöberg, "Ein Selbstpreis des Königs Hammurabi von Babylon," *ZA*, 54 (1961), 51–70.

17. See O. R. Gurney, "The Cuthean Legend of Naram-Sin," *AnSt*, 5 (1955), 93–113, and *AnSt*, 6 (1956), 163f.; J. J. Finkelstein, "The So-called 'Old Babylonian Kutha Legend'," *JCS*, 11 (1957), 83–88.

18. See E. Ebeling, *Bruchstücke eines politischen Propagandagedichtes aus einer assyrischen Kanzlei*, *MAOG*, 12/3 (1938), for a translation; and for added fragments see W. G. Lambert, *AfO*, 18 (1957), 38–51.

19. See H. G. Güterbock, *ZA*, 42 (1934), 79ff.; new edition by R. Borger, *BiOr*, 28 (1971), 3–24.

20. The understanding of this text is based on B. Landsberger's translation, *ZA*, 37 (1927), 88ff.; for an English rendering see *ANET²*, pp. 312ff.

21. See C. J. Gadd, "The Kingdom of Nabu-naʾid in Arabia," in *Akten des Vierundzwanzigsten Internationalen Orientalisten-Kongresses München* (Wiesbaden, 1959), pp. 132–34; *idem*, "The Harran Inscriptions of Nabonidus," *AnSt*, 8 (1958), 35–92. See W. von Soden, "Eine babylonische Volksüberlie-

ferung von Nabonid in den Daniel Erzählungen," *ZATW*, N.F. 12 (1935), 81–89; and for the Qumran texts see J. T. Milik, "Prière de Nabonide et autres écrits d'un Cycle de Daniel," *Revue Biblique*, 62 (1956), 407–15; and, lately, R. Meyer, Das Gebet des Nabonid," *Sächsische Akademie der Wissenschaften, Sitzungsberichte, Phil.-hist. Kl.* 107/3 (Berlin, 1962).

22. For the provinces of the empire see n. 18, chap. i.

22a. In early texts the name is most often spelled phonetically, *Ba-bil-la;* see I. J. Gelb, "The Name of Babylon," *Journal of the Institute of Asian Studies,* 1 (1955), 25–28.

23. On this important period see D. O. Edzard, *Die "zweite Zwischenzeit" Babyloniens* (Wiesbaden, 1957).

24. On the reign of Hammurapi see H. Schmökel, "Hammurabi von Babylon, die Errichtung eines Reiches," in Janus Bücher, *Berichte zur Weltgeschichte 11* (München, 1958). No serious use has yet been made of the considerable textual evidence available for the rule of this king, to study the history of the period.

25. This is the letter ABL 255; see also J. V. Kinnier Wilson, *Iraq,* 18 (1956), pl. 24, r. 12, and the Seleucid text from Sippar BM 56148, for mentions of Hammurapi in late texts. Note also *tēqīt ēnē ša* ᵐ*Hammurapi latku,* "a salve for the eyes from (the time of) Hammurapi, a proven (medication)," BAM 159 iv 22'.

25a. The edition is that of G. R. Driver and J. C. Miles, *The Babylonian Laws* vol. 2 (Oxford, 1955). More than 36 clay tablets containing parts of the text, dating from the Old to the Neo-Babylonian period, have so far been found. For a survey see R. Borger, *Babylonisch-assyriche Lesestücke* (Rome, 1963), Heft 2, pp. 2–4. New texts have since been discussed by J. Nougayrol, *RA*, 60 (1966), 90 (K.10884 = CH XXIVr94–XXVr15); J. J. Finkelstein, "A Late Old Babylonian Copy of the Laws of Hammurapi," *JCS*, 21 (1967, published 1969), 36–48; and E. Sollberger, "A New Fragment of the Code of Hammurapi," *ZA*, 56 (1964), 130–32. Note also J. J. Finkelstein, "The Hammurapi Law Tablet BE XXXI 22," *RA*, 63 (1969), 11–27.

26. See J. J. Finkelstein, "Ammiṣaduqa's Edict and the Babylonian 'Law Codes'," *JCS*, 15 (1961), 91–104.

27. No adequate and systematic up-to-date study of these interesting documents, their importance for the history of law and institutions in Mesopotamia, or investigation of their contribution to our knowledge of religion, art, and language is available. F. X. Steinmetzer's book, *Die babylonischen Kudurru als Urkundenform* (Paderborn, 1922), will have to fill the gap for quite some time.

28. The developments of the early part of this period have now been thoroughly studied by J. A. Brinkman in *The Political History of Post-Kassite Babylonia 1158–722 B.C.* (Rome, 1968). For the later part see M. Dietrich, *Die Aramäer Südbabyloniens in der Sargonidenzeit (700–648)* (= *AOAT*, 7, 1970). The material which sheds light on the Chaldeans of that period is contained for the most part in the contemporary Assyrian royal inscriptions and the royal correspondence found in Nineveh bearing on the political and military situation in and around southern Babylonia.

29. On these late usurpers see A. Poebel. "The Duration of the Reign of Smerdis, the Magian, and the Reigns of Nebuchadnezzar III and Nebuchadnezzar IV," *AJSL*, 56 (1939), 121–45; also R. A. Parker and W. H. Dubberstein, *Babylonian Chronology 626 B.C.–A.D. 75* (Providence, 1956), pp. 10ff.

30. For the chronology of the period, cf. K. Balkan, *Observations on the Chronological Problems of the Kārum Kaniš* (Ankara, 1955), pp. 41–101; and J. Lewy, in *Orientalia*, n.s. 26 (1957), 12–36.

31. For the problem of the location of Šubat-Enlil, cf. J.-R. Kupper, *Les nomades en Mésopotamie au temps des rois de Mari* (Paris, 1957), pp. 7f.

32. On that period see W. W. Hallo, "From Qarqar to Carchemish, Assyria and Israel in the Light of New Discoveries," *The Biblical Archaeologist*, 23 (1960), 34–61.

33. The same policy was already applied by the kings of the Third Dynasty of Ur, as is shown by inscriptions of Šu-Sin published by M. Civil in his article, "Šū-Sîn's Historical Inscriptions: Collection B," *JCS*, 21 (1967, published 1969), 24–38. For evidence concerning these displaced peoples, see S. Schiffer, *Keilinschriftliche Spuren der in der zweiten Hälfte des 8. Jahrhunderts von den Assyrern nach Mesopotamien deportierten Samarier* (*OLZ*, Beiheft no. 1 [1907]); E. Ebeling, *Aus dem Leben der jüdischen Exulanten in Babylonien*, (Berlin, 1914), and J. B. Segal, "An Aramaic Ostracon from Nimrud," *Iraq*, 19 (1957), 139–45.

34. On the problem of the end of the Sargonids see R. Borger, "Mesopotamien in den Jahren 629–621 v. Chr.," *WZKM*, 55 (1959), 62–76.

Chapter IV (pp. 171–227)

1. See W. Andrae, *Das Gotteshaus und die Urformen des Bauens im Alten Orient* (Berlin, 1930); H. J. Lenzen, "Mesopotamische Tempelanlagen von der Frühzeit bis zum zweiten Jahrtausend," *ZA*, 51 (1955), 1–36; E. Heinrich, *Bauwerke in der altsumerischen Bildkunst* (Wiesbaden, 1957).

2. See above, n. 20, chap. ii.

3. On Mesopotamian mythology see the latest discussion in S. N. Kramer (ed.), "Mythology of Sumer and Akkad," *Mythologies of the Ancient World* (Garden City, N.Y., 1961).

4. On the New Year's ritual see F. Thureau-Dangin, *Rituels accadiens* (Paris, 1921), pp. 127ff.; for an English translation, *ANET*[2], pp. 331ff. No adequate study of this important text has been made. See also P.-R. Berger, "Das Neujahrsfest nach den Königsinschriften des ausgehenden babylonischen Reiches," in *Actes de la XVIIe Rencontre Assyriologique Internationale*, ed. A. Finet (Ham-sur-Heure, 1970), pp. 155–59.

5. See for the texts discussed, Thureau-Dangin, *op. cit.*, pp. 11ff.; and *ANET*[2], pp. 336ff.

6. For birds see CT 40 49, CT 41 5, STT 341, and KAR 125; see W. G. Lambert, *Anatolian Studies* 20 (1970), 111–17. The relationship between certain deities of the Mesopotamian pantheon and certain animals, real or mythological, has not been investigated. Some of the animals accompany the deity, other represent it in several ways.

7. For the text CT 24 50 see A. Jeremias, *Handbuch der altorientalischen Geisteskultur* (Leipzig, 1913).

7a. See now Agnès Spycket, *Les statues de culte dans les textes mésopotamiens des origines à la 1ʳᵉ dynastie de Babylone* (= *Cahiers de la Revue Biblique* 9) (Paris, 1968).

8. C. Clerq, *Les théories relatives au culte des images chez les auteurs grecs du 2ᵉ siècle avant J.-C.* (Paris, 1915); and J. Geffcken, "Der Bilderstreit des heidnischen Altertums," *Archiv für Religionswissenschaft*, 19 (1919), 286–315; also H. Eising, "Die Weisheitslehrer und die Götterbilder," *Biblica*, 40 (1959), 393–408.

9. See the text cited, n. 10, chap. iii. Note also the obvious *fraus pia* resorted to in the text BBSt. no. 36 where we are told (col. iii 20ff.) that a clay plaque was "found" on the west bank of the Euphrates showing the correct features and paraphernalia of Šamaš just when royal grants had become available to reinstall a forgotten cult.

10. See A. M. Blackman, "The Rite of Opening the Mouth in Ancient Egypt and Babylonia," *Journal of Archaeology*, 10 (1924), 47–59; S. Smith. "The Babylonian Ritual for the Consecration and Induction of a Divine Statue," *JRAS* 1925, pp. 37–60; and the additional material cited by M. Civil, *JNES*, 26 (1967), 211; E. Otto, *Das ägyptische Mundöffnungsritual* (Wiesbaden, 1960).

10a. On standards of weight regulated by the temples and the king see D. O. Edzard, *Die "zweite Zwischenzeit" Babyloniens* (Wiesbaden, 1957), p. 81 note 398, and compare "two hundred shekels after the king's weight" 2 Sam. 14:26.

11. See the section "Les sacrifices quotidiens du temple d'Anu," in Thureau-Dangin, *Rituels accadiens*, pp. 74–86.

12. See R. de Vaux, *Ancient Israel, Its Life and Institutions* (New York, Toronto, and London, 1961), p. 469. The institution is clearly post-exilic. See also W. Herrmann, "Götterspeise und Göttertrank in Ugarit und Israel," *ZATW*, 72 (1960), 205–16; F. Nötscher, "Sakrale Mahlzeiten vor Qumran," in *Lex Tua Veritas (Festschrift für Hubert Junker)*, H. Gross and F. Meissner, eds. (Trier, 1961), pp. 145–74.

13. This is the text GCCI I 405, but see also ABL 187 rev. 4, referring to Assurbanipal as crown prince.

14. *Passim* in P. Rost, *Die Keilschrifttexte Tiglath-Pilesers III* (Leipzig, 1893).

15. On Old Babylonian prebends see Denise Cocquerillat, "Les prébendes patrimoniales dans les temples à l'époque de la 1ʳᵉ dynastie de Babylone," *Revue Internationale des Droits de l'Antiquité*, Third Series 2 (1955), pp. 39–106.

15a. For evidence attesting to a similar practice in Egypt see H. Kees, *Ägypten* ("Kulturgeschichte des alten Orients," 1. Abschnitt [München, 1933]), p. 248, on the shares and their distribution in the temple of Sobk in El-Lahun.

16. See e.g., A. Vincent, "Les rites du balancement (Tenouphah) et du prélèvement (Teroumah) dans le Sacrifice de Communion de l'Ancien Testament," in *Mélanges Dussaud*, vol. 1, pp. 267–72.

17. For evidence referring to a Western sacrificial practice in a cuneiform

text from Alalakh see D. J. Wiseman, *The Alalakh Tablets* (London, 1953), 126:15, "fire will consume the lambs and the birds," and *ibid.*, 19.

18. The references to blood collected in the *CAD* sub *damu* show clearly that blood was of no importance in Mesopotamian cult or even magic. The ritual use of blood in the Old Testament is widespread for cathartic purposes (smearing and sprinkling); its importance on the mythological level is well known and often crucial.

18a. For an indication that divination, too, was performed behind a curtain note "you draw the curtain as that of the diviner," *ZA*, 51 (1955), 170:25. Drawing the curtain in the temple while the jewelry of the divine image is removed is mentioned in the Neo-Assyrian letter ABL 1094:9.

19. See Thureau-Dangin, *Rituels accadiens*, pp. 89ff.

20. See E. Kantorowicz, "Oriens Augusti—lever du roi," *Dumbarton Oaks Papers*, No. 17 (1963), pp. 119–77, especially pp. 162ff.; and A. Hermann, "Zu den altorientalischen Grundlagen des byzantinischen Zeremoniell," *Jahrbuch für Antike und Christentum*, 7 (1964), 117ff.

21. The pertinent text was published by T. G. Pinches, "The Chariot of the Sun at Sippar in Babylonia," *Journal of the Transactions of the Victoria Institute*, 60 (1928), 132–33.

22. An excellent but far from complete survey of these names is to be found in J. J. Stamm, *Die akkadische Namengebung* (Leipzig, 1939). For a special study on the inventory of names occurring in a specific period, see now R. D. Biggs, "Semitic Names in the Fara Period," *Orientalia*, n.s. 36 (1967), 55–66; H. Limet, *L'anthroponymie sumérienne dans les documents de la 3ᵉ dynastie d'Ur* (Paris, 1968); C. Saporetti, *Onomastica medio-assira* vols. 1–2 (Rome, 1970). For an analytic study of the names of a specific type and provenience, see A. L. Oppenheim, "Die akkadischen Personennamen der Kassitenzeit," *Anthropos*, 31 (1936), 470–88.

23. K. Tallqvist's *Akkadische Götterepitheta* (Helsinki, 1938) allows us a glimpse of the variety and emptiness of the epithets used in the religious literature; the book, however, is rather a collection of pertinent material than a step toward its understanding.

24. Oannes taught man the art of writing and figuring, and all crafts, also to organize in cities, and to establish temples; see P. Schnabel, *Berossos und die babylonisch-hellenistische Literatur* (Leipzig, 1923), p. 253. For an etymology of the name Oannes see W. G. Lambert, *JCS*, 16 (1962), 74, and W. W. Hallo, *JAOS*, 83 (1963), 176, n. 79.

24a. In second millennium texts Šamaš and Adad appear side by side in texts from peripheral regions only. There is a reference to a sacrifice made to them in Arrapha by a king of Ešnunna(?) in the stela RA 7 153 ii 9f. and they are mentioned in the curse formulas of Annubanini and of another king of Lullubum. See E. Sollberger and J.-R. Kupper, *Inscriptions royales sumériennes et akkadiennes* (Paris, 1971), p. 168 IIIG1 and IIIG2. For the Old Babylonian origin of the *tamītu* texts in which they occur as oracle-givers, see W. G. Lambert, *Bibliotheca Orientalis*, 23 (1966), 164.

25. For the material, cf. the translations offered in M. Witzel, *Tammuz-*

liturgien und Verwandtes (Rome, 1935); C. Frank, *Kultlieder aus dem Ischtar-Tamūz Kreis* (Leipzig, 1939); and for a recent attempt at a synthesis, T. Jacobsen, "Toward the Image of Tammuz," *History of Religion*, 1 (1961), 189–213; also O. R. Gurney, "Tammuz Reconsidered, Some Recent Developments," *JSS*, 7 (1962), 147–60.

26. For an inventory of these symbols rather than for an investigation of their cultic and religious functions see C. Frank, *Bilder und Symbole babylonisch-assyrischer Götter* (Leipzig, 1906); also Elizabeth Douglas Van Buren, *Symbols of the Gods in Mesopotamian Art* (Rome, 1945); Ursula Seidl, "Die babylonischen Kudurru-Reliefs," *Baghdader Mitteilungen*, 4 (1968), 7–220.

26a. See also W. von Soden, "Die Schutzgenien Lamassu und Schedu in der babylonisch-assyrischen Literatur," *Baghdader Mitteilungen*, 3 (1964), 148–56.

27. See M. Cohen, "Genou, Famille, Force dans le Domaine Chamito-Sémitique," in *Mémorial Henri Basset* (Paris, 1928), p. 203.

28. On *šimtu*, cf. G. Furlani, "Sul concetto del destino nella religione babilonese e assira," *Aegyptus*, 9 (1928), 205–39.

29. For the basic material used in the preceding discussion see H. Zimmern, "Šimat, Sīma, Tyche, Manīt," *Islamica*, 2 (1926–27), 574–84; S. Langdon, "The Semitic Goddess of Fate, Fortuna, Tyche," *JRAS* (1930), pp. 21–29; W. W. Graf Baudissin, "Alttestamentliches *hajjim* in der Bedeutung von Glück," in *Festschrift Sachau*, pp. 143–61. For the Hittite and the Iranian material see J. Friedrich, *ZA*, 37 (1927), 189–90; and E. Herzfeld, *Zoroaster and His World* (Princeton, 1947), vol. 1, p. 177.

30. This is the poetic composition called after its incipit Lugal. e u₄ me.lám.bi nir.gál which exists in an earlier Sumerian and in a later bilingual version.

31. F. Cumont, "La double fortune des Sémites," in *Études Syriennes* (Paris 1917), pp. 263–76; and J. Gagé, "La théologie de la victoire impériale," *Revue Historique*, 171–72 (1933), pp. 1–43.

31a. An excellent survey of this situation is offered in *La divination en Mésopotamie ancienne et dans les régions voisines*, XIVᵉ Rencontre Assyriologique Internationale (Paris, 1966). Of all the papers collected, attention should be drawn here to A. Falkenstein, "'Wahrsagung' in der sumerischen Überlieferung," *op. cit.*, pp. 45–68; cf. also J. Nougayrol, "La divination babylonienne," in *La divination*, ed. A. Caquot and M. Leibovici (Paris, 1968), vol. 1, pp. 25–81.

32. For the Elamite translation of an astrological omen text see V. Scheil, "Déchiffrement d'un document anzanite relatif aux présages," *RA*, 14 (1917), 29–59; for Hittite omens, cf. A. Goetze, *Kleinasien²*, pp. 148–51; K. K. Riemschneider, *Babylonische Geburtsomina in hethitischer Übersetzung* (= Studien zu den Boğazköy-Texten Heft 9; Wiesbaden, 1970); also, *idem*, *Die akkadischen und hethitischen Omentexte aus Boğazköy* (in MS).

33. For the problems involved see A. Boissier, *Mantique babylonienne et Mantique hittite* (Paris, 1935), and J. Nougayrol, "Les rapports des haruspicines étrusque et assyro-babylonienne, et le foie d'argile de *Falerii veteres*," *CRAI* (1955), pp. 509–17.

33a. Cf. the last treatment of this text category by R. D. Biggs, "A propos des textes de libanomancie," *RA*, 63 (1969), 73–74.

34. See *CAD* sub *isqu*.

35. See J. Nougayrol, *OLZ*, 51 (1956), p. 41 (with reference to LKA 137 and 138).

36. For this practice see Goetze, *Kleinasien²*, p. 150.

36a. This type of divination was practiced by old women just as dream divination in Mesopotamia was originally in the hands of women. See A. L. Oppenheim, *The Interpretation of Dreams in the Ancient Near East* (Philadelphia, 1956), pp. 221f.

37. In addition to Assyrian "bird observers," so important at court that they had to take the oath of loyalty to the king together with other diviners and secretaries (ABL 33), a text (ADD 851) mentions them among Egyptian diviners brought as prisoners to Nineveh.

38. See EA 35.

39. A possible attestation in an Old Babylonian text seems to be preserved in BE 6/1 118, which records that a *ṭupšarru* gave six birds to a diviner. For Alalakh, see D. J. Wiseman, *The Alalakh Tablets*, no. 355; the Hittite LÚ. MUŠEN.DÙ seems to have been concerned with similar divinatory practices, and was probably comparable in function to the Roman *pullarius* who accompanied the army, much as the *bārû* did in Mesopotamia (ARM 2 22:23–6, AKA 551 iii 20, KAR 428 r. 3, etc.).

40. See the passages cited by Erica Reiner in "Fortune-Telling in Mesopotamia," *JNES*, 19 (1960), 28f.

40a. See J. Nougayrol, "Divination et vie quotidienne au début du deuxième millénaire av. J.-C.," in *Acta Orientalia Neerlandica, Proceedings of the Congress of the Dutch Oriental Society Held in Leiden on the Occasion of Its 50th Anniversary, 8th–9th May 1970*, ed. P. W. Pestman (Leiden, 1971), pp. 28–36.

41. Such a statement as "the right half . . . refers to me, the left half . . . to the enemy" (CT 20 44:59)—*pars familiaris* versus *pars hostilis*—is extremely rare in Mesopotamian extispicy. See also in this respect the difficult text (dealing with astrological and terrestrial omens) treated by C. Virolleaud, *Babyloniaca*, 4 (1910), 109–13, and my new edition of it in "A Babylonian Diviner's Manual," *JNES*, 33 (1974), 197–220.

42. The five Old Babylonian tablets YOS 10 57, 58, and 62 as well as CT 3 2ff. and 5 4ff. repeat the same text with slight variants. For texts from Boghazkeui see KUB 34 5 and KUB 37 198. For a selection of oil omens in an Assur text see KAR 151 r. 31ff. The texts have been edited by G. Pettinato (*Die Ölwahrsagung bei den Babyloniern*, vol. 2 [Rome, 1966]) who also utilized a new Old Babylonian tablet (IM 2967).

43. These texts are PBS 1/2 no. 99 and UCP 9 367–77.

44. See, e.g., J. Nougayrol, *RA*, 38 (1941), 87. A slightly different explanation of the communication with the deity speaks out of the text Zimmern BBR no. 98–99:7–9, which tells us that the diviner was to whisper a message into the ears of the animal before it was killed.

44a. For the use of these models see the specific suggestion offered by Oppenheim, *JNES*, 13 (1954), 143f.; for the circumstances under which the diviner was expected to function in Mari see A. Finet, "La place du devin dans la société de Mari," in *La divination en Mésopotamie ancienne*, pp. 87–93.

45. See B. Landsberger and H. Tadmor, "Fragments of Clay Liver Models from Hazor," *IEJ*, 14 (1964), 201–18. For liver models found in the West see C. J. Gadd, *Ideas of Divine Rule in the Ancient East* (London, 1948), p. 92. Models of livers and lungs have also come to us from Ugarit (with Ugaritic inscriptions)—see C. Virolleaud, *CRAI*, 1962, p. 93; C. F.-A. Schaeffer, *AfO*, 20 (1963), 215 (Fig. 34) and 210 (Fig. 29); and M. Dietrich and O. Loretz, "Beschriftete Lungen- und Lebermodelle aus Ugarit," *Ugaritica* 6 (Paris, 1969), pp. 165–79. For literature on such models, also from Alalakh and Megiddo, see Nougayrol, *La divination en Mésopotamie ancienne*, p. 8. Old Babylonian models of lungs are published in YOS 10 4 and 5, for example, and models of the intestines in *ibid.*, 65; see also A. Goetze, *JCS*, 11 (1957), 97f. For drawings of exta on tablets containing omens see J. Nougayrol, *RA* 68 (1974), 61f.

46. Hepatoscopy in Mari seems to have been practiced in a distinctly different way from that of Babylonia proper, witness the three Mari "reports" on extispicies which were published by J. Nougayrol, "Rapports paléo-babyloniens d'haruspices," in *JCS*, 21 (1967, published 1969), 219–35, especially 226–32 (texts L, M, and N), as well as those of the letters ARM 4 54 and 5 65. Let me point out two essential features brought out by this material (which certainly will increase in the future): the antagonism expressed in report M between the native diviners and their colleagues from Babylonia; and the quotation of the specific question at hand (text N lines rev. 6'–11') formulated for a yes-or-no answer, suggesting that no specific apodoses were known. I feel inclined to propose as a hypothesis that in Mari we have Mesopotamian hepatoscopy on the folklore level, while in Babylonia there had evolved scholarly divination characterized by fixed and specific deductions based on distinct features. Apparently in Mari hepatoscopy was used solely to obtain divine approval or rejection. This is corroborated by the Mari letter, *Compte-rendu de la Seconde Rencontre Assyriologique Internationale* (Paris, 1951), pp. 66ff. discussed in my paper, "Divination and Celestial Observation in the Last Assyrian Empire," *Centaurus*, 14 (1969), p. 132 n. 47. It is quite possible that among the Hittites, also, folklore divination was practiced before the scholarly approach was introduced from Babylonia. The existence of a Hittite terminology for parts of the exta and features observed (see E. Laroche, "Sur le vocabulaire de l'haruspicine," *RA*, 64 [1970], 127–39) seems to speak for this theory.

47. See YOS 1 45 and F. M. T. Böhl, "Die Tochter des Königs Nabonid," *Symbolae Koschaker*, pp. 151–78. In this context see A. Lods, "Le rôle des oracles dans la nomination des rois, des prêtres chez les Israélites, les Égyptiens et les Grecs," in *Mélanges Maspéro*, vol. 1, pp. 91–100.

48. See J. A. Knudtzon, *Assyrische Gebete an den Sonnengott für Staat und königliches Haus, etc.*, 2 vols. (Leipzig, 1893); E. G. Klauber, *Politisch-religiöse Texte aus der Sargonidenzeit* (Leipzig, 1913); J. Aro, "Remarks on the practice of extispicy in the time of Esarhaddon and Assurbanipal," in *La divination en Mésopotamie ancienne*, pp. 109–17. The *tamītu* texts, which seem to be much

older though less known since only a few have been preserved, originated in a similar situation; see W. G. Lambert, "The *'tamītu'* Texts," *ibid.*, pp. 119–23.

49. For attempted anatomical identification, we may quote here Mary I. Hussey, "Anatomical Nomenclature in an Akkadian Omen Text," *JCS*, 2 (1948), 21–32; see also A. Goetze, YOS 10 pl. 126; W. L. Moran, "Some Akkadian Names of the Stomachs of Ruminants," *JCS*, 21 (1967, published 1969), 178–82; and R. D. Biggs, "*Qutnu, maṣraḫu* and related terms in Babylonian extispicy," *RA*, 63 (1969), 159–67.

49a. J. Nougayrol, "Le foie d'orientation, BM 50494," *RA*, 62 (1968), 31–50.

50. For the "historical omens" see n. 15, chap iii.

50a. For a special type of extispicy, cf. J. Nougayrol, "Présages médicaux de l'haruspicine babylonienne," *Semitica*, 6 (1956), 5–14. Note also the curious and so far inexplicable combination of dreams and extispicy report in the two Middle Babylonian texts published respectively by H. F. Lutz (in *JAOS*, 38 [1918], 77–96) and V. Scheil (*RA*, 14 [1917], 146, 149f.). For a parallel instance where celestial omens are seen in a dream see A. L. Oppenheim, *The Interpretation of Dreams in the Ancient Near East* (Philadelphia, 1956), p. 205 (referring to YOS 1 39, and RT 19 101f.).

51. A complete modern edition of all the extant fragments of this large and rather well-preserved series was published by E. V. Leichty, *The Omen series* šumma izbu (= Texts from Cuneiform Sources 4; Locust Valley, N.Y., 1970); see also Riemschneider, *Babylonische Geburtsomina in hethitischer Übersetzung*.

52. See Erica Reiner, *JNES*, 19 (1960), 28.

53. See Thureau-Dangin, *Rituels accadiens*, p. 34:16, 36 r. 3f., 38 r. 14ff., and 145:451f. Note furthermore the texts in CT 40 35–40.

54. See B. Meissner, "Omina zur Erkenntnis der Eingeweide des Opfertieres," *AfO*, 9 (1933), 118–22. For Old Babylonian texts of this type see YOS 10 47–49.

55. See Erica Reiner, *JNES*, 19 (1960), 25ff.

56. For this series, one can only refer to the antiquated and incomplete edition offered by F. Nötscher, *Orientalia*, 31, 39–42, and 51–54. See also D. B. Weisberg, "An Old Babylonian Forerunner to *šumma ālu*," *HUCA*, 40–41 (1969–70), 83–104.

57. See Oppenheim, *AfO*, 18 (1957–58), 77, addendum.

58. See Oppenheim, *The Interpretation of Dreams in the Ancient Near East* (Philadelphia, 1956), p. 195. See also E. I. Gordon, *BiOr*, 17 (1960), 129 n. 57. For the literature occasioned by the recently published volume of Mari letters ARM 10, (Paris, 1967) see W. L. Moran, "New Evidence from Mari on the History of Prophecy," *Biblica*, 50 (1969), 15–56, and the literature cited there, pp. 15 and 56.

59. For this dreambook see above, n. 58.

60. See F. R. Kraus, *Texte zur babylonischen Physiognomatik* (Berlin, 1939); also, *idem*, "Weitere Texte zur babylonischen Physiognomatik," *Orientalia*, n.s. 16 (1947), 172–206. For a text from Boghazkeui (Akk. and Hitt.) see E. F. Weidner, *AfO*, 15 (1945–51), 102.

61. See R. Labat, *Traité akkadien de diagnostics et pronostics médicaux* (Paris, 1951). See also J. V. Kinnier Wilson, "Two Medical Texts from Nimrud," *Iraq*, 18 (1956), 130–46; and, *idem*, "The Nimrud Catalogue of Medical and Physiognomical Omina," *Iraq*, 24 (1962), 52–62.

62. See Labat, *Traité akkadien*, p. xlix, and *idem*, "Une nouvelle tablette de pronostics médicaux," *Syria*, 33 (1956), 119–30. For an Old Babylonian text of this type see TLB 2 21.

63. See PBS 2/2 104. For rare types of omens see E. F. Weidner, "Ein Losbuch in Keilschrift aus der Seleukidenzeit," *Syria*, 33 (1956), 175–83, and J. Nougayrol, "Aleuromancie babylonienne," in *Orientalia*, n.s. 32 (1963), 381–86.

64. The latest edition is in W. G. Lambert, *Babylonian Wisdom Literature* (Oxford, 1960), pp. 110–15 and pl. 31–32. For the dating of the documents it is essential to realize that the incipit appears in the catalogue of the omens of the *šumma ālu* series (see n. 56 above), with KAR 407 right column line 21 as the first line of a tablet of this series (tablet 53). See also CT 40 9 Sm. 772:16. For a critical discussion of the content see I. M. Diakonoff, "A Babylonian Political Pamphlet from about 700 B.C.," in *Studies in Honor of Benno Landsberger on His 75th Birthday* (= *AS* 16, 1965), pp. 343–50.

65. See F. R. Kraus, "Ein Sittenkanon in Omenform," *ZA*, 43 (1936), 77–113, and the similar texts CT 51 147 and STT 324.

66. For an Old Babylonian text see *ZA*, 43 (1936), 309–10; for a text from Mari see G. Dossin, *Syria*, 22 (1939), 101, and, *idem, Compte-rendu de la Seconde Rencontre Assyriologique Internationale* (Paris, 1951), pp. 46–48; for a text from Qatna see C. Virolleaud, *Antiquity*, 3 (1929), 312–17; for a text from Susa see V. Scheil, "Un fragment susien du livre Enuma Anu (ilu) Ellil," *RA*, 14 (1917), 139–42 (= MDP 18 258); for the Akkadian material from Boghazkeui see E. Laroche, *RHA*, 62 (1958), 24. See also E. F. Weidner, *AfO*, 14 (1941–44), 173–74. The Hittite translation of the very beginning of the series, preserved in KUB 34 12 (courtesy H. G. Güterbock) shows that the unusual Sumerian introduction to the text (preserved in the library of Assurbanipal with an added Akkadian translation) goes back to an Old Babylonian original. Still, it is difficult to assume that the incipit u_4.an.né:*i-nu* AN *ú* ᵈEN.LÍL of the catalogue in S. N. Kramer, *RA*, 55 (1961), 172: 49f., and also W. W. Hallo, *JAOS*, 83 (1963), 176, refers to the astrological series.

67. See below, n. 21, chap. vi.

68. The text published by E. R. Lacheman, "An Omen Text from Nuzi," *RA*, 34 (1937), 1–8, deals with earthquakes, as do the Boghazkeui tablets KUB 37 163 and 164. For a Middle Babylonian text with meteorological omens see PBS 2/2 123. Both topics are included in the astrological series of the library of Assurbanipal (see below, n. 69).

69. See the discussion by E. F. Weidner, "Die astrologische Serie *Enûma Anu Enlil*," *AfO*, 14 (1941–44), 172–95, 308–18; *AfO*, 17 (1954–56), 71–89; and *AfO*, 22 (1968–69), 65–75. For a survey of the astrological material in Hittite see E. Laroche, *RHA*, 59 (1956), 94–96.

70. For horoscopes in Babylonia see A. J. Sachs, "Babylonian Horoscopes," *JCS*, 6 (1952), 49–75. A very primitive type of divination was based on the date

a child was born. Pertinent texts are attested from Boghazkeui in Hittite (Laroche, *RHA*, 62 [1958], 23) and Akkadian (*ibid.*), and also in the "stream of the tradition" see B. Meissner, "Über Genethlialogie bei den Babyloniern," *Klio*, 19 (1925), 432–34 (ref. to Virolleaud, *Babyloniaca*, 1 [1906], 187, 192f., and TCL 6 14). For the continuation of the tradition cf. the remark of Strabo, "but some of these (the local philosophers), who are not approved by the others, profess to be genethlialogists" (Strabo 16, 1 6, cited in F. H. Cramer, *Astrology in Roman Law and Politics* [Philadelphia, 1954]), p. 5 n. 20.

70a. See R. I. Caplice, *The Akkadian* namburbi *Texts: An Introduction* (Los Angeles, 1974).

71. See O. R. Gurney, "The Cuthean Legend of Naram-Sin, "*Anatolian Studies*, 5 (1955), 103:8off.

72. Dr. Å. W. Sjöberg informs me that the well-attested Sumerian composition dubbed "The Curse over Akkad" shows the same *topos*: the contempt of Naram-Sin for divination and its dire consequences for his capital Akkad. For a somewhat related problem see W. von Soden, "Religiöse Unsicherheit, Säkularisierungstendenzen und Aberglaube zur Zeit der Sargoniden," *Analecta Biblica*, 12 (1959), 356–67.

73. See ABL 46 rev. 8ff.

74. See H. Tadmor, *Eretz Israel*, 5 (1958), 150–63.

Chapter V (*pp. 228–287*)

1. For the hieroglyphic writing systems of Byblos, cf. M. Dunand, *Biblia grammata* (Beyrouth, 1945); for that very rarely attested system from Urartu, cf. A. Goetze, *Kleinasien*[2] (München, 1957), p.194, n. 1. For all other systems to be found in the adjacent civilizations cf. I. J. Gelb, *A Study of Writing*[2] (Chicago, 1963), index. For writings on clay in unintelligible signs, cf. W. Eilers, *Analecta Orientalia*, 12 (1935). For the rare instances of artificially archaizing writings see B. Meissner, "Ein assyrisches Lehrbuch der Paläographie," *AfO*, 4 (1927), 71–73 (and B. Landsberger, *MSL* 3, p. 10). A connected text exists in a still unpublished fragment from Calah.

2. Cf. A. L. Oppenheim, "On an Operational Device in Mesopotamian Bureaucracy," *JNES*, 18 (1959), 121–28. This text comes from Nuzi and dates to the early second half of the second millennium. Much earlier, however, are quite similar devices, that is, clay tokens enclosed in a ball-shaped clay cover, that have been found at such sites as Chogha Mish (see P. P. Delougaz and Helene J. Kantor, *Fifth International Congress of Iranian Art and Archaeology*, p. 27), Susa (P. Amiet, "Il y a 5000 ans, les Élamites inventaient l'écriture," *Archaeologia*, 12 [September–October 1966], 2of., and, *idem*, *Elam* [Auvers-sur-Oise, 1966], pp. 66, 70), and Warka (*XXI. Vorläufiger Bericht . . . Uruk-Warka* [Berlin, 1965], pp. 31f.). They are usually associated with clay tablets containing figures only; see P. P. Delougaz and Helene J. Kantor, *Chogha Mish* (= OIC 23; Chicago, 1976), chap. 5. It should be noted that the Nuzi text might not be as isolated as I had thought when I published it, since my colleague M. Civil informs me that he knows of allusions in Sumerian texts to such a practice. See also the article by O. Eissfeld, "Der Beutel des

Lebendigen" (Berlin, 1960). Note that the description of the commercial activities of Tyre in Ezekiel 27 does not seem to refer to writing among the difficult technical terms used there.

3. See Oppenheim, "Mesopotamian Mythology II," *Orientalia*, n.s. 17 (1948), 44.

4. See Leo Koep, *Das himmlische Buch in Antike und Christentum* (Bonn, 1952).

4a. For Sumerian law codes see F. R. Steele, "The Code of Lipit-Ishtar," *AJA*, 52 (1948), 425–50, and J. J. Finkelstein, "The Laws of Ur-Nammu," *JCS*, 22 (1968–69), 66–82; also M. Civil, "New Sumerian Law Fragments," in *Studies in Honor of Benno Landsberger on His 75th Birthday* (= *AS* 16, 1965), pp. 1–12; and O. R. Gurney and S. N. Kramer, "Two Fragments of Sumerian Laws," ibid., pp. 13–19.

4b. Apart from the Code of Hammurapi (see n. 25a, chap. iii), see A. Goetze, *The Laws of Eshnunna* (New Haven, 1956), and R. Yaron, *The Laws of Eshnunna* (Jerusalem, 1969). For the middle Assyrian period see G. R. Driver and J. C. Miles, *The Assyrian Laws* (Oxford, 1935), pp. 4–373, 380–511; also E. F. Weidner, "Das Alter der mittelassyrischen Gesetztexte (mit 4 Tafeln)," *AfO*, 12 (1937), 46–54—both accessible in a recent French translation by G. Cardascia, *Les lois assyriennes* (Paris, 1969). For the Neo-Babylonian codification see G. R. Driver and J. C. Miles, *The Babylonian Laws* (Oxford, 1955), pp. 324–47; E. Szlechter, "Les lois néo-babyloniennes," *Revue Internationale des Droits de l'Antiquité*, 3ᵉ Série, vol. 18 (1971), 43–107, vol. 19 (1972), 43–126; and H. Petschow, "Das neubabylonische Gesetzesfragment," *Zeitschrift der Savigny-Stiftung für Rechtsgeschichte*, Rom. Abt. 76 (1959), 37–96. What is termed "laws" in Driver-Miles, *The Assyrian Laws* (pp. 1–3, 376–79) represents in fact regulations establishing the obligations and the responsibilities of the court official in the *kārum* of Kaniš; see M. T. Larsen, *The Old Assyrian City-State and Its Colonies* (Copenhagen, 1976), pp. 283ff.

4c. J. Friedrich, *Die hethitischen Gesetze* (Leiden, 1959), with additions in *AfO*, 21 (1966), 1–12. For a recent English translation see A. Goetze in *ANET*, pp. 188–96.

5. For Egyptian collections of laws, cf. H. W. Helck, *Zur Verwaltung des mittleren und neuen Reiches* (Leiden and Köln, 1958), p. 30; and W. F. Edgerton, *JNES*, 6 (1947), 154, n. 5.

6. Cf. H. Junker, *Die Götterlehre von Memphis* (Berlin, 1940); and also W. Erichsen and S. Scott, *Fragmente memphitischer Theologie in demotischer Schrift* (Wiesbaden, 1954).

7. For the books of the Wars of Yahveh, see Num. 21:14.

7a. Under the heading "funerary inscriptions" goes a group of small cone-shaped objects which contain blessings on the person who restores the tomb; see E. Szlechter, "Inscription funéraire babylonienne conservée au Musée Fitzwilliam à Cambridge," *CRAI*, 1965, pp. 429–40. From tombs in Susa come a few clay tablets inscribed with short Akkadian prayers in which apparently the deceased speaks. They have been collected by E. Ebeling in *Tod und Leben*, vol. 1 (Berlin and Leipzig, 1931), pp. 19–22.

8. Cf. C. J. Gadd, *Anatolian Studies*, 8 (1958), 46–57.

9. See I. E. S. Edwards, *Oracular Amuletic Decrees in the Late New Kingdom* (London, 1960).

10. For the execration texts, cf. G. Posener, *Princes et pays d'Asie et de Nubie* (Brussels, 1940).

11. See H. Zimmern BBR 26 iii 5.

12. For an abecedary of that provenience, cf. n. 27, chap. i.

13. See I. M. Diakonoff, "The Origin of the 'Old Persian' Writing System and the Ancient Oriental Epigraphic and Annalistic Traditions," in *W. B. Henning Memorial Volume* (London, 1968), pp. 98–124. For the Elamite system of cuneiform writing see G. G. Cameron, *Persepolis Treasury Tablets* (Chicago, 1948), chap. ix.

14. Only rarely attested practices are the use of phonetic indicators in combination with the sign PI (reading *wa-*, *wi-*, *wu-*), the conventional dissolution of initial clusters which are difficult to render in the existing writing systems, and the judicious use of doubling to differentiate between voiced and voiceless consonants.

15. Such library tags are published in Craig, *AAT*, pl. 1, KAV 130. For such tags from Boghazkeui see H. G. Güterbock, *MDOG*, 72 (1933), 38. Note also *MRS*, vol. 9 p. 2, n. 3. For colophons see the first systematic collection by H. Hunger, *Babylonische und assyrische Kolophone* (= *AOAT* 2; Neukirchen-Vluyn, 1968), with some additions by R. Borger, *WO* 5 (1970), 165–71.

16. Cf. F. R. Kraus apud E. Laroche, *ArOr*, 17/2 (1949), p. 14, n. 2; and for a more recent publication of catalogues, W. G. Lambert, *JCS*, 11 (1957), 11f., and, *idem*, "A Catalogue of Texts and Authors," *JCS*, 16 (1962), 59–77. For Sumerian texts of this type see S. N. Kramer, "New Literary Catalogue from Ur," *RA*, 55 (1961), 169–76; and I. Bernhardt and S. N. Kramer, "Götterhymnen und Kult-Gesänge der Sumerer auf zwei Keilschrift-Katalogen in der Hilprecht Sammlung," *WZJ*, 6 (1956–57), 389–95. See also W. W. Hallo, *JAOS*, 83 (1963), 167–87. For catalogues from Boghazkeui see E. Laroche, *ArOr*, 17/2 (1949), 14–23. Catalogues listing the incipits of a "series" are not mentioned here.

16a. For Aramaic dockets and epigraphs see the catalogue of F. Vattioni, *Augustinianum*, 10 (1970), 493–532. Additional epigraphs, mainly from Nimrud, are published by A. R. Millard in "Some Aramaic Epigraphs," *Iraq*, 34 (1967), 131–37, and epigraphs from Babylon by Liane Jakob-Rost and H. Freydank in "Spätbabylonische Rechtsurkunden aus Babylon mit aramäischen Beischriften," *Forschungen und Berichte*, 14 (1972), 7–35.

17. On such stamps, cf. O. Schroeder, "Gesetzte assyrische Ziegelstempel," *ZA*, 34 (1922), 157–61.

18. See MDP 23 no. 242 and 24 no. 373.

19. See D. J. Wiseman, "Assyrian Writing-Boards," *Iraq*, 17 (1955), 3–13.

20. For Aramaic written on clay with cuneiform signs (TCL 6 58) see C. H. Gordon, "The Aramaic Incantation in Cuneiform," *AfO*, 12 (1937–39), 105–17; and see B. Landsberger, *ibid.*, pp. 247–57. For a reference to an Aramaic document (*kaniku annitu Armitu*) see Saggs, *Iraq*, 17 (1955), 130, no. 13:3.

21. On Sumerian schools see n. 17, chap. vi.

22. The passage in ABL 334 runs "the king, my lord, should read the . . . tablets and I shall place in it (i.e., the library) whatever is agreeable to the king; what is not agreeable to the king, I shall remove from it; the tablets of which I have spoken are well worth to be preserved for eternity," and refers clearly to the library of Assurbanipal. The latter's concern with the content of his collection is illustrated in the famous letter CT 22 1 in which the king instructs his agents to look for specific types of tablets.

23. Cf. E. F. Weidner, "Die Bibliothek Tiglatpilesers I," *AfO*, 16 (1952), 197–215. No recent literature is available on Mesopotamian libraries; see F. Milkau, *Geschichte der Bibliotheken im Alten Orient* (Leipzig, 1935), and J. Schawe, "Der alte Vorderorient," in *Handbuch der Bibliothekswissenschaft*, ed. F. Milkau and G. Leyh, vol. 3 (1955), pp. 1–50; also M. Weitemeyer, "Archive and Library Technique in Ancient Mesopotamia," *Libri*, 6 (1956), 217–38.

24. Published mainly in the series *Materialien zum sumerischen Lexikon*, 13 vols. to date (Rome, 1937–), but also in *AfO*, 18 (1957–58), 81–86, 328–41; *JAOS* 88 (1968), 133–47.

25. The series is published in *MSL* 4 (1956), 1–44. The specific linguistic features of the emesal (lit., "genteel speech," not "women's") dialects have not been studied (see provisionally A. Falkenstein, "Das Sumerische," *Handbuch der Orientalistik* [Leiden, 1959], p. 18). For an Egyptian-Akkadian wordlist cf. S. Smith and C. J. Gadd, "A Cuneiform Vocabulary of Egyptian Words," *JEA*, 11 (1925), 230–39, and a pertinent note of W. F. Albright, *JEA*, 12 (1926), 186–90; for a Kassite-Akkadian wordlist cf. K. Balkan, *Kassitenstudien, Die Sprache der Kassiten* (*AOS* 37 [1954]), 3–11. Note also C. Frank, "Fremdsprachliche Glossen in assyrischen Listen und Vokabularen," *MAOG*, 4 (1928–29), 36–45. Translations of Sumero-Akkadian wordlists into foreign languages are not mentioned here.

26. Published with translation and commentary by B. Landsberger as *MSL* 1.

27. No translation or discussion of this important series is available for which texts are extant only from Assur (see F. Köcher, *Keilschrifttexte zur assyrisch-babylonischen Pflanzenkunde* [Berlin, 1955]), and from the library of Assurbanipal. The Neo-Babylonian commentary fragment CT 41 45 (BM 76487) to Köcher no. 28 represents the only evidence, so far, that the series was known in the south.

28. The series are called, respectively, *abnu šikinšu* and *šammu šikinšu* and are part of the stream of tradition, as their fragments from Assur, Nineveh, and Sultantepe show.

29. See W. von Soden, "Leistung und Grenze sumerischer und babylonischer Wissenschaft," *Welt als Geschichte*, vol. 2 (1936), pp. 411–64, 509–57, and, more recently, "Zweisprachigkeit in der geistigen Kultur Babyloniens," *Österreichische Akademie der Wissenschaften, Sitzungsberichte, Phil.-hist. Kl.* 235/1 (Vienna, 1960); R. Labat, "Le bilinguisme en Mésopotamie ancienne," *GLECS*, 8 (1957), 5–7. My somewhat revised interpretation of the function of these lists appears in "Man and Nature in Mesopotamian Civilization," in *Dictionary of Scientific Biography*, vol. 15 (New York, 1977).

30. See D. D. Luckenbill, *The Annals of Sennacherib* (Chicago, 1924), pp. 43f.

31. See Oppenheim, "Mesopotamian Mythology I," *Orientalia*, n.s. 16 (1947), 228f.

32. See the text BBSt no. 6.

33. See Oppenheim's remarks in "A New Prayer to the 'Gods of the Night'," *Analecta Biblica*, 12 (1959), 290f.

33a. A. Goetze and S. Levy, "Fragment of the Gilgamesh Epic from Megiddo," ʿAtiqot, 2 (1959), 121–28.

34. See J. Nougayrol, *Ugaritica*, vol. 5 (Paris, 1968), pp. 300–304 no. 167, for a fragment that is either part of or belonging to the prototype of the Flood Story as told in the Nineveh version of the epic. The text is republished in W. G. Lambert and A. R. Millard, *Atra-ḫasīs: The Babylonian Story of the Flood* (Oxford, 1969), pp. 131–33.

35. See P. Garelli, ed., *Gilgameš et sa légende*, VIIᵉ Rencontre Assyriologique Internationale Paris, 1958 (Paris, 1960), with an excellent bibliography on pp. 7–27; W. G. Lambert published three new fragments from the library of Assurbanipal, *ibid.*, pp. 53–55; for a new Assur fragment see R. Frankena, *ibid.*, pp. 113–22, and for a number of new Neo-Babylonian fragments, D. J. Wiseman, *ibid.*, pp. 123–35. For the Sumerian cycle of Gilgameš stories see S. N. Kramer, *ibid.*, pp. 59–81. The texts from Sultantepe were subsequently published by O. R. Gurney in *JCS*, 8 (1954), 87–95. See also A. R. Millard, "Gilgamesh X: a new fragment," *Iraq*, 26 (1964), 99–105; and D. J. Wiseman, "A Gilgamesh Epic Fragment from Nimrud," *Iraq*, 37 (1975), 157–63.

36. For the representations of Gilgamesh and Enkidu on seals see P. Amiet, "Le problème de la représentation de Gilgameš dans l'art," in *Gilgameš et sa légende*, ed. Garelli, pp. 169–73; and Graciane Offner, "L'épopée de Gilgameš a-t-elle été fixée dans l'art? *ibid.*, pp. 175–81.

37. The Greek philosopher Aelian (ca. A.D. 170–235) mentions Gilgamos in his collection of excerpts and anecdotes. The story he tells deviates greatly from what we know of the epic.

38. The twelfth tablet renders the Sumerian TuM NF 3 no. 14 and pertinent duplicates.

39. For this topic see G. Castellino, "Urnammu, Three Religious Texts," *ZA*, 52 (1957), 1–57; also in the Epic of Gilgamesh (tablet VII, col. iv); and eventually the late text published by W. von Soden, "Die Unterweltsvision eines assyrischen Kronprinzen," *ZA*, 43 (1936), 1–31.

40. The early version adds another crime against the mores, the exercise of the *ius primae noctis* (referred to in lines 32–33 of the Pennsylvania Fragment, col. iv). The Nineveh version, or the earlier text on which it is based, drops the motif, possibly either because it contained an accusation of misuse of royal power or because it represents an intrusion of a foreign custom not understood any more.

41. The praise of city life and the pride in such rustic activities as hunting and intimacy with wild animals seem to reflect a very specific cultural situation. One could propose that it fits the milieu of the Amorite rulers

before they moved into the capitals of Mesopotamia to assume their royal power over the city dwellers, when the desert was still their home and the city's splendor a lure on their horizon.

42. First, Gilgamesh fails to pass the test of keeping awake for six full days; next, he fails to realize that he has washed himself and his attire in the "Fountain of Youth"—instead of drinking of its miraculous water whose qualities had been pointed out to him obliquely; and last, he loses the "Plant of Life" to the snake who thus acquires power of rejuvenation.

42a. A new text (CT 46 43) has been published that offers a local theogony which is novel in many respects; see W. G. Lambert and P. Walcot, "A New Babylonian Theogony and Hesiod," *Kadmos*, 4 (1965), 64–72.

42b. Cf. T. Jacobsen, "The Battle between Marduk and Tiamat," *JAOS*, 88 (1968), 104–8.

43. See Luckenbill, *The Annals of Sennacherib* (Chicago, 1924), pp. 139ff., although the text is in need of a new edition which should yield a better translation.

44. On this topic see W. von Soden, "Gibt es ein Zeugnis dafür, dass die Babylonier an die Wiederauferstehung Marduks geglaubt haben?" *ZA*, 51 (1955), 130–66; also, *idem, ZA*, 52 (1957), 224–34.

45. Recent discovery of abundant new text material has resulted in a new text edition by W. G. Lambert and A. R. Millard, *Atra-ḫasīs: The Babylonian Story of the Flood* (Oxford, 1969), and a spate of interpretational essays, listed in R. Borger, *Handbuch der Keilschriftliteratur*, vol. 2 (Berlin, 1975), pp. 157ff.

45a. H. Freydank, "Die Tierfabel im Etana-Mythus. Ein Deutungsversuch," *MIO*, 17 (1971), 1–13.

46. For the problem of the wisdom of Adapa and the seven sages see Erica Reiner, "The Etiological Myth of the 'Seven Sages'," *Orientalia*, n.s. 30 (1961), 1–11. The suggestion offered there on pp. 7ff. concerning the figure of the wise vizier Ahiqar has been confirmed by a text found in Uruk and published by J. J. A. van Dijk, *UVB*, 18 (1962), 44–52.

47. Latest edition by L. Cagni, *L'epopea di Erra* (= Studi Semitici 34; Rome, 1969.)

48. The largest of these texts is *The Lamentation over the Destruction of Ur*, published by S. N. Kramer (Chicago, 1940); the *Lamentation over the Destruction of Sumer and Ur* is translated by the same author in J. B. Pritchard, ed., *ANET*³ Supplement, pp. 611–19.

48a. Revelation of a poem in a dream seems to have become a topos, as shown in a colophon written in 733 B.C.; see Hunger Kolophone no. 290.

49. For the reading Anzu proposed by B. Landsberger see *WZKM*, 57 (1961), 1–21.

50. See, in addition to the text EA 357 coming from Amarna, O. R. Gurney, "The Myth of Nergal and Ereshkigal," *Anatolian Studies*, 10 (1960), 105–31, a Sultantepe text.

51. To the two extant copies from respectively Assur and the library of Assurbanipal has now been added an earlier and somewhat deviant

Assyrian fragment, LKA 62 r. 10ff., published by E. Ebeling, *Orientalia*, n.s. 18 (1949), 36–37. See A. Falkenstein, "Der sumerische und der akkadische Mythos von Inannas Gang zur Unterwelt," in *Festschrift Werner Caskel* (Leiden, 1968), pp. 97–110; A. D. Kilmer, "How was Queen Ereshkigal Tricked? A New Interpretation of the Descent of Ištar," *UF*, 3 (1971), 299–309.

52. For these difficult texts see n. 25, chap. iv.

53. For this text see the edition of W. von Soden cited above, n. 39 and his reinterpretation in *Welt des Orients*, 7 (1974), 237f.

54. See, for example, the hymns (in German translation) assembled in A. Falkenstein's *Sumerische und akkadische Hymnen und Gebete* (Zürich and Leipzig, 1953), pp. 85–114.

55. For the texts see G. Meier, *Die assyrische Beschwörungssammlung Maqlû* (Graz, 1937); Erica Reiner, *Šurpu, A Collection of Sumerian and Akkadian Incantations* (Graz, 1958); also E. E. Knudsen, "A Version of the Seventh Tablet of Shurpu, from Nimrud," *Iraq*, 19 (1957), 50–55; and W. G. Lambert, "An Incantation of the Maqlû Type," *AfO*, 18 (1958), 288–99.

56. See the article cited above, n. 33.

57. On this and many of the texts quoted thereafter see W. G. Lambert, *Babylonian Wisdom Literature* (Oxford, 1960).

58. For the understanding of this literary composition, Assyriology is indebted to B. Landsberger, "Die babylonische Theodizee," *ZA*, 43 (1936), 32–76. For an English rendering see Lambert, *Babylonian Wisdom Literature*, pp. 70–89.

58a. Other examples of this device, which show that the opus was destined for readers rather than listeners, are known, such as the hymn to Babylon published by T. G. Pinches, *Texts in the Babylonian Wedge-writing* (London, 1882), pp. 15–16 no. 4, and the hymn to Marduk published by J. A. Craig, *Assyrian and Babylonian Religious Texts*, vol. 1 (Leipzig, 1895), pp. 29–31, as well as smaller, fragmentary texts. For a rare double acrostic see R. F. G. Sweet, "A Pair of Double Acrostics in Akkadian," *Orientalia*, n.s. 38 (1969), 459–60.

59. For an evaluation of the text by an historian of literature see A. Hofer-Heilsberg, "Ein Keilschrifttext, der älteste Mimus der Weltliteratur, und seine Auswirkung," *Theater der Welt*, 3–4 (1937), 1–16.

60. Cf. O. R. Gurney, "The Tale of the Poor Man of Nippur," *Anatolian Studies*, 6 (1956), 154–64; V. Julow, "The source of a Hungarian popular classic and its roots in antiquity," *Acta Classica Univ. Scient. Debreciniensis*, 6 (1970), 75–84; O. R. Gurney, "The Tale of the Poor Man of Nippur and its Folktale Parallels," *Anatolian Studies*, 22 (1972), 149–58.

61. For a short Sumerian composition which could possibly be compared in tenor and milieu to the "Poor Man of Nippur" see A. Falkenstein, *Indogermanische Forschungen*, 60 (1952), 114–20, ref. to TCL 16 80:1–19.

62. For a publication of the pertinent texts with a discussion of similar compositions from other literatures, I refer here to a forthcoming publication by M. Civil.

63. For the Sumerian proverb collection, reference has to be made to the labor of E. I. Gordon who has already presented us with a number of publications dealing with this extremely difficult material. His latest article, "A New Look at the Wisdom of Sumer and Akkad," *Bibliotheca Orientalis*, 17 (1960), 122–51, offers an excellent survey.

64. For a survey of most of the material published to date see A. L. Oppenheim, *Catalogue of the Cuneiform Tablets of the Wilberforce Eames Collection in the New York Public Library* (New Haven, 1948), pp. 215–24. For a continuation of this bibliography see Tom B. Jones and John W. Snyder, *Sumerian Economic Texts from the Third Ur Dynasty* (Minneapolis, 1961), pp. 347–52.

65. For the typical Mesopotamian letter style see O. Schroeder, "Ein mündlich zu bestellender altbabylonischer Brief," *OLZ*, 21 (1918), 5–6; also F. R. Kraus, "Briefschreibübungen im altbabylonischen Schulunterricht," *JEOL*, 16 (1959–62), 16–39. Stylistic or literary studies dedicated to Mesopotamian epistolography are rare; see E. Salonen, *Die Gruss- und Höflichkeitsformeln in babylonisch-assyrischen Briefen* (Helsinki, 1967). See also J. Friedrich, "Die Briefadresse in Ras Schamra," *AfO*, 10 (1935–36), 80–81.

66. See A. Falkenstein, "Ibbīsīn-Ishbiᵓerra," *ZA*, 49 (1949), 59–79. For a much later example of a political letter see Weidner, *AfO*, 10 (1935–36), 2–9; and B. Landsberger, *ibid.*, pp. 140–44. For a literary device making use of the form of a political letter see the text STT 40–42 published by O. R. Gurney, "A Letter of Gilgamesh," *Anatolian Studies*, 7 (1957), 127–36. For the "first" political letter see the tongue-in-cheek description in S. N. Kramer, *Enmerkar and the Lord of Aratta* (Philadelphia, 1952), lines 504–26.

67. The best introduction to this corpus of letters is contained in L. Waterman's *Royal Correspondence of the Assyrian Empire* (Ann Arbor, 1936), vol. 4, pp. 9–13. Those written in the Assyrian dialect by scholars and experts are republished by S. Parpola, *Letters from Assyrian Scholars to the Kings Esarhaddon and Assurbanipal* (= *AOAT* 5/1; Neukirchen-Vluyn, 1970). It may be noted that about 2,000 letters of this type and provenience are still unpublished in the Kuyundjik Collection of the British Museum.

68. See R. C. Thompson, *The Reports of the Magicians and Astrologers*, 2 vols. (London, 1900), badly in need of re-edition. For a unique (because private) reference to astrological matters see the Neo-Babylonian letter UET 4 168.

69. See A. Falkenstein, "Ein sumerischer 'Gottesbrief'," *ZA*, 44 (1938), 1–25; and, *idem*, "Ein sumerischer Brief an den Mondgott," *Analecta Biblica*, 12 (1959), 69–77; see also F. R. Kraus, *JCS*, 3 (1951), 78, n. 40; C. J. Gadd, *Divine Rule*, p. 27, and n. 3; cf. UET 4 171 (see von Soden, *JAOS*, 71 [1951], 267), and its duplicate KAR 373; YOS 2 141 (see Stamm, *Namengebung*, p. 54). See also ARM 1 no. 3, Dossin, *Syria*, 19 (1938), 126, and Syria, 20 (1939), 100f. For an excellent survey of all texts see now R. Borger, "Gottesbrief," *RlA*, vol. 3 (1957–71), pp. 575–76, and add F. R. Kraus, "Ein altbabylonischer Privatbrief an eine Gottheit," *RA*, 65 (1971), 27–36. For late Egyptian letters to gods see G. R. Hughes, *JNES*, 17 (1958), 3f.

70. See Oppenheim, "The City of Assur in 714 B.C.," *JNES*, 19 (1960),

133–47, and note also the letter (*šipirtu*) of Assurbanipal CT 35 44–45 (Th. Bauer, *Das Inschriftenwerk Assurbanipals* [Leipzig, 1933], vol. 2, 83), which, however, belongs to a different literary category.

71. See S. N. Kramer in *ANET*, p. 382, with literature. In a corpus of letters, edited by F. A. Ali, "Sumerian Letters: Two Collections from the Old Babylonian Schools" (Ph.D. diss., University of Pennsylvania, 1964), there appear also "business letters." For such letters see now C. J. Gadd and S. N. Kramer, *UET* 6/2 (1966), nos. 173–83 and *ibid.*, "Introduction," 3ff.

72. For a good introduction to Mesopotamian law, see M. San Nicolò, *Beiträge zur Rechtsgeschichte im Bereiche der keilschriftlichen Rechtsquellen* (Oslo, 1931); also P. Koschaker, "Keilschriftrecht," *ZDMG*, 89 (1935), 1–39, and G. Cardascia, "Splendeur et misère de l'assyriologie juridique," *Annales Universitatis Saraviensis*, 3 (1954), 159–62.

73. For such texts see I. L. Holt, *AJSL*, 22 (1910–11), 209f.

74. For an interpretation of certain features of the legal texts from Susa (MDP 18, 22–24, and 28) as reflecting formal utterances, see Oppenheim, "Der Eid in den Rechtsurkunden aus Susa," *WZKM*, 43 (1936), 242–62.

74a. See H. Petschow, "Die neubabylonische Zwiegesprächurkunde und Genesis 23," *JCS*, 19 (1965), 103–20.

75. See M. San Nicolò, "Der neubabylonische Lehrvertrag in rechtsvergleichender Betrachtung," *Bayerische Akademie der Wissenschaften, Sitzungsberichte, Phil.-hist. Kl.*, 1950, no. 3, and note the pertinent texts from Nuzi JEN 572 (weaver's craft) and HSS 19 59 (smith's craft).

76. *AASOR* 16 no. 56.

77. See Oppenheim, "'Siege Documents' from Nippur," *Iraq*, 17 (1955), 68–79.

78. The importance of this document was first pointed out by S. Feigin in *Hatequfah* 32/33 (1947), pp. 746–65; see T. Jacobsen, "An Ancient Mesopotamian Trial for Homicide," *Analecta Biblica*, 12 (1959), 130–50, on the basis of newly excavated duplicates. See also E. Szlechter, "La peine capitale en droit babylonien," in *Festschrift Emilio Betti*, vol. 4 (1962), pp. 147–48.

79. The instances cited come from *ZA*, 43 (1936), 315–16; ARM 6 43; D. J. Wiseman, *Alalakh* no. 17; E. F. Weidner, *AfO*, 17 (1954–56), 1–9. See also Kohler and Ungnad, *Assyrische Rechtsurkunden* (Leipzig, 1913), nos. 659 and 660. For a political law suit see *AASOR*, vol. 16 nos. 1–14 and E. A. Speiser, "The people of Nuzi vs. Mayor Kushshiharbe," *ibid.*, pp. 59–75. See also Sybille von Bolla, "Drei Diebstahlsfälle von Tempeleigentum in Uruk," *ArOr*, 12 (1900), 113–20; W. F. Leemans, "Some Aspects of Theft and Robbery in Old Babylonian Documents," *RSO*, 32 (1957), 661–66; E. Ebeling, "Kriminalfälle aus Uruk," *AfO*, 16 (1952), 67–69. A theft is also reported in the Neo-Assyrian letter from Calah, ND 2703, published by H. W. F. Saggs in *Iraq*, 27 (1965), 28f. no. 81.

80. See MDP 11 no. 83. See also W. Hinz, "Elams Vertrag mit Narām-Sîn von Akkade," *ZA*, 58 (1967), 66–96.

81. See D. J. Wiseman, *Alalakh*, no. 2.

82. See E. F. Weidner, "Der Staatsvertrag Aššurnirâris VI. von Assyrien mit Matiʾilu von Bît-Agusi," *AfO*, 8 (1932–33), 17–34.

83. See the most recent treatments by J. A. Fitzmyer, "The Aramaic Inscription of Sefire I and II," *JAOS*, 81 (1961), 178–222.

83a. See A. L. Oppenheim, "'The Eyes of the Lord'," *JAOS*, 88 (1968), 173–80.

84. See H. Winckler, *Sammlung von Keilschrifttexten* (Leipzig, 1894), vol. 2, no. 1.

85. See E. von Schuler, *Hethitische Dienstanweisungen für höhere Hof- und Staatsbeamte* (Graz, 1957). For other instances see E. Laroche, *RHA*, 59 (1956), 88–90.

86. See E. F. Weidner, "Hof- und Harems-Erlässe assyrischer Könige aus dem 2. Jahrtausend v. Chr.," *AfO*, 17 (1954–56), 257–93.

87. See HSS 15 no. 1.

88. See F. R. Kraus' book cited n. 41, chap. ii, *in fine*; see also J. J. Finkelstein, "Some New *misharum* Material and Its Implications," in *Studies Landsberger*, pp. 233–46; and "The Edict of Ammiṣaduqa: A New Text," *RA*, 63 (1969), 45–64, 189–90; also F. R. Kraus, "Ein Edikt des Königs Samsu-iluna von Babylon," in *Studies Landsberger*, pp. 225–31.

88a. See Maria de J. Ellis, "Ṣimdatu in the Old Babylonian Sources," *JCS*, 24 (1972), 74–82.

89. See the book cited in n. 27, chap. iii.

90. On the problem of the number of stelae with the laws of Hammurapi that have been taken to Susa see J. Nougayrol, "Les fragments en pierre du Code Hammurabien," *JA* 245 (1957), pp. 339–66, and *JA* 246 (1958), pp. 143–55.

Chapter VI (pp. 288–331)

1. For the impression left by textiles on metal objects see J. de Morgan, *La préhistoire orientale*, vol. 3 (Paris, 1927), pp. 59–61.

2. There are certain exceptions which deserve mention. First, the texts dealing with the training of horses (extant in Akkadian as well as in Hittite), for which reference should be made to Anneliese Kammenhuber, *Hippologia Hethitica* (Wiesbaden, 1961), then the Akkadian texts with instructions for making perfumes and glasslike substances, and third, a Sumerian pharmaceutical text. A Sumerian composition, known as the *Georgica*, should be characterized as instructions to the administrator of a large estate producing cereals with the help of serfs, rather than as a farmers' "handbook." The efficiency of the agricultural operation is insured by detailed numerical indications as to seed, furrows, size of tools, and so on. There is no trace of concern of the farmer for the soil by which he lives, nor for the gamut of agricultural possibilities of the region. Only what is economically the most profitable method, making maximum use of manpower, is discussed.

3. The majority of the medical texts from the library of Assurbanipal are published by R. C. Thompson in *Assyrian Medical Texts* (London, 1923); see also E. Ebeling, "Keilschrifttafeln medizinischen Inhalts," *Archiv für Geschichte der Medizin*, 13 (1921), 1–42, 129–44; also, *Archiv für Geschichte der*

Mediʒin, 14 (1922), 26–78. The texts from Assur are scattered through the older publications (KAR and LKA) and are now being presented by F. Köcher in "Die babylonisch-assyrische Medizin," 4 vols to date (Berlin, 1963–).

4. See n. 27, chap. v.

5. See R. Labat, "A propos de la chirurgie babylonienne," *JA*, 242 (1954), pp. 207–18.

6. See A. L. Oppenheim, "A Caesarian Section in the Second Millennium B.C.," *Journal of the History of Medicine and Allied Sciences*, 15 (1960), 292–94.

7. See W. von Soden, "Die Hebamme in Babylonien und Assyrien," *AfO*, 18 (1957–58), 191–221.

8. See Oppenheim, "On the Observation of the Pulse in Mesopotamia," *Orientalia*, n.s. 31 (1962), 27–33.

8a. On these two experts see Edith K. Ritter, "Magical Expert (= *Āšipu*) and Physician (= *Asû*): Notes on Two Complementary Professions in Babylonian Medicine," in *Studies in Honor of Benno Landsberger on His 75ᵗʰ Birthday* (= *AS* 16, 1965), pp. 299–321.

9. No evidence is available for dental surgery or for those ingenious mechanical appliances for keeping false teeth in place (see for the West, D. Clawson, "Phoenician Dental Art," *Berytus*, 1 [1934], 23–28). For references to the care of teeth see B. R. Townend, "An Assyrian Dental Diagnosis," *Iraq*, 5 (1938), 82–84.

9a. Some recipes were designated as *niṣirti šarrūti* 'royal secret,' e.g., Köcher BAM 50 r. 23 and the references cited AHw. 796 s.v. *niṣirtu* 4c.

10. The first publication of this important text was that of L. Legrain, "Nippur Old Drugstore," University Museum, *Bulletin*, 8 (1940), 25–27; and see also *American Journal of Pharmacy* 1947, pp. 421–28. It is superseded now by M. Civil, "Prescriptions médicales sumériennes," *RA*, 54 (1960), 57–72. The latter contributed further Sumerian material in *RA*, 55 (1961), 91–94. For medical texts in Sumerian coming from Boghazkeui see KUB 4 19 and 30, also KUB 37 10.

11. See W. G. Lambert, "The Gula Hymn of Bulluṭsa-rabi," *Orientalia*, n.s. 36 (1967), 120–21.

12. See *Harper Memorial Volume*, 1, p. 393. Diviners from Isin are mentioned also in the Old Babylonian letter, TCL 18 155.

13. See H. Zimmern, "Der Schenkenliebeszauber," *ZA*, 32 (1919), 164–84. The characteristic of genuine urbanization—the practice of buying bread in a store—is tellingly illustrated in the Old Babylonian letter VAS 16 50 (see P. Kraus, *MVAG* 36/1 [1932] 48f.), probably from Sippar, where someone complains, "I have no hired man who would grind the barley (for me) so we have been eating bought bread." This parallels the Pliny passage, *Pliny Natural History* XVIII 107, which speaks of the appearance of bakers in Rome after the inhabitants had stopped making bread for themselves.

14. See for the woman physician the Old Babylonian text TCL 10 107:27; for the eye doctor the Neo-Babylonian text VAS 6 242:8 and 17; note the designation of a veterinarian as A.ZU.GUD.ḪI.A in TCL 1 132:7 (Old Babylonian) instead of the literary expression *munaʾišu*.

15. See KAR 213 and *CAD* sub *agašgû*. For the relation between scribe and physician in Egypt see H. Junker, "Die Stele des Hofarztes ꜢIrj," *ZÄS*, 63 (1928), 53–70.

16. The Šulgi hymn in praise of himself, now published in UET 6/1 p. 81, refers to this king's knowledge of divination (máš.šu.gíd.gíd dadag. ga me.en in line 9) and the extispicy tablet KAR 384 speaks in rev. 45 of the sacred lore of Šulgi (*nişirti* ᵐŠulgi). Note eš.bar.kin, for which see A. Goetze, "The Chronology of Šulgi again," *Iraq*, 22 (1960), 151–52, and máš in Gudea Cyl. A 12:16ff., 13:17, and 20:5.

17. For the Sumerian é.dub.ba texts see the basic publication of S. N. Kramer, "Schooldays, a Sumerian Composition Relating to the Education of a Scribe," *JAOS*, 69 (1949), 199–215; and A. Falkenstein, "Die babylonische Schule," *Saeculum*, 4 (1954), 125–37. For the bilingual material see C. J. Gadd, "Fragments of Assyrian Scholastic Literature," *Bulletin of the School of Oriental and African Studies*, 20 (1957), 255–65, LKA 65, PBS 5 132; and a group of texts, called "Examination Texts" by B. Landsberger, two of which have been published by Å. W. Sjöberg, "In Praise of the Scribal Art," *JCS*, 24 (1972), 126–31, and "Der Examenstext A," *ZA*, 64 (1975), 137–76. For women scribes see B. Landsberger, *MSL*, vol. 9 (1967), p. 148.

18. See Anne Draffkorn Kilmer, "Two New Lists of Key Numbers for Mathematical Operations," *Orientalia*, n.s. 29 (1960), 273–308.

19. It is worth noting that there is little interest in Mesopotamia in the calendar and its problems. A primitive method of intercalating months, which was refined later on, is already attested for the beginning of the second millennium B.C. in Babylonia. No evidence for such practice is found in the native Assyrian calendar system, where the lunar months seem not to have been adjusted to the solar year, as is also the case in the Muslim calendar.

20. For this series see E. F. Weidner, *Handbuch der babylonischen Astronomie* (Leipzig, 1915), vol. 1, 35–41, 141f. For an ivory prism containing a part of this series (lengths of shadow for measuring time) see *ZA*, 2 (1887), 335–37 (= S. Langdon, *Babylonian Menologies and the Semitic Calendars* [London, 1935], p. 55).

21. For the importance of omen passages, which mention observations of the planet Venus and date them to the Old Babylonian king Ammişaduqa, see S. Langdon and J. K. Fotheringham, *The Venus Tablets of Ammiza-duga* (London, 1928); and B. L. Van der Waerden, "The Venus Tablets of Ammişaduqa," *JEOL*, 10 (1945–48), 414–24. For an evaluation see O. Neugebauer, *JAOS*, 61 (1941), 59. A new edition, with a critical evaluation, is now presented by Erica Reiner and D. Pingree in *Bibliotheca Mesopotamica*, 2/1 (Malibu, 1975).

22. For the earliest astrological texts see n. 32, n. 66, chap. iv.

23. For the palm tree, cf. the literature given in Ingrid Wallert, *Die Palmen im Alten Ägypten* (Berlin, 1962).

24. See P. Leser, "Westöstliche Landwirtschaft," in *Festschrift Publication d'hommage offerte au P. W. Schmidt* (Wien, 1928), pp. 416–84; and, *idem*, *Entstehung und Verbreitung des Pfluges* (Münster, 1931).

25. For the use of rubble from ruined hills as fertilizer see *CAD* sub *eperu*, mng. 6 ("an unidentified substance").

26. The term *karû* is used in Neo-Babylonian to denote such a storage pile. Cf. E. F. Weidner, in *Mélanges Dussaud*, vol. 1, p. 924, n. 5.

27. See L. F. Hartman and A. L. Oppenheim, "On Beer and Brewing Techniques in Ancient Mesopotamia," *JAOS*, Supplement no. 10 (Baltimore, 1950), and M. Civil, "A Hymn to the Beer Goddess and a Drinking Song," in *Studies Presented to A. Leo Oppenheim* (Chicago, 1964), pp. 67–89.

28. For the problems related to the domestication of the camel, see *CAD* sub *gammalu, ibilu*. See also B. Brentjes, "Das Kamel im Alten Orient," *Klio*, 39 (1960), 23–52.

29. See E. Ebeling, *Parfümrezepte und kultische Texte aus Assur* (Rome, 1950). For a Neo-Assyrian fragment from Calah see *Iraq*, 13 (1956), 112, ND 400.

30. For the rich evidence in cuneiform texts concerning the manufacture of glass and glasslike substances, see A. L. Oppenheim *et al.*, *Glass and Glassmaking in Ancient Mesopotamia* (Corning, N.Y., 1970). See also A. L. Oppenheim, "Mesopotamia in the Early History of Alchemy," *RA*, 60 (1966), 29–45.

31. See J. L. Kelso, "The Ceramic Vocabulary of the Old Testament," American Schools of Oriental Research, *Supplementary Studies*, no. 5–6 (New Haven, Conn., 1948). A corresponding study of the textual and archaeological evidence from Mesopotamia is still needed.

31a. There are indications, however, that palaces were not supposed to stand on higher terraces than temples: Assurbanipal (M. Streck, *Assurbanipal* vol. 2 [Leipzig, 1916], p. 86 x 78–80) mentions that he did not increase by much the height of the palace of the crown prince for fear that it would rival the temples.

32. For the earlier periods see H. J. Lenzen, "Mesopotamische Tempelanlagen von der Frühzeit bis zum zweiten Jahrtausend," *ZA*, 51 (1955), 1–36.

32a. For theories about these towers see Th. A. Busink, "L'origine et l'évolution de la ziggurat babylonienne," *JEOL*, 21 (1969–70), 91–142; E. Heinrich, "Von der Entstehung der Zikurrate," in *Vorderasiatische Archäologie. Studien und Aufsätze, Anton Moortgat zum fünfundsechzigsten Geburtstag gewidmet* (Berlin, 1964), pp. 113–25; H. J. Lenzen, "Gedanken über die Entstehung der Zikurrat," *Iranica Antiqua*, 6 (1966), 25–33.

33. For a description of such a banquet see K. F. Müller, *Das assyrische Ritual* (Leipzig, 1937), pp. 58–89. Reference should be made here to the important Assyrian royal ritual called *tākultu*, during which the king was apparently host to the gods and goddesses of the official pantheon whom he greeted in solemn "toasts," asking them to bestow blessings on his royal person and the entire realm. See n. 26, chap. ii.

Bibliographical Notes

Chapter I

For anyone who wants to obtain a well-balanced and straightforward, if somewhat pedantic, view of Mesopotamian civilization as seen by the philologist, B. Meissner's *Babylonien und Assyrien* (2 vols.; Heidelberg, 1920 and 1925) still offers more reliable information than more recent books of this kind, which all use secondary if not tertiary sources.

No comprehensive study of the peoples of the ancient Near East is available. Strange as it may seem to the outsider, the several Semitic-speaking peoples who lived in Mesopotamia from the third millennium B.C. on—the Akkadians and the subsequent waves of immigrants and invaders, including the Arameans and the Chaldeans—have not been made the subject of an extensive study by any competent scholar from the points of view of cultural or physical anthropology (but note H. Field, *The Anthropology of Iraq* [Chicago, 1940–50] and E. Wirth, *Agrargeographie des Irak* [Hamburg, 1962]). S. Moscati's *Ancient Semitic Civilizations* (London, 1957) however, offers a resumé of the assumptions that have currency at the moment.

For the Sumerians we have an enthusiastic presentation in S. N. Kramer, *History Begins at Sumer* (London, 1958), and, *idem*, *The Sumerians* (Chicago, 1963). One may also refer to H. Schmökel, *Das Land Sumer*, 2d ed. (Stuttgart, 1956), although it is removed from any direct contact with original text material. This is also true of the same author's *Ur, Assur und Babylon, Drei Jahrtausende im Zweistromland* (Stuttgart, 1955).

Note also M. Vieyra, *Les Assyriens* (Paris, 1961); H. Schmökel, *Kulturge-schichte des alten Orients* (Stuttgart, 1961), 1–310; H. W. F. Saggs, *The Greatness that was Babylon* (London, 1962); *idem, Everyday Life in Baby-lonia and Assyria* (London, 1965); K. Jaritz, *Babylon und seine Welt* (Bern, 1964); J. Laessøe, *People of Ancient Assyria* (London, 1963); B. Brentjes, *Land zwischen den Strömen* (Heidelberg, 1963); J. Klíma, *Gesellschaft und Kultur des alten Mesopotamien* (Prague, 1964).

The story of the decipherment of the cuneiform systems of writing is extensively presented by A. Pallis, *The Antiquity of Iraq* (Copenhagen, 1956), chaps. ii and iii.

As for the languages of Mesopotamia, A. Falkenstein, *Das Sumerische* (*Handbuch der Orientalistik*; Leiden, 1959) and his more representative *Grammatik der Sprache Gudeas von Lagaš*, 2 vols. (Rome, 1949–50) offer the latest in the study of the Sumerian language. W. von Soden's *Grundriss der akkadischen Grammatik* (Rome, 1952; 2d ed. with Ergän-zungsheft, 1969) will remain for a long time a basic tool of the Assyriolo-gist. A linguistically oriented structural presentation is available in Erica Reiner, *A Linguistic Analysis of Akkadian* (The Hague, 1966); note also *idem*, "Akkadian," in *Current Trends in Linguistics*, vol. 6, ed. T. A. Sebeok (The Hague, 1970), pp. 274–303 with bibliography. Akkadian dictionaries have been few and far between for more than half a century. The usefulness of those published has been quickly reduced by the steady influx of new text material, even where they had not been de-ficient from other points of view. The situation promises to be remedied at long last by the appearance of the extensive *Assyrian Dictionary*, ed. I. J. Gelb *et al.*, 12 vols. to date (Chicago, 1956–), and the much shorter *Akkadisches Handwörterbuch* of W. von Soden, 12 fascicules to date (Wiesbaden, 1959–), which utilizes the collections made by the late B. Meissner. For many years to come, the active Assyriologist will have to rely on his own collections until the large projects are terminated, and possibly thereafter, unless provisions are made to keep the contents of these dictionaries abreast of new text material and continuous progress in the field. A Sumerian dictionary in the proper sense of that term does not exist. The work of A. Deimel, *Šumerisches Lexikon* (Rome, 1925–37), is to be considered a still useful relic of the early days of Assyriology.

Considering other languages written in one or another of the cunei-form systems of the ancient Near East, we may simply refer to *Altklein-asiatische Sprachen*, with contributions of J. Friedrich on Hurrian and Urartian, Erica Reiner on Elamite, and Annelies Kammenhuber on Hittite, Palaic, Luwian, and Hattic (*Handbuch der Orientalistik*, Erste Abteilung, II. Band, 1. und 2. Abschnitt, Lieferung 2; Leiden/Köln,

1969), with the important review by I. M. Diakonoff and I. M. Dunayevskaya in *OLZ*, 68 (1973), 5–22; J. Friedrich, *Hethitisches Elementarbuch*, 2d ed. (Heidelberg, 1960); C. H. Gordon, *Ugaritic Handbook* (Rome, 1955); R. G. Kent, *Old Persian Grammar* (New Haven, 1950); E. A. Speiser, *Introduction to Hurrian* (New Haven, 1941); and I. M. Diakonoff, *Hurrisch und Urartäisch* (München, 1971).

As for the civilizations which flourished in contact with or under the influence of Mesopotamia: for Asia Minor, which includes the Hittite and other civilizations of that region, we have a model handbook in A. Goetze, *Kleinasien*, 2d ed. (München, 1957), also H. Otten in Schmökel, *Kulturgeschichte des alten Orients*, 313–446, and Thomas Beran on Urartu, *ibid.*, 606–57; cf. O. R. Gurney, *The Hittites* (Pelican Book A 259). See also G. Walser, ed., *Neuere Hethiterforschung* (Wiesbaden, 1964); M. Mayrhofer, *Die Indo-Arier im Alten Vorderasien* (Wiesbaden, 1966); "Die Arier im Vorderen Orient—ein Mythos?" Mit einem bibliographischen Supplement (*Österreichische Akademie der Wissenschaften, Sitzungsberichte, Phil.-hist. Kl.* 294. Band, 3. Abhandlung (Wien, 1974). No informative and scholarly guidebook is available for those interested in the civilization of Elam, whose capital, Susa, lies toward the foothills north of southern Babylonia (see n. 25, chap i.) The several ephemeral civilizations which at one time or another grew up between the western bend of the Euphrates and the Mediterranean coast and often used the Akkadian language and system of writing, likewise remain without convenient presentation. Eventually, one may quote W. F. Albright, *From Stone Age to Christianity*, 2d ed. (Baltimore, 1946), as the most readable introduction into the thorny problem of the relationship of the Bible to Mesopotamian civilization; two articles by E. A. Speiser—which I consider representative—"Ancient Mesopotamia" in *The Idea of History in the Ancient Near East* (New Haven, 1955), 37–76, and "Three Thousand Years of Bible Study," *The Centennial Review*, 4 (1960), 206–22; and—for the eastern contact zone—S. Piggott, *Prehistoric India* (Pelican Book A 205) and R. E. M. Wheeler, *Civilizations of the Indus Valley and Beyond* (London, 1966).

To obtain information about the predominant interests of the scholars in the field of Assyriology, their aspirations, standards, and methodological orientation, one has to turn to the articles and book reviews which are published in a constant stream in various scholarly periodicals in the United States, Europe, and Asia. They reflect in their variety the shifting directions of topical predilections and the interplay of schools and local traditions. Some of those periodicals are entirely dedicated to Assyriology and related subjects, and the rest offer articles of Assyriological interest among others in the field of Oriental studies.

To the former belong, as the two oldest, the *Zeitschrift für Assyriologie und verwandte Gebiete* (published since 1886), and the French *Revue d'Assyriologie et d'Archéologie orientale* (since 1886). Also in this group are the *Archiv für Orientforschung* (since 1923) and the *Journal of Cuneiform Studies* (since 1947). Others, such as *Orientalia*, Nova Series (since 1932), the *Journal of Near Eastern Studies* (since 1942), *Iraq* (since 1934), *Sumer* (since 1945), *Die Welt des Orients* (since 1947), and *Anatolian Studies* (since 1951), present much Assyriological material, while a number of journals of Oriental societies offer such material from time to time. Two regularly published bibliographies carefully keep track of these numerous articles; the bibliography in the *Archiv für Orientforschung* covers the period from 1925 until now and is organized in geographical and topical subdivisions; that in the periodical *Orientalia*, Nova Series, published by the Pontificium Institutum Biblicum in Rome, was begun in 1939 (by A. Pohl, S.J., now continued by R. Caplice, H. Klengel, and C. Saporetti) and periodically contains indexes of the names of authors and topics. An excellent bibliography of all published cuneiform texts now exists in R. Borger, *Handbuch der Keilschriftliteratur*, vol. 1 (Berlin, 1967); vol. 2 (Supplement to vol. 1, Berlin, 1975); vol. 3 (Berlin, 1975).

The overwhelming majority of cuneiform texts are published by the large museums such as the British Museum in London, the Musée du Louvre, Paris, the Staatliche Museen in Berlin, and the University Museum of the University of Pennsylvania—to mention only the largest collections—in extensive series of volumes which contain only handmade copies. This also holds true for most of the publications of smaller museums and private collections. Especially welcome is the text publication project of the Iraq Museum, in which volumes have been published since 1964. The series *Texts from Cuneiform Sources* (Vol. 1 in 1966) publishes critical editions of cuneiform texts which are either part of a literary corpus or delineated by topic or provenience. Uncounted and often important texts have been scattered through scholarly journals, sometimes in unexpected places, and make life difficult for a scholar who does not have at hand one of the very few first-class Assyriological libraries. Sooner or later it will become imperative to collect those texts in some easily available form.

The obvious question for any outsider concerns the accessibility of all this material in translation. There are, of course, a number of books and articles in which certain texts and even larger groups of texts of the same or related nature have been translated. To list them systematically would require, however, more space than can be allowed here. Suffice it to state that the number of texts available in up-to-date editions and translations is small indeed. For a representative cross section of the material one has to go back through the publications of the last half century.

A systematic collection of volumes in which, let us say, historical, epical, ritual texts, prayers, and hymns were presented in transliteration, translation, and commentary for the use of the scholars of other disciplines as well as for Assyriologists would meet a real need. If carefully kept up by revised editions, a "Loeb Classical Library for Assyriologists" would contribute far more to the advance of the field than many a costly archaeological expedition. Such an attempt was made some fifty years ago, but the influx of new texts dwarfed this short-lived effort. No anthology of translated and commented-on texts exists which offers a representative and serious cross section of cuneiform literature in its manifold aspects. In J. B. Pritchard's *Ancient Near Eastern Texts Relating to the Old Testament*, 2d ed. (Princeton, 1955), 190 of 516 pages are given to Assyriology. The effectiveness and value of the translated texts is greatly reduced by the fact that the Assyriological material was assembled solely to illustrate the relationship to the Bible, a restriction to which neither the Egyptian nor the Hittite materials were subjected; in consequence these offer a far more representative selection.

Chapter II

In the field of social institutions, very few books and articles can be listed here; their mention does not imply necessarily an acceptance of their views. On kingship see R. Labat, *Le caractère religieux de la royauté assyro-babylonienne* (Paris, 1939); H. Frankfort, *Kingship and the Gods, a Study of Ancient Near Eastern Religion as the Integration of Society and Nature* (Chicago, 1948); T. Jacobsen, "Early Political Development in Mesopotamia," *ZA*, 52 (1957), 91–140; *Le palais et la royauté*, ed. P. Garelli, XIXᵉ Rencontre Assyriologique Internationale (Paris, 1974); on slavery see I. Mendelsohn, *Slavery in the Ancient Near East* (New York, 1948); B. J. Siegel, *Slavery During the Third Dynasty of Ur* (*American Anthropologist*, n.s. 49/1, pt. 2, 1947). On economy see W. F. Leemans, "The Trade Relations of Babylonia and the Question of Relations with Egypt in the Old Babylonian Period," *JESHO*, 3 (1961), 21–36; A. L. Oppenheim, "A Bird's-Eye View of Mesopotamian Economic History," in *Trade and Market in the Early Empires*, ed. K. Polanyi, C. M. Arensberg, and H. W. Pearson (Glencoe, 1957), pp. 27–37; W. F. Leemans, *Foreign Trade in the Old Babylonian Period as Revealed by Texts from Southern Mesopotamia* (Leiden, 1960). On the temple see F. R. Kraus, "Le rôle des temples depuis la troisième dynastie d'Ur jusqu'à la première dynastie de Babylone," *Journal of World History*, 1 (1953-54), 518–45 (with bibliography on p. 54off.); A. Falkenstein, "La cité-temple sumérienne," *ibid.*, pp. 784–814 (English translation: *The Sumerian Temple City* [Los Angeles, 1974]); *Le temple et le culte.* Compte rendu de la Vingtième Rencontre Assyriologique Internationale (Istanbul, 1975). On the city and urbanism see *City Invincible, A Symposion on Urbanization and Cultural Development in the Ancient Near East*, ed. C. H. Kraeling and R. McC. Adams (Chicago, 1960); R. McC. Adams, "The Origin of Cities," *Scientific American* (1960); *idem, The Evolution of Urban Society, Early Mesopotamia and Prehispanic Mexico* (Chicago, 1965), and *Land Behind Baghdad: A History of Settlement on the Diyala Plains* (Chicago, 1965); *idem*, with H. J. Nissen, *The Uruk Countryside: The Natural Setting of Urban Societies* (Chicago, 1972); C. J. Gadd, "The Cities of Babylonia," *The Cambridge Ancient History*, I, pt. 2 (3d ed.; Cambridge, 1971), chap. 13, with bibliography on pp. 894–902; A. L. Oppenheim, "A New Look at the Structure of Mesopotamian Society," *JESHO*, 10 (1967), 1–16; W. J. van Liere, "Capitals and Citadels of Bronze-Iron Age Syria and Their Relationship to Land and Water," *Annales archéologiques de Syrie*, 13 (1963), 109–22.

It seems to me to be not only appropriate but indispensable to indicate here a number of pertinent Assyriological studies written by Russian scholars. I have selected these entries from a much larger list compiled by Professor I. M. Diakonoff. They are arranged alphabetically.

I. M. Diakonoff, *Razvitiie zêmêl'nych otnošênii v Assirii (The Development of Agrarian Conditions in Assyria)* (Leningrad, 1949); "Rêformy Urukaginy v Lagašê" ("The Reforms of Urukagina in Lagaš"), *Vêstnik Drêvnêi istorii*, 1951, 1, 15–22; *idem*, Ia. M. Magazinêr, and I. M. Dunaievskaia, "Zakony Vavilonii, Assirii i Chêttskogo carstva" ("The Laws of Babylonia, Assyria and the Hittite Kingdom"), *ibid.*, 1952, 3, 199–303; 4, 205–320; I. M. Diakonoff, "*Muškēnum* i povinnostnoie zêmlêvladêniie na carskoi zêmlê pri Chammurabi" ("The *Muškēnum* and Conditional Tenure of Crown Land in Hammurabi's Time") (summary in English), *Eos*, 48 (1956), 37–62; *Obščêstvênnyi i gosudarstvênnyi stroi drêvnêgo Dvurêc'ia. Sumer* (Social and State Structure in Ancient Mesopotamia) (summary in English) (Moscow, 1960); M. L. Heltzer, "Novyie teksty iz drêvnêgo Alalacha i ich značêniie dlâ social'noekonomičêskoi istorii drêvnêgo Vostoka" ("New Texts from Ancient Alalakh and Their Importance for the Social-Economic History of the Ancient Orient"), *Vêstnik drêvnêi istorii*, 1956, 1, 14–27; N. B. Jankowska, "Nêkotoryie voprosy ekonomiki assiriiskoi dêržavy" ("Some Questions of the Economy of the Assyrian Empire"), *ibid.*, 28–46; "Zêmlêvladêniie bol'šêsêmêinych domovych obščin v klinopisnych istočnikach" ("The Landownership of Extended Family House Communities in the

Cuneiform Sources"), *ibid.*, 1959, 1, 35–41; Y. B. Yusifov, "Kuplâprodaža nêdvižimogo imuščêstva i častnoje zêmlêvladênije v Elamê II tys. do n. e." ("Sale of Immovables and Private Landownership in Elam in the II mill. B.C."), *Klio*, 38 (1960), 5–22; L. A. Lipin, "The Assyrian Family in the Second Half of the Second Millennium B.C.," *CHM*, 3 (1961), 628–45; G. Kh. Sarkisian, "Samoupravlâjuščijsâ gorod Sêlêvkidskoj Vavilonii" ("The Self-governing City of Seleucid Babylonia"), *Vêstnik drêvnêj istorii*, 1952, 1, 68–83; W. Struve, "Problêma zaroždênija razvitija i upadka rabovladêl'čêskogo obščêstva drêvnêgo Vostoka" ("The Problem of the Rise, Development, and Decline of the Slave-holding Society of the Ancient Orient"), *Izvêstija Gosudarstvênnoj (Rossijskoj) Akadêmii istorii matêrial'noj Kul'tury*, 77 (1934); "K voprosu o specifikê rabovladêl'-čêškich obščêstv drêvnêgo Vostoka" ("On the Problem of the Specific Character of the Slave-holding Societies of the Ancient Orient"), *Vêstnik Lêningradskogo Univêrsitêta (sêrija istorii, jazyka i litêratury)*, 9 (1953), 81–91; A. I. Tiumenev, *Gosudarstvênnoje chozâjstvo drêvnêgo Sumêra* ("The State Economy of Ancient Sumer") (Moscow-Leningrad, 1956). English versions of some of the cited articles and of others appear in *Ancient Mesopotamia: Socio-Economic History. A Collection of Studies by Soviet Scholars*, ed. I. M. Diakonoff (Moscow, 1969).

Chapter III

Only a few books are suggested here to familiarize the reader with the history of the region: A. Moortgat, "Geschichte Vorderasiens bis zum Hellenismus," in *Ägypten und Vorderasien im Altertum*, ed. A. Scharff and A. Moortgat (München, 1950); H. Schmökel, "Geschichte des alten Vorderasiens," in *Handbuch der Orientalistik*, ed. B. Spuler, (Leiden, 1957); Elena Cassin, J. Bottéro, and J. Vercoutter, eds., *Die Altorientalischen Reiche*, vols. 1–3 ("Fischer Weltgeschichte," 1956–67), with chapters by J. Bottéro, Elena Cassin, D. O. Edzard, A. Falkenstein, P. H. J. Houwink ten Cate, R. Labat, A. Malamat, and H. Otten; P. Garelli, *Le Proche-Orient asiatique: Des origines aux invasions des Peuples de la Mer* (Paris, 1969); second part, *idem*, with V. Nikiprowetzky, *Les empires mésopotamiens—Israël* (Paris, 1974). All are provided with ample bibliographical notes. In the *Propyläen Weltgeschichte*, "Sumer, Babylon und Hethiter bis zur Mitte des zweiten Jahrtausends v. Chr.," pp. 525–609, and "Der nahe Osten im Altertum," pp. 41–133, W. von Soden availed himself of the traditional privilege of the Assyriologist to write on Mesopotamian history. For a treatment of the complex chronological problems see the summaries of M. B. Rowton, "The Date of Hammurabi," *JNES*, 17 (1958), 97–111, and in *The Cambridge Ancient History*, I pt. 1 (3rd ed.; Cambridge, 1970), chap. 6, "Ancient Western Asia."

On the history of special periods or regions, only a few works will be mentioned here: D. O. Edzard, *Die zweite Zwischenzeit Babyloniens* (Wiesbaden, 1957); J. A. Brinkman, *A Political History of Post-Kassite Babylonia: 1158–722 B.C.* (Rome, 1968); J. Oates, "Assyrian Chronology, 631–612 B.C.," *Iraq*, 27 (1965), 135–59; J.-R. Kupper, "Northern Mesopotamia and Syria," *The Cambridge Ancient History*, II pt. 1 (3d ed.; Cambridge, 1973), chap. 1; O. R. Gurney, "Anatolia c. 1750–1200 B.C.," *ibid.*, chap. 6; R. Labat, "Elam c. 1600–1200 B.C.," *ibid.*, II pt. 2 (1975), chap. 29; H. Klengel, *Geschichte Syriens im 2. Jahrtausend v. u. Z.*, 3 vols. (Berlin, 1965–70).

Chapter IV

The latest book with the grandiose aim of presenting what is customarily referred to as "Mesopotamian" or "Assyro-Babylonian" religion is E. Dhorme, "Les religions de Babylonie et d'Assyrie," *Les anciennes religions orientales: "Mana"* (Paris, 1945), vol. 1, 1–330. Note also F.M.T.de Liagre Böhl, "Die Religion der Babylonier und Assyrer" in *Christus und die Religionen der Erde* (Wien, 1951), vol. 2, 441–98; R. Follet, "Les aspects du divin et des dieux dans la Mésopotamie antique," *Recherches des sciences religieuses*, 38 (1952), 189–208; J. Bottéro, *Les divinités sémitiques anciennes* (Rome, 1958); G. Contenau, "Les religions de l'Asie occidentale ancienne" in Drioton, Contenau, Duchesne-Guillemin, *Les religions de l'Orient Ancien* (Paris, 1957), pp. 55–98; R. Largement, "La religion suméro-akkadienne," *Histoire des religions*, 4 (Paris, 1956), 119–76; and G. Furlani, "Religioni della Mesopotamia e dell'Asia Minore," *La Civiltà dell'Oriente* (Rome, 1958), pp. 53–134. S. H. Hooke's *Babylonian and Assyrian Religion* (London, 1953) should also be mentioned. An attempt at a profile of a god is E. von Weiher's *Der babylonische Gott Nergal* (= *AOAT* 11, Neukirchen-Vluyn, 1971).

As a characteristic example of an attempt to use a much wider angle and a more abstract outlook, we may quote here T. Jacobsen, "Mesopotamia," in *The Intellectual Adventure of Ancient Man*, ed. H. and H. A. Frankfort, J. A. Wilson, T. Jacobsen, and W. A. Irwin (Chicago, 1946), also to be found in *Before Philosophy* (Penguin Books A 198), and, *idem*, "Ancient Mesopotamian Religion; the Central Concerns," *Proceedings Am. Philosophical Society*, 107 (1963), 473–84. As a sample of a personal approach one may add C. J. Gadd, *Ideas of Divine Rule in the Ancient East* (London, 1948); H. Frankfort, *The Problem of Similarity in Ancient Near Eastern Religions* (Frazer Lecture; Oxford, 1951); and A. L. Oppenheim, "Analysis of an Assyrian Ritual," *History of Religions*, 5 (1966), 250–65.

On more special problems related to religion in the wider sense of that term see W. G. Lambert, "Morals in Ancient Mesopotamia," *Ex Oriente Lux Jaarbericht*, no. 15 (1957–58), pp. 184–96; T. H. Gaster, "Mythic Thought in the Ancient Near East," *Journal of the History of Ideas*, 16 (1955), 422–26; Morton Smith, "The Common Theology of the Ancient Near East," *JBL*, 71 (1952), 135–48; W. von Soden, "Das Fragen nach der Gerechtigkeit Gottes im Alten Orient," *MDOG*, 96 (1965), 41–59.

Chapter V

Many of the books mentioned in the Bibliographical Note to chap. i, as well as the numerous books and articles cited in the notes to the present chapter, will provide additional information on the problems presented here. For those interested in literary history, attention should be drawn to *Sumerische und akkadische Hymnen und Gebete* (Zürich and Stuttgart, 1953), which offers not only translations of these texts but also an "Einführung" by A. Falkenstein and W. von Soden, pp. 1–56, as well as copious notes, pp. 361–407, and a short bibliography. Additional information offered by the same authorities is contained in A. Falkenstein, "Zur Chronologie der sumerischen Literatur, Die nachaltbabylonische Stufe," *MDOG*, 85 (1953), 1–13, and W. von Soden, "Das Problem der zeitlichen Einordnung akkadischer Literaturwerke," *ibid.*, pp. 14–26.

In the discussion of Mesopotamian literature, the rendering of the contents of the individual works has been held to a minimum in order to concentrate on features which were considered relevant for the type of presentation planned. The interested reader is referred to the translations given in J. B. Pritchard, ed., *Ancient Near Eastern Texts Relating to the Old Testament*, 3d ed. (Princeton, 1969) or to the abbreviated version, J. B. Pritchard, *The Ancient Near East, An Anthology of Texts and Pictures* (Princeton, 1958).

A selection of official, business, and private letters in translation is found in A. L. Oppenheim, *Letters from Mesopotamia* (Chicago, 1967).

Chapter VI

For nearly all the important fields of the history of science and technology, Assyriology can contribute data of unique antiquity. This is especially true for the fields of mathematics, astronomy, and medicine. It so happens that the first two are covered with unparalleled excellence by O. Neugebauer, *The Exact Sciences in Antiquity*, 2d. ed. (Providence,

R.I., 1957), and, *idem*, "The Survival of Babylonian Methods in the Exact Sciences of Antiquity and the Middle Ages," *Proceedings Am. Philosophical Society*, 107 (1963), 528–35. The historian of medicine who looks for a serious introduction to cuneiform medical texts has a harder task. He has to rely on translations that are either antiquated or inadequate, and this makes even the work of such a scholar as H. E. Sigerist, *A History of Medicine* (New York, 1951), pp. 377–492, difficult to use. On medicine, chemistry, and technology see my essay, "Man and Nature in Mesopotamian Civilization," *Dictionary of Scientific Biography*, vol. 15 (New York, 1977).

Apart from the books and articles cited in this chapter, a number of additional bibliographic references should be given here: Owsie Temkin, "Beiträge zur archaischen Medizin," *Kyklos*, 3 (1930), 90–135; R. Labat, "La Mésopotamie," in *La Science antique et médiévale, Histoire générale des sciences*, vol. 1 (Paris, 1957), 73–138; J. Nougayrol, "Présages médicaux de l'haruspicine babylonienne," *Semitica*, 6 (1956), 7–14; R. Labat, "La pharmacopée au service de la piété (Tablette assyrienne inédite)," *Semitica*, 3 (1950), 1–18; *idem*, "La médecine babylonienne" (Conférence faite au Palais de la Découverte, Université de Paris, 1953); A. Finet, "Les médecins au royaume de Mari," *Annuaire de l'Institut de Philologie et d'Histoire Orientales et Slaves*, 15 (1954–57), 123–44; R. D. Biggs, "Medicine in Ancient Mesopotamia," *History of Science*, 8 (1969), 94–105; J. V. Kinnier Wilson, "Organic Diseases of Ancient Mesopotamia" and "Mental Diseases in Ancient Mesopotamia," in *Diseases in Antiquity*, ed. D. and A. T. Brothwell (Springfield, Ill., 1967), pp. 191–208 and 723–33; M. Leibovici, "Sur l'astrologie médicale," *JA*, 244 (1956), 275–80; also D. Pingree, "Astronomy and Astrology in India and Iran," *Isis*, 54 (1963), 229–46.

As for Mesopotamian art, I restrict myself to H. Frankfort, *The Art and Architecture of the Ancient Orient* (The Pelican History of Art, 1954); M. N. van Loon, *Urartian Art, Its Distinctive Traits in the Light of New Excavations* (Istanbul, 1966); and J. A. Potratz, *Die Kunst des Alten Orient* (Stuttgart, 1961), which contains a systematic bibliography, pp. 404–17.

Glossary of Names and Terms

As indicated in the Foreword, this glossary of names and terms should facilitate the reading of the book. It is not intended to be complete but rather to supplement the General Index.

ACHAEMENIDS   The dynasty of the Achaemenids ruled Iran from the middle of the sixth century B.C. (after having overcome the Medes) to 331 B.C. They conquered an empire, extending into Anatolia and Syria, under Cyrus (II) the Great, who took Babylon from Nabonidus in 539 B.C. His son, Cambyses II, conquered Egypt and Cyprus, while Darius I (521–486 B.C.) extended the empire into India in the east and Lybia in the west; he fought with the Greeks and the Scythians across the Black Sea.

ADAB   Situated halfway between Telloh and Nippur, the mound of Bismaya, the site of the town of Adab, suffered a short and not very successful excavation by E. J. Banks in 1903–4. It yielded tablets from the pre-Sargonic to the Neo-Babylonian period, many of them still unpublished. The mention of a king of Adab as an early ruler in the king list and the evidence from the Akkad and Ur III periods show that the city has slowly lost importance, although Hammurapi lists it in the introduction to his Code. See E. J. Banks, *Bismaya or the Lost City of Adab* (New York and London, 1912).

AKKAD (Agade)   A city in northern Babylonia which Sargon (2334–2279) either founded or from where he ruled his empire. It has not been located, although texts from as late as the sixth century B.C. mention it and even its ruined buildings. The linguistic contrast between the south and the north, which the designation "Sumer and Akkad" reflects, assumed political importance under the kings of the Third

Dynasty of Ur. It was from then on used to designate *per merismum* the entire region of Babylonia proper.

The term Akkad Period refers to the political as well as to the artistic achievements which can be related to the *floruit* of the dynasty of Sargon of Akkad.

AKKADIAN   Designation of the closely related Semitic dialects which are also called Assyrian and Babylonian (Assyro-Babylonian). It is derived from the adjective *akkadû*, i.e., "(language) of the city/region of Akkad," which was used in the Old Babylonian period to denote the Semitic version of a Sumerian text.

ALALAKH   Tell ʿAṭshānah in the plain of Antioch in Turkey, excavated by Sir Leonard Woolley in 1936–49, has yielded a body of written material second in importance only to Ugarit among the sites of Syria and Palestine (see also Ugarit, Qatna, Neirab, and Hazor). Apart from the publication of the inscribed statue of Idrimi (q.v.) by Sidney Smith, the main part of the treaties and legal and administrative tablets has been made available by D. J. Wiseman, *The Alalakh Tablets* (London, 1953), followed by the same author's contributions in *JCS* 8 (1954), 1–30, and *JCS* 12 (1958), 124–29. Apart from the Akkadian material (which comes from two layers separated by about three centuries), a Hittite letter and a divination text were found in Alalakh. Among the non-economic Akkadian texts are word lists, fragments of astrological omens, bilingual compositions and conjurations, and an anepigraphic liver model.

ALEPPO   An important center in northern Syria on the route between the Orontes and the Euphrates valleys, which has not been touched by the archeologists' spade. From Hittite, Egyptian, and Assyrian sources we know that Aleppo was fought over by the empires in the second millennium B.C. It is also mentioned in the texts from Ugarit and Alalakh.

ALISHAR   A mound southeast of Boghazkeui where in 1927–32 a small number of "Cappadocian tablets" were excavated by the Oriental Institute, Chicago. The published 53 texts (I. J. Gelb, *Inscriptions from Alishar and Vicinity, OIP* 27, 1935) are somewhat younger than the bulk of the texts from Kaniš (Kultepe); their contents are the same.

AMARNA PERIOD   Designation taken from the modern name of the site of the capital of Egypt under Amenophis IV (1369–1353 B.C.), also called Akhnaton, on the Nile, two hundred miles south of Cairo. For Assyriological purposes, the term is taken to denote the period of the mentioned Pharaoh and his predecessor Amenophis III (1398–1361 B.C.), a period during which the cuneiform letters found in Amarna shed light on Babylonia, Assyria, the Hittite and Mitanni kingdoms, Syria,

Palestine, and Cyprus. The now scattered archive of more than three hundred letters (and a few literary and lexical texts) contains letters written by Kadašman-Enlil I (ca. 1370 B.C.) and Burnaburiaš II (1359–1333 B.C.) of Babylon, Aššur-uballiṭ I of Assyria (1365–1330 B.C.), and Tušratta of Mitanni and Šuppiluliuma of Hatti (ca. 1380–1340 B.C.). It also contains a large body of texts coming from princes, officials, and local rulers in Syria, Palestine, and Cyprus as well as copies of letters sent by the Egyptian kings.

AMORITES   The term, taken from the Bible translation, refers as a rule to one or more ethnic groups speaking Semitic but not Akkadian languages, within Mesopotamia and to the west of it. The Akkadian designation *amurrû* (Sumerian, m a r. t u) denoted in the course of the second millennium B.C. not only an ethnic group but also a language and a geographical and political unit in Upper Syria.

ARBELA   The city now called Erbil (earlier Urbilum, Arbilum, Arbail(u)) is situated north of the Upper Zab and is known from the Ur III period on to Assurbanipal's reign. Its political importance is difficult to gauge for lack of documentation, but as a cult center within Assyria it was second only to Assur. The modern city lies over the ancient, and no excavations have been made there.

ARRAPHA   A city (modern Kirkuk) attested from Hammurapi to Nabonidus, situated east of the Tigris on the Radânu River, belonged since Adad-nirari II (911–891 B.C.) to the Assyrian empire. From a mound in its vicinity (Yorghan Tepe) come the tablets known as Nuzi tablets because the name of the excavated city was Nuzi. The main find of several thousand tablets made by the expeditions led by Edward Chiera has been nearly completely published (by E. Chiera, R. H. Pfeiffer, E. A. Speiser, but mainly E. Lacheman). They all date from the middle of the second millennium B.C. and shed light on an interesting hybrid civilization which evolved among Hurrian and other alien social patterns and Babylonian scribal and administrative techniques. Below this stratum were found tablets which mention a city named Gasur (q.v.). For literature see M. Dietrich, O. Loretz, and W. Mayer, *Nuzi-Bibliographie* (=AOAT Sonderreihe 11; Neukirchen-Vluyn, 1972).

ARSACID (Dynasty)   The Parthian kings of the Arsacid Dynasty conquered Mesopotamia under King Mithradates I (ca. 171–138 B.C.) and ruled from their capital Ctesiphon, near today's Baghdad, for more than three centuries (up to ca. 224 A.D.).

ASSUR   Situated on a bluff on the west bank of the Tigris about forty miles south of the Upper Zab, the old capital of Assyria (*Aššur*) was thoroughly excavated by the Deutsche Orient-Gesellschaft from 1903 to 1914; the epigraphic and archeological màterial is being published in an impressive series of volumes. A good survey of the urban features of the city (temples, palaces, gateways) is offered by E. Unger in *RLA* I 170–195. Though Aššurnaṣirpal II (883–859 B.C.) moved his capital to Calah, Assur remained until its fall (614 B.C.) a city for which the Assyrian kings showed great concern.

ASSURBANIPAL   The reign (668–627 B.C.) of this last great king of Assyria is characterized by the war he had to lead against his brother, Šamaš-šum-ukin, whom his father had installed as king of Babylon, and the curious gap in the documentation which blacks out the last ten years of Assurbanipal's rule. The civil war ended with the defeat of Babylon. In other victorious campaigns, Assurbanipal showed the military might of Assyria from Thebes to Susa, as the last achievement after nearly half a millennium of Assyrian warfare against all its neighbors. The dates given here are based on the references to Assurbanipal in the inscription of Nabonidus' mother.

BABYLON   This great metropolis has a long and complex history for which there exists much textual evidence apart from the findings of the archeologists, mainly the Deutsche Orient-Gesellschaft. R. Koldewey worked at the site from 1899 to 1917. Among the documents referring directly to the city are a long text describing systematically the entire city, several maps on clay tablets, a hymn to the city, and the famous description of the city by Herodotus (in Greek) (cf. O. E. Ravn, *Herodotus' Description of Babylon*, Copenhagen, 1942). For an attempt to handle this vast material see E. Unger, *Babylon, die heilige Stadt* (Berlin, 1931), and, by the same author, *RLA* I, pp. 330–69.

BABYLON, FIRST DYNASTY OF   See Hammurapi Dynasty.

BAHRAIN   See Telmun.

BOGHAZKEUI   See Hattuša.

BORSIPPA   An important ancient city south of Babylon, attested from the Ur III period (mentioned there beside Babylon) to the Seleucid and even Arabic periods. Although hardly any scientific excavations have been conducted on the site, marked by the impressive ruin of its temple tower, many legal tablets and a number of literary and astronomical texts are known to come from Borsippa. They are dated mainly from the late periods (from the Chaldean Dynasty on). For the layout of the city see E. Unger in *RLA*, vol. I, pp. 402–29, and R. Koldewey, *Die Tempel von Babylon und Borsippa* (*WVDOG*, 15; Leipzig, 1911). Borsippa was as a rule politically dependent on Babylon and was one of the few larger cities of lower Mesopotamia which was never the seat of any political power.

CALAH (*Kalḫu*)   Founded by Aššurnaṣirpal II in 883 B.C., this capital of Assyria on the east bank of the Tigris (about twenty-two miles south of modern Mosul and of ancient Nineveh) attracted the attention of the earliest excavators (A. H. Layard, H. Rassam, W. H. Loftus) more than a hundred years ago. Work in Nimrud, the modern name of the site, was resumed by the British School of Archaeology in 1949 and has yielded important results. For an instructive survey see M. E. L. Mallowan, *Twenty-five Years of Mesopotamian Discovery* (London, 1956), pp. 45–78. For the history of the city see W. W. Hallo, "The Rise and Fall of Kalah," *JAOS*, 88 (1968), 772–75.

CAPPADOCIAN TEXTS   See Kaniš.

CARCHEMISH   Important city on the Upper Euphrates but definitely outside the realm of Mesopotamian civilization. Light on its history is shed by Hittite (from Hattuša and Ugarit), Assyrian, and Babylonian historical texts. With Damascus and Palmyra (*Tadmur*) it shares a still undefined role in the international trade that linked Mesopotamia to the Mediterranean littoral during and after the Hittite domination of the city and its subsequent conquest by Sargon II (717 B.C.)

CHAGAR BAZAR   A site in northeast Syria, in the upper Habur Valley, excavated by the British School of Archaeology from 1934 to 1937. The tablets found (see C. J. Gadd in *Iraq*, 7 (1940), 22–61) are datable to the rule of Šamši-Adad I of Assyria and are administrative in nature.

CHALDEAN DYNASTY   This last native dynasty was founded by Nabopolassar (625–605 B.C.), continued by his eminent son Nebuchadnezzar II (604–562 B.C.), and terminated in the quick succession of the latter's son Evil-Merodach (561–560 B.C.), his son-in-law Neriglissar (559–556 B.C.), and the latter's son Labaši-Marduk (556 B.C.). It saw the downfall of the Assyrian Empire, the coming of the Medes and the rise of Babylonia (now often called Chaldea) which, for a short time, replaced Assyria as the foremost military power in the Near East. Royal inscriptions, chronicles, and a large number of private, legal, and administrative texts and letters (from Sippar, Nippur, Babylon, Uruk, and Ur) amply document this period, which represents in many respects the acme of Babylonia's wealth and political power. It is customary to include the usurper Nabonidus (555–539 B.C.) in this dynasty.

CTESIPHON   See Arsacid (Dynasty).

DAMASCUS   City in an oasis in Syria, attested in Egyptian texts and the Amarna correspondence ever since the sixteenth century B.C. Much of our information concerning the city comes from the Old Testament, which describes the relation between the Hebrew kingdoms and Damascus in war and peace. The Arameans, who conquered it in the last quarter of the second millennium, were followed by David, and by the Assyrians in the eighth century. Eventually, Damascus became the capital of a Nabatean kingdom (85 B.C.). Throughout the history of the city, trade with foreign countries seems to have played an important role.

DARK AGE   A term coined by B. Landsberger in his article "Assyrische Königsliste und 'Dunkles Zeitalter'," *JCS* 8 (1954), 31–45, 47–73,

EAST LUWIAN   In Asia Minor, mainly south of the Halys River extending west toward the Euphrates and, south, to the Orontes and the Mediterranean, widely scattered objects, stelae, and rocks have been found inscribed with a system of hieroglyphic signs. They are attested for about a millennium (from 1800 B.C. on) and their language has been termed East Luwian. It is often thought that the "Hieroglyphic Hittite" is related to the Luwian of southwest Asia Minor, preserved on clay tablets in cuneiform signs.

ECBATANA   Summer capital of the Achaemenid and Parthian rulers of Iran under today's Hamadan at the foot of the Elvend Mountain.

EMUTBAL   See Der.

ENMERKAR   A mythical ruler (Sumerian e n) of Uruk, the hero of several Sumerian epic poems among which "Enmerkar and the Lord of Aratta" is the best preserved (translated by S. N. Kramer). Enmerkar's name appears also in the Sumerian king list.

ERIDU   The Sumerian king list assigns to Eridu the oldest dynasty of Mesopotamia, and this claim has been confirmed, to a certain extent, by excavations which yielded important evidence for the antiquity of the site (Abu Shahrain, seven miles southwest of Ur). The city was once on the seashore or an inland lake, and its main god was Enki, the Sumerian counterpart of the water god Ea. It is mentioned throughout the entire history of Mesopotamia in economic, administrative, historical, and literary texts.

ESARHADDON   King of Assyria (680–669 B.C.). After the still mysterious murder of his father Sennacherib, Esarhaddon fought with his brothers for the throne and gained it after a short civil war. His main campaigns were directed against Egypt which, under his rule, came for the first time under Assyrian domination. Ample documentation allows the historian not only to establish the outlines of the political history of Esarhaddon's rule but also to obtain an impression of the personality of this king.

ESHNUNNA (Tell Asmar)   Capital of the country of Warum, one of the several kingdoms which flourished before and during the Old Babylonian period in the fertile region between the Tigris and the mountains. After the collapse of the empire of Ur III, the kings of Eshnunna strove for political power and expansion until first the kingdom of Isin, then the victories of Hammurapi barred their aspirations. Eshnunna, however, is mentioned, although quite rarely outside literary texts, in later periods. While the main bulk of the tablets excavated by the Oriental Institute of the University of Chicago in Tell Asmar remains unpublished, two tablets containing the laws of Eshnunna have been found at another site in Tell Harmal (old name

106–33, to refer to the spectacular gap in documentation
Babylonia, sets in with the last kings of the Hammurapi Dyn
lasts nearly to the midpoint of the Kassite Dynasty. In Assyria,
with the end of the dynasty founded by Šamši-Adad I and
Aššur-uballit I. In both instances, however, the king lists
tenuous thread across the gap. Many problems related to the c
logy of Mesopotamia are intimately linked to the span of time a
to the "Dark Age." There are different schools of thought, "shor
"long" chronologies, and intermediary solutions. None of the
based on more than circumstantial evidence. The discussion is su
continue until more evidence and synchronisms will allow us to fi
few available facts into a more reliable time sequence.

DER   Although attested not infrequently from the Old Akkadia
the Seleucid period, the town of Der, situated beyond the Tigris tow
Elam (see S. Smith, *JEA* 18 [1932], 28), was politically important only
a short time in the early Old Babylonian period as capital of the regi
called Emutbal. Since its mound has not been excavated, nothing can
said about its history or about its pantheon which, according to th
literary sources, seems to have been rather atypical.

DJEMDET-NASR   A mound fifteen miles northeast of Kish where in
1925–26 tablets with very archaic inscriptions were discovered together
with characteristic pottery (form and decor) as well as a special type of
thin bricks. The pottery has been fitted into the early Mesopotamian
sequence after Warka Level IV.

DREHEM   See Ur, Third Dynasty of.

DUR-KURIGALZU   The ruins of ʿAqarquf to the west of Baghdad mark
the site of the temple tower of a new city probably founded by the
Kassite king Kurigalzu II (1332–1308 B.C.). It was called Dur-Kurigalzu
and is mentioned in contemporary texts from Nippur. Tablets found in
excavations have been published by O. R. Gurney in *Iraq* 11 (1949),
131–49; for fragments of a large statue inscribed with the difficult and
artificial Sumerian of the period, see S. N. Kramer in *Sumer* 4 (1948),
1–28; see also Kramer's translation in J. B. Pritchard (ed.), *ANET²*,
pp. 57–59.

DUR-ŠARRUKIN (Khorsabad)   Capital of Assyria, founded by Sargon
II (721–705), twelve miles northeast of Nineveh on the site of another
city. The mound has been investigated by excavators ever since 1842.
The city had been built toward the end of the reign of Sargon and
seems to have been maintained as seat of a governor for nearly a
century thereafter. The excavations yielded the plan of the city and its
citadel, a number of monuments, and some tablets among which the
Assyrian king list is outstanding.

Šaduppum) and were published by A. Goetze, *The Laws of Eshnunna*, *AASOR* 31 (1951–52).

FARA Site of the Šuruppak of the Flood story, a city on the old course of the Euphrates, twelve miles southeast of Nippur, where a large collection of early Sumerian texts, seals, and seal impressions were excavated in 1902–3.

GASUR Name of the Old Akkadian settlement or manor which lies underneath the later city of Nuzi. Texts found there have been published by T. J. Meek in *HSS* 10. At the same site, a few Old Assyrian ("Cappadocian") tablets were found which belong to the very few texts of that type coming from outside Asia Minor. (See Kaniš.)

HAMMURAPI DYNASTY (First Dynasty of Babylon) This dynasty—called by the native historiographers "Dynasty of Babylon"—comprises eleven kings and extends over three centuries (1894–1595 B.C.) with all but the very first ruler belonging to the same family, son always following father. Under the second king the dynasty moved into the previously attested settlement, called Babil, and enlarged its political domain and power until it reached its apogee under the sixth king (Hammurapi, 1792–1750 B.C.). From then on, the sphere of influence of the kings of Babylon shrank constantly under external and apparently also internal pressures. The entire period was of crucial importance for the artistic, literary, and intellectual development of Mesopotamia. Later literary texts repeatedly mention the name of Hammurapi as representing an old and glorious phase of Mesopotamian history.

HARRAN A city in northern Upper Mesopotamia, attested first in the Hittite texts from Boghazkeui, then in the Old Testament and in the Assyrian royal inscriptions from the last third of the second millennium onward. It was conquered by the Assyrians pushing toward the west but became (under Sargon II) an integral part of Assyria, rivaling in importance the old cities of the Assyrian heart land. Its main deity was the moon god whose temple was sumptuously rebuilt by the Babylonian king Nabonidus. From Sultantepe, a large mound in the plain of Harran, came an important collection of literary texts published by O. R. Gurney, J. J. Finkelstein, and P. Hulin. For important stelae found there see C. J. Gadd, "The Harran Inscriptions of Nabonidus," *Anatolian Studies*, 8 (1958), 35–92; W. Röllig, "Erwägungen zu neuen Stelen König Nabonids," *ZA*, 56 (1964), 218–60.

HATRA Seat of an Aramaic kingdom in the desert of Upper Mesopotamia, apparently engaged in caravan trade. It was possibly under Parthian domination and defended itself repeatedly and successfully against Roman attacks (Trajan) but fell to the rising power of the Sassanian rulers (Shapur I). Its site shows a striking circular circumvallation and the ruins of a large palace.

HATTUŠA   The capital of the Hittite Empire situated on fortified mountain spurs in eastern central Anatolia (near the modern village of Boghazkeui) somewhat north of the center of the circle made by the bend of the Halys River. It is attested from the time of the Assyrian colonies to the disappearance of the Hittite kingdom in the thirteenth century B.C.

HATTUŠILI III   Hittite king of the early thirteenth century, famous for his treaty with Ramses II of Egypt and for his correspondence with the latter and the Kassite kings of Babylonia, Kadašman-Turgu and Kadašman-Enlil II. He is known to have rebuilt Hattuša and enjoyed a reign characterized by peace and prosperity. He is the author of a unique literary document, his autobiography.

HAZOR   An old and large city mound in the Plain of Huleh north of the Sea of Galilee. It is mentioned in the texts from Mari, in the Amarna correspondence, and also once in the texts of the literary tradition (dream omen). For the important results of recent excavations made there see Y. Yadin, *James A. de Rothschild Expedition at Hazor* (Jerusalem, 1958 and 1960).

HYKSOS   In modern scholarly usage this term (applied first by Manetho in his third century B.C. Egyptian history) refers to a people or group of peoples actively involved in a complex succession of migrations, conquests, and acculturations which took place in the first half of the second millennium B.C. in Lower Egypt, Palestine, and Syria. It deeply affected the political and cultural development in this region, and it involved several ethnic and linguistic groups apparently penetrating from outlying regions. The Hyksos left far more archeological than textual evidence and have been, and still are, the subject of much discussion. For the latest presentation, see A. Alt, *Die Herkunft der Hyksos in neuer Sicht* (Leipzig, 1954).

IDRIMI   A king of Alalakh in the third quarter of the second millennium who has left us, inscribed all over a seated statue, a unique document in which he gives an account of his youth, his rise to the throne, and his political and military achievements.

ISIN   The kings of the first dynasty of Isin ruled this city in central Lower Mesopotamia for more than two hundred years (2017–1794) after the collapse of the empire of Ur III. Under the leadership of a usurper of "Bedouin" extraction, Išbi-Irra (2017–1985), and his immediate successors, the power of the city extended rapidly toward Nippur, Telmun, Elam, Ur, and Der so that its kings could rightly claim the succession of Ur as foremost power of the region. After the time of Išme-Dagan (1953–1935 B.C.) and Lipit-Ištar (1934–1924), whose names are intimately linked with legislation concerned with the social problems of their kingdom, the extent of Isin's sphere of influence shrank constantly under the pressure of the upcoming kings of Larsa. Rim-Sin of Larsa conquered Isin in the twenty-ninth year of his reign, two years before Hammurapi ascended the throne in Babylon.

Kaniš (Kultepe)   Apart from a small number of tablets found in Alishar and nearby Boghazkeui (see also Gasur), all tablets written by the Assyrian traders of the beginning of the second millennium B.C. come from the mound Kultepe near Kayseri south of the Halys. The city of Kaniš, which lies under and around this mound, has yielded more than 16,000 tablets of which only roughly 2,000 have been published between 1882 and 1963. The main body of texts, excavated by the Turkish Historical Society since 1948, has remained unpublished but for a handful of tablets and is not accessible to scholars. The understanding of these difficult texts in philological and historical respects was pioneered, following their decipherment and identification, by Benno Landsberger and Julius Lewy.

Kassites   Rulers with foreign names sat on the throne of Babylon for about half a millennium down to 1155 B.C. The circumstances of their rise to power are hidden in the "Dark Age" (q.v.). When its shade lifts, Babylonia under Kassite rule has emerged again as a political power in the Near East, although its stability and military strength were far from constant for many centuries. Eight among the last kings of the "Kassite Dynasty" have Akkadian personal names. The contributions of this foreign element to Mesopotamian civilization are still being studied.

Khorsabad   See Dur-Šarrukin.

Kirkuk   See Arrapha.

Kish   Before the incorporation of Kiš into the growing kingdom of nearby Babylon (at that time under its third ruler), the old and famous town does not seem to have had any importance in the period after the collapse of Ur III. Its role in the Akkad period cannot yet be adequately understood. At that time, its possession gave the kings of Lower Mesopotamia the title of "King of Kish," which was interpreted as *šar kiššati* "king of the (entire) world," a title used henceforth by kings in and around Mesopotamia who thus laid claim to the hegemony of the region.

Kultepe   See Kaniš.

Kuyundjik   See Nineveh.

Larsa   About the same time as in Isin a ruler of foreign extraction (Naplanum, 2025–2005 B.C.) took over the southern Babylonian city of Larsa. Under his fourth successor, Gungunum, Larsa rose to political importance mainly by the conquest of Ur and by assuming the latter's role in commercial relations (reaching as far as Telmun). Much of the political ambition of the subsequent rulers was spent in competition with Isin, mainly in the fight for the possession of Nippur. After new usurpers coming from east of the Tigris, sons of a sheik of Emutbal who had an Elamite name, assumed power in Larsa, Isin was conquered and a short period of flowering was brought to the kingdom of Larsa under its long-lived last king Rim-Sin (1822–1763 B.C.). Hammurapi's conquest of Larsa terminated the period of city states in lower Mesopotamia.

LAGAŠ (Telloh)   The large complex of mounds at and near Telloh in eastern Lower Mesopotamia contains the old city of Lagaš made famous by its ruler Gudea, with its sister cities. The lower layers date from such early periods as that of Ubaid and Uruk, with the name of the city appearing already in pre-dynastic texts. The documentary evidence reaches if sparingly to the time of Samsuiluna, the successor of Hammurapi. Over the ruins, an Aramaic ruler (*Adad-nadin-aḫḫe*) established a palace in the third century B.C. with bricks inscribed with his name in Greek and Aramaic characters. See A. Parrot, *Tello* (Paris, 1948).

LULLUBU (Lullu)   A mountain people comparable to the Quti but without the stigma which the early Mesopotamian tradition has attached to the latter due to their invasion of the lowlands. An inscription and a representation of Ištar found on a rock shows that the Lullu people had been in contact with Mesopotamia in the Old Akkadian period. See E. A. Speiser, *Mesopotamian Origins* (Philadelphia, 1930), pp. 88–96.

MAGAN AND MELUHHA   In the geographical nomenclature of Mesopotamia, these two geographical names appear often side by side, although when used to identify persons or objects (plants, metals, etc.), the scribes differentiate carefully. It is here assumed that there exists a definite difference between the second and first millennium uses of the two toponyms. In the second millennium they referred to the outmost eastern fringe of the known world, i.e., to eastern Arabia and India. In the first millennium they were exclusively used to denote, only in literary contexts, Ethiopia and perhaps the region beyond. A few scholars insist that the early references deal likewise with these African countries supposed to have been in contact with Mesopotamia via the Indian Ocean.

MALGIUM   A city and its region on the east bank of the Tigris south of the mouth of the Diyala River which flourished in the Old Babylonian period, fighting against the kingdom of Isin (Gungunum) and participating in the great alliance of the kingdoms beyond the Tigris against Hammurapi (mentioned in the year names of the latter from the year 30 to 39). It disappeared toward the end of Old Babylonian period.

MANNEANS A group of tribal states and migrating peoples pressing at the beginning of the first millennium toward Urartu and Assyria from the east. Their relationship to native groups and to Iranian-speaking peoples is difficult to establish. See the very explicit review by R. Ghirshman in *Bibliotheca Orientalis*, 15 (1958), 257–61, of I. M. Diakonoff's *Istoria Midii* (Moscow-Leningrad, 1956).

MARI The tablets coming from Tell Hariri, the site of Mari, on the Euphrates before it enters today's Iraq, exhibit all the characteristics of cuneiform texts coming from a peripheral site. Among the large number of administrative documents and letters—allegedly 20,000—stand out an interesting royal ritual, some bilingual and literary texts (unpublished), and a few tablets in Hurrian. The majority of the texts deal with the short period from the rule of Jahdun-Lim of Hana, who conquered Mari, to the collapse of the kingdom of Šamši-Adad I (1813–1781 B.C.) of Assyria under his son Išme-Dagan I and the short-lived restoration under Zimri-Lim, son of Jahdun-Lim. These tablets, mostly letters and administrative documents, and a group of legal texts have been made available in the series "Archives royales de Mari" (Paris) since 1946. A parallel series offers transliterations and translations since 1950. Fourteen volumes have thus far been published with more than 2,500 texts by G. Dossin, Ch.-F. Jean, J.-R. Kupper, J. Bottéro, G. Boyer, M. Birot, M. Burke, and A. Finet. A number of inscribed statues and administrative texts illustrate the history of the city back to the pre-Sargonic period. The importance of the texts from Mari lies not so much in the superficial parallels they offer to the Old Testament background as in the light they shed on the clash between two cultures, that of Mesopotamia and that of the "barbaric West." See M. Noth, *Mari und Israel* (Tübingen, 1953).

MELUHHA See Magan.

MESOPOTAMIA The term is used in this book in two ways: to refer to the civilization which arose along and between the two rivers, Tigris and Euphrates, in the fourth millennium B.C., whatever the ethnic and linguistic nature of its carriers was or from wherever they came, i.e., including Sumerian and Akkadian as well as earlier and later contributors, and secondly, to refer to a geographical concept. The latter is meant to denote more or less strictly the region bordered by the two rivers from their mouth to the point where they approach each other upstream of Baghdad (termed Lower Mesopotamia) and, beyond that point, the entire extent of land along and between the rivers (Upper Mesopotamia), including the strip of piedmont on the left bank of the Middle Tigris, i.e., Assyria proper.

MITANNI An important kingdom whose power extended over much of Upper Mesopotamia and Northern Syria from the sixteenth to the fourteenth centuries. Its sphere of influence, ever since it emerged from the "Dark Age," was constantly infringed upon by the Hittites, who in the New Kingdom pressed again toward northern Syria and the Euphrates, and by the Egyptians, who moved in the same direction. In the middle of the fourteenth century, the kingdom of Mitanni collapsed, but it took the Assyrians more than two centuries after their liberation from Mitanni domination to conquer the regions in which the Mitanni had held sway for such a long time. The language of Mitanni, or of the several smaller kingdoms that belonged to it, seems to have been Hurrian; the ruling class, however, showed definitely Indo-European personal names. The capital, Waššukanni, has not yet been located.

MURŠILI II Hittite king, ruling from 1339–1306 B.C., father of Muwatalli who fought with Ramses II the famous battle of Qadesh.

MUṢAṢIR City of Urarṭu (residence of the national god Khaldi), whose conquest by Sargon II is described in a long text (TCL 3). Interestingly enough, an Assyrian relief depicts the specific features of this city with apparent accuracy; see F. Thureau-Dangin, Une relation de la huitième campagne de Sargon (Paris, 1912).

NABATEANS One of several hybrid civilizations created by groups of Arabic extraction from the outgoing second millennium until deep into the first millennium B.C. at the edges of the Syro-Arabic desert region in a circle from the lower Euphrates to the south of the Dead Sea. The Nabateans are attested for about three or four centuries in the region of Edom and Moab with their capital in Petra, and begin to play a role of international political importance after Alexander the Great liberated them from Persian domination until the annexation of their kingdom by Trajan. In a characteristic fusion of native elements (pantheon) and foreign elements (Aramaic and Greek language and script), the Nabateans combined agriculture, based on a sophisticated use of the extremely scarce water supply at their disposal, with international trade through which their caravans linked the Persian Gulf and the Red Sea to the Mediterranean Sea.

NABONIDUS Last king of Babylonia (555–539 B.C.), a native of Harran who usurped the Babylonian throne probably due to the difficult internal situation created by the short-lived reigns of the unfortunate successors of Nebuchadnezzar. The reign of Nabonidus seems to have been characterized by a series of unprecedented acts of the king of which we know only a few, and those in a vague way; such as his prolonged absence from Babylon while staying in Tema (Arabia), the joint rule with his son Belshazzar, his obvious preference for the cult of the moon god of his birthplace (Harran), and other acts to which allusions are made in contemporary cuneiform texts. His tragic role as last king of Babylonia appealed to classical authors (Herodotus, Xenophon, and Josephus) and his unconventional behavior made him the "mad king of Babylon," known all over the Near East.

NEBUCHADNEZZAR II   King of Babylonia (604–562 B.C.), succeeding his father, Nabopolassar, who founded the Chaldean Dynasty and won liberation from Assyrian domination. Babylonia began to assume Assyria's functions in military and political respects under Nabopolassar, but Nebuchadnezzar II led the country on to an apogee of power in the ancient Near East after his victory over the Pharaoh Necho II at Carchemish (605 B.C.). He extended Babylonian supremacy to the west, conquering Jerusalem and Tyre (597 and 586 B.C.) and fighting against Egypt. The numerous inscriptions of this king and the abundant legal and administrative documents dated to his reign do not shed much light on specific events during his rule or on his personality or on the social and economic background of this apparently most prosperous period in Babylonian history.

NEIRAB   In 1926 and 1927, the French Fathers Carrière, Barrois, and Abel excavated a mound near Aleppo which revealed a small city of the Assyrian and Neo-Babylonian period, called Niribi. Two Aramaic stelae, found earlier, mention the same name and the names of Akkadian and Sumerian deities connected with the moon cult. The texts have been published by E. Dhorme, "Les tablettes babyloniennes de Neirab" *RA*, 25 (1928), 53–82.

NIPPUR   The city of Nippur (Sum. N i b r u) in central Babylonia occupies a special position in the history of Mesopotamia up to the middle of the second millennium B.C. Like Sippar, it was hardly ever the seat of any political power, but its god Enlil and his famous temple Ekur belonged to a phase in the development of religious institutions in Mesopotamia which set them off against all the other cities and local cults. From the early Sumerian period on, Nippur was also a center of intellectual activities. Much of what we know of Sumerian literature comes from finds made in Nippur. Excavations by several American institutions have been going on since 1889 and have yielded literary, historical, administrative, and legal documents which cover nearly all the stages of the history of the city up to the Parthian period. The tablets excavated in the last century have been made available to a large extent to the scholarly world, but only a few of those found in the last fourteen years have been published.

NINEVEH   When Sennacherib made the city Ninua the capital of his empire at the end of the eighth century B.C., it could already look back on more than two millennia of history, covered by archeological and epigraphic (Naram-Sin, Šamši-Adad I) evidence. Much of the city's importance seems to have been related to the cult of the Ištar of Ninua, who already in the Amarna Age was famous as far away as Egypt. Nineveh's political power was short-lived; it fell in 612 B.C. to the Medes. Its size and prosperity as well as its sudden destruction is reflected in a number of passages in the Old Testament. The extensive ruins of the city with its long walls and the two large mounds, Kuyundjik and Nebi Yunus, quite early attracted the attention of archeologists and have repaid their efforts with reliefs and cuneiform documents.

Nuzi   See Arrapha.

Parthians   An Iranian tribe from the region of the Caspian Sea which rebelled in the middle of the third century B.C. under their leader Arsaces (see Arsacid Dynasty) against the Seleucids, conquered Iran and eventually Mesopotamia.

Persepolis   The famous ruins of a royal residence, founded by Darius I (521–486 B.C.) in southwest Iran and destroyed by Alexander the Great (330 B.C.), have attracted European travelers since the beginning of the seventeenth century (Pietro della Valle).

Persian Period   This period extends in Babylonia from Cyrus' entry into Babylon (539 B.C.) to Alexander the Great. Tablets dated to the Persian rulers come from Sippar, Babylon, Borsippa, Nippur, Ur, Uruk, and a number of smaller sites. The presence of the conquerors makes itself felt only in a very limited number of foreign words, referring mainly to officials (see W. Eilers, *Die Iranischen Beamtennamen in der keilschriftlichen Überlieferung*, Leipzig, 1940). Apart from a traditional clay cylinder assigned to Cyrus, only inscriptions in which the Akkadian appears beside an Old Persian and, at times, an Elamite version are known. For these texts see R. G. Kent, *Old Persian Grammar, Texts, Lexicon* (New Haven, 1950), and O. Rössler, *Untersuchungen über die akkadische Fassung der Achämenideninschriften* (Berlin, 1938).

Ptolemies   A Hellenistic Dynasty which ruled Egypt from 306 to 30 B.C., from Ptolemy I Soter, a general of Alexander the Great, to Ptolemy XIV Philopator and Cleopatra. Its rule saw the flowering of Hellenistic civilization and the last phases of Egyptian civilization.

Qatna   A site halfway between Damascus and Aleppo at which a small number of Akkadian cuneiform tablets (several inventories and an omen text) from the middle of the second millennium were found. The city is mentioned in the Amarna correspondence, in the texts from Boghazkeui, and possibly in the Mari tablets. See G. Dossin "Iamhad et Qatanum" *RA*, 36 (1939), 46–54.

Quti (Guti)   A people with a distinct language, at home in the

Zagros Mountains (probably near today's Luristan) whose invasion into lower Mesopotamia brought about the disappearance of the remnants of the empire of Sargon of Akkad. Their kings are listed as having ruled Akkad for about one hundred years. Their personal names and a few words preserved in lexical texts are the only linguistic evidence available. Their influence on Mesopotamian civilization cannot be gauged. See E. A. Speiser, *Mesopotamian Origins. The Basic Population of the Near East* (Philadelphia, 1930), pp. 96–119, for a presentation of the material pertaining to the Quti and their possible identity with the Kurds; also W. W. Hallo, "Gutium," in RLA, vol. 3 (1957–71), 708–20.

SAMʾAL (Zenjirli) The site of a small kingdom in the Taurus Mountains where the Arameans who conquered the region from Luwian-speaking natives erected a well-planned city in the tenth century B.C., which after a century or two fell into the Assyrian sphere of influence and was eventually incorporated into the Assyrian Empire. It was excavated by a German expedition.

SARGON OF AKKAD The fifty-six years of rule which the Sumerian king list assigns to this powerful king of the late third millennium B.C. have left their imprint on Mesopotamian history, political concepts, and literature. The expanse of territory which he and his grandson Naram-Sin either conquered or ruled at times is extensive enough according to the (mostly secondary) sources available to us but was further enlarged by a body of lengendary tales which attached themselves to these two heroic figures. Sargon's birth, his rise to kingship, his long and adventurous rule were well remembered in Mesopotamia and Asia Minor. Sargon's claim to the region from the Lower Sea and its islands to the Upper Sea and its islands, i.e., from Telmun to Cyprus, fashioned the political goals of many a Mesopotamian empire-builder after him.

SARGON II King of Assyria (721–705 B.C.), Sargon II ascended the throne after the very short rule of his brother (Shalmaneser V) and was forced to fight hard to re-establish the empire ruled by his father (Tiglath-Pileser III). After ten years of warfare against the enemies to the west (Syria and Asia Minor) and north (Urartu), Sargon turned his attention to Babylonia and chased Merodach-Baladan II into Elam and made himself king of Babylon in 709 B.C. Sargon was killed in battle in a minor engagement in Iran, and his own new city Dur-Šarrukin (Khorsabad) near Nineveh was left unfinished.

SARGONIDS Convenient term to refer to the last kings of the Assyrian empire from Sargon II (721–705 B.C.) to the disappearance of Assyria as an empire. Their numerous inscriptions, their diplomatic and court correspondence as well as their monuments make four of these kings

(Sargon II, Sennacherib, Esarhaddon, and Assurbanipal) the best-known royal figures of Mesopotamian history.

SASSANIANS   An Iranian dynasty (224–651 A.D.) which replaced that of the Arsacids and ruled for more than three hundred years an empire extending from Syria to northwest India. They fought the Romans victoriously on their western front and for a long time succeeded, in spite of their difficulties with their eastern neighbors, in acting as a cultural center relating East and West while maintaining the Iranian and Mesopotamian cultural heritages.

SEALAND   Literal translation of the Akkadian designation for the marshy region around the head of the Persian Gulf and the rivers flowing into it. The king lists mention ten or eleven kings of a Dynasty of URU.KÙ^{ki} who have either Akkadian or very artificial Sumerian names. In their very few inscriptions they call themselves king of the Sealand and seem to have been contemporary with the early Kassite rulers in the north. Although nothing is known directly about the survival of this ephemeral political entity, there is enough evidence from Babylonian sources of the latter part of the second millennium and the first half of the first (the king lists place a brief "Second Dynasty of the Sealand" in the eleventh century) that a southern province of the Babylonian kingdom was called Sealand and continued to exist, actively participating in the fight against Assyrian domination. The study of R. P. Dougherty, *The Sealand of Ancient Arabia* (New Haven, 1932) is largely obsolete.

SELEUCIA   Situated on the western bank of the Tigris downstream from today's Baghdad, Seleucia in Mesopotamia (one of the several Near Eastern cities of that name) was founded in 312 B.C. by Seleucus I Nicator and destroyed in 164 A.D., flourishing thus for nearly half a millennium as the political and cultural center of a large kingdom.

SELEUCIDS (Seleucid Period)   Next to nothing is known of the interesting hybrid civilization which seems to have grown out of a fusion of native Mesopotamian, imported Syrian (or Aramean), and superimposed Greek elements under the reigns of the kings of the family of Seleucus I Nicator (murdered 281 B.C.), ruling large stretches of the Near East from the new capital of Mesopotamia, called Seleucia. The cuneiform sources covering this period are few indeed. Apart from a number of contemporary copies of texts containing the literary tradition (omen texts, literary tablets in Akkadian, and bilingual texts), we have a small group of legal documents (mainly from Uruk), a few historical inscriptions (among them two king lists), and mathematical and astronomical tablets. Inscriptions on papyrus and other perishable writing materials which have preserved for us so much of the contemporary Graeco-Egyptian civilization have all perished in Mesopotamia.

SENNACHERIB   King of Assyria (704–681 B.C.). Heir to an empire consolidated by his father Sargon II, the entire reign of Sennacherib was marred by a series of bitter wars, with defeats and victories, waged against Babylonia and its main ally, Elam. It ended apparently with the destruction of Babylon in 689 B.C. It is not unlikely that the assassination of Sennacherib by one or more of his sons has to be related directly to the conflict with Babylonia which, although enacted overtly on the political and military levels, served also to express internal and intellectual stress within the Assyrian ruling circles. The expedition to the west which brought Sennacherib into contact with Hezekiah of Judah and which is reported in the Old Testament was only a minor punitive expedition to assure payment of tribute.

SIDON   An important harbor on the Phoenician coast twenty-five miles north of Tyre, mentioned in the Amarna correspondence and in Egyptian and Old Testament sources. It was destroyed by Esarhaddon in 677 B.C. after a series of conflicts with Assyria beginning at the time of the death of Sargon II.

SIPPAR   This northernmost of the cities of Lower Mesopotamia has yielded more texts bearing on the Old Babylonian and the Neo-Babylonian periods than any other site in Mesopotamia, in addition to important literary tablets. Originally, Sippar seemed to have had the function of a trading center far off the settled regions of southern and central Lower Mesopotamia, which, under the protection of the sun god Šamaš, harbored an agglomeration of compounds used by nomadic and seminomadic people. Peace and peaceful trade relations seem to have been much more the concern of this rich city than political ambitions. Some names of short-lived "kings" are attested for Sippar in the pre-Hammurapi-Dynasty period, but, with the coming of that dynasty, Sippar clearly became an integral part of the empire, sharing its fate to the very end. The Sippar of the Neo-Babylonian (Chaldean) period is known by many administrative and legal texts; only a fraction of these tablets have been published.

SULTANTEPE   See Harran.

SUSA   Capital of Elam, situated in the Mesopotamian plain on the Ulai River, the site of Šušan was occupied for more than five millennia, and excavations on the mound have now been going on for about one hundred years. An administrative center of Elam, the site has yielded all the known Elamite inscriptions of historical and literary content and a number of Old Akkadian and Sumerian Ur III texts as well as several hundred legal texts which date from the late Old

Babylonian period or the subsequent centuries. A few literary and omen texts, word lists, and school tablets show that Akkadian was taught in Susa in that period. First among the monuments excavated at Susa ranks the Codex Hammurapi of which two or perhaps three copies together with a number of Babylonian *kudurru*-stones were once brought as spoils to their capital by victorious Elamite kings.

TELMUN (Bahrain)   The islands of the archipelago near the Arabian coast in the eastern part of the Persian Gulf have played an important role throughout the duration of Mesopotamian civilization as an emporium linking the shipping lanes of the Gulf to those of the east. Evidence for the role of Telmun is available from the pre-Sargonic to the Neo-Babylonian period, although it leaves long and crucial gaps. Plants, stones, metals, and animals came into Mesopotamia via Telmun from the east, and the relationship of the island to the regions called respectively Magan and Meluhha is still a moot question. See Magan and Meluhha.

TEMA   An old oasis city (modern Teima) in northwest Arabia where the caravan routes cross which lead from the west and the south to the head of the Persian Gulf and from Damascus to Medina. It is mentioned as a caravan trade city in the Old Testament, in Assyrian royal inscriptions (Tiglath-Pileser III), and in later administrative texts. Nabonidus lists Tema together with other caravan cities of Arabia in an inscription and is said to have stayed there, for unknown reasons, for several years.

TYRE   Island city on the Phoenician coast, closely linked in its experiences in history with its sister city to the north, Sidon. Its strategic position on an island—only Alexander the Great laid siege to Tyre and conquered it (332 B.C.)—increased the political importance which extended to Cyprus as well as to the mainland. Its first contact with the Assyrians pressing to the Mediterranean was with Aššurnaṣirpal II to whom Tyre paid tribute in 876.

UGARIT   A city-state near the coast of the Mediterranean Sea due east of the nearest point of the island of Cyprus. The mound (Ras Shamra) covers the remains of a series of civilizations of which only those using clay as writing material are of direct interest to this book. A number of these tablets are inscribed with signs that bear no direct relation to those of the Mesopotamian writing system. Their language is a Semitic dialect whose relationship to the other languages of this group is still under discussion. Other tablets unearthed in Ugarit contain Akkadian texts and word lists in which appear Sumerian, Akkadian, and Hurrian transliterations of words in the language of Ugarit, legal, epistolary, and literary texts. Lastly, Hittite texts were also found.

UR   Between Eridu and the present course of the Euphrates lies the extensive mound which covers the "Ur of the Chaldees." After several earlier attempts, systematic excavations started under Sir Leonard Woolley in 1922 and yielded as their most spectacular result the famous royal tombs. The site furnished, moreover, a rich harvest of historical inscriptions, legal and administrative documents, and literary and scholarly texts which date from archaic texts (somewhat younger than those from Djemdet Nasr) to those of the Persian and Seleucid periods. Like Uruk, Ur spans the entire known history of Mesopotamia.

UR, THIRD DYNASTY OF (abbrev. Ur III) The dynasty, founded by Ur-Nammu soon after the liberation of the country from the Quti invasion, reached its climax during the long rule of his son Šulgi, followed by his short-lived successors Amar-Suen and Šu-Sin. It disappeared with Ibbi-Sin who was taken as prisoner to Elam. Building inscriptions, royal hymns, and the large bulk of administrative documents fail to yield a comprehensive view of the history or the political nature of the empire. Neither can the numerous names of governors, officials who managed establishments, administrated herds (in Puzriš-Dagan, now Drehem), commodities, luxury goods (mainly in Umma, now Djokha), or who were connected with the capital (tablets from Ur) or other administrative centers, be made to yield any adequate insight into the economic structure of the empire.

URARTU An important kingdom, centered in the region around Lake Van with a *floruit* which lasted from about 900 to 600 B.C. The Assyrian kings from Aššur-bel-kala (1073–1056) to Sargon II (714 B.C.) fought against Urartu either directly or against its political influence in northern Syria, which extended at one time as far as Aleppo. Numerous inscriptions in the Urartian language using cuneiform signs on rocks, objects, and clay tablets, a bilingual text (Urarto-Assyrian), remnants of temples, city walls, and objects made of stone and metal attest the importance of the Urartian civilization.

URUK The history of Uruk in southern Babylonia (Sumerian U n u g, Biblical Erekh, modern Arabic Warka) parallels that of Mesopotamia from its earliest to its latest phase. The earliest Sumerian documents (published and interpreted by A. Falkenstein) stand at its beginning and large bodies of legal and scholarly tablets of the Seleucid period at its end. Such famous primeval figures as Enmerkar, Gilgamesh, and Tammuz, such history-making kings as Lugalzagesi and Utuhegal ruled in the city whose ruins impress us by their extent and the accumulation of temples. German expeditions began work in Uruk before World War I, but the yield in published documents has not been rich.

VOLOGESIA A city near Babylon founded by the Parthians in the first century A.D. See the recent article by H. Treidler in Pauly-Wissowa (ed.), *Realencyclopädie der classischen Wissenschaften, Zweite Reihe*, 17 (Stuttgart, 1961), 767–71.

WARKA See Uruk.

ZENJIRLI See Samʾal.

Index